D0242018

IN TEARING HASTE

IN
TEARING HASTE

*Letters between Deborah Devonshire
and Patrick Leigh Fermor*

Edited by
CHARLOTTE MOSLEY

JOHN MURRAY

First published in Great Britain in 2008 by John Murray (Publishers)
An Hachette Livre UK Company

1

Drawings of the view from Patrick Leigh Fermor's house in Mani (page xvii)
and Lismore Castle (page xxi) by John Craxton

A CIP catalogue record for this title is available from the British Library

ISBN 978-0-7195-6858-9

Typeset in Bembo by Palimpsest Book Production Limited,
Grangemouth, Stirlingshire

Printed and bound by
Clays Ltd, St Ives plc

John Murray policy is to use papers that are natural, renewable and recyclable products and
made from wood grown in sustainable forests. The logging and manufacturing processes are
expected to conform to the environmental regulations of the country of origin.

John Murray (Publishers)
338 Euston Road
London NW1 3BH

www.johnmurray.co.uk

CONTENTS

ACKNOWLEDGEMENTS

It is unusual for a book of letters to be published during the lifetime of its authors and this one has greatly benefited from their contribution. My first thanks, therefore, are to Debo and Paddy for being unfailingly generous with their time and memories.

I owe a huge debt to Helen Marchant who typed all the letters, not only at record speed but with preternatural skill when it came to deciphering Paddy's handwriting.

I am particularly grateful to Artemis Cooper, who is preparing a biography of Paddy, and to Olivia Stewart for her help with the photographs.

I would also like to thank the following: Ginnie Airlie, Stuart Band, Anne Pauline de Castries, Caroline Cranbrook, Derry Moore, Katie Edwards, Anne Egerton, Ian Else, Magouche Fielding, the Clerk to the Worshipful Company of Fishmongers, Bridget Flemming, Nicholas Henderson, Hussein Hinnawi, Kate Kee, Jeremy Lewis, Jean-Noël Liaut, Elizabeth Longman, Mary S. Lovell, Michael Mallon, Sophie Caroline de Margerie, Peter Miller, Diane Naylor, Charles Noble, Henri and Sybil d'Origny, Jane Ormsby Gore, Andrew Parker Bowles, Andrew Peppitt, Christine Robinson, Serena Rothschild, Penelope Skarsouli, Mary Soames, Archie Stirling, Mario Testino and Teresa Wells.

EDITOR'S NOTE

Patrick Leigh Fermor's first sight of Deborah Mitford left a lasting impression. She did not even notice him. It was at a regimental ball in 1940 when he was a twenty-five-year-old officer in the Intelligence Corps and she the twenty-year-old fiancée of Andrew Cavendish, recently commissioned into the Coldstream Guards. She had eyes only for her husband-to-be.

They met again as acquaintances at parties in London in the early 1950s, but their friendship truly blossomed in 1956 when Paddy took up a long-standing invitation to stay with Andrew and Debo – by now the Duke and Duchess of Devonshire – at Lismore, their magnificent neo-Gothic castle overlooking the Blackwater Valley in County Waterford, Ireland. This fairy-tale setting with its rich historical associations cast a spell over Paddy's romantic spirit, stirring his love of pageantry and heraldry, of wild open country and odd encounters, of archaic language and local lore. He also fell for Debo. It was not an exclusive love – he was devoted to Joan Eyres Monsell, the woman who was to become his wife – but a deep, platonic attraction between two people who shared youthful high spirits, warmth, generosity and an unstinting enjoyment of life.

Debo was the youngest of the six beautiful Mitford sisters, whose exploits and extreme political opinions made them household names; she was also the most well-adjusted. The family's rather isolated upbringing in the Oxfordshire countryside, immortalised in Nancy Mitford's novels, suited Debo and she considered her childhood to have been happy. Unlike her sisters, she never resented not being sent to school – dreaded the idea in fact – and followed them into the schoolroom where they were taught by a succession of governesses. From her mother, Lady Redesdale, who after her own mother's death had taken over the running of her father's household at the age of fourteen, Debo inherited an excellent head for business and a natural talent for organ-ising, qualities that proved useful when, in 1950, Andrew inherited the dukedom and the vast Devonshire estates. In 1959, he and Debo decided to move back into Chatsworth, the family's magnificent house in the Peak District of Derbyshire, which had not been redecorated since the First World War and had been occupied by a girls' school during the Second. Andrew devised a way of paying off the death duties that were owing after his father's death, amounting to some eighty per cent of the estate, and Debo threw herself with gusto into restoring the house and reopening it fully to the public. She started shops and a restaurant, a children's playground and a farmyard, helping to transform a debt-ridden inheritance into a thriving enterprise. In the early 1980s, she embarked – rather unexpectedly given her claim never to have read a book – on a writing career. *The House*, an account of the restoration work, was the first of ten highly individual books she has produced about Chatsworth and the estate.

When Debo and Paddy began to write to each other, in 1954, Paddy's reputation rested on an impressive war record and two books: *The Traveller's Tree: A Journey through the Caribbean Islands* and *The Violins of Saint-Jacques*, his only novel. He had spent most of the war in Crete where, after the Allied retreat from the island in 1941, he was among a small number of British agents who stayed to help organise resistance to the Nazi occupation. In 1944 he led the successful abduction of Major-General Heinrich Kreipe, the German commander in Crete, a daring operation that won him the DSO. The exploit became famous, not because Paddy himself has ever written or even talked much about it, but because in 1950 his second-in-command, William Stanley Moss, published a best-selling book, *Ill Met by Moonlight*, which was later made into a film.

After the war, wanderlust took Paddy to the Caribbean, Central America, France, Spain, Italy and, most often, to Greece where he and Joan decided to settle in 1964. They built a house in the Peloponnese, in an olive grove overlooking the sea, camping for two years on a plot of land while the house, which they designed themselves, rose up around them. With its classical and oriental features, and a cloistered gallery that leads into a huge, light-filled drawing room opening on to a terrace, the building fits so well into its surroundings that when a white goat wandered in one day, followed by six more in single file, they looked quite at home as they trooped across the floor, into the gallery, down twenty steps and into the landscape again, neither the goats nor the house seeming in any way out of countenance.[1]

Mani and *Roumeli*, published in 1958 and 1966, revealed Paddy's deep regard for his adopted country and were well received, but *A Time of Gifts* and *Between the Woods and the Water*, the first two volumes of a projected trilogy published in 1977 and 1986, made him known to a far wider reading public. His extraordinary account of an eighteen-month journey on foot across Europe, from Holland to Constantinople, which he embarked on in 1933 at the age of eighteen, is the stuff of a *Bildungsroman*; but whereas in coming-of-age novels the youthful protagonist emerges wiser but often disenchanted by the tough process of maturity, Paddy's real-life journey did nothing to dent his infectious enthusiasm and capacity for wonder.

Paddy, like Debo, is apolitical by nature. Hitler's Brownshirts remained on the periphery of his awareness as he walked across Germany in 1934, the year after the Nazis came to power. And there is barely a mention in his letters of the *coup d'état* in Greece in 1967, when a military junta seized power and suspended civil rights until parliamentary democracy was restored seven years later. Debo's lack of interest in politics is partly due to temperament and partly to choice. After witnessing how radical politics tore her family apart, separating her parents and dividing her sisters, she decided that they were not for her.

Paddy and Debo began to correspond in 1954, not very regularly at first – there would be a volley of exchanges then silence for several months – but when something caught their interest and they knew the other would be amused, they sent off a letter in the hopes of a reply. Both were natural writers and storytellers, and kept up with a number of other correspondents: Debo mainly with her four sisters, Nancy, Pamela, Diana and Jessica, and with her two closest friends, Daphne Bath, who married Paddy's comrade-in-arms Xan Fielding, and Kitty Mersey, affectionately nicknamed 'the Wife'. Paddy wrote chiefly to Joan (whenever he was away from home), to his friends Ann Fleming and Diana Cooper, and to Balasha Cantacuzène, a Romanian painter with whom he had fallen in love when he was twenty. Gradually, as their circle of family and friends grew smaller, their letters to each other grew more frequent. Diana Cooper and Ann Fleming died in the 1980s; Kitty Mersey and Daphne Fielding in the 1990s; in 2003, Paddy lost Joan, and Debo lost her last surviving sister, Diana.

As writers, they were perfect foils for each other. Unless Paddy was making a plan or asking a quick question – in which case he would scribble a few lines headed '*In unbelievable haste*' or '*With one foot in the stirrup*' – his letters are sustained pieces of writing, as detailed and beautifully wrought as his books. With the eye of a painter, the pen of a poet and a composer's ear for language and dialogue, in his letters he often sounds like a musician practising scales before launching into a full-blown symphony, and indeed two of his books, *A Time to Keep Silence* and *Three Letters from the Andes*, were based on letters to Joan. In complete contrast, Debo's letters are breezy and spontaneous. Dashed off almost in telegraphese at times, they are sharp, idiosyncratic and funny. Where Paddy is dazzlingly erudite, widely read and a polyglot, Debo is defiantly (at times disingenuously) a non-reader, puncturing any intellectualising or use of a foreign word with, '*Ah oui*', or '*quelle horrible surprise*'. Paddy has an omnivorous interest in culture, while Debo is interested in the countryside, preferring country fairs to literary salons. Agricultural and horticultural jargon is the one linguistic area where she can outshine Paddy.

Much of the charm of the letters lies in their authors' particular outlook on life. Both are acutely observant and clear-sighted about human failings, but their lack of cynicism and gift for looking on the bright side bear out the maxim that the world tends to treat you as you find it. On the whole, the people they meet are good to them, the places they visit enchant them and they succeed splendidly in all they set out to do. This light-heartedness – a trait that attracted many, often less sunny, people towards them – gives their letters an irresistible fizz and sparkle.

Some six hundred letters between the two correspondents have survived, and many more must have been written, particularly by Debo during the first decade of their friendship. Paddy's peripatetic life before 1964, when he settled in the Mani, meant that letters occasionally went astray. Even after making Greece his home, he was often travelling and not always able to keep track of papers. There is a gap of four years at the end of the 1990s where no letters at all from Debo have been found.

Each correspondent reacted very much in character to the editing of their letters. Debo, unconcerned about perfect style or syntax, let hers stand as she wrote them, while Paddy's exacting standards made it impossible for him to let any glaring infelicities slip through and he has polished his, changing word order here and there, deleting repetitions and rectifying punctuation.

The choice of letters is mine and so are the excisions. As in any correspondence between friends, there were many plans for meeting, reports on health, grumbles about the weather and the slowness of the posts, all of which make for dull re-reading. Paddy and Debo also kept up a running exchange of riddles, ditties and jokes that have, on the whole, lost their freshness, and they have mostly been excluded. These cuts have been made silently and any ellipses are Paddy and Debo's own.

One of the great advantages of having both correspondents at hand during the editing of their letters is that I have been able to draw on their memories of people and events, and, where possible, have used their recollections in the footnotes. At times, re-reading a letter evoked a longer, more detailed reminiscence and these have been added in italics in the main body of the letters.

1 Patrick Leigh Fermor, 'Sash Windows Opening on the Foam', *Architectural Digest*, November 1986, reprinted in *Words of Mercury*, edited by Artemis Cooper (2003), pp. 126–30.

PATRICK LEIGH FERMOR
by Deborah Devonshire

I am told Paddy was born in 1915. Not possible! Hardly a grey hair, upright, trudging for miles up and down dale, or swimming for hours according to whether he is in England or in Greece, he is adored by my youngest grandchild as well as by his own generation; an ageless, timeless hero to us all.

I first saw him at a fancy-dress party in London. He was a Roman gladiator armed with a net and trident, and his get-up suited him very well. I had heard of him, of course. Everyone had. By 1957, the story of his exploits in occupied Crete had been made into the film *Ill Met by Moonlight* with Dirk Bogarde as Paddy. It is still shown on television from time to time.

It was in 1942 and '43, living so closely to them in shared danger, that he became deeply devoted to the Cretans, and the bond between him and his old comrades is as strong as ever.

For eighteen months, Paddy and his great friend Xan Fielding lived in the mountains of Crete disguised as shepherds (I wouldn't put him in charge of my sheep, but never mind) and in constant danger of being caught by the enemy. Then came the spectacular coup in 1944 when he and Billy Moss, an officer in the Coldstream Guards, kidnapped the German general, Heinrich Kreipe.

Their prize was bundled into the back of the German official car: Moss drove them through a town in the blackout, Paddy sitting on the front seat wearing the general's cap, in case anyone should glance at the occupants. After a four-hour climb on foot to the comparative safety of a cave in the mountains, they spent eighteen days together, moving from one hiding place to another and sharing the only blanket during the freezing nights. When the sun rose on the first morning and lit up the snow on the summit of Mount Ida, the general gazed at the scene and quoted a verse of an ode by Horace. His captor completed the next six stanzas. Such a duet under such circumstances must be unique in the history of war.

When he was sixteen and a half, Paddy was expelled from The King's School, Canterbury, for holding hands with the greengrocer's daughter, sitting on a crate of veg. What to do next? A military crammer was tried but didn't seem to suit, so he mooned around London, making friends who lasted a lifetime. At the age of eighteen ('and three-quarters', he says, for accuracy) he yearned to go to Greece. He could not afford the fare so he walked there. What a lesson to young people now, who write to strangers asking for money to enable them to travel.

Years later, his walk inspired *A Time of Gifts* and *Between the Woods and the Water*, perhaps the two most acclaimed of all his books, winners of endless literary prizes and translated into more languages than probably even Paddy knows. His love of Greece prompted him and his wife Joan to build their glorious house on the sea in the Mani, living in a tent and working with the masons till it grew into the idyllic home it now is.

He is one of those rare birds who is exactly the same with whoever he is talking to. Children recognise him as a kindred spirit. With his formidable scholarship and prodigious memory, he is just as able to spout Edward Lear or 'There was an Old Woman as I've heard tell, who went to market her eggs for to sell' for them, as Marvell or Shakespeare, via Noël Coward, for grown-ups.

Try to get him to sing 'It's a Long Way to Tipperary' in Hindustani with his Italian translations of 'John Peel' and 'Widdecombe Fair'. John Peel's hounds – Ruby, Ranter, Ringwood, Bellman and True – turn into Rubino, Vantardo, Rondo Bosco, Campanelli and Fedele.

> Tom Pearse, Tom Pearse
> Lend me your grey mare,
> All along, down along, out along lee,

becomes:

> *Tommaso prestami tua grigia giumenta*
> *Tutti lungo, fuori lungo, giù lungo prato.*

And Cobley's gang are:

> *Guglielmo Brewer, Jacopo Stewer, Pietro Gurney,*
> *Pietro Davey, Daniele Whiddon ed Enrico 'awke.*
> *Ed il vecchio zio Tommaso Cobley e tutti quanti* etc.

Or get him to recite the longest palindrome, 'Live dirt up a side track carted is a putrid evil', delivered, for some unknown reason, in the broadest Gloucestershire accent. Just the entertainment for a winter's night.

Handsome, funny, energetic and original, Paddy is a brilliant, shining star – how lucky my family and I are to have had such a friend for so long.

Adapted from an article written for PLF's eighty-fifth birthday, Daily Telegraph, *10 February 2000.*

DEBORAH DEVONSHIRE
by *Patrick Leigh Fermor*

In autumn 1940, Smedley's Hydro at Matlock in Derbyshire – a bleak, castellated and blacked-out Victorian pile, perched high above the rushing Derwent (whose mineral springs, it was said, could turn a bowler hat into a crystalline fossil overnight) – was crammed with polyglot officers of all ages and origins. It was the Intelligence Training Centre, which sounds more important than it was. The war wasn't going well and it was thought that a ball would cheer us all up, so we did our best with balloons, chrysanthemums and streamers. Many of the officers were musical, so we had a band and it went with great brio.

Henry Howard, one of the instructors, brought over a spectacular couple from nearby: a tall, slim ensign in blues and an incredibly beautiful girl; nobody could look at anyone else. They were both twenty. There was nothing showy about their dancing – rather the reverse. We all wished we knew them, but it was out of the question: they seemed to be sleep-dancing, utterly rapt, eyes shut as though in a trance. He was called Andrew Cavendish and she was Deborah, the youngest Mitford sister.

'Funny, Howard bringing that Mitford girl over,' a crusty old student said when they had gone. 'After all, this *is* meant to be the Intelligence Training Centre, and there *is* a war on.'

The war had been over for a few years when we met again at a fancy-dress drinks, and then at a party with two fast boats sailing up the Thames laden with eccentrically dressed passengers. Andrew had been through the war with the Coldstream Guards and won an MC in northern Italy. Deborah had been busy with a score of tasks, and both were at grips with bringing Chatsworth back to life. I was very pleased to be asked to stay, having already visited Lismore. 'Our dump looms when you turn left after the church. You can't miss it. It sticks out like a sore thumb.'

There is no need to describe that amazing house; everyone knows Chatsworth. It was an unexpected heirloom: Andrew's older brother had been killed in action in 1944, and his father had died in 1950. This brought a stack of new duties, and new things to enjoy (and see that everyone else enjoyed). He dealt with all tasks with seriousness, speed and decision. When he served as Minister of State for Commonwealth Relations in the Macmillan Government ('pure nepotism of Uncle Harold's'), he did it with impressive ability.

In the country, Andrew had a genius for marking historical and family events with enormous gatherings. The house and all hotels for miles around filled up with guests, staff and tenants; vast tents went up all over the grounds, and there were fountains, music, feasting, tumblers, sword-swallowers and players of obsolete instruments. There were pageants, ballets, cantatas. It was a sort of Field of the Cloth of Gold – all to be blown away, except from memory, with the smoke of the last firework: scenes so magical that departing cars had to go several miles before they could safely turn back into pumpkins. I can see Andrew, like a tired youthful Prospero, in his study – a vast cave full of books – planning new splendours, ticking off a list of new engagements, perhaps brooding on almshouses for grey-beards yet unborn.

How different from the winds and snow of the Huantay mountain range in Peru! Andrew and I had been included, as minor amateurs, in a mountaineering expedition in the Andes. It was so congenial that the same party clambered all over the Pindus. We then tackled the Pyrenees with Xan Fielding, and were about to try the not very arduous Elburz range in Iran, when the Ayatollah came to power.

Lismore Castle, the Devonshires' home in Ireland – built by King John, lived in by Sir Walter Raleigh and plumbed by Andrew's aunt by marriage, Adele Astaire – looks like a castle out of *Le Morte d'Arthur*. I was allowed to stay ('in order to write') in the tallest tower, where there was no sound but the admonitory gurgle of bathwater climbing up its pipe before dinner, the flutter of a flag overhead and thousands of birds. It looked down on treetops and a bridge over the Blackwater River with a strange echo. Files of salmon shimmer upstream towards the Knockmealdown Mountains and herons glide by almost in touching distance.

LISMORE

In the village lived Dervla Murphy, the great travel author, and a few fields away grazed the beautiful Grand National winner Royal Tan, a present to Debo from Aly Khan. He had run four times in the great race, and had come in first, second and third, and fell only at the last fence in the fourth, which he would otherwise have won. This fine horse had fallen platonically head-over-heels in love with a very small donkey and they were inseparable. However, I made a good impression by wheedling the horse away by hours of stroking and soft talk, then furtively slipping a bridle over his head. I felt sorry for the little donkey as we went down the lane to the blacksmith's, who welcomed Royal Tan like a prince. 'Arrh! He's seen a lot of crowds in his day!' he said, and then, as an afterthought, 'I'll just put a light slipper on him.'

Later, there was a lot of riding through the spring woods with Debo, my wife Joan, and Robert Kee. There was a picnic under the fairy oak at Abbeyleix, and an afternoon when we were bent on having a shrimp tea. A sort of spell hung over the whole region. Nobody was at home when we went to nearby Dromana House. It was oddly silent. No Villiers, no Stuarts. There was an open window, so we clambered in like Bruin Boys of riper years. A few old letters were scattered about and a dismembered double-barrel gun and some moulting foxes' brushes. Dusk was falling, so we tiptoed away.

Equally vain to try and reproduce the comedy of Debo's and her sister Nancy's exchanges, much of it schoolroom reproach. When the fire at Lismore had gone out, Nancy said, 'I note no bellows', and, imploring Debo to stop whatever she was doing, 'Borah, I beg!'

Thanks to Nancy's books we know a lot about the Mitfords. 'Our lives were absolutely secure and regular as clockwork' (this is Debo writing, not Nancy). 'We had parents who were always there. An adored Nanny who came when Diana was three months old and stayed for forty years. Mabel in the pantry and Annie the house-keeper. Animals were as important as humans – mice, guinea pigs, a piebald rat belonging to Unity, poultry and goats, and the animals of farm and stable.'

Debo's fondness for animals has never left her. Chickens seem to have been her first love, and they are still high on the list. Sheep are particular favourites; she knows all about them, every variety and breed, and she haunts sheep sales. Rare breeds abound at Chatsworth. For a time there was a whole troop of tiny horses. She is shadowed everywhere by two whippets.

Shops have always held particular glamour for her – her favourite book is Beatrix Potter's *Ginger and Pickles* – and this has given rise to shops full of country food, butchers' shops, carpenters', shops selling rustic tackle and pretty well everything an estate can produce.

Although she hates books and has never read any of mine, or those of any other writer friends, she has written several books about Chatsworth and its surroundings. She writes with ease and speed, and wonders what all the fuss is about.

Adapted from an article written for DD's eightieth birthday, Daily Telegraph, *31 March 2000.*

INDEX OF NAMES AND NICKNAMES

LETTERS

1954–2007

21 March 1954

Fitzroy House[1]
Fitzroy Square
London W1

Dear Paddy Leigh Fermor,

I'm beginning like that chiefly because Nancy[2] says one mustn't, but as she says I'm mental age of 9 it doesn't signify how one begins. I'm ever so excited about you coming to Ireland. Do really come & don't just say you are.

Daph[3] & Xan[4] are coming to stay at Chesterfield St[5] on Monday, v exciting.

Best love
Debo

---

1 DD was in a nursing home, recovering from a minor operation.

2 Nancy Mitford (1904–73). DD's eldest sister, the novelist, biographer and arbiter of correct usage, used to address her letters to '9, Duchess of Devonshire', the basis of her teasing being the accusation that DD was illiterate. 'Unfounded, it's my theory, because, though never seen to read, she's so full of surprises.' PLF, unpublished letter to Harold Acton, 5 November 1974.

3 Daphne Vivian (1904–97). Tall, beautiful, libidinous author of popular books on London society, including *The Duchess of Jermyn Street: the Life and Good Times of Rosa Lewis of the Cavendish Hotel* (1964), *Emerald and Nancy: Lady Cunard and Her Daughter* (1968) and two volumes of autobiography. Married to 6th Marquess of Bath 1927–53 and to Xan Fielding 1953–78.

4 Alexander (Xan) Fielding (1918–91). Wartime secret agent, writer and translator who shared with PLF a natural aversion to most forms of constraint. They had been friends since the war when, as Special Operations Executive (SOE) agents, they built up guerrilla and intelligence networks in Nazi-occupied Crete. A 'gifted, many-sided, courageous and romantic figure, at the same time civilized and bohemian.' PLF, Foreword to *A Hideous Disguise* (Typographeum, 1994), p. 9. Married to Daphne Bath, née Vivian, 1953–78 and to 'Magouche' Phillips, née Magruder, in 1979.

5 The Devonshires' London house.

26 April 1955   c/o Niko Ghika[1]
                                                 Kamini, Hydra
                                                 Greece

Dear Debo,

I've just heard from Daphne on the point of departure to stay with you. Why does everyone go to that castle[2] except me?

My plan is this: there is a brilliant young witch on this island (aged sixteen and very pretty), sovereign at thwarting the evil eye, casting out devils and foiling spells by incantation. It shouldn't be beyond her powers to turn me into a fish for a month and slip me into the harbour. I reckon I could get through the Mediterranean, across the Bay of Biscay, round Land's End and over the Irish Sea in about 28 days (if the weather holds) and on into the Blackwater. I'm told there's a stream that flows under your window, up which I propose to swim and, with a final effort, clear the sill and land on the carpet, where I insist on being treated like the frog prince for a couple of days of rest and recovery. (You could have a tank brought up – or lend me your bath if this is not inconvenient – till I'm ready to come downstairs. Also some flannel trousers, sensible walking shoes and a Donegal tweed Norfolk jacket with a belt across the small of the back and leather buttons.) But please be there. Otherwise there is all the risk of filleting, *meunière* etc, and, worst of all, *au bleu* . . .

Please give my love to Daphne if she's with you. You can let her

in on this plan, if you think it is suitable, but nobody else for the
time being. These things always leak out.

  Love
    Paddy

P.S. Please write & say if this arrangement fits in with your plans.

---

1 Nikos Ghika (1906–94). The well-known Greek painter and sculptor, a great
friend of PLF, had lent him his house on the Aegean island of Hydra. Married to
Barbara Hutchinson in 1961.
2 Lismore Castle, Co. Waterford, overlooking the Blackwater River, has been the
Irish home of the Dukes of Devonshire since 1753.

30 April 1955   Lismore Castle
                                                 Co. Waterford
                                                 Eire

Dear Paddy L F,
    I was v v excited to get your letter with the swimming plan in it.
It is a *frightfully good* plan, but the pestilential thing is that you would
find, not me, but Fred Astaire[1] installed in this pleasant residence.
However if you could swim a bit further to the right and land in
England and then be like an eel & get a bit across the land you can
have the freedom of my bath in Derbyshire & I will have the
sensible shoes etc ready.

I would like it like anything, so have a try and I will instruct any salmon around your route to see that you aren't filleted or meuniered or bleued.

I heard they set on you at a ball and broke you up, oh it was a shame.[2]

Is it jolly in Greece? I bet it is.

Love from

Debo

---

[1] Fred Astaire (1899–1987). The dancer and choreographer's sister and stage partner, Adele, married DD's uncle by marriage, Lord Charles Cavendish, and lived at Lismore Castle 1932–44. When her husband died, she returned to America but continued to visit Lismore each year, during which time Fred Astaire was a frequent visitor.

[2] PLF got into a fight at a hunt ball in Ireland and was badly cut.

2 March [1956]   Gadencourt[1]

Pacy-sur-Eure

Eure

Dear Debo,

Thank you very much for your letter in January, also for asking me to stay in Ireland in April. It's frightfully rude not having answered earlier, and I can't quite think how it's happened. Anyway, if it is still open, I would simply love to – if I could come towards the end of this month, as Daph and Xan are coming here on their way back to the Kasbah.

The cold here has been worse than Baffin Land. It got so bad about three weeks ago that I baled out and went to Paris. I had a delicious luncheon with your sister Mrs Basil Seal[2] with lots of vodka beforehand – O for a beaker full of the cold north! – and then lots of a wine called Château Chasse-Spleen. This was very nice; then I took sanctuary at Chantilly,[3] and had a paralysing, but most luxurious attack of lumbago. Don't be spellbound by the beauty of the name – it's as though a mastiff had mistaken your spine for an ordinary bone, and given it the usual treatment. This was dispelled by heavenly drugs, thrust in

like bayonet practice by a jovial nun resembling a Merry Wife of
Windsor.

Annie Fleming,[4] Judy Montagu,[5] Ld Gage[6] & Peter Quennell[7]
came to stay, and we had lovely protracted meals by candlelight,
discussing poetry, sex, heresy and kindred themes. The big castle
looked like some tremendous Russian Winter Palace in a park
peopled by statues posturing under loads of snow. All the lakes were
frozen and covered with ducks and swans mooching about rather
awkwardly, wondering what on earth had gone wrong. There were
also a number of displaced herons.

I had a rather dispiriting return to Normandy. The Normans are
an awful lot really. My heart bleeds at the thought of the nice easy-
going Saxons suddenly, in 1066, having to put up with an influx of
these bossy and humourless louts.[8] What *was* rather curious was the
discovery, in the house, of two tortoiseshell butterflies walking about
the place with wings ajar. They were tottering in a most inexpert
way as though they'd had a few. I can't think where they have been
all through the winter or what living on; furtively grazing in their
stunned way, I suppose, on dark pastures of Harris Tweed and Lovat
mixture . . .

Do, please, let me know about Ireland. It really would be
lovely.

Best love from
Paddy

---

1 PLF and Joan had been lent the Normandy house of Sir Walter Smart (1883–
1962), Oriental Secretary in Cairo before the war, and his Lebanese painter wife,
Amy, daughter of the Cairo newspaper mogul Fares Nimr.
2 Evelyn Waugh's caddish anti-hero Basil Seal, described in *Put Out More Flags*
as 'an obstreperous minority of one', was largely based on Nancy Mitford's husband,
Peter Rodd.
3 PLF's hosts in Chantilly were Duff and Lady Diana Cooper, who settled at the
Château St Firmin, near Chantilly, in 1947, after his retirement as ambassador in
Paris.
4 Ann Charteris (1913–81). Social and political hostess who became friends with
PLF and DD in the 1950s. Married Ian Fleming, the creator of James Bond, as her
third husband, in 1952. Intelligent, beautiful and witty, she had 'a flair for tossing
in the right word to start people capping each other or throwing down gauntlets'.
PLF, unpublished letter to Mark Amory, 3 April 1983.

5 Judy Montagu (1923–72). The daughter of Venetia Stanley, confidante of Prime Minister H. H. Asquith, married art historian Milton Gendel in 1962. 'She wasn't remotely like anyone else . . . Some lives must be assessed by the warmth with which friendship is lavished and returned, and, in these rare terms, Judy's was an entire success.' PLF in *H. H. Asquith: Letters to Venetia Stanley*, edited by Michael and Eleanor Brock (OUP, 1982), p. 611.
  6 Henry Gage, 6th Viscount Gage (1895–1982). Lord-in-Waiting to King George V 1925–39, who possessed, according to his *Times* obituary, 'strong Christian beliefs, fortified by a considerable knowledge and erudition in the Scriptures'.
  7 Peter Quennell (1905–93). Biographer and critic, editor of the *Cornhill Magazine* 1944–51 and *History Today* 1951–79.
  8 PLF was alluding to a letter he had received from his great friend, the novelist Rose Macaulay, 'my one aim on landing in France with my car, is to hurry through Normandy *AUSSI VITE que possible* . . . How awful it must have been for us (the Saxons and Britons) when the Normans arrived; so boring, heavy-handed and dreary.' Rose Macaulay, unpublished letter to PLF, 23 January 1952.

6 March [1956]   Edensor House[1]
                                                 Edensor, Bakewell
                                                 Derbyshire

Dear Paddy,

I am so pleased you will come to Lismore, *any* time would be terribly nice.

It *is* unfair you having Daph & Xan, they won't come to us. I'm booking for the Kasbah though, I can see one has to book a long way ahead or some horrid counter-hon[2] would get there first.

Sorry about it being so cold, anyway there are crocuses now. Also calves.

Don't forget to come to Lismore. Explain to the Fieldings how one worships them, as a matter of fact I suppose they know.

Love,
    Debo

1 A rambling village house within Chatsworth Park where DD and her family lived 1946–59.
  2 The Society of Hons was invented by DD and her sister Jessica when they were children. They met in a linen cupboard, a haven of warmth in their Oxfordshire home, Swinbrook House – later immortalised as the 'Hons' Cupboard' in Nancy Mitford's novels. Anyone not an Hon was a 'horrible Counter-Hon'.

Saturday [May 1956]   Gadencourt
                                                       Pacy-sur-Eure

Darling Debo,

I'm not going to attempt to say thank you in this letter for that
lovely Paradise stay in Lismore – only that I still exist in a glorious
afterglow of it, and find myself smiling with the inane felicity of a
turnip lantern whenever I think of it, which is almost the whole
time: it must astonish passers-by . . .

Millions of hugs & love to Xan and Daph. I'm writing to them
this afternoon.[1]

And Glorious love & devotion to you, from
        Paddy

1 The letter follows.

Saturday [May 1956]   Gadencourt
                                                       Pacy-sur-Eure

Darling Daphne & Xan,

Lismore was beyond all expectations, absolute bliss throughout.
Thank heavens no one else there most of the time except Debo,
Emma & Stoker,[1] Andrew[2] & Eliz[3] half the time, then Ran,[4]
Debo's Wife[5] for a night, and three heavenly days with nobody but
Debo and those sweet & comic children, for whom I fell like
anything, also for Andrew, but most of all, as you might guess, for
your best friend, Debo, who is funny, touching, ravishing and
enslaving, an exquisite and strange deviation. With all this, there was
another quality that I like more than anything, a wonderful and
disarming unguardedness in conversation, and an intuitive knack –
which you'd both mentioned – for people's moods and feelings.
Well, as you see, it's as I feared! These graces and charms must really
be enormous, because they even compensate for an engagingly
unashamed Philistinism.

Anyway, all that flair and instinct, coupled with so many pretty
ways, nearly makes up for the gaps left by Shakespeare etc. As you can
imagine, we talked lots about you both, an orgy of body-worship[6]

all round. I long to hear how it all went, the descent on Tangiers. I thought for one wild moment of inflicting myself on you – or the neighbourhood – but had, ruefully, to come back here.

There was hardly a drop of rain all the time and the whole castle and the primeval forest round it were spellbound in a late spring or early summer trance; heavy rhododendron blossom everywhere and, under the Rapunzel tower I inhabited, a still leafless magnolia tree shedding petals like giant snowflakes over the parallel stripes of an embattled new-mown lawn: silver fish flickered in the river, wood pigeons cooed and herons slowly wheeled through trees so overgrown with lichen they looked like green coral, drooping with ferns and lianas, almost like an equatorial jungle. One would hardly have been surprised to see a pterodactyl or an archaeopteryx sail through the twilight, or the neck of a dinosaur craning through the ferns and lapping up a few bushels out of the Blackwater, which curls away like the Limpopo, all set about with fever-trees . . . Anyway, you know it all so well, and Debo must have told you all our adventures and peregrinations: lovely gorse burning; visits to cows, drinking Guinness as one went; watching salmon hauled in below Dromana, finding bones in a graveyard overgrown with giant broccoli, while ravens croaked in a ruined tower; two swans nesting on the mudflats in front of Ballinatray, the falling house where the housemaid is a keen huntswoman; the little Gaelic-speaking lobster harbour of Helvik – a Norse name – then my search for a shrimp tea (what was shrimp in Irish we wondered? – sráoimph? At last we found an old boy in Ardmore, who scratched his head and said, as if he was imparting a treasonable secret: '*Birawny* is what they call ut'). Then, on the last day, a wonderful picnic three miles from Bridget's[7] house, outside a witch's hut in a magical wood containing a *fairy tree*, and a *queen's tree*, so the witch said. She had a small boy there, a grandchild: 'my dartur doid in the bearin of him, and left us in poor circumstances . . .' Then Aer Lingus, London, and the 400[8] in the space of 3 or 4 hours.

Darling Daph & Xan, must stop now. Do sit down (unlike me!) and write at once with lots of details and news. I'm feeling *un poco adagio* & lonely as you might say at the moment. Thank heavens Joan[9] gets back in a few days.

Fondest love

Paddy

1 DD's elder daughter, Emma Cavendish (1943–), and son, Peregrine Hartington (1944–), always known as 'Stoker'.

2 Andrew Cavendish, 11th Duke of Devonshire (1920–2004). Politician, racehorse owner, keen collector of contemporary British art and passionate book collector. Married DD in 1941. Having lost his older brother, Billy, in 1944, he succeeded to the title and Devonshire estates after his father's death in 1950. PLF described him as 'infectiously spontaneous, stylish and funny', with a 'baseless feeling of unworthiness for the wholly unexpected succession to his great heritage'. *Spectator*, 12 June 2004.

3 Lady Elizabeth (Deacon) Cavendish (1926–). DD's unmarried sister-in-law. Long-time companion to the Poet Laureate John Betjeman.

4 Randal McDonnell, 8th Earl of Antrim (1911–77). Chairman of the National Trust 1965–77. A great friend of the Devonshires who nevertheless always addressed him, for reasons forgotten, as 'Lord Antrim'.

5 Lady Katherine (Kitty) Petty-Fitzmaurice, Baroness Nairne (1912–95). DD's closest friend's nickname, 'Wife', originated from an involved family joke which began when a man repeatedly referred to his wife as 'Kitty my wife' in one breath. It was adopted by DD to describe any great friend of either sex. Married 3rd Viscount Mersey in 1933.

6 An expression applied by DD to anyone – or anything – that she happened to like.

7 Lady Bridget Parsons (1907–72). 'Beautiful, silent and often grumpy friend of my sisters and my brother Tom.' (DD) Her widowed mother, the Countess of Rosse, was married to 5th Viscount de Vesci of Abbeyleix. It was in their woods that the picnic took place.

8 A nightclub off London's Leicester Square. Owing to the licensing laws at the time, it was not possible to buy individual drinks, only whole bottles, 'but they would keep it for you for your next visit. I finished a bottle in 1945 that I had begun in 1940.' (PLF)

9 Joan Eyres Monsell (1912–2003). PLF first met the beautiful, highbrow amateur photographer in wartime Cairo and they were eventually married in 1968. She was first married, 1939–47, to John Rayner. Naturally self-effacing, it was her 'elegance, luminous intelligence, curiosity, understanding and unerring high standards that made her such a perfect muse to her lifelong companion and husband'. John Craxton, *The Times*, 10 June 2003.

[Postmarked May 1956]   Tangiers
[Postcard]

I *am* having a jolly time, no one goes on at me about learning to
read but there is ever such a lot to hear. V. pleased with your
telegram in Frogland. We are going on a Mystery Trip into the
hinterland and to a grand dinner party, Daphne has made a
wonderful holiday. Xan is being a terrific Hon, very gullible.

Come back to Lismore.

Much love

Debo

✱

(DD)

*Daphne Weymouth – as she was when I first knew her – was synonymous
with enjoyment, laughter, fun and high jinks. She was one who lifted the spirits
with her energy and overflowing good nature. She went in for almost childlike
excesses of all kinds which, with her beauty, courage and imagination, made her
an irresistible companion.*

*Sturford Meade, Henry and Daphne's house near Longleat, was a refuge of
luxury and pre-war gaiety made more immediate by the friends ordered abroad,
often never to return. For Andrew and me it was a second home while he was
stationed at nearby Warminster in 1942–3.*

*Many marriages failed to survive wartime separation and when Henry came
back after five years in the Middle East both had changed and theirs sadly
stuttered to an end.*

*Daphne alone and in the prime of her life meant lovers; one or two serious,
some here today and gone tomorrow. Her admirers were legion. She remained
a great friend of us both, as did her second husband, Xan. She was married
for twenty-five years to both her husbands. Two silver weddings must be
unusual.*

*Wherever Daphne and Xan settled – like migrating birds they were often
on the move – they made you feel happy and at home. Their company, the chat
and the fun overcame any physical discomfort or rough edges which might be
found in a hired house.*

Tangiers was one of their stops and I stayed with them there. Their little, damp and badly lit house was squashed in a busy street so narrow that the continuous noise never got out, roamed by packs of dishevelled children with runny noses, and no Europeans nearby.

We went into the hinterland in the hopes of seeing the Blue Men of the desert, crossed mountains and drank too much coffee. With Xan one always felt safe, however hazardous the road.

We had lunch with the best-known ex-pat, David Herbert,[1] a lifter of mood, so quick and funny. I felt he must have been very homesick. One side of his life could flourish unchecked, but there were few kindred spirits to entertain his whizzing social side, which was such a feature of life at Wilton and its neighbourhood. I loved him until his disloyalty and cattiness about my sister Diana[2] ended our friendship.

1 David Herbert (1908–95). Immensely hospitable son of the 15th Earl of Pembroke, who grew up at Wilton House in Wiltshire. He first visited Tangiers in 1933 and settled there permanently after the war.

2 Diana Mitford (1910–2003). DD's sister left her first husband, Bryan Guinness, for Sir Oswald Mosley, leader of the British Union of Fascists, whom she married in 1936. Her political views and her refusal to repudiate her friendship with Hitler led many people to turn their backs on her.

Sunday [1956]   Gadencourt
                                                    Pacy-sur-Eure

Dearest Debo,

I really must try and get hold of a travelling brain-sharpener[1] (the size of one of those old bucket-shaped helmet-cases of japanned leather or tin, usually found in attics), because I was convinced you were leaving London a day later than you did. So you must picture my sorrow and dismay at the end of the telephone when I discovered that I was wrong, and that you had left an hour and a half before. It was little comfort to think that you were staying at the Continental. I hope you got a telegram from me there – also another and a stop-gap letter to Tangiers begging you to stop in Paris on the way back in order that we might spend a lovely evening guzzling and then dancing till cockcrow and finally eating onion-soup in the Halles as dawn broke.

The truth is I simply long for you, and hate the idea of changing jokes etc. You know, the sort of mood when nobody else will quite do. I'm still basking in a felicitous hangover of Ireland, and constantly discover vast smiles bisecting my rough-hewn features at the thought of all the fun and enchantment there. You, Andrew, Emma & Stoker seem saints and angels in human form. It's a miracle you're allowed to live, so do beware of traffic, falling flagpoles, mushrooms, lighting rockets and undercurrents when bathing; and a billion thanks for letting me come & stay.

I've just written a long letter to Xan and Daph about all this and about you, and piled it on pretty thick – but no thicker, I hasten to say, than the truth, which is glorious. I long to hear from you and from them about Tangiers, so please don't be sparing, and write almost at once and let it rip. I wish you could fly to Paris just for fun so that my splendid scheme can come into operation. Otherwise, I doubt if I shall survive, and that would never do. I'm down with Blackwater fever as it is, and the doctors are pulling long faces.

I say, wasn't it marvellous discovering that wobbly echo – Fermor's echo – under the bridge?[2] I wish I really had written down all I wanted to remember, instead of only a few, but I'll get them all straight in time. At the moment they are all dotted about my brain like bits of Meccano to be assembled some time . . .

I spent the weekend at Ad. Lubbock's,[3] then dined with Judy Montagu, Peter Quennell and the girl, called Spider Monkey,[4] who he is about to marry. She's very beautiful but etiolated and looks like Alice after finishing the bottle labelled DRINK ME. Then I came to Paris, and spent the evening, till 3 a.m., talking to Diana Cooper[5] in a café, only to discover as we left that the key of her car had been pinched . . . Luncheon with Nancy next day, when, by request and accompanied by her silver peal of laughter, she sang me 'the bubbling of the glands';[6] a sound for sore ears. Then I came out here, where my darling Joan arrives on Teusday.

It might be still summer, and I'm scribbling away under an apple tree up to the ankles in long grass, daisies and dandelion clocks, those infallible timepieces. Thousands of birds whizz to and fro, an oddly

English sounding cuckoo lives close and a frenzied rattle indicates that several woodpeckers are taking toll of many an elm trunk. Although it is only 6 in the evening, an untimely nightingale sets me a-swoon with forlorn thoughts. In fact, I'm going indoors to get a swig of calvados. How lovely it would be if, on coming back, I saw you mooning about under these branches in that saffron kilt and black stockings, like an Edwardian girl who's just finished a fencing lesson. One of the nicest bits at Lismore was walking through the wood above the river just before dinner on the last night, with a sunset streaming through the branches.

I saw Ran at Lady Bridget [Parsons]'s and we almost wept with nostalgia. It would be lovely if you came to Paris, so please try – I'd be there hot foot! But please write hourly, or I'll pine away, I do believe.

With fondest love and devotion, darling Debo from
Paddy

1 'A mythical device invented by Andrew to get a quicker response from dim friends. It was a metal headpiece from which two razor blades penetrated the skull and sharpened the wits of the wearer. Often accompanied by a mind broadener, a gentler mechanism, that stretched the mind in all directions.' (DD)

2 'The bridge over the Blackwater at Lismore has several arches crossing fields that are regularly flooded. When the river is low you can walk under them. The highest arch echoes loudly and was called after Paddy, who used to sing there for the satisfaction of hearing his amplified voice.' (DD)

3 Adelaide Stanley (1906–81). A friend of PLF and cousin of DD, who lived near Sevenoaks in Kent. Married Maurice Lubbock in 1926.

4 Sonia (Spider) Leon (1928–). Nicknamed for her long-limbed elegance by Peter Quennell, whom she married in 1956.

5 Lady Diana Manners (1892–1986). The reigning beauty of her age, greatly admired by PLF, married Alfred Duff Cooper, 1st Viscount Norwich, in 1919. Flouting the convention that a retiring ambassador should not return to the country of his former post until at least a year after his departure, the Coopers settled at St Firmin immediately after his retirement in 1947 and remained there until Norwich's death in 1954.

6 'Nancy used to tease me mercilessly about the tuberculin gland in my neck, which she said would put off prospective suitors as it "hubbled and bubbled" at night. She sang to the tune of a popular song, "The hounds and the horses, galloping over the land, all stopped to hear the hubbling and the bubbling of the gland", which induced tears.' (DD)

[May 1956]   Gadencourt
                                                    Pacy-sur-Eure

Darling Debo,

Your letter was a marvel and a lovely fat one. I revelled in every single word, and laughed a lot and love your flat-out, headlong way of writing. It plunged me back in Lismore – staying there and all the fun, jokes and everything were by far the nicest thing for me this year – and also gave me a dash of the gloom of an exile wandering far away from Eden. I say, what do you mean about me not liking gardens? I love them, and that one especially, in particular with a glass in hand and the key lost, lawns in stripes, but some grass under trees so long that one gets back slightly late for dinner, festooned up to the knees in cuckoo-spit.

Alas, I ought to resist the temptation to implore you to come to Paris now, as I am bombarded by my publisher daily to have the manuscript of the book[1] in within the fortnight, or else it won't be able to come out this year – and I've only got this house till the end of June. However, if you *did* come to Paris, I need hardly say that I'd be there faster than an arrow from a bow . . . I thought of trying to get you to come and stay here, but it wouldn't be sensible at the moment, as I'd have to be closeted with this blithering book in a muck sweat of creative fever, leaving you and Joan alone all day in double agony of shyness. *BUT*, I do hope you'll be in London for the last half of June, when I'm coming over purely on pleasure bent, and rather hoping to be practically inseparable from your side. *DO PLEASE TRY!* We could do innumerable glorious things. I long to do lots more dancing for one thing, and make you stay up long past bedtime, also to take that river steamer to Greenwich. Do let me know about this, and what hopes there are. I do hope you haven't got a million beastly thwarting plans! The truth is I worship & long to see you, and keep thinking of things to talk about.

The sun pours down here and I scribble a lot in the garden, planning to arrive in London brown and gimlet-eyed, ready to win friends and influence people. Two swallows flew into my room this morning and circled round for twenty minutes. I suppose it's too late, but it would be nice if they built a nest against one of the beams that cross the ceiling. The windows would have to be left open even in a deluge. One of them kept banging against a window instead of flying out. I put it in my pocket, went out to the lawn where some people were. I said 'Watch me throw a stone over that enormous tree', took it out and threw it up into the air. It fluttered up into the firmament and everyone was amazed!

Do please write at once and tell your plans, and an autobiography of your immediate past.

With lots of love from
    Paddy

A published report recalls in 1952 that fornication was responsible for over 32,000 illegitimate births. So *THAT'S* what it's caused by! I'm glad they've put their finger on it at last . . .

1 *A Time to Keep Silence* (1957). An account of PLF's sojourns in monasteries in France and Cappadocia, where he retreated to work on his first book *The Traveller's Tree: A Journey through the Caribbean Islands* (1950).

2 June 1956   Edensor House
                                                        Bakewell

Darling Paddy,

V nice to get a letter. V v sad to leave Ireland. The Wife and I are so overcome with shyness, we find it difficult to speak to strangers, even dogs, just like you & I did when we felt funny about going to a restaurant.

It is midwinter here, quite a nice day for February, & one needs woollen knickers. The Wife has got on orchid pink, it will get dirty in the coal dust of the industrial north.

When are you coming to England, what I mean is when are you *really* coming, not saying one day & meaning something quite else. Then I can get on with my plans for going to Greenwich by boat etc. Get yr travelling Wit Sharpener on in good time.

Let one know all.

Much love
    D Devonshire

8 June 1956
[Postcard]

My address of Ensor Lodge was a v bad shot. It is *Edensor House*, Bakewell, Derbyshire.

Al Khan[1] was v v good & came to Harvey Nichols to buy stays & stockings & gloves. He knows unexpected things like how gloves shrink. I looked in the pig house here – *what do you think I found?* A little pig. I'll show you if you come here.

Wife & I were sitting, thinking no ill of anyone when what should my eye light on but that great fat green book you wrote,[2] so I had a look in it. Meanwhile I've got to page 18 of *Hide & Seek*.[3]

Do you always spell Tues Teus, is it Greek or something?

Diana Cooper looked smashing at a ball I went to, about 16.

Just got a P.C. from Xan so my day is made.

---

1 Prince Aly Khan (1911–60). The racehorse-owning playboy, father of the present Aga Khan, was reputed to be able to handle more women simultaneously than most men can in a lifetime. His marriage to his second wife, the actress Rita Hayworth, ended in 1953. He was often DD's host in Paris and at the Château de l'Horizon in the South of France.

2 *The Traveller's Tree*. The book grew out of captions PLF wrote to accompany photographs of the Caribbean, taken by his friend the Greek photographer Costa Achillopoulos.

3 Xan Fielding, *Hide and Seek: The Story of a War-time Agent* (1954).

Monday, 12 June 1956   c/o Julian Pitt-Rivers[1]
                                              Château du Roc
                                              Fons, Lot

Darling Debo,

I'm sorry about Ensor Lodge.

Yes, I've always had trouble with Teusday; I expect you make mistakes about different shapes of cattle cake sometimes.

It would be lovely to have a transparent and invisible brain-sharpener that one could wear all the time, or even a small pocket one like a hearing aid, self-stropping, stainless with a set of refills.

I set off with Joan last week in a Bentley she's got, so old as to be practically a fossil but fast as the wind. We stopped the first night

at a small town called Valençay, where there's a huge castle that used
to belong to Talleyrand. In the park are numbers of strange birds that
ought to be put in the book: scores of different-coloured peacocks
forever perching on pinnacles and stone urns; secretary-birds that
sound more useful than they really are and glorious-coloured cranes
from Sardinia and the Cape of Good Hope, with headdresses like
Red Indians, and a number of flamingos.

   Lots of love from
      Paddy

1 PLF was staying with the anthropologist Julian Pitt-Rivers (1919–2001) and his
second wife, Margarita, former wife of Miguel Primo de Rivera, son of the Spanish
dictator.

26 August 1956   Aix en Provence

Darling Debo,
   I'm terribly sorry not having written half a century ago, after
telephoning you on the eve of leaving to join Xan and Daph in the
South of France. Things there were such turmoil that I don't think any
of the hundred-odd people engaged on making that film[1] wrote so
much as a postcard the whole time. D, X & I talked it over and
decided you would have hated it. I did, rather, and buggered off after
about a week.
   It was all pretty queer. First things first: Dirk Bogarde,[2] the actor
who is doing one in the film, is absolutely charming – slim,
handsome, nice speaking-voice and manner, a super-gent, the ghost
of oneself 12 years ago. He and Daph & Xan had become bosom
friends by the time I got there, and he and his equally nice manager
(rather a grand thing to have?) are going to stay with them for
Christmas in Tangiers. We all lived – us, the other actors, directors,
cameramen etc – in a vast chalet, miles above the clouds in the
French Alps, leagues away from anywhere and at the end of an
immeasurable tangle of hairpin bends. The film itself, what I saw of
it, is tremendously exciting – tremendous pace, action galore, staggering
scenery, with the guns of whiskered and turbaned Cretan guerrillas

jutting down from every rock and miles of peaceful French roads
choked with truckloads of steel-helmeted Germans bawling 'Lili
Marlene'. It'll certainly be a thumping success, and when it finally
appears at the Odeon or elsewhere, I propose to sneak in and see
it in a false beard night after night. Some bits – not yet filmed,
fortunately – turn Bogarde-Fermor into a mixture of Garth[3] &
Superman, shooting Germans clean through the breast from a
dentist's chair, strangling sentries in an offhand manner – *all totally
fictitious*! I'm having a terrific tussle getting them to change these bits
in the film, not because I really mind, but because anyone who
knows anything about the operation knows that it's all rot. There are
scores of small things dead wrong, & Xan and I are having a death
struggle to get them put right, mostly for the sake of Greek and
Cretan friends. It's all v. rum. The main trouble is that once a film
script is written, the authors themselves bow down and worship it as
though it were Holy Writ. *IT* becomes the truth and anyone trying
to change it (like X or me) incurs the horror of heretics trying to
tamper with the text of the Gospel.

Well, I baled out of this mountain madhouse after 7 days and
retreated to a minute Provençal village called Auribeau, where I
stayed in the pub and scribbled all day (against time) in the priest's
leafy garden overlooking a forested valley along which flowed a
swift and icy river with deep green pools dappled with the shadows
of leaves where I splashed and floated between paragraphs for hours
among the dragonflies. There was never anyone there except occasionally a solitary fisherman with a straw hat and never a bite.*

Then everything changed 100%, when Annie Fleming went to
stay with Somerset Maugham[4] (not Willy to me) at Cap Ferrat, where
he inhabits a gorgeous villa. It was a concerted plan that she should
try and wangle my staying there for fun, for a few days. She duly got
me asked there to luncheon, and afterwards, as if by clockwork, Mr
Maugham asked me to stay several days and everything looked like a
triumph of Annie's engineering and plain sailing. *But there were rocks
ahead.* (Do you know Somerset Maugham? He is 84, and his face is

---

* Perhaps because of the splashing I mentioned.

the wickedest tangle of cruel wrinkles I have ever seen and so discoloured and green that it looks as though he has been rotting in the Bastille, or chained to the bench of a galley or inside an iron mask for half a century. Alligator's eyes peer from folds of pleated hide and below them an agonizing snarl is beset with discoloured and truncated fangs, but the thing to remember is that he has a very pronounced and noticeable stutter that can seize up a sentence for 30 seconds on end.)

All went better and better – a sort of honeymoon – as the day progressed. But at dinner things began to go wrong. Two horrible and boring guests arrived (publishers) called Mr & Mrs Frere.[5] Mr Frere made some sweeping generalization and

Me 'I love generalizations – for instance, that all Quakers are colour-blind (you know the line) – or that all heralds stutter!'

Mrs Frere 'Stutter?'

Me 'Yes.'

Mrs Frere 'How do you mean, stutter?'

Me 'Stutter . . . you know, stammer . . .'

Later on, after that fatal 8th glass of whisky, I was in trouble again: –

Somerset Maugham 'It's a c-c-confounded nuisance t-t-today b-b-being the F-feast of the As-as-as-assumption. N-none of the g-gardeners have d-done a s-s-stroke . . .'

Me 'Ah yes! The Feast of the Assumption of the Blessed Virgin! Just after the Pope gave out the dogma a few years ago, I was going round the Louvre with a friend of mine called Robin Fedden[6] (who, by ill luck, has a terrible stammer) and we paused in front of a huge picture of the Assumption by (I think) Correggio (*ah, oui*) & Robin turned to me and said "Th-th-that's what I c-c-call an un-w-w-warrantable as-s-s-sumption".'

There was a moment's silence, the time needed for biting one's tongue out. When bedtime came my host approached me with a reptile's fixity, offering me a hand as cold as a toad, with the words: 'W-w-well I'll s-s-say g-good-b-b-bye now in c-case I'm not up b-by the t-time y-you l-l-leave . . .'

Annie helped me pack next morning, and as I strode, suitcase in hand, to the door, there was a sound like an ogre's sneeze. The lock of the suitcase had caught in the sheet, leaving a jagged yard-long rent across the snow-white expanse of heavily embroidered gossamer. I broke into a run and Annie into fits of suppressed laughter.

As a result of bullying by Annie & Diana Cooper (who turned up in the area, where I had settled in a horrible hotel, soon after) I was asked by W.S.M. to a meal of reconciliation and amends, where we met as affable strangers. It was really a gasbag's penance and I, having learnt the hard way, vouchsafed little more than a few safe monosyllables.

The rest of my short stay in that area was spent with D. Cooper, Annie, Robin & Mary,[7] & Hamish[8] (who were all staying with Mrs Fellowes).[9] *I hate it* – the Côte d'Azur I mean – and will never set foot there again.

I've taken rooms here for a week – ending tomorrow – in a pretty, retired midwife's house, in whose garden I write. This ravishing town, full of chimes of bells, fountains, peasants playing *boules* in the shadow of lime trees and splendid decaying palaces and churches, is a wonderful disinfectant after that awful coast. All is splendid or dilapidated, nothing smart.

In two days time I set off on the great yacht Diana has borrowed[10] with Duff, Joan, Alan Pryce-Jones[11] and a couple called Frank & Kitty Giles:[12] Corsica, Sardinia, Sicily. It really would be a kind act were you to write c/o British Consul, Cagliari, Sardinia. Meanwhile, please give my love to Andrew, to Emma & Stoker (angels in human form) & to your Wife.

Lots of love from
    Paddy[13]

---

1 *Ill Met by Moonlight* (1957), produced and directed by Michael Powell and Emeric Pressburger. A romanticised version of the daring abduction, led by PLF, of General Heinrich Kreipe in Nazi-occupied Crete, based on the book by PLF's comrade William Stanley Moss (1950).

2 Dirk Bogarde (1921–99). The actor was apprehensive about meeting the real-life character he was playing but was soon won over by PLF's charm and adroitness.

3 Muscle-bound hero of a strip cartoon which ran in the *Daily Mirror* 1943–97.

4 W. Somerset Maugham (1874–1965). The writer bought the Villa Mauresque on the French Riviera after his divorce from his wife, Syrie, in 1927.

5 Alexander Frere-Reeves (1892–1984). Publisher, for many years head of William Heinemann, Maugham's publishing house. Married to Patricia Wallace, daughter of the thriller-writer Edgar Wallace. 'Frere (nasty man) made us all angry by saying that no author wrote for anything but profit, this put my voice up by several octaves as well as Paddy's.' *The Letters of Ann Fleming*, edited by Mark Amory (Collins, 1985), p. 185.

6 Robin Fedden (1908–77). Gifted writer, poet, traveller and mountaineer who was Historic Buildings Secretary at the National Trust 1951–73. Married Greek-born Renée Catzeflis (d. 1992) in 1942.

7 Lady Mary St Clair-Erskine (1912–93). Wayward daughter of 5th Earl of Rosslyn. 'She could get away with almost anything through her charm, and was always forgiven; and there was often plenty to forgive.' Daphne Fielding, *Mercury Presides* (Eyre & Spottiswoode, 1954), p. 159. Married to Sir Philip Dunn 1933–44, to Robin Campbell 1946–58, to Charles McCabe 1962–9 and again to Sir Philip Dunn in 1969.

8 James Alexander (Hamish) St Clair-Erskine (1909–73). Son of 5th Earl of Rosslyn with whom Nancy Mitford, in spite of his homosexuality, had been infatuated when young.

9 Marguerite (Daisy) Decazes (1890–1962). Well dressed, sharp-tongued daughter of the 3rd Duc Decazes, and heiress through her mother to the Singer sewing-machine fortune. She owned the luxurious villa Les Zoraïdes on Cap Martin, near Monaco. Married Reginald Fellowes, as her second husband, in 1919.

10 Diana Cooper had been lent the 103-foot *Eros II* by Greek shipping magnate Stavros Niarchos (1908–96).

11 Alan Pryce-Jones (1908–2000). Writer, critic and editor of the *Times Literary Supplement* 1948–59, who had once been engaged to Joan Leigh Fermor. Married Thérèse Fould-Springer in 1934.

12 Frank Giles (1919–). Author and journalist, Paris correspondent of *The Times* 1953–60. Married to Lady Katherine (Kitty) Sackville in 1946.

13 PLF reworked this letter at a later date, providing further details of his fateful visit to Somerset Maugham. It was published in an article by Ben Downing, *Paris Review*, Spring 2003.

1 October 1956   Easton Court Hotel
                                                 Chagford, Nr. Exeter
                                                 Devon

Darling Debo,

I've been at this pub in the heart of Andrew's damp duchy for about a week, ever since leaving that yacht (which was perfect), and I'm scribbling away like mad. Outside, the rain thrashes down as though out of sheer spite, and I wish there was somebody I could complain to, and have something done. I don't mind as much as I would at other times, though, as it stops me from mooching endlessly about the moors (which I might otherwise do) instead of writing.

It's rather strange and mysterious country, and whenever there's a couple of hours that look faintly possible, I go tittupping over the moors and through the woods on a black horse called Flash that lives hard by; usually getting soaked by sudden showers or by crashing along overgrown rides where each leaf one collides with seems to shed a tablespoonful of rainwater. Very steep hills are separated by rapid streams flowing with Guinness-dark water. The banks are full of rowan-berries, Lords and Ladies run to seed, ragged-robin and willowherb dribbling with the spit of cuckoos long flown. The woods are thick with moss & lichen (like Lismore), turning into the same green coral. Occasionally they open into glades where many vixens would be decadently gloved in magenta. Stone bridges as uncouth and angular as early heraldry span these streams and ring hollow under-hoof, and the dampness, darkness and greenness gives them a submarine & legendary feeling. One should be dressed in full armour under shoals of green-haired mermaids drifting through the oak branches on slow and invisible currents, all to the sound of harps, if you catch my drift.

Above this, Dartmoor is dotted with rings of druidical stones or jutting at a slant from a sea of red bracken, and above this bracken, like chessmen or T'ang (*ah oui!*) objects, peer the heads of wild ponies the size of large dogs, gazing as though mesmerized, as one approaches cautiously. Most are bay but others are black, chestnut, roan, grey, dappled, skewbald or piebald in bold geographical designs, one or two practically striped like zebras, many with blond flapperish manes & tails. One raffish grey stallion, obviously of standing and authority, has one of his mad eyes surrounded by a piratical black patch. Up you creep till suddenly they are off helter-skelter in a flurry of flying hoofs and horsehair, the burglarious stallion taking advantage of the disorder by attempting to inflict the last outrages on minute mares at the gallop: the foals pounding anxiously after them are so small that they only make a ripple on top of the bracken. At a safe distance they freeze again, as in grandmother's steps. They must have been caught and branded and let loose again, and now various

owners are rounding them up by their brands for the annual pony
fair in Chagford later this month. They are broken-in & sold as pets
or for children or for circuses – formerly to costermongers and –
too awful to think of, after their free and dashing life on the moors
– sent down coalmines; or, worse still, shanghaied on to tramp
steamers for Belgians to munch.

I went on one of these raids yesterday: Mr French, a local stable
owner with a well-nigh incomprehensible Devon accent, & a ragged
gang of farm boys on steeds & self. It was a long job. The stableman
warned me that these ponies were contrary and artful buggers. The
afternoon wore by in stealthy encircling advances through the bracken,
long waits in the howling wind with nothing to do but stuff with
blackberries, and sudden gallops, whips cracking like mad while the
boys made shrill noises like barking dogs & owls hooting. At last we
had about a hundred cornered in a lane, kicking, leaping, whinnying
and trying to clamber over each other. Thirty were picked out by their
brands and we set off through a ten-mile labyrinth of lanes as the sun
was setting, half of us in front to block escape routes at crossroads.
Night had fallen by the time we drove this cavalcade of pigmies
through the streets of Chagford. The aborigines emerged, beer mug in
hand, from brightly lit pubs to watch these artful buggers pound by. It
was past ten when we trotted them into a field where three sleek elderly
giants were already grazing. They raised their heads in amazement as
though a horde of Teddy Boys, stunted with gin, had suddenly
rocked'n'rolled into the Athenaeum. (What lies ahead of these problem
ponies? Will they settle down?) I'm glad to say that by the time we
left them there in the dark, one of the fogeys was diffidently rubbing
noses with the little patch-eyed stallion (looking no bigger than a
dachshund) which I though particularly decent.

Lots of love,
    Paddy

P.S. I had dinner with Mrs Basil Seal on the way back, and was
pleased & flattered at her learning the saga of Mr Maugham *via* you;
but sorry she had written back saying all his wrinkles spelt nothing
but kindness & benevolence.

[5 November 1956]   Easton Court Hotel
                                               Chagford

Darling Debo

I've just got your letter from Sardinia. It's a lovely letter, only
marred, as was your last one, by this business about pall-bearers. You
tell me all about enlisting wonderful John[1] & Xan, with never a hint
of asking me, when I am exactly the right medium height, own a
dark suit and a measured tread, and would really look sad (not that
your other candidates wouldn't). So please put me down, should I
outlive you and there are still any vacancies. I'll do a '*PLF writes:* –'
in *The Times* if you like and say that all our wishes go out to your
widow, Baroness Nairne[2] etc.

I'm still chained to this never-ending book, it is nearly finished
and marvellous. I think. I wish Edensor House was three miles away
– I could tittup there in the evenings on Flash, on whose back I
pound rather aimlessly across the moors, which grow steadily bleaker
and more menacing as the days draw in. It's just the sort of place
where, some windy night, I might help some poor and infirm old
woman bent double under a load of sticks, who would turn out to
have supernatural powers and grant three wishes . . . But not a soul
so far. I ought really to have two older brothers who had already
ridden that way and not only not helped her, but mocked her age &
infirmity.

With lots of love
Paddy

[1] Lieut.-Col. John Silcock; the Devonshires' land agent at Lismore for many years.
[2] DD's 'Wife', Katherine Mersey.

12 November 1956   Easton Court Hotel
                                          Chagford

Darling Debo,

I say, how exciting about that baby.[1] I do think you are clever.
Have you thought of names? Boys: Tarquin, Clovis, Comus, Spiridian.
Girls: Pomona, a minor rustic goddess of orchards and walled gardens.
But perhaps Geo., Harry, Betty, Peg and Polly, etc are safest.

I would *simply love* to come for the chatting, when I'm out of
this literary forest. My egress is being held up a lot by this Crete
film. I've just been to another one, trying to instruct Cypriot waiters
(who are dubbing – as they say – the voices of Cretan guerrillas) to
talk in a Cretan dialect, which is about as hard as telling a Bakewell
gamekeeper to talk like a Co. Waterford poacher. I'm going to do all
the Greek-speaking bits done by Dirk, i.e. he makes the shapes with
his mouth, laughs superciliously, lifts his eyebrows or shouts at the
top of his voice – all in dead silence – while I, concealed in a bush,
make all the noises . . . rather an intimate relationship. But most of it
is in English. It's all very queer.

HORSY INTELLIGENCE: On one of these rural rides yesterday
afternoon, my horse (Flash) stopped at a gate and an immense
carthorse came thundering over the grass to rub muzzles. They
alternately put their nostrils end to end – not a very good fit, owing
to the size of the newcomer – and blew hard, sending out great
clouds of steam as it was a frosty evening. They seemed very keen on
this and I'm thinking of taking it up.

Stranger still, in the middle of last night – at 2 a.m. – I heard a
cavalcade of horses trotting and cantering under my window, jumped
out of bed and peered out like Old Mother Slipper Slopper, but it
was pitch-dark and windy and nothing to be seen, eerie, like
smugglers or highwaymen or a troop of hired assassins off for an
ambush with dark lanterns. I told the rather credulous maid Barbara
about it next morning, who said it must have been ghosts or –
rather wittily I thought – nightmares. It turned out in the end to be
a fast set of Dartmoor ponies. Sometimes on very windy and cold
nights, they come tooling down – 'It must be terrible cold for them

up there' – and clatter about in the villages, waking all the dogs and setting cocks crowing prematurely. There have been times when swarms have even galloped through Exeter in the small hours, whinnying in the Cathedral Close and causing many a citizen and minor canon to sit up in the dark with their eyes rolling in wild surmise.

Lots of love from
    Paddy

---

1 DD was expecting her younger daughter, Sophia, born on 18 March 1957.

[1956]   Easton Court Hotel
                                          Chagford

Darling Debo,

I hunted yesterday, the first time since the war, and enjoyed every second of it. Scarcely any jumps, which was a comfort, except a few ditches over which nimble Flash sailed as lightly as a moth. It was a lovely day of bright rainy sunlight, what they call a fox's wedding in Northamptonshire. There were only about 15 people, all squire farmers and their mates, a bit dull, but very nice and friendly. All except one, perhaps, who I later learnt was not quite all there. After pounding for miles I found myself stationary beside him outside a spinney inside which a lot of yelping, horn blowing and whip cracking was going on. He was a great lantern-jawed, sombre man on a huge horse. Just in front of us, turning his back on all the flurry in the wood, sat an idle hound smothered in filth and, as it were, with legs akimbo, gazing from one to the other of us with benevolent interest, his tongue lolling amiably and occasionally scratching behind his ear with his right paw. After about 10 minutes the silence began to weigh, so I pointed at this hound with my borrowed crop and said, in a voice that wasn't my own: '*That hound's taking it very easy.*' My companion roused himself from a brown study, his great mug swivelled slowly in my direction and fixed me with large bloodshot eyes; but uttered never a word. In County Kildare he would have clapped spurs to his steed and given me two black eyes.

The going was very fast; hell for leather; but no foxes were killed.
Our cavalcade now and then made a very impressive noise, as troops
of heifers, fifty strong, kept joining us and hammered along through
the bracken at our sides. They seem very keen. Anti-bloodsport flocks
of sheep, however, dispersed at once with massed baaa's of protest.
Towards the end, ten of those ponies I've mentioned before – (they
look rather dismal at this time of the year, embedded in sodden
bracken, blinded by their manes and always wringing wet) – joined
the hounds and careered along in their midst. This particular gang
were black, white and marmalade skewbalds; in fact, slightly larger
hounds, looking like hounds' uncles at a rather hearty parents' match.
Lots of seagulls wheeled about mewing overhead, enjoying an inland
holiday. We ended up following the hounds and the ponies round
and round a wood till it began to get dark, and then chucked it.
I trotted home with the hunt secretary and his simple face was
puckered with surmise. 'Funny kind of a fox, that last one' he kept
murmuring between meditative puffs at his old briar. 'Didn't seem
able to make up his mind, somehow . . .'

Do (please) write to London (Travellers) as I think I've practically
finished here. I hope to see Nancy in the capital. Andrew has been
writing and speaking up manfully.[1] I do envy him his certainty.

Love from
Paddy

1 Andrew Devonshire fervently supported Prime Minister Anthony Eden's
contentious policy of military intervention during the Suez Crisis and had made
it the subject of his maiden speech in the House of Lords.

[April 1957]   13 Chester Row[1]
                                          London SW1

Darling Debo,
Do take care of Sophia. The great thing, I'm told, with children
of that age is to see they are not stolen away by gypsies and replaced
with a changeling, while the rightful baby is stained brown with
walnut juice and brought up to rob hencoops and tell fortunes, and

heaven knows what besides. Fancy that nurse threatening to put her outside for the crows . . .

I feel rather gloomy, and long to be out of this wretched town.

Lots of love from
    Paddy

1 PLF and Joan's London house.

Monday [24 June 1957]   13 Chester Row, SW1

Darling Debo,

I got a lovely letter from Emma this morning, praising a vasculum I had sent her.[1] She writes jolly well and funnily, and please give her my love. I hope it was the right size. My father[2] used seldom to be without one, and my sister and I, being snobbish and unbotanical, used to trail along a few feet ahead or behind, pretending there was no link.

Of course there were geological hammers, cameras, butterfly nets, map cases, sketching blocks, field glasses, reference books, steel-rimmed spectacles and a vole-skin cap like half a pumpkin with side flaps as well, and pepper-and-salt knickerbockers and boots with colossal studs, which he was always oiling. The great thing, I think I remember, is to put lots of damp moss in the vasculum before setting off on a stately botanical journey.

Please write at once.

Love
    Paddy

1 PLF had sent DD's daughter, a keen gardener from childhood, a container used by botanists to hold field samples.
2 Lewis Leigh Fermor (1880–1954). Distinguished geologist, author of *Memoir on the Manganese-Ore Deposits of India* (1909), who spent most of his working life as Director of the Geological Survey of India.

Saturday   Dumbleton Hall[1]
[Postmarked 7 July 1957]   Dumbleton, Evesham
                                            Worcestershire

Darling Debo,

Staying with Annie Fleming near Dover two weeks ago, half the English Channel flowed into my right ear and it's been feeling pretty queer ever since. Yesterday, my fierce Orangeman doctor from Belfast thrust into it a silver ice-cream cone or scoil sign[2] fitted with electric light, and said 'Why, you've got a fungus there!' What can he mean? I see a forest of toadstools, the sort that elves shelter under in summer showers, Arthur Rackham's world; so now weed killer is being pumped in. Rather glamorous, you'll allow.

They are mowing the hay here and everything smells marvellous. When this is finished, I sneak off to the village for a meditative glass of Ind Coope.

Lots of love from
    Paddy

1 A neo-Jacobean house belonging to PLF's father-in-law, Bolton Eyres Monsell, 1st Viscount Monsell (1881–1969), Conservative MP for Evesham 1910–35. John Betjeman recorded his memories of the Eyres Monsells in 'Dumbleton Hall', published in *Uncollected Poems* (1982).
2 The Irish school warning road-sign resembled an ice-cream cone on fire.

12 o'clock   13 Chester Row, SW1
[Postmarked 18 July 1957]

Darling Debo,

Bridget [Parsons]'s out alas.

But the real purpose of this letter is to tell you something I've just read, viz. that in ancient times in Sicily the smell of the flowers was so strong that hunting dogs used invariably to lose the scent and wander about for hours at a loss, bemusedly sniffing with half closed eyes, with the quarry happily grazing several miles off. Poor fuddled Bellman & True . . .[1]

Lots of love
    Paddy

1 Two of the foxhounds in the eighteenth-century hunting song 'D'ye ken John Peel'.

5 August [1957]   Hôtel Prince de Galles
                                                33 Avenue George V
                                                Paris

Darling Debo,

Everything's fixed. I only finished reading the book[1] three minutes
before meeting Mr Zanuck,[2] but it didn't matter, because he burst
into his suite at the Savoy like a rifle bullet saying: 'Swell to see you,
Mr Feemor, it's really swell. I'm off to the Belgian Congo in three
days, and I've just taken two yellow pills & three injections and don't
make much sense, so you mustn't be sore at me if I talk a whole lot
of boloney.'

He's tiny, with bright blue minute eyes glinting with mad intensity,
a ragged sandy moustache and his injections had clearly incapacitated
him from judging distances, as the colossal cigar in his mouth – as
irremovably there as part of his anatomy – was snapped in the middle,
one half hanging at right angles and belching volumes of smoke, like
the funnels of one of those Thames steamers going under Chelsea
Bridge. He must have charged into a door or a wall or perhaps a
mirror.

I can't remember if I told you that the whole of the book is a
plea against elephant shooting, in case the species becomes extinct.
The villain of the book goes berserk and shoots them by the score
in a sort of demon's passion. This is obviously the bit Mr Zanuck
likes best, because when I met him next day he said: 'It's a swell
book, Mr Feemor, a wonderful book. The best bit is when they
bump off all those elephants. But we'll run into difficulties here
because of all that goddam humanitarian hooey in England and
America. I'd like to do the thing properly, and shoot a whole lot of
them, a whole lot . . .' his blue eyes kindled dreamily. 'I doubt if I get
permission to shoot more than a dozen.' He looked rather dejected
for a second, but then said, cheering up, 'I tell you what we'll do!
We'll only shoot a dozen or maybe fifteen, but I'll put lots and lots
of cameras about at different angles so it'll look as if it were killing
hundreds! But what a book!'

There never seemed to be a second's question of my *not* doing the thing, so now I've got to start work full steam ahead and hope for the best. It's rather an alarming, but v. exciting assignation.

I had luncheon with the old French authoress[3] the day before yesterday and with Mark Grant,[4] and there was much loving talk of you, and swapping of Athenian for Irish tales. Otherwise, Paris seems stripped of all my friends and has become one of the major tropical cities of the world. The policemen are in shirtsleeves and khaki solar-topees, as though it were Khartoum. I wandered around by myself till 7 a.m. in Montmartre the first night in countless bars full of negroes, soldiers, sailors, toughs and tarts of all colours and a few noseless pimps, and on the second night till 8 a.m. in Montparnasse and Les Halles. Here, very strangely, I fell in with two Australian nurses who seemed a bit lost, and fed them onion soup as day broke, surrounded by porters and butchers in blood-stained smocks as though they had just been helping at the guillotine. I am writing this in the mosaic courtyard of this luxurious hotel, with a bogus Spanish fountain tinkling in the middle. The Frogs and Americans here look awful, exactly like pigs, with tiny pig's eyes. I have just caught a sobering glimpse of my own reflection, and so, alas, do I. Circe has done a thorough job.

How I wish you had been here! Just think of the night prowling and dark dancing, all the fun. I long for you like anything, and *yearn* and gaze towards the dividing Channel with hate.

Meanwhile, a billion tons of love, Debo darling, and promise to write hourly.

     Paddy

1 Romain Gary, *Les Racines du ciel* (1956). Set in French Equatorial Africa, the Goncourt Prize-winning novel tells the story of Morel, an idealistic ex-soldier, who sets out to save the African elephant from extinction. PLF was asked to work on the screenplay of the novel, adapted as the film *The Roots of Heaven* (1958).

2 Darryl F. Zanuck (1902–79). Hollywood producer of *The Roots of Heaven*.

3 One of DD's many nicknames for her sister Nancy, sometimes varied to 'the Old French writer'.

4 Mark Ogilvie-Grant (1905–69). A friend of PLF and all the Mitfords, who was posted to Greece with SOE and taken prisoner in the Mani soon after landing. Settled in Athens after the war, where he worked for BP and was 'a great friend of everyone interesting. He loved music and had a passion for the singing of Dame Nellie Melba and, late at night, would burst into imitations of her, half worship, half skit.' (PLF)

17 August 1957   Château de St Firmin
                                            Vineuil
                                            Oise

Darling Debo,

I *say* what an adventure with Evelyn Waugh![1] I can see those
pale eyes burning. He has the most peculiar expression of mouth,
eye-socket and nostril, as though they were all recoiling from
his own aroma, which would be a blend of tweed, claret,
cigar smoke and incense. Freud[2] too, eh? I suppose it's alright.
H'm.

I'm writing this in bed, and was woken up an hour ago by
hunting horns playing lovely melancholy tunes, soon followed by
hounds giving tongue, as they say, and, sitting up in bed with one
ear cocked, lo and behold, three men in scarlet coats were moving
across the park in the middle distance, with those horns that go
round the body like lifebelts. Ever since, there has been a distant
rumour of muted baying & fanfares. Is it stag hunting *already*, I
wonder, or just a sort of exercise? I wouldn't half mind doing it in
France sometime, just for the oddity. They hunt for truffles in the
oak forests of Périgord, in the south west, with specially trained
truffle hounds. It would be rather smart to be an MTH,[3] even a
joint one.

A Basque woman called Jacqueline looks after Joan and me here.
All her front teeth are missing, otherwise she's rather handsome in a
dark wild way – she's having a new set made by a dentist round the
corner. One has to look her hard in the eye when giving orders, and
none of one's usual diffidence; as, I imagine, with some animals like
lions or jaguars; otherwise she might turn and rend one, with her
back (perforce) teeth joining in one's jugular. Perhaps she's only
waiting for the dentist's work to be done before leaping and rolling
one over and over.

I'm rather enjoying this work, and am writing apace. It's all about
French Equatorial Africa, elephants, tom-toms and jet-black witch
doctors with spectacles painted on to their faces very eerily with
white clay.

I must go and borrow the gardener's bike, and spin through the rain to the post.

So lots of love, darling Debo, and polar bear hugs from
    Paddy

---

1 Evelyn Waugh (1903–66). The novelist, a difficult and demanding guest, announced that he had found an unemptied chamber pot in his bedside table when staying at Edensor with DD.
2 Lucian Freud (1922–). The artist painted six members of the Devonshire family. 'Very attractive, an original. As well as his prodigious talent, he is delightful company, can be very funny, always unexpected. He was a will o' the wisp, appearing and disappearing in a disconcerting way, day and night were the same to him. Scathingly critical of those he does not like, he is a real friend to his loved ones. Admittedly he does discard them sometimes, but Andrew and I were lucky in that we remained friends for more than fifty years.' (DD)
3 Master of Truffle Hounds.

Wednesday [1957]   Hôtels St James & d'Albany
BOO HOO   202 & 212 rue de Rivoli
                                    Paris 1er

My darling Debo,

I *do* feel glum and downcast at your not coming to Paris! I somehow felt sure you would, and could already see us toddling about the streets arm-in-arm, two jolly bachelors, rolling from one lovely meal to another and dancing till daybreak and then stoking up on *soupe à l'oignon* in the Halles and then, after a suitable pause, beginning all over again. It's lunatic to be so sad about it. I *wish* you didn't love everyone else more than me – it wouldn't matter if I didn't rather love you, as I suppose I do, otherwise I wouldn't feel so selfish and possessive. The thing is, no one else will quite do, it's too idiotic. But I do adore you. I mustn't go on grumbling and groaning like this.

It's lovely here – we play *boules* under the moulting trees below, with long-legged girls pelting after them squealing with flying plaits followed by small teams of barking dogs. There are also quite a lot of small children who stagger about the grass opposite as though they were the worse for drink; suddenly falling flat on their faces. When this happens, I count three slowly, and then the first perfunctory wail sails through the Tuileries.

I'm having lunch today with Françoise Sagan,[1] the rather pretty mop-headed near-teenage prodigy who wrote *Bonjour Tristesse*. I wonder what that will be like. Pretty awful, probably.

Nothing more for the moment, darling Debo, except love and hugs and fond and loving thoughts by the bushel, from

    Paddy

---

[1] Françoise Sagan (1935–2004). The novelist's first book, *Bonjour Tristesse* (1954), was published to great acclaim when she was only eighteen.

Teus [1957]   Hôtels St James & d'Albany
                                     202 & 212 rue de Rivoli, 1er

Darling Debo,

Lunch with Françoise Sagan went OK – at least I think it did. She's so shy that it rather infects one too. She perches like a bird on the edge of the chair with eyelids fluttering up and down timidly over nut-brown eyes, talks quickly and hesitantly, frequently breaking off, has a nice giggle, and looks about 15, with occasional hints that she might be 50, stunted by gin for a travelling circus by gypsies. All this rattled me a bit, but we talked away more or less consecutively about literature and kindred subjects. There seems little, at a first glance, to hint at the existence of volcanic passion and the torments of love. We're going to listen to Gréco[1] singing at a music hall tomorrow. They are great pals. After that, supper with these two & Zanuck, which will be interesting. I rather love Juliette Gréco.

Last night at about 8 in the evening I saw an enormous limousine in a traffic block in the Boulevard Haussmann, with an old-world chauffeur at the wheel, and, lolling among the upholstery in the back, like Cleopatra in the poop of her barge, Coccinelle,[2] the prettiest of the performers at the Carousel. 'She' was wearing a tremendously low-cut white satin dress, emerging from a vast sea of white fur falling off her shoulders; long diamond earrings, and the

long white-gloved arm that hung on to the old-fashioned acorn-ended
tassel at the side of the window had an elaborate pearl necklace twisted
round it. I couldn't help it, my heartbeats broke into double-time.

No more news for the present, but lots of love from
    Paddy

[1] Juliette Gréco (1927–). The French actress and singer appeared in Otto
Preminger's film of *Bonjour Tristesse* (1958), singing the title tune. She and PLF
became lifelong friends.
[2] Jacques-Charles Dufresnoy (1931–2006). Transsexual singer and entertainer who
became Jacqueline-Charlotte Dufresnoy, better known as 'Coccinelle'; a fixture at
the fashionable Carousel nightclub.

Wednesday [1957]   Hôtels St James & d'Albany
                                    202 & 212 rue de Rivoli, 1er

Darling Debo,

You *were* an angel to come to Paris, and I do wish I hadn't
made such a hash of it somehow. I meant it to be a glorious time
for you. Probably trying too hard! As you say, there's plenty to
chew on.[1]

I went to a tremendous Shakespeare reading by Sir John Gielgud[2]
(forgive me for making you jealous) on Monday night with Diana
Cooper and Horrible Mrs Fellowes and another Frog, then to a
supper in this knight's honour at the Embassy, which was no good at
all because the wine flowed like glue.[3]

I'm spending a fascinating evening tonight with a writer called
Michel Leiris,[4] who is head of the Black Africa section of the Musée
de l'Homme, and a pal of his who is the world authority on drum-
language in central Africa, how messages are beaten out, the range of
what they can say by drum beats, speeds, distances, and so on, which
you will freely admit[5] is exciting.

I long to see you again, for lots of reasons. I've chewed like mad
but there still remains a faint lump of something that won't quite
dissolve, try as one may. You know the sort of thing I mean. I'd
really like to be anywhere but here at the moment, and think
longingly of Flash last winter and pounding about those stony

ravines in Devonshire soaked to the skin; but fear the only fox I shall see this year will be Twentieth-Century.

I do wish you were here, as I miss you like anything, so please write fairly steadily starting with now; and lots and lots of true love, darling Debo, from

     Paddy

1 Neither DD nor PLF, after racking their brains, have the faintest recollection of what this was about.

2 John Gielgud (1904–2000). The actor was knighted in the 1953 coronation honours.

3 Britain's ambassador in Paris at the time was Gladwyn Jebb, 1st Baron Gladwyn (1900–6).

4 Michel Leiris (1901–90). The noted French writer and ethnographer worked at the Museum of Mankind in Paris for over fifty years.

5 'I freely admit' and 'Do admit' were expressions often used by DD and adopted by her family and friends. 'I freely admit that the best of my fun I owe it to horse and hound', the Whyte-Melville quote, was on the cover of *Horse & Hound* magazine, 'my bible when I was a child'. (DD)

Sunday   Chantilly
late November 1957   But really St James & d'Albany

Darling Debo,

I came here yesterday afternoon with Cecil Beaton,[1] after a lovely luncheon with the French authoress at Véfour, where we had marrow and mushrooms on bits of toast and two wonderful soles floating in pale beige. How nice Cecil is. We gassed away in the motor-car about everyone we could think of; mostly him dissecting and dismembering person after person with that astonishing needle-thin voice.

The house is absolutely full, and I've been shoved miles away from anywhere in a claustrophobic attic, a terribly depressing one, where I woke up a couple of hours ago in a rage: the rage of an out-of-date bowler hat in a hat box, forgotten for several generations in a box-room; but soon got over it when I came down and found a brilliant, cloudless frosty morning with scores of swans circling over the lake and settling with the noise of an express train gathering speed. The lawns are stiff and brittle and shiny with frost, and when one walks across them, it leaves a dark track of footprints, as across sand. These swans made me think of peering down from that big window during happy hols at Lismore. I wish you were here.

    Love from
       Paddy

P.S. Don't think I'm not taking your horrible silence hard, because I am. I telephoned to you in London in a sudden access of depression yesterday, but they said you would be at a Newbury number after seven. I almost telephoned there too, but thought it might be rather silly, so didn't in the end.

---

1 Cecil Beaton (1904–80). After winning a Tony Award for his costumes for the Broadway production of *My Fair Lady* (1956), the photographer was at work on the film *Gigi* (1958).

New Year's Day, 1958   Island of Porquerolles
(Happy New Year)   VAR
                             but as from Hôtels St J & d' A
                             Paris (back tomorrow, alas)

Darling Debo,

CHAP I.

    As you were toiling north with Cyril,[1] I was walking across the road on a fine frosty morning from Diana Cooper's house, feeling pretty smart; dressed to kill, as I thought, to uphold our island honour among the Frogs, but not daring yet to clap on that velvet cap, because I wasn't sure whether in France the little bow at the back should be tied or untied. I found my new horse-owning chum, a jolly, tall, very good-looking, slightly bounderish Brazilian called Jean de Souza-Lage, waiting over a wonderful breakfast of omelettes, kidneys, liver, mushrooms and a bottle of claret. He was so gloriously got up that the subdued correctness of my rig at once looked like the female version of some splendidly plumaged male bird, i.e. he had on a scarlet waistcoat with gold buttons, a long royal-blue wide-skirted coat smothered with gold and silver braid round the collar and cuffs and scalloped pockets, huge gold and silver buttons, white buckskin breeches and gleaming jack-boots coming halfway up the thigh like the Household Cavalry; his stock was fastened with a stag's head in rubies, and when he set off, he had a murderous gold-mounted crop slipped into a belt, one of those lovely strange horns over one shoulder and under the other, a gold embroidered belt and a silver-hilted short-sword in a gleaming scabbard. (I furtively unpicked the bow at the back of my cap after a glance at his, and let the ribbons dangle.)

Off we set on two mares of almost Trojan size – mine was called Herodiade – and soon arrived at the Abbey of Royaumont, where Alan Pryce-Jones' rich relations in law[2] live. The courtyard was full of haughty steeds neighing under coroneted blankets and menacing black and white hounds, dribbling and barking, were leashed in and thrashed by bottle-nosed hunt servants; also numbers of gorgeously clad swells, glass in hand, were striding about with their mates in habits and gold-trimmed three-cornered hats, looking spiffing. Lots of greeting, hand-kissing, sweeping flourishes of those velvet caps and general hobnobbing. The Master is a fine old boy called the Marquis de Roualle[3] who told me 'Most of zese 'ounds come from Badminton. *Down Rrrover!*' – crack, slash. The male members, all with their horns the size of orchestral instruments, play a hundred different & stately tunes on them, all together and very well, to mark the different incidents of the chase – slightly hair-raising and drenched in romance. We moved off in a fanfare and were soon in some fields surrounded by forest. Almost at once, two stags came leaping out of the trees and crossed the field the other side of a stream with immense bounds, heads tilted back under their antlers. One was a '*royal*', as they say, with a vast scaffolding of antlers, the other a '*six*' (rather professional, all this?). The whole scene was just what I'd been longing for and very like something on a tapestry.

I stuck to my pal all day, as he's considered a great expert. I may say it was not nearly as wild as I had thought. There was no jumping except one or two little brooks, but miles of hell-for-leather galloping through thick undergrowth and under low branches till you are striped like a zebra with marks of twigs and brambles, the horses smothered

with sweat. Two hours later, after heavy pounding (part of it through a
built-up area like Welwyn Garden City), we found ourselves in the
middle of a swampy tract full of pampas grass and reeds ten feet high,
with a great shindy of hounds somewhere in the middle. Down we
got, gave our horses to a peasant girl in clogs, and plunged into the
middle on foot. Jean loaded me up with horn, crop, belt and scabbard,
and charged ahead, brandishing his naked blade. I plodding after, 2ft
deep in slime – all right for him, just like his native Amazon, but it
nearly killed me. We came on the '*six*' stag at bay surrounded by
hounds, S-L advanced on it, to stab it in the breast, but it broke away
and was killed a mile away by one of the huntsmen with a special
gun, as it was in a village full of children, and they slash out like
anything, it seems. The poor slain quarry was put in a cart, taken back
to the Abbey and cut up. Joints of venison were distributed to the
peasants who had helped; the rest was wrapped in a bundle with the
antlers, while we swigged champagne & ate caviar & smoked-salmon
sandwiches. Then it was the hounds' turn, a grizzly banquet of innards
on the grass, while, for ¾ of an hour, ceremonious laments were
blown on the horns. Overpoweringly strange and medieval it all
seemed. '*Dieu, que le son du cor est triste au fond des bois!*'

Lots and lots of love & fond & loving thoughts from
Paddy

1 Cyril Connolly (1903–74). Shortly before Christmas, the author and critic had
driven with DD to Edensor, where he spent two nights. DD had thought his
manners 'unforgivable' on a previous visit to Lismore, but 'he got such glowing
references from his friends that I tried again. This visit was not a success either.
He was a good friend of Andrew, who appreciated his company more than I did.'
(DD)
2 Royaumont, the Palladian Abbot's Palace near Paris, was lived in by Baron Max
Fould-Springer, whose sister Thérèse was married to Alan Pryce-Jones.
3 Marquis Jean de Roualle (1890–1973). Master of the Piq'avant Nivernais Hounds.

(PLF)
After a spell slogging away at the scenario for The Roots of Heaven, *some
of it with Joan at Duff and Diana's house in Chantilly, we went to Andros,*

and when it was finished flew back to London. I deposited the 'treatment', as agreed, for Darryl Zanuck at the Savoy. Next morning I turned up at his suite, which was full of smoke. 'Come in, Mr Feemor,' he said, 'sit down.' He puffed at his cigar in silence. I asked him if he had got the treatment. After a few more silent puffs he said, 'It's a whole heap of crap', then, after another pause, he said, 'IT'S NO GOOD!' There was a further pause, and several puffs. Oddly enough I felt rather relieved. It wasn't my world, after all. But after more silence and several puffs, he said, 'We're going to the races.' I looked a bit puzzled, so he went on, 'We go to Paris tomorrow and I'll get you a suite like mine in the Hôtel Prince de Galles and a bottle of whisky and a nice-looking typist, and we'll get down to it. Is your passport OK for French Equatorial Africa?'

30 March 1958   Twentieth Century Fox
                                                 Boîte Postale 83
                                                 Maroua, Cameroon
                                                 Africa

My darling Debo,

I've not behaved very well about writing. I'm abroad, and take up my pen feeling a bit hangdog.

Well. I flew out to French Equatorial Africa – with Darryl Zanuck and John Huston.[1] We got there about 6 a.m., to a town called Fort Lamy, in a lovely turquoise dawn, full of priests calling the Moslems to prayer. But soon day broke and revealed a fly-blown town of mud walls inhabited by dejected looking negroes, the air a-swoop and a-flutter with vultures, the heat giving you a straight left like a boxing glove. We settled for three weeks in an immense stockade by the banks of the Shari River – about 50 huts with, in the middle, a six-roomed bungalow with a wide and shady verandah in which the six VIPs lived. I was staggered to discover – and I bet you are too – that I was one of these. The inhabitants were John Huston, Darryl Zanuck, Juliette Gréco, Trevor Howard[2] – who plays the male lead – Errol Flynn[3] and me. Rolling savannah – and on one side, the river – surrounds this stockade; the region teems with elephants, lions, jaguars, panthers, buffaloes, baboons and crocodiles, no stranger fauna than the inhabitants, however.

We came here, to the Cameroon, two weeks ago, to a second stockade. I couldn't bear camp life any more, so took a house in the negro quarter of the town, and I am writing under a huge mango tree, with a jet-black Foulbé tribesman in the middle distance. I have hired him for a month and he is beating a rush mat with infuriating slowness and deliberation: whack! wait for it; whack! w.f.it; w! etc. The town is a labyrinth of mud walls surrounding conical thatched huts and the population consists entirely of coal black enormous Foulbés, very fine looking, clad in splendid robes – their faces slashed by ceremonial scars, and they ride horses with medieval tilting saddles and black-and-white checked caparisons down to their fetlocks. Curly scimitars glitter from the saddles. They are ruled by a feudal chieftain called the Lamido of Maroua who lives in a sort of mud Lismore on the outskirts of the town. His subjects approach him kneeling and when he sallies forth surrounded by his horsemen, trumpeters sound fanfares. He has many slaves and concubines and a subterranean jail where his prisoners lie in chains.

The country is rolling and volcanic, full of tall mountains and deep valleys of enormous blackish boulders that look like fossilized stampedes of mastodons. It is full of troglodyte villages and fetish-worshipping primitives who never leave their caves without a bow, a quiver full of arrows and a long sharp spear. They gather all round us on the rocks, drinking in all our strange equipment, the clothes and the unfamiliar noises – 'Roll it, please!' 'Cut!' 'Action!' – with utter bewilderment. I think they are convinced that we are members of a strange sect connected with making the sun set, as, the moment it dips beyond the hills, we pack up.

But of course what you want to know about is the people. It's pretty complex, but here goes.

John Huston. Wildly bogus, charming, complicated, boastful and ham. I like him very much and don't trust him a yard. He has to be kept under pretty strict control; he would trample on one if he saw the faintest flicker of a flinch, and does so when he does see it. This entails keeping on the offensive quite a lot, i.e. diagnosing his weak points and, when occasion arises, hitting hard and often. This establishes an equivocal and amusing kind of truce and makes life quite fun, a rather dangerous game which both sides divine by an amused look in each other's eyes: thin-ice work & figure skating. He sings 'Johnny, I Hardly Knew You'[4] beautifully.

Darryl Zanuck. In spite of the rasping voice and the huge cigar, I think he probably has a heart of gold. The sheen of the gold is obscured at the moment by his demented jealousy of Juliette Gréco. He follows her everywhere with his eyes or in person, suspects her almost entirely without reason and attempts to incarcerate her in vain. It is quite obvious that she can't bear to be touched by him any more. This leads to scenes and blows. Last night he knocked her out cold, then, in a fit of anxiety, threw a bucket of water over her and sobbed for an hour. It's all rather pathetic and awful, and our world crackles with anger and unhappiness at its very core.

Trevor Howard. Have you ever seen him? – sorry, of course you have. I only asked because *I'm* so ignorant in such matters. He is playing the lead – Morel, the elephant defender – and seems to me wonderful. A very nice man, but as with nearly all actors, there is something missing: – 'A bit of a bore' doesn't quite cover it, somehow. It's something missing somewhere else, which I have yet to put my finger on. He drinks like Hell, starting at breakfast, and goes through his part in a sort of miraculous trance.

Errol Flynn. All the above strictures about actors do not apply here. He poses as the most tremendous bounder – glories in being a cad – but is intelligent, perceptive and, in a freak way, immensely likeable. We are rather chums, to my bewilderment. Sex rules his life, and very indiscreet and criticisable and amusing he is about it.

Juliette Gréco. By far the most interesting of the lot. Extremely well read, unspoilable, wild, rather like a panther, a tremendous sense of humour. The camp is divided up into cliques within cliques, and the French one, consisting of six, to which I unpatriotically belong, is the most exciting, and, I rather suspect, the most hated. We became great pals at once. She is utterly bohemian, and incorruptible by the richest film company in the world; or so I should think. Her involvement with Zanuck is a bit of a mystery, which I have not yet fathomed. It's queerly out of character.

On the whole, with one or two exceptions – apart from those
mentioned – I hate the lot of them. The standard of conversation
and jokes is deplorable, and I sometimes feel on the brink of
weeping. The staggering sums which I suppose I am earning are
really not worth it. The only justification will be if it's a really
tremendous film.

How I long for you and all my friends. So please write *at once*,
in spite of my awfulness on the same count. Please, please, at
once!

And lots of love from
   Paddy

---

1 John Huston (1906–87). The American film director and actor, who was directing
The Roots of Heaven, had chosen PLF to write the screenplay.
2 Trevor Howard (1913–88). The British actor played Morel, hero of the film.
3 Errol Flynn (1909–59). The actor's last major film appearance was as Major
Forsythe in *The Roots of Heaven*.
4 The Irish traditional anti-war song, the basis for the American popular song
'When Johnny Comes Marching Home'.

11 April 1958   Darryl F. Zanuck Productions Inc.
                                     Maroua

IN HASTE

Darling Debo,

This is scribbled at high speed in the hopes of shaming you into
writing.

I'm sitting under a mango tree, turning a deaf ear to an old negro
whose nostrils syphilis has quite eaten away; he is trying to sell me a
sheaf of fiendish-looking assegai-heads with spikes and cruel barbs
and grooves for poison. He spends nearly all day trying to do this
and his mumbled litany is seldom out of earshot; cries of Old
Maroua: 'Who'll buy my sweet spearheads?'

Lots of love
   Paddy

Middle of July [1958]   Paros
                                         As from:
                                         c/o Hon. Alan Hare,[1] MC
                                         British Embassy, Athens

Darling Debo,

    Nine days ago Joan, Maurice Bowra,[2] his professor pal,[3] Mark
[Ogilvie-Grant] and I set off at noon for this island in a hell-ship, a
sort of Ægean *Altmark*, the decks a-cluck with poultry and awash
with vomit; a black-and-white cow kept sticking its head through
the dining-room porthole and mooing. This was the only nice thing.
At Syra, the first island where we dropped anchor, at 9 p.m., Mark
and I went ashore and made a bee-line for a wine shop that also
sold *kokoretsi*, entrails stuffed with good things, twisted round a
skewer and roasted over charcoal. We had some, then a second
helping, when lo and behold! the ship was sailing away. We leapt into
a dinghy, the boatman pulling like Grace Darling, but the ship
churned hard-heartedly off into the night with our loved ones,
leaving us feeling pretty foolish. No boat for another two days! We
settled down on the waterfront, drank endless jugs of retsina and
wandered oafishly along the quay. Our fancy was taken by a handsome yacht, which had moored at the quay and was locked in sleep.
We pretended it was Ran's one, on which he had set off in a
different direction that morning, and began shouting 'Wake up you
beasts! Don't think we can't see you!', and, like the children of
Bethel to Elisha, 'Go up thou bald head' and so on. Shadowy figures
began to stir indignantly on the deck and finally up through the
opening double doors of the companionway emerged a bald pate
a-gleam in the soft starlight. Lord Antrim! They had changed course,
tying up there silently while Mark and I were busy drinking. Odd,
eh? Ran was ashore in his pyjamas in a twinkling and drinking
continued, I'm sorry to report. Our troubles were over, and we
arrived in Paros in style next morning.

    Lots and lots of love
        Paddy

1 Alan Hare (1919–95). Former SOE operative in Albania and future chief executive and chairman of the *Financial Times* who was working for the Secret Intelligence Service in Athens. PLF had known him since they shared lodgings in Cairo during the war. Married to Jill North in 1945.

2 Maurice Bowra (1898–1971). The legendary Oxford don, an old friend of Joan Leigh Fermor, was Warden of Wadham College from 1938 until his death and Vice-Chancellor of the University of Oxford 1951–4.

3 Ernst Kantorowicz (1895–1963). German historian, author of a controversial biography of the Holy Roman Emperor Frederick II; he had been a friend of Bowra since they met at Oxford in 1934.

(PLF)

When the others had left, Truman Capote[1] and a friend came to see us (told by someone to look in). He was very small and frail, and wearing a tartan tam-o'-shanter, and carrying an enormous woolly dog, almost larger than him, under his arm. He was very amusing and told us all sorts of stories in a rather high and fluting voice, accompanied every so often by a deep bass laugh. It was hard to think that the two sounds came out of the same small frame.

1 Truman Capote (1924–84). The American author, whose novella *Breakfast at Tiffany's* was published later that year, was travelling in Greece with the writer Jack Dunphy (1915–92).

22 July 1958   Edensor House
                                                Bakewell

Darling Paddy,

V nice to get your letter with an account of falling on your feet again, viz Ld Antrim's ship being there to fetch you away.

Much has occurred since you left, but nothing tremendously important. I mean no new bodies to worship, it's the same crew so far.

Desmond[1] has given notice. They are busy with the hay. An army of workmen have moved into Chatsworth[2] & are making a great deal of dust and noise, nothing to show for it of course. It's alternately bitter and boiling.

My love affair with Ann Fleming prospers. Sometimes I get this sort of telegram 'Warden of All Souls Dining Monday Please Come' (didn't go of course) so that should put that ancient French writer in her place.

I went to dinner with her (Ann) the other night and sat by Harold Nicolson[3] and Angus Wilson[4] who is perfect. Andrew came, & Robert,[5] & he sat by *Diana Cooper & Judy Montagu* and I'm sorry to say we resorted to making a face or two at each other.[6]

I had been to Percy St before to make sure of forcing him to come as he is such a slippery customer, and there was Augustus John,[7] goodness he is like my father both to look at and in the things he says, things like 'Great Scott'. I told him how Emma wants to give a skeleton for a leaving present to St Elphin's so he said she could have his, but then admitted it might not be ready by August.

Andrew was on *The Brains Trust*[8] yesterday. You must say that was brave. The chairman was that v nice person with a beard in a wheelchair who we saw on the stage doing songs & things with one other person.[9]

Give Joan my love & lots to you.

Debo

1 Michael Desmond; the Devonshires' butler.
2 The Devonshires had decided to move into Chatsworth and were restoring the house completely.
3 Harold Nicolson (1886–1968). The diplomat and politician was working on one of his last books, *The Age of Reason* (1960).
4 Angus Wilson (1913–91). The distinguished novelist had published *The Middle Age of Mrs Eliot* earlier in the year.
5 Robert Kee (1919–). Writer, broadcaster and great friend of the Devonshires and PLF. Author of *The Impossible Shore* (1949), *A Sign of the Times* (1955) and *Ireland: A History* (1980). Married to Janetta Woolley 1948–50, to Cynthia Judah 1960–89 and to Kate Trevelyan in 1990.
6 Neither Diana Cooper nor Judy Montagu, both great friends of PLF, were favourites of DD.
7 Augustus John (1878–1961). The painter lived at 14 Percy Street, in London's Fitzrovia, where Robert Kee also lived for a time. 'I met him once with Robert Kee in a Soho street. He looked me up and down and said, "Have you got children?" "Yes." Another long look. "*Did you suckle them?*"' (DD)
8 The popular BBC programme, in which a panel answered listeners' questions, had transferred from radio to television in the early 1950s.
9 Michael Flanders (1922–75). Actor and singer who performed in a wheelchair after contracting poliomyelitis. One-half of the comic duo Flanders and Swann.

(DD)

Andrew loved walking and Bolton Abbey, our estate in Yorkshire, was his opportunity. He scorned Land Rovers and ritzy Range Rovers, which have replaced legs in the last twenty-five years, and often arrived at a distant line of butts before they did. But as we got older and most of the regular guns no longer came he went elsewhere in August, saying the place was full of ghosts.

A pheasant shoot is a bait for persuading people to travel a long way for a winter weekend. Describing a shoot to a non-participant is as bad as going over games of golf or bridge, so I spared Paddy the bother of reading about it. But my gun took me from Sussex to Devon, from Anglesey to Norfolk and home via Northumberland. I loved it and all the people who went with it.

Paddy never took to shooting and a good thing too. I can't imagine a more terrifying thought than Paddy let loose with a 12-bore in high excitement untutored in the rules of safety. But he occasionally stayed with us for a shooting weekend and came out and took it all in. After a good lunch, he was a dangerous obstacle in my butt, sound asleep and oblivious of the loud bangs immediately above him.

He was always the star of the evenings. Most of our contemporaries had been in the army and were thrilled to meet the Cretan legend.

12 August! [1958]

Kamini
Hydra

Darling Debo,

How clearly I spy you at this very moment, in my mind's little eye, in shooting rig but well muffled against wind and rain, flanked by Lord[1] and two dogs straining at the leash with their tongues hanging out and breathing hard with a tweed-clad troop of well-breakfasted peers heading for the drizzling moors. I discern the glint of gun barrels and the fly-looking rough-hewn North Country beaters deploying; equally, hosts of birds enjoying the end of their hols but wondering uneasily what's up and not knowing what's coming to them in a few minutes' time . . . The rain falls inexorably, zero hour is nigh . . . There is a whirr of wings . . . then bang! bang! bang! (thud, thud, thud . . .) I see faithless

Ran, his sunburn almost all gone, not many yards away; not your Uncle[2] though, who must be discussing Cyprus in London; and Andrew, making all welcome and pointing out likely clumps, but gunless; Emma and Stoker looking pretty serious over their special weapons; Martyn Beckett,[3] perhaps, slightly blood-shot from the Bag o' Nails[4] . . . I taste slugs of raw whisky by proxy, smell gunpowder, observe tweed collars turned up against wind and rain, and, as the dark and bloodthirsty afternoon wears on, matchless eyes beginning to run with the blast and bulbous or alabaster noses turning more ruby than the port they will soon be sniffing . . . I see the maids of Bolton scuttling through the downpour for lack of a way indoors and Desmond, who must have wisely thought better of his notice, arranging ice-cubes in a hollow metal apple . . . the gurgle of baths filling up . . . (Please strike out or amend anything that doesn't apply. But admit it's not far out.)

It's all very different here. I'm back in the vast white studio on our old island, scribbling away. The cicadas outside are deafening. Below, the tiled roofs go cascading down to the sea which is covered with islands and the sun rides rough-shod over all. The thing is this: don't you think you'd better come for a bit, when there is a truce with those birds? I think we'll be here till the end of September, I wish you would. Joan pines for you and sends love. You could bring Robert [Kee] if he would like it (I'm not sure I approve but I suppose I've got to lump it!) I think he'd like it too. I could meet at the airport and bring you out here after a very short gay Athenian spell. Please ponder the matter. There's no one to see, really, except us. I'd get Mark [Ogilvie-Grant] & Coote[5] to vary the danger of boredom. It seems sad to bury the summer so soon.

Last week Joan and I, with Alan the Spy and Roxane Sedgwick,[6] climbed to the top of Mt Olympus. It took four days, sleeping out on various ledges and it nearly did us in. The last day was real hand-over-hand stuff, till at last we were on the highest point of S.E. Europe, with the whole of Greece below like a map. It was very strange and rather wonderful and the air was like whisky & soda (don't think I didn't hear you say Ugh). Tony Lambert, councillor at the Embassy and great bird expert, had told us to look out for some rare birds, the Wall Creeper and the Sombre Tit. We saw lots of the latter, none of the former. Numbers of choughs, though. But we were slightly under-eagled. Joan grumbled a certain amount, and said she was to be buried there if she fell down a crevasse; not lugged back by train to Athens. I made up an epitaph for her:

> Bury me here on Olympus
> In the home of the lonely wall-creeper
> But don't take me back to Athens, please,
> Stretched out on a second-class sleeper . . .

At an open-air hangout by the sea on our return (us, Mark, Coote, the Spy & wife and others) Coote reminisced happily about her RAF days, smoking a cigar the while. She is very good on the slang (Wing Commander = Winko, Group Captain = Groupie, etc). This evoked these lines:

> 'What's happened to Winko?' asked Groupie.
> The Mess Corporal wagged his old head:
> 'He said that he'd fancy a Bass, sir,
> But he went for a Burton instead . . .'

The Muses are not absent, as you see.

I do wish we were all a bit closer together. Do try and remedy this.

Anyway fond love to Emma, Stoker & Andrew and lots and lots to you, from

Paddy

---

1 Tom Lord; the Devonshires' head keeper.

2 Harold Macmillan, 1st Earl of Stockton (1894–1986). Conservative Prime Minister 1957–63. Married Lady Dorothy Cavendish, Andrew Devonshire's aunt, in 1920, and was always called 'Uncle Harold' by DD.

3 Sir Martyn Beckett (1918–2001). Architect, enthusiastic amateur pianist and an old friend of the Devonshires. Married Priscilla Brett in 1941.

4 A nightclub in London's Regent Street.

5 Lady Dorothy (Coote) Lygon (1912–2001). Youngest of the Lygon sisters, daughters of 7th Earl Beauchamp, whose family and house, Madresfield Court, inspired Evelyn Waugh's *Brideshead Revisited* (1945). Served in the WAAF 1940–5. After the war, she worked in Istanbul as a governess, in Athens as social secretary to the British ambassador, and lived for a while on Hydra before returning to England to work as an archivist at Christie's. Married Robert Heber-Percy in 1985.

6 Roxane Sotiriadi; Greek wife of Alexander Sedgwick, *New York Times* correspondent for the Middle East.

31 August 1958   Estate Office
                                                  Chatsworth
                                                  Bakewell

Darling Paddy,

I did love your description of shooting. It was *nearly* all right but
slipped up over one or two things, like a Hollywood film about
England, so I am afraid it's your American blood lately infused by
Huston & Zanuck which has put you wrong.

The other thing was that the weather Thank God was much
better than usual, with the result that one sweated into one's Devil's
Suit (red wool from neck to ankle under everything else) and was
bitten to death by midges & harvest bugs & other counter-honnish
denizens of those benighted moors.

The *waits* are terrific. Some drives take two hours & one can't
have a sit down with one's eyes shut because one NEVER KNOWS,
suddenly without a word of warning (as their wings fail to whirr &
are deathly quiet) those blasted birds have come & gone & the other
guns, keepers etc give one NASTY LOOKS if one is asleep.

Conversations with the loaders are nice, viz. Jones, from the Swiss
Cottage here,[1] tells one about what touches him, things like hares
screaming. He knows the partridges on his beat individually. One day
he found one with her legs all twisted up in a bit of sheep's wool,
couldn't fly & was hopping about, so he took the wool off & let her
go & said he didn't see her for four days. But then of course he did
& all was well.

John Wyndham[2] came to Bolton in waiting to the Prime Minister.
He is a marvel. I forget between seeing him how much I love him.
One night at dinner he pushed me off my chair quite hard so I fell
with a flump on the floor & Desmond solemnly picked me up with
a hurt look as though it was he who had been shoved.

I talked secrets one day with the PM. Most jolly & educational.
He has become much more human all of a sudden and talks about
things like Adultery quite nicely.

Much love to Joan & you write & tell all.
    Debo

1 Harry Jones; one of a family of gamekeepers who lived at Swiss Cottage, an isolated house on the Chatsworth estate. 'Their philosophy of life was different to that of any other people I have known; they saw little but nature in the raw.' (DD)

2 John Wyndham, 1st Baron Egremont (1920–72). A great friend of both Devonshires. Private Secretary to Harold Macmillan for many years. Married Pamela Wyndham-Quin in 1947. 'I have never been much good at *place à table* – John Wyndham used to do it by weight, which didn't go down too well with smart foreigners.' DD, *The House: A Portrait of Chatsworth* (Macmillan, 1982), p. 167.

9 (?) September 1958   Kamini
                                                          Hydra

Darling Debo,

Your letter arrived in the nick of time. I was about to settle down, with a curling lip, to some fairly brisk remarks about calloused trigger-fingers too tired for penmanship etc when in comes Vasiliki, the tragedy-queen cook, with your splendid letter and takes all the wind out of my sails. Coote and Mark are staying and I read out sundry and chosen bits to them and Joan and caused much happy laughter. Mark said enviously, 'I say, that's a much longer letter than the ones I get from Nancy,[1] you are lucky.' I didn't let on about the long wait.

I went into Athens a couple of weeks ago and went on board the S.S. *Hermes*, which was carrying D. Cooper, Rose Macaulay,[2] Juliet Duff[3] and various others to Constantinople, then a trip round the Black Sea touching at various Russian ports, then back. This was all very convivial – the Grande Bretagne Hôtel suddenly became a rather jolly lunchtime Ritz, with the above-mentioned, Mark, Gladys Stewart-Richardson,[4] Coote, Cecil Beaton (who was just back from staying in Paros with Truman Capote).

A sudden passion for astronomy has sprung up here. I got a huge star atlas sent out by Heywood Hill,[5] it's wonderful for sleeping out on the terrace. One just lies there with the atlas on one's lap, torch in hand to flash on the page – it's hardly needed – spotting constellation after constellation blazing away overhead. We're becoming pretty good at hobnobbing with and bandying about the names of stars. You'll probably have cause to complain of this anon. I want to invent, and have patented, Fermor's Heavenly Brolly: a vast black-lined

umbrella with all the stars embroidered inside in silver, the ferrule
being the Pole Star. You would just open it at night, point it at the
Pole Star, and the heavens become an open book.

Fond love from

Paddy

1 Mark Ogilvie-Grant was one of Nancy Mitford's oldest friends and they kept
up a regular correspondence.
2 Rose Macaulay (1881–1958). The prolific novelist and journalist died shortly
after returning from this cruise.
3 Lady Juliet Lowther (1881–1965). Daughter of 4th Earl of Lonsdale, married
Sir Robert Duff in 1903.
4 Gladys Stewart-Richardson (1883–1966). Descended from an old Scottish highland family, she drove lorries and ambulances in Macedonia during the First World
War. Settled in Athens and set up a factory producing fine raw silk for clothing.
5 The bookshop, founded by Heywood Hill (1906–86), opened in London's
Mayfair in 1936.

27 July 1959   (Castello di Passerano[1]
                                            Gallicano nel Lazio
                                            Provincia di Roma)
                                            Abruzzi

Darling Debo,

This non-writing won't do at all; so bags I break silence, in order
to seize the advantage and put you in the wrong, before this sly
move occurs to you.

Don't be fooled by the splendour of the address at the top of this
paper; I set it myself at a local printers. This castle is a huge empty
thing of spell-binding beauty on top of a leafy hill overlooking
a froth of treetops and cornfields surrounded on three sides by
classical mountain ranges whose names need not concern us, and
on the fourth by the Roman Campagna and the dome of St
Peter's in the distance, indicating – too near! – great Rome itself.
The castle hadn't been inhabited for 600 years, so it meant putting
windows in and borrowing, buying or hiring furniture (all of
which has ruined me). It *looks* rather marvellous, but there is not a
drop of water running. Two beautiful girls called Loredana and
Gabriella come wobbling gracefully up the castle ramp twice daily

with great brass pitchers on their heads. I won't enlarge on the loo situation . . .

Some nuns in Tivoli sewed me a huge heraldic banner, which I fly from a mast on a tower (Fermor's answer to Lismore). I have been building up a fictitious character for myself: the Black Bastard of Passerano, and like to think that when I unfurl my banner from the topmost battlements, all the trembling peasants of the valley look askance and cross themselves, dowse their lights and hide their cattle and bolt up their dear ones. Actually, most of my time is spent driving car-loads of white-clad little girls or Fauntleroys into nearby Gallicano nel Lazio for first communion, or the castle women – there is a farm grovelling at the foot of the ramparts – to market: the Black Sucker of Passerano, *Il Succho Nero*.

There used to be masses of nightingales, but they've vanished now, but there are plenty of owls which sometimes get in and flap silently round for hours among the oil lamps and candles, having rashly flown down a spiral stair inside a tower; also frogs, crickets and nightjars. The atmosphere at night is like the castle in *Hamlet* by William Shakespeare.

The discomfort is almost beyond sufferance. Some of this is caused by rats, which, rather intimidated at first by my usurping their age-old suzerainty, are getting the upper hand again. I think Joan was rather taken aback by all this. The other night, hoping to foil the ants (which I forgot to mention), she put a basin of water on a table, and inside this, a jug with a plate on top containing a loaf for breakfast tightly wrapped in brown paper, and, balanced on top of this, a saucer with butter in. Next morning I was reading early by a window in the same room – the banqueting hall! – when I was roused by a rustle; there, his hind legs on tiptoe on the basin's rim, stood a tall rat carefully unfolding a hole in the bread paper with his forepaws and nibbling in felicity. I threw my book at it – *The Age of Elegance* by Arthur Bryant – but missed. The rat sloped off perfunctorily, but turned back halfway to the door and resumed his post in half a minute. I thought I'd better let it rip. So there he crunched, the butter wobbling to and fro on top, looking at me out of the corner of his eyes with a victor's glance . . . Next night, Joan found a large scorpion nestling on her. So I suppose it's time to draw stumps.

We are now in the cool heights of the Abruzzi, great Alpine mountains about 100 miles E. of Rome, in a village called Ovindoli. The cattle here are a wonderful body of cows. At dusk, a bell is rung from the church tower, and, quite unaccompanied, all gather from their fields at a never changing rendezvous, and head for the village by the hundred. Once in the market square, they split up and mooch off along various lanes to the houses where they live and tap on the door with their horns and out comes a girl or a grandmother and lets them into a comfortable cellar for the night.

Lots and lots of love from
     Paddy

1 PLF had been lent this castle in the Alban Hills.

9 August 1959   Edensor House
                                              Bakewell

Darling Paddy,

I *was* pleased to get your letter and to know you have not departed this world.

I never really believe in foreign addresses, for instance that well known old French writer my sister is at a hang out called S. Vio & then a number, Venice.1 Well, admit that doesn't sound real. So of course I'm not going to spend hours writing fascinating things, or boring ones either, for the delectation of the lost letter box somewhere or other. Yours sounds a bit more true though damned affected.

Anyway it was v v nice to get it.

I did once have millions of things to tell, like sitting next to John Huston one night at dinner. *My word* he is awful. I can't think how you spent so long near him without smashing him. He said ghoulishly embarrassing things like We Irishmen ought to get together. Well he's American and I'm English, but I didn't like to enlarge on that.

Otherwise I can't think of much except that Sophy was portrayed by Epstein.[2] They had to go every day for two hours for 14 days, so Diddy[3] & Sir Jacob became terrific friends & Diddy said 'I think Sir Jacob's fallen for me – he likes a ton weight.' I thought that a *very good joke* & so would you if you could have seen them in that studio surrounded by ½ finished monster nudes with droopy bosoms & such like curios.

I saw a good bit of Ann Fleming. I truly love her & kept going to dinner, sometimes in the wrong clothes, like when she took us all to a recep. at the Tate after dinner. I didn't know it was grand & went in a cotton frock & when I got there found all the women in dresses to the ground & pearls. Then we got to the Tate & to my horror Cake[4] advanced on unseen feet in crinoline & diamonds glittering from top to toe & I was in her path like a rabbit & a snake & she made the sign to go & talk to her & it was wicked work with the dread wrongness of get-up & Sir J Rothenstein[5] looking at one as though one was a v small bit of dirt & then her saying 'isn't that wall lovely' meaning a lot of daubs by famous painters & me being speechless because of being honest & after a bit I heard myself saying 'Oh dear now I'm *stuck*' which of course was v v rude indeed.

That's the sort of thing that's been happening, nought of great interest.

The children are here, very tall, very lazy & very nice. Emma is in revolt about most things but that is the disease of her age I think (16).

I am engrossed with Chatsworth, v boring for everyone else.

Next week the moors loom (not William Shakespeare's Venetian variety – would that they were) & Uncle Harold and his followers. Oh dear, well never mind.

Where will you be the 2nd ½ of Sept? I might be able to do something nice about then, & Nancy's Colonel[6] has v kindly asked me to his Palace which I would like except what about my fat ankles, deformed thumb[7] & Harvey Nichols clothes.

Much love – & send a P.C. or so – from

Debo

1 Nancy was staying with her Venetian friend, Countess Anna-Maria Cicogna.
2 Jacob Epstein (1880–1959). The sculptor's bust of DD's daughter was his penultimate work.
3 Ellen Stephens; nanny to DD's children 1943–63.
4 DD's nickname for the Queen Mother, which she gave her after being lastingly impressed by her enthusiasm at a wedding when the cake was cut.
5 John Rothenstein (1901–92). Director of the Tate Gallery 1938–64.
6 Gaston Palewski (1901–84). The love of Nancy's life, whom she always teasingly called 'Colonel' after his rank in the Free French army, was posted as ambassador in Rome in 1957. 'Gaston brought life and laughter to the magnificent Palazzo Farnese when he was ambassador. I loved his company because of his understanding of English humour – somehow so unexpected in an out-and-out Frenchman (or an out-and-out French politician).' (DD)
7 Nancy used to tease DD that her thumb was deformed from sucking it as a child, and warned her that she would never find a husband as a result.

29 September 1959   Lismore Castle
                                                     Co. Waterford

Darling Paddy,

Thank you *so much* for my lovely visit. I did love every minute of it and I do think it was kind of you to have me on top of all those others. I think the most surprising thing was Mr Tom[1] looking up from *The Times* (only for a minute I admit) to look at The Green Grotto on Capri. He said it was Awfully Nice, which was going it I thought.

We did miss you after you had gone off.

I've boasted to E Sackville West[2] that I am an intimate of Sir W Walton[3] but I didn't tell him how Sir W admitted the true horror of his and others' music.

I spoke to Ann F[leming] for a moment in London but then had to rush for the train, but I gathered she had been poisoned by the Colonel in Rome as they had Fish for dinner on a Monday, which she says is well-known to be fatal.

Much love
    Debo

1 Thomas Egerton (1918–98). A lifelong friend since schooldays of Andrew Devonshire, with whom he shared a passion for racing. During the war, he served in the Coldstream Guards in North Africa where he was famous for saving the Officers' Mess marmalade during the Siege of Tobruk. Married Anne Cobbold in 1962. 'His quiet charm and humour endeared him to his contemporaries.' (DD)

2 Edward Sackville-West, 5th Baron Sackville (1901–65). Music critic and writer who shared Long Crichel House in Dorset, a sort of all-male Bloomsbury, with a circle of writers and artists. In 1956, he moved to Cooleville House, Co. Tipperary, and was a neighbour of the Devonshires at Lismore. 'He adored playing Freda, the game on the billiard table. It sometimes involved running round to get your shot in, so he did not risk his dinner jacket and brought a change of clothes for the evening's entertainment.' (DD)

3 William Walton (1902–83). After his marriage to Argentine-born Susana Gil Passo in 1949, the British composer settled at La Mortella on Ischia.

6 October 1959   Bar da Filipo
                                                  Forio d'Ischia
                                                  Prov. di Napoli

Darling Debo,

I say, it *was* decent of you to come. It cheered me up like anything, and I'd really thought I'd never smile again after the rigours of the first half of the month.

It was blowing a ghastly sirocco here when I got back, for days, the air full of headaches and limbs turning to lead, suicidal depression and demoralisation. Then, all of a sudden, lovely crystalline autumn weather, a touch of chill in the air, pale clear blue skies, emptying towns and bare beaches, all's well.

Henry and Virginia Bath[1] are staying at the San Francesco, and we had a nice noisy meal at Filipo's last night. Iris[2] said that, much as she dislikes people chewing gum, she thinks chewing tobacco is an attractive and manly habit – especially the sort of talk that goes with it. I asked her what on earth she meant. She thereupon fixed me with those ice blue eyes, scowled, and began slowly and ruminatively to munch, her whole face assuming the leathery lineaments of a frontiersman. She then said in a deep and husky voice, '*There ain't no rattlers there, ma'am*' and squirted a ghost-jet of tobacco juice out of the corner of her mouth, fixing me challengingly in the eyes.

No more now, dearest darling Debo, except lots and lots of love from

  Paddy

---

[1] Henry Thynne, 6th Marquess of Bath (1905–92). 'Extraordinarily handsome, a romantic's idea of an aristocrat. He brought wild animals to Longleat when it was opened to the public after the war, calling it his Safari Park. It still brings thousands of sightseers to that beautiful place.' (DD) Married to Daphne Vivian 1927–53 and to Virginia Tennant in 1953.

[2] Iris Tree (1897–1968). Bohemian daughter of the celebrated actor Sir Herbert Beerbohm Tree. Married the screenwriter Curtis Moffat in 1916 and the actor Count Friedrich Ledebur in 1934.

14 October 1959   Train (not rapido)

Darling Paddy,

I nearly wrote to you from the Hebride[1] which I've been on but somehow didn't & when I got back to London last night I found your letter & was v glad to hear that Iris Tree admires tobacco chewers. I agree with her I'm afraid. V brave of you to dine at Filipo's.

Since I wrote there has been the election. The jolly thing was driving people to the poll at home, keepers' wives who live at the back of beyond, old ladies who were hard of hearing, two wives of farm workers (who lived 300 yards from the polling station but said they must be fetched) and such like. The interesting thing was they all wore their best and put on hats to perform the ritual (which I freely admit makes one feel rather funny).

Evie Waugh has done a good joke on me (& probably others). His new book arrived,[2] all wrapped in bits of other books as they do, & I thought how nice & felt rather superior, NOT BEING A GREAT READER, to get the damned thing straight from the horse's mouth as it were, so I undid it & read something like 'To Darling Debo, in the certainty that not one word of this will offend your Protestant persuasion'. Naturally I didn't look any

further, but Emma and my Wife who were sitting there bagged it
& started to turn the pages which were ALL BLANK, just lovely
sheets of paper with gold edges & never a word on one of them.
That's the sort of book which suits me down to the ground.
Good Old Evie.

1 DD had been staying with her mother on Inch Kenneth, a small island off the
coast of Mull in the Inner Hebrides, where Lady Redesdale spent several months
a year.
2 *The Life of the Right Reverend Ronald Knox* (1959).

[October 1959]   Bar da Filipo
                                                       Forio d'Ischia

Darling Debo,

We – Iris, Joan, Iris's staggering ex-husband Friedrich[1] and I –
got back from Capri yesterday. There are all sorts of things we
didn't see there, notably a dining cellar with the walls painted to
simulate falling plaster where the curly-haired waiters repair the
nylon cobwebs daily with a special solution and give a final whisk
round with the dust-gun before opening time. It is the prototype
of all those 'continental' restaurants or bistros in Sloane St and
Elizabeth St: –

> He served me some *ravioli*
> Under a cardboard ham,
> The shirt on his back was from Capri
> The hairs on his chest were sham
> And the apron across his codpiece
> Was the colour of strawberry jam.
>
> 'In Sloane St they call me Tonino
> In Sydenham they call me Ted'
> The hair that curled on his bosom
> Was died blue-black from red:
> – Nest for a holy medal,
> (*Nest for a diner's head!*)

The place is full of similar splendours.

A lot of migrating geese flew overhead for Africa half an hour ago, but I'm staying on for a bit.

Love

    Paddy

---

1 Count Friedrich Ledebur (1900–86). Actor known for his roles in *Alexander the Great* (1956), *Moby Dick* (1956) and *Slaughterhouse-Five* (1972). 'Whenever the studios needed a picturesque or stately figure, or a deep voice to whisper, "All is not vell", they sought him out.' (PLF)

10 November 1959   Hairdressers

Darling Paddy,

I can't quite think what's been happening except that Chatsworth is now like a job, 9–6 with an hour for lunch, so there is no time for anything except being horrid to people on the telephone (radiator people & that kind of thing) & suddenly it's become November & shooting is toward.

Daphne and Xan came for a nice stay. I do love them both in their various ways. As for Xan he becomes nobler, smarter, more beautiful & less confident as the years go by & I WORSHIP HIS BODY, but what's the good, one never gets past idiotic chat & one has the strong feeling that he is hating it all, that he knows one knows he is (& he isn't the only one) but that's the end of it, v annoying as I would like to settle down to an orgy of depth plumbing but it's no go & I can't think of a single thing to say. What a waste.

Next day   Train 11 November

Today I had a Business Lunch with Lucian [Freud], to arrange about him coming to Chatsworth to paint the walls of the bathroom which belongs to the bedroom which is stuffed all up to the ceiling with Sabine Women being tweaked. It is Horrific, so whatever Lu does will go nicely. When we got on to the price we both got rather nervous, so the Business part of the lunch was a failure.

Andrew's Granny has gone potty. Her maid suggested moving her

to the middle of her bed when she was dangerously near the edge &
she said 'I won't be moved, I have been just here in this bed ever
since I re-married.'

Much love
Debo

26 February 1960   Chatsworth
                                                    Bakewell

Darling Paddy,

I have found a lot of bunches of wax crocuses, like one sees on
graves in France, and have planted them skilfully among Andrew's
real ones and am waiting on tenterhooks for them to be noted. As
they are slightly larger than life size I feel they can't be missed.

I *might* fall in love with John Freeman.[1] He is an exerciser of
fascination of rabbit & snake variety. Never met him of course.

Much love
Debo

1 John Freeman (1915–). Labour MP, ambassador in Washington 1969–71 and
interviewer on *Face to Face*, the celebrated BBC live television show.

28 March 1960   Lismore Castle
                                                 Co. Waterford

Darling Paddy,

V v glad you will come here. We will have old No Eye[1] and his
daughter for one night, Laure by name. Also her hubby. *Quelle belle
surprise.*

My sister Decca has written a book,[2] and the burden of its song
seems to be to steal all you can lay hands on and then be v proud
that you have done it. I suppose that's one way of going on. She's a
bit batty of course. It seems a bit hard on Lady Redesdale[3] who is
an honest type.

Don't not come.

Much love
Debo

I believe the ageing French writer will be at Mr Eddy [Sackville-West]'s for May so we can have Intellectual Evenings. *Quelle dread surprise.*

---

[1] Viscount Charles de Noailles (1891–1981). DD became friends with the patron of the Surrealists and expert gardener through her sister Nancy. Married Marie-Laure Bischoffsheim in 1923. They had two daughters: Laure (1924–79), married to Bertrand de La Haye Jousselin in 1946, and Natalie (1927–2004), who married Sandro Perrone, owner of the Italian newspaper *Il Messaggero*, in 1949.

[2] Jessica (Decca) Mitford (1917–96). The fifth Mitford sister's first volume of autobiography, *Hons and Rebels* (1960), recounted her childhood, conversion to Communism, and elopement and marriage to Esmond Romilly, who died in 1941 when his plane went missing over the sea. In 1943, she married American attorney Robert (Bob) Treuhaft.

[3] Sydney Bowles (1880–1963). DD's mother. Married David Mitford, later 2nd Baron Redesdale (1878–1958) in 1904.

Sunday [1960]   Dumbleton[1]
                                                      Evesham

Darling Debo,

I went for a long walk with Joan & Graham[2] in the Dumbleton woods yesterday, and we found a young fox caught in a trap by one fore-pad. It snarled and glared as I approached to release him, so I had to pull him by the brush with one hand, opening the trap with the other. Free at last he paused and fixed me with a glance of implacable hatred, then limped off, sensibly, into a jungle of foxgloves. If it had been a lion, far from saving my life like with Androcles years later in the Coliseum, he would have swallowed me there and then. I minced on my way rather crestfallen.

Lots of love from
     Paddy

---

[1] After the death of PLF's mother-in-law in 1959, Dumbleton Hall was sold to the Post Office as a convalescent home for employees and the family moved into the agent's old house.

[2] Graham Eyres Monsell, 2nd Viscount Monsell (1905–94). PLF's unmarried brother-in-law, an accomplished pianist, was very close to his sister Joan.

23? 24? October 1960   c/o Niko Ghika
                                              Hydra (temporary)

My darling Debo,

A brief autobiography follows, hoping you'll put me up to date in return.

AUTOBIOGRAPHY

Off we set in Joan's Sunbeam Rapier, hood down, singing at the wheel, heading from Le Touquet to our old friend Lady Smart's, spent three days there, then into a deserted dusty summer Paris, so bare that it might have been emptied by a Bedouin raid, and south to Fontainebleau, for a further three days of utmost luxury and pleasure at your old pal Charles de Noailles and Natalie's house.[1] I can't remember whether you've been or not, but *if* not, do hasten. The house is probably more Nancy's Mecca than yours, but it seems enchanting to me, all that's best in froggery. Natalie darted about the place seeming almost as nervy, frail, small and wide-eyed as her Chihuahua, whirling us at the speed of light from one cousin's castle to another; but the real treat of course was Charles de N., pottering and talking and smiling and clipping and prodding from one strange and wonderful plant to another, clad in mole-coloured corduroys and gym shoes, with a wonderful basket in one hand, slotted for trowels, forks, secateurs, labels, bast string, gloves and indelible pencils. I wished you had been there and then thanked my stars you weren't, for the conversation would have soared into such a rarefied empyrean of botanical expertise that we wouldn't have understood a single word, instead of the lovely told-to-the-children tour we had. He worships your body, as you know (and rightly).

At dinner the first night I asked him about the Irish tour and, do you know, the most extraordinary and eerie thing happened. It was *word for word*, or so it seemed to me, what we imagined he might say, when, without having met him, I improvised what it might be, at Lismore! I couldn't believe the evidence of my ears. The only thing in which I was a bit out was in being too snobbish, which he wasn't. But the rest was uncanny. You were his favourite by far. His

horticultural high point, after a long pause for thought, turned out to
be Annes Grove.[2] I felt very bucked I'd been there that day with
Eddy [Sackville-West] and the French Writer. Anyway, it was a
glorious stay, with no one else there, except François Valéry's son,[3]
which was perfect. I felt it had all been rather a click: but one never
quite knows.

(This para. can be skipped) Then off hot wheel eastwards to
Châtillon-sur-Marne, to see the Vix Vase, a huge Greco-Etruscan
amphora dug up seven years ago, an amazing object, and further east
to Colmar in Alsace-Lorraine to gaze for the 5th time at Grünewald's
Issenheim altarpiece, the most amazing crucifixion in the world.

Then across the Rhine, through the Black Forest, one night on
the shores of Lake Constance surrounded by Germans; south into the
Austrian Tyrol, on into Italy at Bolzano, then *clean through the
Dolomites*, hundreds of miles of sheer and dizzy spikes a-gush with
streams out of which beautiful trout virtually leap straight on to
frying pan, grill and saucepan; north of Venice into Yugoslavia at last;
through Slovenia to Lubliana, through Croatia to Zagreb, then east
along a billiard table *autostrada* towards Belgrade. Now, a travel tip for
motoring in Yugoslavia: there are only about three petrol pumps in
the country, and scarcely any motors. We ran out hundreds of miles
from one on this *autostrada* in the heat of the day and settled for
hours under an acacia tree (shittim-wood in the Old Testament) until
at last a caravan of twelve Cadillacs drew up and succoured us by
siphoning petrol out of their tanks. They were a party of Persian
princes with their sloe-eyed princesses on the way from Claridge's to
Teheran. They partook freely of our wine flask, asked us to stay in
their palaces (the competition began to look ugly) and then slipped
into gear for Iran.

We continued south into wildest Bosnia, where mountains began
to rise and minarets to sprout in every village, each alive with
Moslem invocations intoned thrice daily. The roads became dust
tracks across plains or twisty ledges of rubble little wider than
eyebrows along the rims of deep gorges at the bottom of which
huge rivers curled and swooped through echoing and forested
ravines, with here and there an old Turkish bridge spanning them as

thinly and insubstantially as a rainbow. The food became odd and wonderful, stuffed with garlic and paprika and the sunlight and our breath got stronger with every mile. So on to Sarajevo, scene of the Archduke's murder, and, through range after range of mountains to Dubrovnik on the Dalmatian coast, a terrific medieval walled city full of renaissance palaces and belfries and winding columns and cloisters, and oysters too – huge and wonderful ones. South of this is the old kingdom of Montenegro, now part of Yugoslavia, reached after a three-hour zigzag up a sheer and cloud-topped wall of mountain, looking down on to strange rock fjords caked with water lilies and with pyramid-shaped mountains that hover on mist like the ones in Japanese pictures, and plenty of gliding storks. Then comes a wilderness of rock, in the heart of which lies the old capital, Cetinje, and the king's palace, the size of Edensor. Long Byronic gorges a-swoop with eagles brought us down into Southern Serbia and an Albanian population: baggy-trousered women heavily veiled, and tall, raffish, guarded mountain men in red and white fezzes, all selling watermelons to each other. They are always in a crowd, always moving compactly along the streets, as though to or from a public execution. Then we came to Serbian Macedonia and wonderful lakes with frescoed Byzantine monasteries on the shores, and deeper and darker mountains and more fearsome gorges and hotter sun. These monasteries and frescoes held us up for days. We were playing it slow but not cool.

Into Greek Macedonia at last, and then by familiar roads to Athens. Here we found Gladys [Stewart-Richardson]'s house (now Joan's) a great deal smaller than we remembered. It is, in fact, a bedroom, a living room, and a kitchen, a sort of old cottage in the middle of Athens (much smaller than Mark [Ogilvie-Grant]'s), with a nice terrace. It's very pretty, but much too small for two. What are we to do? Worse, a colossal road is being built outside, with fifty pneumatic drills, giant steel claws for rubble, hydraulic pumps, steamrollers and blasphemy. One has to talk in bellows. I have now bought some pink wax ear plugs, which makes everything even eerier. I see massed drills a-shudder, rollers a-crunch, and ten tons of broken concrete crashing from suddenly gaping steel claws, all only a few yards off, *and all in dead silence*; lorries hurtle by as soundlessly as minnows. Meanwhile, one's heart sounds like a steam hammer, and one's own steps like nail-clad footfalls in a cathedral.

END of Autobiography. Pause for tea break.

In spite of all this, it's lovely being back in Greece. Mark was away when we arrived, chez Joan, and then, which made one feel wistful, chez you. Diana Cooper and Cecil [Beaton] had just been through, missing by the skin of all our teeth. But waiting on the mantelpiece was a huge stuffed seagull Diana had bought, and two stuffed hoopoes with pearl necklaces about their necks, as a housewarming present.

Well, after wandering about a bit in various islands and mountains, vaguely looking out for a permanent writing nest, we rendezvous-ed with Mark in Leivadia and headed for fateful Arachova and Delphi, and set off next dawn from A by car to the plateau, thence towards the summit with a nice guide and one mule. Mark veering to right and left with his sawn-off trident in one hand, polythene botanist's bag in the other, through Niebelungen-clouds and fir-forests to the bare rocks, when we discovered that the guide did not realize we wanted to go down via the Carysian Cave to Delphi as well. There would be no time to make the summit and this as well, so we turned down into the Devonshire country,[4] waded across the plateau – Mark pointing out all the points of that Way of the Cross, where the wrong turning was taken in your journey etc. We sat by a well, very thirsty. The guide lowered his waterbottle on the end of his belt. Mark bent in to prod it below the surface with his stick, hoping to fill it, and out of his breast pocket and into the depths dropped his very expensive spectacles. There's obviously a sort of blight on the place. Then up to the cave, and down through the woods that everyone missed on last year's return journey. Mark dug up several colchicums and a centauria (impressed?) and we saw two lovely black squirrels, getting down to Delphi just after dark, Mark pointing out with his trowel where you had waited and craned like Sister Anne.

Our search was begun in Hydra, but we're back in Athens now

after about three weeks of hot and cloudless October and early November weather, our last bathe there was on 3rd Nov. Well, since Niko Ghika has settled there with Barbara, it's been transformed – more terraces flung out, glorious paintings, strange sweet-smelling plants in amphorae, awnings like striped yacht sails, and the most glorious view in Greece, often described to you in the past. How I *wish* you'd come there when we lived there, as now we only come as guests now and then. Barbara and Niko have become more fervent bed dwellers than ever, those happy faces always seem to be gazing brightly at one from twin pillows whenever their door is open. The other day they were actually up and about for five hours on end, which is a record. It made me a bit anxious; I wondered if it was cracking up . . . But no, next day they were more lovesick than ever, unable to keep hands unclasped for long, either chatting, walking or at meat, keeping in touch by foot when knives and forks got in the way. It made one feel rather protective and a bit sad: such ages since one was in such a plight, at least overtly.

But the main and immediate thing is, write at once please.

Lots and lots of love from

Paddy

Late Night Final

You've probably heard all about Stavros N's island from Anne Tree.[5] Last week he came over on the wonder yacht *Créole* to Hydra to pick us up for dinner and a rather luxurious night on board, so off we skimmed to Spetsopoula, his island off Spetsai, through the sunset. This wild island is now a network of roads, and up one of these we rambled in a couple of brightly coloured waiting dodgems, to a large new and pretty ugly villa, but v. luxurious, and found some French friends playing tric-trac, a M. Bonnet and his bride (née Dubo Dubon Dubonnet) and Porfirio Rubirosa, his beautiful but inane wife,[6] and Tina Onassis & Eugenie Niarchos[7] (v. nice indeed). After a deluge of drinks there, we en-dodgemed again, tooled down to the shore and into Criss Crafts and swished round to a gorge-like cove a mile away, the beach glittering with specially imported sand and about 100 blazing pine torches stuck into the rocks, looking very wild and

magnificent. A jukebox in the rocks jived away non-stop, and we
settled down to caviar round a circular table out of doors. At the end
of the meal, Stavros, who had been drinking non-stop all day,
suddenly leapt on to the table, sending candles and gold plate flying,
and danced like a wild thing, seizing Tina O, Mrs P.R. and Mrs B, all
four whirling then stamping and leaping by torchlight, till Stavros, all
the day's drinks now churning up to an inner whirlpool, staggered
down to the imported sand again and rocketed off to repose.

There was drinking, eating, bathing and jiving all next day, then a
tour of the island by dodgem, thousands of imported pheasants
whirring through the branches (mown down daily by S), and
imported stags trotting under the trees. One of these tried to rape a
lady last year, but she strangled it (its head now glowers down from
the drawing room wall – a stuffer stuffed). Then a visit to a grass
factory, which turns out seventy trays of forced grass a day, to be left
about for the pheasants, and a review of a vast cage full of Prussian
Elkhounds (the Baskerville department) all barking fit to bust and
used as gun dogs. Then farewell to red-eyed Stavros and a quiet
yacht-borne return to Hydra and sanity by moonlight.

1 Natalie Perrone lived at the Hôtel de Pompadour, an exquisite folly designed
by the architect Gabriel for the Marquise de Pompadour in 1749.
2 Annes Grove Gardens in Co. Cork; created in the early twentieth century by
Richard Grove Annesley.
3 In fact PLF's fellow guest was François Valéry himself, son of the writer Paul
Valéry.
4 While on a Hellenic Cruise earlier in the year, Andrew Devonshire, his daughter
Emma, Mark Ogilvie-Grant and other friends had got lost walking above Delphi.
DD, who had not gone on the walk, spent many anxious hours waiting for them
while the cruise ship left without them. 'Passengers are warned to this day not to
stray like the Duke of Devonshire.' (DD)
5 Lady Anne (Tig) Cavendish (1927–). Married Michael Tree in 1949. DD's sister-
in-law and husband had a house on the Aegean island of Spetsai, adjoining the
small island of Spetsopoula which was owned by Stavros Niarchos.
6 Porfirio Rubirosa (1909–65). The well-endowed Dominican playboy was married
to his fifth wife, twenty-three-year-old French actress Odile Rodin.
7 Athina (1926–74) and Eugenia Livanos (1927–70). In 1947, Eugenia married
Stavros Niarchos as his third wife. After her death, Niarchos married her sister,
Athina, who had previously been married to Aristotle Onassis.

17 November 1960   Chatsworth
Train to London – Pity   Bakewell

Darling Pad,

Well I was pleased to get that fat letter.

Several bits were v praiseworthy viz. letting one know when to skip (always grateful for that sort of inf). All most educational.

Things here are exactly the same. It is November, thank God, but not the 28th day of yet. Andrew has got a job[1] & a pay packet, an office, a phone and a BOSS. Did you ever know five more unexpected things. The result is Happiness, Fury at having speeches mucked about by the aforesaid boss, & the High Commissioner for Ghana looming for lunch at Chatsworth on Sunday. Very odd, & very good really as he loves the regularity of offices and the civil servants who make tea for him.

I think it was just in the nick myself, as he was killing himself with rushing about England ridding himself of guilt by pace.

I'm dying to meet his top boss, feller called Duncan Sandys,[2] because everyone who knows him loathes him. He is a tiger for work (o else to do I guess; you know, lives in Surrey & doesn't hunt).[3] He is Interested in Women but probably for only one horrid thing. We'll soon see because I'm going to have lunch with him in a minute or so. I'll report.

We went to a recap for diplomats & officials at B Palace. It beat cockfighting for (a) a long wait (b) the unpleasant shock of a whole passage of Topolski horrors[4] commissioned by the Duke of Edinburgh & (c) the following conversation with a lady called Mrs Alport, wife of Minister of State,[5] a job between Sandys' & Andrew's.

She I've been longing to meet you as I came out with your sister Jessica.

Me Oh lor.

She You know, you'll find you'll like all the people you'll have to meet, they are very kind really and you'll have no reason to be shy.

Me Oh. (*Thinks* Haven't been shy for 20 years.)

She Of course you'll join the CROWS.

Me What?

She Crows – Commonwealth Relations Office Wives.

Me Oh. Well I live in the country & I don't go about much any more.

She Oh, don't worry, you'll enjoy it.

Well, really, you see what it's like. *RUBBISH*. Making women have anything to do with politics, it makes me very angry. I shall speak to Uncle Harold about it & let Sandys have the rough side of my tongue when at last we meet. But as long as Andrew enjoys it I'm all for it, but CROWS, oh dear.

The well-known French lady writer is in England. It's so nice having her & I hope the book[6] is making her rich, & that the Portfolio will benefit.

Lady Mosley is also about & with those two, Lady Redesdale & Woman[7] we had a very fine unveiling of a memorial thing to my Dad in Swinbrook Church. We cried a good deal & laughed even more of course. It's rare for four of us to meet.

I had a very jolly time in Scotland with Col Stirling,[8] a visit after my own heart. No books were mentioned, no one asked if one was happy & the other guests were two sweet generals, one called de Guingand[9] & famous for the war. On a very wet day it was a fine sight to see those generals in their mackintosh knickers on hands & knees down a road stalking grouse on stubble.

I'd never seen or heard wild geese before. Have you ever? A fantastic noise, like a lot of women at a cocktail party in the sky, tumbling over each other for the best place in the air. The oddest & most impressive nature note for years.

I'm going back there in Jan – can't wait. Col Stirling has gambled away all his Spanish pictures, I believe there used to be El Grecos, Goyas and Velasquez by the doz, but there is only a dolly's sized Velasquez left, v enviable all the same.

Love to all, masses to you

Debo

Important P.S. Saw Diana Cooper's point for more or less the first time at a pretty ghastly dinner at the Hamish Hamiltons' for Nancy's book.

1 Andrew Devonshire had been appointed Parliamentary Under-Secretary for Commonwealth Relations. 'He always used to say that no one who had not held that office knew quite how dim an under-secretary's job was. He enjoyed it all the same.' (DD)

2 Duncan Sandys (1908–87). Minister in several Conservative governments, Secretary of State for Commonwealth Relations 1960–4. Married to Winston Churchill's daughter Diana 1935–60.

3 DD was quoting the 10th Duke of Beaufort, Master of the Beaufort Hounds, who could not imagine what James Lees-Milne, one of his tenants, did all day. 'Pointless man, the feller doesn't even hunt.'

4 The Polish painter Feliks Topolski, official artist for the coronation of 1953, was commissioned to produce a record of the event to hang at Buckingham Palace.

5 Cuthbert Alport (1912–98). Parliamentary Under-Secretary of State, Commonwealth Relations Office 1957–9, Minister of State 1959–61. Married Rachel Bingham in 1945.

6 Nancy Mitford's last novel, *Don't Tell Alfred*, published by Hamish Hamilton in 1960.

7 Pamela Mitford (1907–94). DD's second eldest sister, nicknamed 'Woman' by her family, was best-known for being the unknown Mitford. Married to Derek Jackson 1936–51.

8 William (Bill) Stirling (1911–83). Scotch landowner, farmer, soldier and entrepreneur. Led the 2nd Special Air Service regiment while his brother, David Stirling, founded and led the 1st (the SAS was dubbed Stirling and Stirling at the time). 'He was a brilliant game shot and the best host of the best shoot at Keir. I was lucky enough to be invited for the last week of January for many years. This unmatched entertainment became known as The Festival.' (DD)

9 Francis (Freddie) de Guingand (1900–79). Distinguished soldier who had been Chief of Staff to Field Marshal Montgomery.

8 December 1960   Chatsworth
                                                  Bakewell

Darling Pad,

I can't remember when I wrote, or whether Andrew had got a job by then.

Anyhow, we've had the first small dose of official entertaining & I can tell you I shall put my foot in it soon as I can't understand (a) protocol (b) sucking up and (c) not saying very loud what one thinks about (a) the government & (b) Uncle Harold & his troupe.

Anyway what's happened so far is an official dinner at the High

Commissioner of Ceylon's & lunch, in his own dump, with the Boss.

It's a new world, and a rum one.

The Ceylons live in a plain house in Addison Road, never an ornament to be seen, but many chairs placed about the room like those lounges where television interviews take place. No fire, not even electric, but bright lights & central heating.

Very well then. I thought it wd be Andrew & me & some Ceylonese people. Not at all. It was for grandees like Ld Home,[1] Ld Mountbatten,[2] Mrs Pandit,[3] Ld Soulbury[4] laced with a few gloomy faces like Mr & Mrs Creech Jones[5] & various anonymous but high up civil servants.

I was lucky & sat by Ld Home. He is *sweet* & looks like an amiable goat but does not smell or anything. Lady Home is one of those large English county ladies with a loud voice, but comforting because of their unchangingness, usually to be seen & heard on saints' days at Eton. She wore an electric blue dress of strange shape & nameless stuff & huge dirty diamonds on a huge clean bosom.

Ld Mountbatten shouted about the bag at Six-Mile Bottom to me across the table & scarcely addressed a word to the lady in a sari whose dinner it was. When the pudding loomed – jelly – he said very crossly to the hired waiter 'What on earth's all this.' It makes one despair of the behaviour of some hopeless English people.

When we'd all stuck it till 11, Ld Home was very polite & said to the host*ess* 'I'm afraid we must very reluctantly tear ourselves away.' I thought that was better.

Lunch with the boss was most educational. He gives one pretty straightforward looks & he's got everything red, except for his teeth which were vaguely yellow. He paints, in his pyjamas, before getting up, or so he says.

I will ask him to stay & report further. I don't think it's any good pretending that one can like or understand ambitious politicians.

I'm so awfully sorry about Ralph Partridge[6] – what it means to all our friends. I wonder what his poor wife will do, if she can stay on at that house – all that. It is sad.

OH how I wish you were coming for Christmas. Poor old
Andrew is faced with Lady Redesdale, Mrs Hammersley,[7] my m in
law and Woman – no man to leaven them.

　　Much love
　　　Debo

1 Alexander (Alec) Douglas-Home, 14th Earl of Home (1903–95). The Conservative politician and future Prime Minister was Foreign Secretary at the time.
Married Elizabeth Alington, daughter of his headmaster at Eton, in 1936.

2 Earl Mountbatten of Burma (1900–79). The former Viceroy and Governor-
General of India was Chief of the Defence Staff 1959–65.

3 Vijaya Lakshmi Pandit (1900–90). Politician and diplomat. Indian High Commissioner to Great Britain 1955–61.

4 Herwald Ramsbotham, 1st Viscount Soulbury (1887–1971). Conservative politician. Governor-General of Ceylon 1949–54.

5 Arthur Creech Jones (1891–1964). Labour politician who, as Secretary of State
for the Colonies, presided over Ceylon's independence in 1948. Married Violet
Tidman in 1920.

6 Ralph Partridge (1894–1960). One of the Bloomsbury quartet that consisted
of Lytton Strachey, who was in love with Partridge; Dora Carrington, whom
Partridge married; and Frances Marshall, who became Partridge's wife after
Carrington's suicide. They lived at Ham Spray House, on the borders of Berkshire
and Wiltshire. Frances Partridge moved to London after her husband's death and
died in 2004, aged 103.

7 Violet Williams-Freeman (1877–1964). A childhood friend of Lady Redesdale
and a favourite of DD and her sisters.

28 or 29 December 1960   Chatsworth
                                                    Bakewell

Darling Pad,

　　Our Sunset Home have departed. Woman brought four dogs (one
of which was incontinent) and her days are spent cooking for them,
feeding them what she has cooked, then going out to make messes. I
know this is a natural cycle but it's repeated in such quick succession
that there was no time to do anything else. It must be a strange life.

　　Going out with the oldsters was a job. They never learn where
the front door is and so many shawls, scarves, sticks, rugs and deaf
aids have to be collected that it's pretty difficult and there are specs

down every chair. The housemaid had a heart attack on Christmas Day & was rushed to Bakewell Cottage Hosp, where I must say I wouldn't mind a week or two as there are only three beds in a room. Think if the Wife & Lady Mosley were in the other two. It would be the fittest thing going.

I sent the Wife a book (empty) with COMPLAINTS heavily engraved in gold, companion to the visitors' book. She sent me a Landseer drawing and a basket. I gave Stoker a cashmere jersey. He gave me some Beecham's powders and a loofah. That's the best of the Christmas news, except that we had some fine cards from people like MR AND MRS SCRIPP KELLOGG printed inside.

No signs of (a) R Kee (b) Daphne and Xan (c) Ann Fleming who has been taken by her ridiculous husband to Switzerland for a whole month.

Much love
      Debo

5 January 1961   12 Kallirhoë Street
                                                   Makriyannis
                                                   Athens

Darling Debo,

I got stuck in the mountains the other night, miles up in clouds and snow, with the huge white starlit peaks of Mt Helmos and Mt Kyllene outside the shepherd's hut that sheltered me. My hosts were two old boys, Uncle George and Uncle Dimitri. I asked them about ghosts, centaurs, Nereids and other familiar spirits of the Greek countryside. U. Dimitri said that was all rot, but Uncle George came across with reams of absorbing lore. When he had finished, Uncle Dimitri said, gazing thoughtfully into the brushwood fire: 'I don't believe a word of it. But demons are another thing. Plenty of them about.'

U. George Rubbish.

U. Dimitri Rubbish my foot. My own niece Maria, my sister's daughter, was bothered by one for years.

U. George What was it like?

U. Dimitri A small black dog with one eye in the middle of its forehead. It followed her about everywhere, talking to her in a low voice, and she would answer it – a continuous mumbling, it was. Then my sister bought a miniature New Testament on a loop of blue string, and went to find Maria in the forest, where she had been cutting wood. She was just starting home, with a load of logs and faggots tied behind her, on the back of her mule, and on top of them this wretched dog was sitting, mumbling away without a break. My sister slipped the Testament round her neck, and the dog suddenly stopped talking and shot like a sky rocket to the top of Mt Kyllene where it burst like a bomb with a report you could hear all over the Peloponnese. She was alright after that, and now she's married with eleven children.

This completely floored U. George, who sat in silence, clicking his tongue in appreciation.

No more for now, except heaps of fond love from
Paddy

18 January 1961   4 Chesterfield Street
                                                    London W1

Darling Pad,

A slightly ghoulish prospect looms today. Andrew & I bugger off to America for Jack Kennedy's coronation[1] – back Sunday I'm happy to say. I can't tell you how queer it is getting a visa – they send you a jolly invitation from The President to his crowning & then proceed to ask you all sorts of cheeky questions & insist on *seeing* you to make sure you're not a Communist. Well how can they know just by looking at one's ugly mug. On one of the many forms was printed ORIGIN & the clerk wrote CAUCASIAN. I asked Look here what's that & he said without a flicker of anything Means you're white. I didn't know I was a jolly Georgian in floppy trousers & a cuirasse wildly dancing & tweaking people left & right. The Consul in Manchester said Take all your pretties – you'll see some fabulous gowns and toilets. Bet I will.

We're staying at the English embassy – I'll report.

Life with the Creature of the Mist[2] was v strange indeed, smashing shoot, we got 1050 objects in four days but I have lost the art & have made up my mind (vaguely) not to go away & shoot any more, only do it at home.

My train arrived at 5.15 *a.m.* & who came lumbering up the platform in the meeting dept but the Great & Good man himself. I worship his body but he doesn't notice.

I sat next to him for thirteen meals out of fourteen & the talk was the same each time, most restful & a refreshing change from the intis,[3] viz. Will you all come back in the summer & we can look for the flowers which only grow on Ben something or other (the local Parnassus). This said in a leaning towards one confidential way & it was so exciting knowing what was coming.

Sincerely (practising for America)

D Devonshire

---

1 DD had known the Kennedys since Joseph P. Kennedy, ambassador in London 1938–40, brought his family to live at Princes Gate where they were neighbours of the Mitfords. Andrew's older brother, William (Billy), married Kathleen Kennedy in 1944. The presidential inauguration, which took place on 20 January 1961, was described by Andrew Devonshire as 'all rather engagingly schoolboyish, but infectious'. *Accidents of Fortune* (Michael Russell, 2004), p. 87.

2 William Stirling.

3 Intellectuals.

25 January 1961   Chatsworth
                                                       Bakewell

Darling Pad,

Two new bodies to add to the list of worshipped – a *sweet* ambassador called Sir Harold Caccia,[1] and Jack Kennedy.

I lay beside Mr Gaitskell[2] for six happy hours in the plane to London & scraped his bottom (strange expression from a French friend who is not too good at English describing confidences received on a journey) & we became vague friends.

He was a Friend in Tweed is a Friend Indeed in Washington when our Austin Princess (1950) broke coming away from the Inaugural Ball at a place called The Armoury which is a vast hall about twice as big as Olympia & was the venue for many a Presidential festivity last week.

The last day of our fantastic outing we were taken to the Senate & Andrew was led into the Chamber (as they have a reciprocal agreement about govt people from foreign parts) & before you could say Robert Kee, two Senators were making speeches of welcome to him. I was sweating with fright in case he would make one back but thank goodness he only bowed. Good old Andrew.[3]

Jack Kennedy was *marvellous*, chiefly because he was so marvellous to us & summoned me from the back of his stand to sit with him during the Parade & it fuddled the commentators on the telly as they only know politicians & film stars & when strange English ladies loom they are stumped.

I can't even tell you what an odd feeling it was sitting there with him like a Consort while majorettes from Texas & crinolined ladies on silver-paper floats went by by the thousand in the bitter cold. An Air Force contingent marched by & one broke ranks, whipped out a camera, took a snap of the President & rejoined the others. I wish I could see a Coldstream Guardsman do that one day.

Jack asked me what I do all day. Stumped. I asked him if he was going to see Uncle Harold – he'd never heard of him. He is lovely – face & hair look as if it had been dipped in the same sand, eyes only different.

We went in a bus labelled 'Kennedy Family' to The White Ho & they all cheered as we went through the gates.

White Ho is very pretty, proper rooms covered in proper silk, green, red, yellow & ghastly blue put by Mamie[4] (I think).

The Gala (seats 1000 dollars, for party funds!) was a literal galaxy of stars, Frank Sinatra, Ella Fitzgerald, Durante, Nat King Cole, the kind of music was SO NICE compared with the usual ghouls, viz. Willie Walton. I appreciated.

At the ball Jack Kennedy climbed over seven rows of cinema seats to say goodbye, to the astonishment of the people next to us & who were nicer from then on.

He is surrounded like a queen bee by photographers, detectives, nexts of kin & fans so if he breaks out of the phalanx of people to come & talk to ONE, one nearly faints with pleasure & surprise.

It was so hot in & so cold out it's a wonder people survive.

V odd to be back here, shooting cock pheasants out of the car like today.

I went to a shop with the secretary to the Ambassadress & saw some lovely gloomy shirts, khaki & black stripes, & said out loud oh those are perfect for Robert & Lucian & the sec said Are they your sons? Oh how I wish they were.

 Much love
  Debo

1 Harold Caccia (1905–90). British ambassador in Washington 1956–61. Created Baron Caccia of Abernant 1965.

2 Hugh Gaitskell (1906–63). Leader of the Labour Party from 1955 until his death.

3 'The Cavendishes were well known to be silent and spoke only when there was something worth saying. The Cecils were the opposite, talk, talk, talk from earliest childhood. My mother-in-law was a Cecil, born and brought up at Hatfield House where everyone had their say on every subject. Andrew took after her and started the Cavendishes talking – something Chatsworth had not known before.' (DD)

4 Mamie Eisenhower's favourite colour was, in fact, pink. During her husband's presidency, the White House was often referred to by the press as the 'Pink Palace'.

16 February 1961   Metsovo
(Feast of SS Pamphilius   Epirus
and Seleucus, Martyrs)   NW Greece

Darling Debo,

I *was* impressed by your coronation trip (did you get a *mug*?), and so were others I imparted the proud news to. It was a wonderful description of J. Kennedy. He seems to have done *jolly well* so far. I wish he weren't so much younger than one. You *do* write good letters, you know, you really do, in that whizz-bang planchette style, hitting the nail on the head again and again without even looking. Please persevere through the coming decades, only another forty years or so, if all goes well.

You'll never guess where I am. Last year in Rome, I got a fan-

letter from Mr Avéroff[1] (the Gk Foreign Minister, now in your
midst) saying he thought *Mani*[2] was glorious (he's better read than
some), and would I *and my party* go and stay in his house in
Metsovo any time, as long as I liked, to write. So here I am, and
Joan too. It's what they call an ancestral Epirot house, in the Turkish
style, huge rooms surrounded by divans, with carved wooden ceilings
giving one the feeling of being inside a cigar box, jutting out in
storey after storey, overlooking the snow-covered roofs of the *highest
village in Greece*, bang on the top of the Pindus Mountains in fact,
almost the wildest and remotest bit of the wildest and remotest range
in Greece. These cigar-box rooms, thank heavens, each have
enormous porcelain stoves, so it's piping hot within, and just as well
as snow falls and swirls without and icicles dangle a foot thick. The
lanes outside have that marvellous winter smell of snow, cattle, straw,
pee, dung, pines, hay, ice, and cigars, appropriately being smoked by
me. The inhabitants are *Koutzovlachs** who speak a v. queer Latin
dialect akin both to Rumanian and Italian. Some say they are
Rumanian nomad shepherds who wandered here centuries ago with
their flocks and never found their way home again. Others, more
plausibly, say that they are the descendants of Roman legionaries,
speaking a corrupt camp Latin, stationed here to guard the high
passes of the Pindus, miles from anywhere; and that when the
Emperor Honorius** recalled the legions to Rome in 410 A.D., they
never got the order; and here they have been stuck ever since, rather
bewildered little rock pools of Romans, wondering wistfully if their
absent centurions know as much as they should about Care of Men.
They wear ribbed velvet pill-boxes, black goat's-hair boleros, black
ditto kilts, black leggings of the same, and pom-pommed shoes, with
hooded full-length capes so stiff that they can step out and leave
them standing like sentry-boxes. They are semi-nomads, and now half
of them are down in the plains with thousands of black sheep and
goats, the last two devouring the delicious grass there, while their
masters moon the winter through in numberless snug wigwams made

* DON'T SKIP
** *ditto*

of plaited willow and brushwood. The rest of my party (Coote and, I
hope, Mark [Ogilvie-Grant]) roll up tomorrow: by plane to Yanina,
the capital of Epirus, and then up here by bus, bringing newspapers
and whisky, & perhaps letters from you and other dear ones. It's
quicker by bus than by car, because a bulldozer-cum-snow plough
goes before the bus. We were blocked in a howling blizzard on the
way here, in spite of heavy chains, in the highest and windiest part of
the pass. It was awful watching the snow blowing higher and higher
as we cowered gazing through the fan-shaped bits the wipers made
on the caked windscreen, till a snow plough came along, and let us
through – creatures of the snow – finally delivered at this warm
casket of a house, with books and carpets and whisky and shaded
lamps and roaring stoves. It seemed a true miracle.

   Did you come across Mr Avéroff – I thought you might because
of Andrew's uncle, perhaps. He's an odd kind. (*PRIVATE*) I scarcely
knew him; but I took my courage in both hands (knowing he had
just wangled an old friend of mine out of Rumania – more of this
anon) and asked if he could do anything about my old love, Balasha
Cantacuzène:[3] and he has promised to, if he can! I can't believe it,
though it may take a year or two. She was over ten years older than
me when I was twenty – so still must be! – which means over fifty-
five (-six since last week). There was a faint chance of her getting
out two years ago, but she didn't want to, because, after prison for
two years (for trying to escape) and living in utter hardship as a
pauper for 15 years in forced residence & little to eat in a remote
village, she said she dreaded seeing anyone again – painfully thin,
teeth and hair dropping out fast. It's too awful. Poor Balasha! But I'm
sure something could be done about all this, and thank heavens,
there are several old friends who will cough up something to begin
with. And indeed go on. She's a painter. She always adored Greece,
and would probably want to settle here. How wonderful it would be
if she did make it! We haven't met for 22 years. She used to be so
beautiful. The one who *did* get out through Mr A – he's called
Nicky Cryssovelóni, a very old friend of mine – says that in spite of
all these calamities, she's quite unchanged in character, just as funny
and intelligent and charming as ever.

I was amazed by how little *he* had changed after countless imprisonments and beatings up. He was, and still is, amazingly good looking, ½ English with a great fascination, I think. Bridget [Parsons] used to be terribly in love with him, & I think would have liked to have married him. But (alas for poor B!) the only one he asked after in England was 'Ann O'Neill',[4] so I've put him on the right track. I've given him a letter for *you* – is this alright? I wish you'd organise a meal or something with Robert [Kee] and perhaps A. O'Neill, as I think his accounts of occupied Rumania and the Communist regime would fascinate him. It's quite something; a lot of it, unexpectedly, is side splitting. Judging by what's going on outside the window – I've let the curtain fall with a shudder – my party are going to have a pretty rough ascent tomorrow.

Heaps of love
Paddy

1 Evangelos Avéroff (1910–90). The Greek Foreign Minister was on a three-day official visit to Britain.
2 PLF's account of his travels in the southern Peloponnese, first published in 1958.
3 Princess Marie-Blanche (Balasha) Cantacuzène (1899–1976). PLF met the Romanian painter in Athens in 1935. Her marriage to the polo-playing Spanish diplomat Francisco Amat y Torres had ended, and she and PLF spent several months together in Greece before returning to live at Baleni, her ancestral home in Moldavia, south-eastern Romania. PLF was at Baleni in 1939 when war was declared.
4 Ann Fleming was married, firstly, to 3rd Baron O'Neill 1932–44.

30 June 1961

Cliff Cottage[1]
Fforest Farm
Dinas, Newport
Pembrokeshire

Darling Debo,

I ffeel ffrightfully guilty about being so ffearffully slow in writing to say thank you for that lovely weekend. It was glorious, and I really loved it.

It was a bit gloomy here to begin with – the deed-box smell of long-closed rooms as Joan and I tiptoed in, and the wriggle of moths' larvae. (But they've all been slain now.) Also, it poured to begin with and, whenever one went out of doors, great cotton-wool clouds weighed down on one, making one feel like a bird's egg packed against breakage and, where flowers ought to be, nothing but tares: *not* at all a case of (please intone this like a psalm):

> 'As he *swore* unto *our* fore*father*:
> *Sutton* and his *seeds* for*ever*.'

Glorious meals, as you rightly guessed, so that one longs to be at meat. A giant lobster, caught an hour before, last night, with raspberries and cream to follow; and these cliffs are one vast Nature Note, puffins, choughs, guillemots, kittiwakes, shearwaters, buzzards and the like, and deep chasms running down to the sea choked with tropical vegetation where foxes and badgers live. Also, there are low but wild mountains behind, the scene of bleak and bracing gallops, then heavenly rides homeward along winding lanes between hayfields and through farmyards where cottagers talk to each other, in Welsh no doubt, about music, wizards, rarebits and kindred themes.

I suppose it's too far to drive from Derbyshire, but, were it not, one might explore further down the coast.

Lastly, work is going like a fire hydrant and about time too.

Lots of love from
    Paddy

---

1 PLF had borrowed the house from Barbara Ghika (1911–89), née Hutchinson, who married the painter Nikos Ghika in 1961. She was married previously to Victor, 3rd Baron Rothschild 1933–46 and to Rex Warner, writer, painter and translator of Greek tragedies, in 1949.

17 July 1961   Chatsworth
                                                         Bakewell

Darling Pad,

Re. Iris Tree. She came for the weekend. Well, she arrived with the *Exchange & Mart* under her arm so I was knocked all of a heap. I never saw such a lady, such sequin ties, such golden evening outfits (chain mail), such memory for poetry, such *company*. She is the fittest thing this side of Tipperary. No wonder you love her so much. The reactions, the being an American, saying 'Well what d'you know', the words used describing things, my goodness, & all this & the *Exchange & Mart.*

I spoke about Ivan Moffat[1] being one of the three people left I want to meet (others are Lds Beaverbrook & Birkenhead).[2] She said one must have three goes at him. I believe he's getting married & that sometimes makes people different for, say, three months so we must hang on. Anyway his dear old mother takes a bit of beating.

Keep in touch.

Much love

Debo

1 Ivan Moffat (1918–2002). Screenwriter, son of Iris Tree and grandson of the actor Sir Herbert Beerbohm Tree. PLF had known Moffat since 1940: 'All his life, with his high forehead, tousled hair and large eyes, he had the look of an intelligent, rebellious, finely-strung and charming boy. His quiet, urgent style was spaced out by pauses and changes of pace and pitch and interrupted by bursts of all-consuming and infectious laughter.' PLF, *Daily Telegraph,* 2 August 2002.

2 The powerful press baron Max Aitken, 1st Baron Beaverbrook (1879–1964), and the historian Frederick Smith, 2nd Earl of Birkenhead (1907–75). 'Beaverbrook was such a *person.* Of course I wanted to meet him, so much spoken of – devil incarnate or irresistible charmer, depending on who you talked to. Freddie Birkenhead was Tom [Mitford]'s great friend. Hearing about him was enough to make me very curious.' (DD)

17? November 1961

Poste Restante
Nîmes
Gard

My darling Debo,

Feeling a bit low. It's Saturday night in this town, pouring with rain, and here I am in this café, unknown and unloved. I wish you were here, and Xan and Daph, Ran, several other people, let alone Joan. Think what lovely drinks and talks we'd have, followed by some smashing guzzle somewhere, then more drinks and a great deal more talks and jokes, and finally pretty tight to bed, and off into dreamland, knowing a glorious day was about to dawn on the morrow, rain or shine.

I did lots of work in Brittany but it got too damp and dark and sad, so I thought, off to the glowing south and pitch camp there, with any luck somewhere near my old pal Larry Durrell.[1] (Not here of course.) But the journey, though solitary, was marvellous, all through S. Brittany, then down to Nantes, over the Loire to La Rochelle, a very pretty arcaded town where, in a bar late at night, I fell in with a delightful old boy who seemed to know everyone anybody's ever met anywhere, and is also curator of the local Natural History Museum, which we went over next day. We sat up in his very pretty book-lined house in the port drinking whisky till 4 a.m. and next day he gave me a thumping lunch with clarets almost too fabulous to drink. He'd just read Nancy's book, and asked me who everyone was so I was able to score rather heavily.[2] Why I go on about him is that, when he was a very young man in La Rochelle, your uncle Jack Mitford[3] was there learning French, a tremendous dasher apparently, with a small pack of hounds for hunting cats. He used to send out cards asking all the smart world of La Rochelle to the meets, and then, hell for leather all over the town, to the wonder of the citizens.

So, on down the west coast of France to Bordeaux, which might have been at the bottom of the sea, it was so rainy. I stopped here at an old-fashioned, quite empty hotel, all long passages, brass bedsteads and threadbare plush, overlooking the submerged cathedral. The maid who helped me up with my luggage – mostly in baskets, the advantage of motor travel – was a tall fair sad beauty, no make up, in a severe black dress and starched white apron. Peering into the rainy square I quoted two lines of Verlaine about the monotonous noise of the rain, which she promptly continued for several more lines. She turned out to be enormously well read, from Paris, lonely and gloomy in Bordeaux, not liking the burghers much. I asked her advice about where to go on one's own in this strange town, and ended up by meeting her round the corner in a bar (it wouldn't do in the hall of the hotel) as it was her night off: black and white now replaced by suede jacket, black jersey & skirt and flat shoes; then lots of oysters and things at another place, and lots of a rather sad life story. It turned out that the happiest time she'd had in her life, so far (she's 24), was last summer, with her greyhound Dick, at Arcachon in the estuary of the Garonne, where the oyster beds are. She would hang about till after sunset when everyone had left the sands, and then swim out with Dick and dive into the oyster beds and pinch the oysters; then turn back to the shore, where she had a plastic bag with a knife, bread, butter and lemon in, and have a solitary feast. Dick didn't like them, fortunately, but is a wonderful oyster-spotter, for after rough weather quite a lot are washed inshore and scattered about the sand, so off dashes clever Dick, to halt panting over some scaly trove, Annie following hot foot.

Kindred themes kept us up late, after which, at two in the morning, we went to a Spanish bar, already shut, but bursting with noise – claps, stamps, wails, guitars etc. We managed to get in and it consisted entirely of the family, about fifteen strong, all reeling, except a boy of four called Juanito who would tell them every quarter of an hour or so, and in vain, that it was long past his usual bedtime, then catch our eyes to commiserate on their hopelessness. The thing about this girl was, apart from her marvellous watermaiden looks, the ingrained *sadness* (as though her heir had gone down in the White Ship). I felt I'd won a prize whenever I made her laugh. One of her reasons for gloom was that, being solitary and nice-looking, she had a pretty rotten time with chaps, none of whom knew anything about Verlaine etc but were all after You Know What, and drifted off when nothing was doing; which cast a blight over all, & ruined most evenings – '*Not like with you!*' she said, eyes wide with grateful candour. This, of course, completely tied one's hands, SHOULD there have been any question of a Thurber-like lunge; and so it continued through next day Sunday off – indeed from beginning to end – and a great drive with Dick to St Emilion & the castle of Montaigne, and some more oysters. The *next* day, descending to depart, there was a discreet farewell wave in a passage, behind the other maids' backs, from this tall figure – black and white again. Then away, to discover on the seat of the Standard Companion[4] a surreptitiously placed present of a Mozart record I'd said the day before was one I liked, and hadn't got; with a covering note saying thanks for some of the '*heures les plus heureuses de mon existence*'. Wasn't that nice? I'll often think of that alluvial, estuary scene of Dick pounding across the sunset dunes under a mother of pearl sky, followed by this beautiful honey-coloured biped with knife, lemon, bread and butter.

So, on through Toulouse, Narbonne, finally here, where I'm staying in a rather gloomy hotel, but hope to move into a nice room in a courtyard of an old arcaded house once owned by a cardinal whose name I won't burden you with. Nobody writes (plainly a conspiracy).

In Brittany, I saw a plough being drawn by a huge black-and-white *bull*, yoked behind a carthorse, rather an unusual sight, especially as there was a rainbow at the same time.

Do write at once, darling Debo, and lots of love and hugs from
    Paddy

What of Daph & Xan?

---

[1] Lawrence Durrell (1912–90). The writer was living in Sommières, a small village in Provence. 'When all seems to languish and droop, his arrival acts like a stiff dose of Eno's or Kruschen Salts and everyone is suddenly ready to clear five-bar gates.' PLF, 'Observations on a Marine Vulture', *Twentieth-Century Literature*, vol. 33, no. 3, Autumn 1987, pp. 305–7.

[2] In *Don't Tell Alfred*, Nancy used aspects of her nephew Alexander Mosley for Basil; Diana Cooper for Lady Leone; Susan Mary Alsop for Mildred Jungfleisch; Lord Redesdale for Uncle Matthew; Eddy Sackville-West for Davey Warbeck and DD for Northey.

[3] John (Jack) Mitford, 4th Baron Redesdale (1885–1963). 'One of my father's younger brothers. He was famously snobbish and was much laughed at in the family for this failing, which he took in good part. When King Edward VII stayed at Batsford, Jack followed him round the garden with a chair in case he wanted to sit down. He made the mistake of marrying a German arms heiress in the spring of 1914, a union which was almost immediately annulled and never mentioned again. He made one or two half-hearted attempts at finding a job, but never stuck at anything and rubbed along as good company – he could be very funny.' (DD)

[4] 'The Standard Companion was the first car I ever had. I revelled in it! Humble and undashing, but dear to me. "Dr Piquard goes up, goes up / Captain Cousteau goes down / But my shark-blue Standard / Carries me all round the town!"' (PLF)

27 November 1961   Chatsworth
                                                   Bakewell

Darling Pad,

I'm going to America on Friday for a spell. I had a v nice letter
from J Kennedy, asking me to go, signed Yours ever Jack Kennedy,
and then below in his own writing President JF Kennedy, The
White House, Washington DC, USA. Well I must say I may be a 9
yr old but I had heard of him *and* his bonne addresse. So I'm going.
I've got cold feet now & heartily wish I was staying here pulling
triggers.

What *will* it be like in Washington? I know, one will go all that
way & then be asked to tea, once, at The White Ho. I'm staying with
David & Sissy,[1] that'll be nice.

Think of me, & I'll send a P.C. if I think Post Resting Nîmes is a
sensible place to send things off to.

I saw Daph & Xan last week, both recovering from bronchitis
and both perfect of course. I think Xan looked very nice but I
couldn't look at him, never can for at least two days as you
know.

The Wife's not too fit, and Mrs Hammersley is very cross about
me going to America. She thinks no one ought to interfere with
that gentleman & that he ought to be left to fry his fish day &
night. Ass.

Keep writing, vaguely.

Much love
    Debo

---

[1] David Ormsby Gore, 5th Baron Harlech (1918–85). Ambassador in Washington
1961–5. The politician and diplomat had been a close friend of J. F. Kennedy since
Kennedy's pre-war years in London during his father's embassy. 'It was JFK's suggestion to Uncle Harold [Macmillan] that he should go to Washington. David had
the best sense of humour and so did the President. This lightened their load and
often surprised their officials. The friendship between the two men was deep and
the relationship between them very different from the conventional formality of
their roles.' (DD) Married to Sylvia Lloyd Thomas from 1940 until her death in a
car crash in 1967, and to Pamela Colin in 1969.

19 January 1962   Easton Court Hotel
Nearly Full Moon   Chagford

My darling Debo,

I *did* love Christmas so and you were kind and angelic to have
me; and I feel a shocking laggard not having written before – only
idly phoning – to say so. I'll never forget all those icicles and frosty
statues and the lovely blaze and the heavenliness of everyone indoors
afterwards; nor the lovely *longness* of it, although it seemed over in a
trice.

When I got back, I found, which I'd completely forgotten, that
I'd been asked to stay for a rustic ball at Mary Campbell's ages
before; so got a lift down with Janetta[1] and great fun it was. Can
you imagine it, there were nearly thirty people staying in the house.
Lots of them very young and in sardine-like dorms. Lots of the
neighbouring quality came over for the ball, which was pretty
informal to say the least, to a gramophone, and got very wild and
lively. Among the guests was Magouche's[2] ex-hub, a tall, very handsome,
Harvardish looking man. Well in the small hours, I was dancing with
Magouche when the tune suddenly changed and Magouche cut a
bold and light-hearted caper and fell to the floor, full length, with a
bump. I chivalrously – it wasn't my fault a bit – reclined on the floor
beside her, leant on one elbow, and there we remained as a joke for
a minute or two, with the dance swirling all round, like two stone
crusaders on a tomb or two recumbent Etruscans, quietly conversing.
All at once I felt a vice-like grip on my nape, and someone shaking
me as a mastiff shakes a rat, as I believe they say. It was Jack (ex-hub)
who said '*I'm going to clobber you*'. I told him not to be a perfect
idiot but to come and have a drink instead, which he grumblingly
did, on condition that we had a 'clobbering match' next morning at
eleven. It was fortunately completely forgotten – a dark demon
called Hangover was whirling through the snowflakes and beating his
foul wings overhead by then – so nothing happened.

No more now, dearest Debo, except love to one and all and 1000
thanks, and lots and lots of love to you from
    Paddy

1 Janetta Woolley (1922–). 'Janetta has a marvellous fine-boned beauty which, when she was fifteen, smote Eddy Sackville-West so hard (in spite of his ordinary lack of such inclinations) it prompted him to propose to her. There is something magical and quiet about her; she had – has – qualities that turned her into a treasured and lifelong friend. I can never help remembering that a distant ancestor of hers was a Lord Ruthven, anti-Mary Queen of Scots, who, though old and ill, got out of bed, put on black armour and, with several other suffering grandees, climbed the stairs of Holyrood Palace and murdered Rizzio, the Queen's Italian favourite, a friend from her earlier life as Queen of France. A grim tale.' (PLF) Married to Humphrey Slater, to Robert Kee 1948–50, to Derek Jackson 1951–6, and in 1971 to Jaime Parladé, Marqués de Apesteguía, a Spanish architect with whom she settled near Ronda in Andalusia.

2 Agnes (Magouche) Magruder (1921–). Boston-born daughter of a US naval officer. Married to the artist Arshile Gorky 1941–8, who nicknamed her 'Mougouch', an Armenian term of endearment; to John C. Phillips Jr in 1950; and to Xan Fielding in 1979.

26 January 1962   Fitzroy House
Telegrams: *Antiseptic*, sinister   Fitzroy Square, W1

Darling Pad,

V v nice to hear from you, specially as I'm incarcerated in this dump, which is terribly nice, but a nursing home nevertheless. I've only had my inside seen to as usual. It must be the most hopeless inside this side of anywhere the way it carries on. Anyway the anaesthetic was marvellous. I said to the anaesthetist the next day how jolly it was & he said yes it's an addiction drug. Well no wonder. Have you ever had it? They give it an hour before the real thing & one floats in a marvellous state through all that's jolly in life, trying to hold on to every minute & savour it to the full.

That dear old President phoned the other day. First question was 'Who've you got with you, Paddy?' He's got you on his brain.

Keep in close touch.

Much love
    Debo

Teusday [August 1962]   Dumbleton

Darling Debo,

I've spent the last two months trying to find somewhere to live in
S.W. Greece, and, the trouble is, I've found it; trouble, because I don't
think we'll be able to get it; owned by too many people, scattered all
over the globe, who, though none of them live there, are unlikely to
want to sell it; but I live in hopes. It's in the Mani, a peninsula in the
middle of a steep deserted bay, pointing S.E., E., S.W. and W., with a
great amphitheatre of mountains which turn a hectic red at sunset.
The peninsula descends like a giant, shallow staircase of olive groves,
plumed with cypress trees, platform after platform dwindling to a
low cliff thirty feet above deep blue-green glittering sea, with trees
and wild sweet-smelling shrubs to the very brink, full of beehives,
olives, woodpigeons, and with a freshwater spring. The cliff is
warrened with a great sea cave into which one swims, under
stalactites and strange mushroom limestone formations. Not a house
in sight, nothing but the two rocky headlands, an island a quarter
of a mile out to sea with a ruined chapel, and a vast expanse of
glittering water, over which you see the sun setting till its last gasp.
Homer's Greece, in fact. But I've not given up hope. It would mean
building a rambling peasant house, with huge airy rooms, out of the
local limestone, on one of those ledges of olive-trees . . .

So much for all that. I flew back to Rome last week, then drove
back alone, stopping two nights at Fontainebleau with your pal ✂ [1]
who sends loving greetings.

My bust wrist[2] came out of plaster of Paris in Palermo, but still
seems jolly stiff and inflexible, and I bet it never quite gets right
again, the way they don't. I wonder what this entails. Balinese
dancing's out, for a start; so, should I ever succeed to a throne, is
holding an orb; the other drawbacks will surface with time.

Tons of love & hugs from
    Paddy

[1] No-eye = Noailles.
[2] Broken in a hunting fall.

28 October 1962 [British Embassy
Washington]

Darling Pad,

Several tons of rubble I'm afraid.[1] It's an *horrible surprise* par
excellence because the poor old Loved One[2] is vaguely taken up
with his work instead of messing about with one.

Much comical stuff to report. Andrew came for two short nights
& one long day & during the long day we were summoned to the
presence for an official call. There were some fiddling little crowds,
pickets etc, outside the White House, our car was stopped at the gate
& a policeman put his head in & said What group are you? Well,
what group are we, I don't know.

A rich lady said to me she needed a secretary who understood
her 'nervouswise'. The lingo is very nice indeed but takes a bit of
learning.

I've been to dinner at the White Ho twice. Jackie Kennedy was
there. She is a queer fish. Her face is one of the oddest I ever saw. It
is put together in a very wild way.

Last night was the dinner for the opening of the exhib of our
drawings.[3] Tom Wragg got completely drunk. I introduced him to
Sargent Shriver.[4] I said this is the brother-in-law of the President,
perhaps you remember his wife Eunice Kennedy, to which he replied
No I don't, but then I meet so many people I can't remember them
all.

Makes one's heart vaguely sink. He was drunk at a cocktail party
& very loudly suggested he & I should go to San Francisco. Well
when you think how he hates me it was rather telling.

You can buy Plastic Feather Rocks for your garden. Huge
Paxtonian objects weight 2oz each. Admit it would be a help to have
a few for the old home.

Much love
Debo

1 'The Cuban crisis was at its height and Paddy sent a telegram to me in
Washington saying, "Blimey we're in trouble, 'arf a ton of rubble", hence my
reply.' (DD) Bernard Cribbins' song 'Right Said Fred', about three removal men

struggling to remove a piano and 'half a ton of rubble' falling on top of their heads, was a favourite of DD and PLF.

2 President Kennedy had telephoned DD on Thanksgiving and asked, 'Have you got all your loved ones around you?'

3 A loan exhibition of Old Master drawings from Chatsworth was on show at the National Gallery in Washington. Tom Wragg, the librarian from Chatsworth, accompanied DD to the opening.

4 Sargent Shriver (1915–). Married Eunice Kennedy in 1953.

9 January 196[3]   Chatsworth
                                                       Bakewell

Darling Pad,

I've been in bed for a week, alright again now. I can quite easily see about taking to drugs, for instance the marvellous feeling of well being & the happiness when going off under a sleeping pill, one feels one *could do anything* far better than anyone else. Dangerous I call it & once a year is the sort of amount of times to resort to them.

The sweet Loved One is on the telly today unveiling the *Mona Lisa*. I guess he'd rather be unveiling a spot of real flesh & blood. What do you think? He'll be bored stiff by the evening at The Nat Gallery.[1] I can't wait to see his honest face acting enjoying it.

Much love
    Debo

1 The *Mona Lisa* was on a three-month loan to the US. It went on show at the Washington National Gallery and the Metropolitan Museum in New York.

6 May 1963   13 Chester Row, SW1

Darling Debo,

I'm feeling rather odd this morning, and it's a feeling whose oddity I can't hope to convey to you. I woke up this morning, after a lively weekend at Bruern,[1] feeling rather weighed down by the flesh and the devil and decided, for a day, to give up smoking and drinking, and, except for a bare minimum, eating. It's noon now, and I feel very strange and rather lost: don't know what to do with my hands. I suppose I'd better just fold them in my lap and gaze in front of me with a quiet and contemplative smile. It's all very queer; very chastening.

Tons of love, Debo darling, from
    Paddy

[1] PLF had been staying at Bruern Abbey in Oxfordshire with Michael and Pandora Astor.

Sunday [May 1963]   Easton Neston[1]
                                                     Northamptonshire

My darling Debo,

I write in a state of some excitement. *I haven't smoked since Monday.* You don't know what this means, it's the equivalent of reeling drunkenness and euphoria and airy rashness in you or Nancy. I feel low, twilit and anti-climactic (if that's the word I seek) but, at the same time, odd, pure, clean, and with a tongue like a Maréchal Niel rose petal and breath like that of high-born kine.

I don't know what's to become of me.[2]

Tons of love,
    Paddy

[1] PLF was staying with his friend Christian (Kisty), Lady Hesketh (1929–2006).
[2] PLF soon took up smoking again and did not give up completely until some twenty years later.

18 or 19 May 1963   Inch Kenneth
                                                     Gribun
                                                     Isle of Mull

Darling Pad,

I loved your NO SMOKING letter on the beautiful paper. It was most cheering. I *do* wonder if you're still at it, or not at it, if you see what I mean.

We (Diana, Woman, the French Lady & me) are all here and have been for ten days because my mother had a sort of collapse after her journey here from London & we were sent for. Oh Whack,[1] the

sadness of it to see her. Thank goodness the Dr has now arranged
various sleeping things every few hours so a lot of the time she is
asleep but when she is awake it is AWFUL because one of the things
which has more or less given up is the swallowing bit of her throat
so she is fearfully hungry & cries for food & then can't manage it,
like a ghastly torture.

There is awful moaning, but the strange thing is we have got *sort
of* used to that. Three times we have thought she was dying but
each time she has rallied & then blames us, sadly, for what she calls
dragging her back from the grave. Isn't it strange it should be so
difficult to be born and so difficult to die.

Between the sad times she has had a few moments of laughing,
jokes about her will, & the others say I go round looking for any small
valuable objects I can see & drop them in a bottomless black bag.

We take it in turns to be in her room 24 hours of the day. What
do people do who have less than four daughters – it unnerves me
when I think of Emma & Sophy. What a lot of deathbeds they will
have to see to.

My sister Woman is excelling herself, cooking gammon in
champagne & droning & intoning about the very wonderful sauce
that she's going to make next. The wonderful thing about her is she
doesn't mind how much we laugh at her. It's v luxurious being with
all the others, such a thing hasn't happened for years.

One simply doesn't know how long it may go on & none of us
can leave as she asks for us by name sometimes.[2] The last two days
another horror has come which is it's almost impossible to hear or
understand what she says. We live for the post which arrives in the
evening with the papers (but on rough days they can't go for it &
that is bitter).

There are two nurses, both saints & both young & jolly.

Being on this island is odd enough in itself, but under these
circumstances it is gruelling. (Except for being with the sisters which
is HEAVEN.)

I must go & find driftwood for the fire.

Much love
    Debo

1 A nickname given to PLF by Nancy Mitford, from the refrain 'Knick-Knack, Paddy Whack', in the song 'This Old Man Came Rolling Home'.
2 'My mother died a few days later, on 25 May, and was buried at Swinbrook in Oxfordshire on one of the first days of glorious weather that year.' (DD)

Teusday [June 1963]   Dumbleton

Darling Debo,

I say the Loved One's doing alright, isn't he? What a pity no Lismore.[1] But I suppose it would seem a bit odd, as the visit is more or less to commemorate his great grandsire's flight from the wicked English yoke.

    Tons of love,
        Paddy

1 President Kennedy, who was on an official visit to Ireland, told DD that his helicopter had circled low over Lismore several times but had not landed. On his way back from Ireland he did, however, stop off at Edensor to visit his sister Kathleen's grave, en route for talks with Harold Macmillan.

Teusday [November 1963]   Katounia
                                                       Limni, Euboea
                                                       Greece

Darling Debo,

Absolutely shattered, like everyone by the awful news of Kennedy's death. Greece has gone into three days mourning; so I can well understand — or probably can't — how infinitely more ghastly and tragic it must be for a great friend. You talked about him and described him so well and vividly — making him seem so vital and astonishing and so much fun, that it was like knowing someone by proxy. And what's everyone going to do *now*, I'd like to know?

    What a beastly age to live in.
    Tons of fond love as ever,
        Paddy

6 December 1963   Chatsworth
                                                            Bakewell

Darling Pad,

We went to Washington for his funeral. Oh it was strange, Americans aren't suited to tragedy. They like everything to be great. I was more or less alright in church till his friends came in & their crumpled miserable faces were too much & it was floods all the way after that.

I never wanted to leave anywhere so quickly as that town. It was so sad David & Sissy [Harlech] having to remain. I suppose they'll have to stick out another year but the whole point of the thing has gone.

If it hadn't been for such a sad sad reason the journeys there & back would have been rather fascinating. We got a lift off the Prime Minister[1] who had a chartered Boeing 707. The passengers were him & Lady Douglas-Home, the Duke of Edinburgh, Mr Wilson,[2] Sir Philip de Zulueta,[3] Sir Timothy Bligh,[4] Sir Harold Evans,[5] 2 girl typists, 2 detectives, the D of E's ADC & Andrew & me & 150 empty seats behind.

I had one of the strangest dinners of my life, with the D of E & Mr Wilson, Andrew at another table with the Homes.

Coming back we were without the D of E, Andrew & Wilson (they came straight back, I stayed for two days) but plus Mr Grimond.[6] So dinner that night was the Homes & me & Mr Grimond. When we got west of Ireland they said it was too foggy to land in London & we fetched up at Manchester.

NO SLEEPERS for the PM & Co so they all (11 of them) came here for the night. When I showed Mr Grimond into the Red Velvet room unkind Sir P de Zulueta said all the Liberal Party could get into bed with him.

It was all very odd indeed & Alice in Wonderlandish.

On Monday we go to Kenya for five days. Andrew starts at Zanzibar but there isn't room for women there, so I go straight to Kenya.

I hope they'll hold their pangas & won't do us all in at the State Garden Party.

The first engagement is a Civic Ball. I'll save the last dance for Jomo.[7]

Oh dear I do feel so sad about J Kennedy, but really the fantastic luck was knowing him at all, such an extraordinary person, so funny, so touching, clever, brave & sort of good, & such marvellous company.

Are you coming back before Xmas?

Much love

Debo

[1] Sir Alec Douglas-Home, Conservative Prime Minister from October 1963 to October 1964.

[2] Harold Wilson (1916–95). The Labour MP had been elected leader of his party earlier in the year. Prime Minister 1964–70 and 1974–6.

[3] Philip de Zulueta (1925–89). Private Secretary to the Prime Minister 1955–64. 'JFK described him to me as "that Spaniard who looks after Uncle Harold".' (DD)

[4] Timothy Bligh (1918–69). Principal Private Secretary to the Prime Minister 1959–64.

[5] Harold Evans (1911–83). Chief Information Officer at the Colonial Office 1953–7, Public Relations Adviser to the Prime Minister 1957–64.

[6] Joseph (Jo) Grimond (1913–93). Leader of the Liberal Party 1956–67.

[7] Jomo Kenyatta (1894–1978). First Prime Minister of Kenya after independence was declared on 12 December 1963. President of Kenya 1964–78.

1 January 1964   Katounia
                                                      Limni, Euboea

Happy New Year, Darling Debo,

Something awful has happened. Aymer Maxwell's[1] dog, a frightfully nice bitch called Turka that he and Joan and I adore (a sandy coloured basic dog) came in last night looking fat as a barrel (she has a wonderful figure normally) with dark marks on her muzzle, which we wiped; it turned out to be blood. We hoped it was a hare, as she's a great one for chasing them. Just now a furious shepherd came down from the mountain saying five of his goats and two kids had been killed last evening. (It's lambing – kidding time? – here.) She's been *suspected* before, but had a sort of alibi. I suppose I'll have to shoot her. This is agony (a) because she's A. Maxwell's, (b) because she's such a heavenly dog. What *is* one to do? It is like that awful story in *Wild Animals I have Known*.[2] Do pity me.

Here's a riddle to change the subject: what English catch–phrase, indicating someone is better than he seems, would *also* apply to a yacht owner whose vessel is even more dangerous than the inlet in which she is anchored?*

No more now, Debo darling, except wishes for a marvellous year.

And lots of love from

    Paddy

* His barque is worse than his bight.

1 Sir Aymer Maxwell (1911–87). A 'serious but congenial' friend of PLF and Joan who settled in Euboea, off the coast of Attica, and sailed the Aegean in his caïque, the *Dirk Hatterick*.

2 Ernest Thompson Seton, *Wild Animals I have Known* (1898). In 'Wully, The Story of a Yaller Dog', a trusty mongrel sheepdog, turned ferocious sheep-killer, attacks its owners and has to be destroyed.

22 January 1964   4 Chesterfield Street, W1

Darling Pad,

Thanks v much for (a) your Christmas telegram & (b) your New Year letter. V kind to send same & deeply appreciated by all.

Now something really important. We've had to put a new door with false book-backs in the Library at Chatsworth and we've got to think of 28 titles. The one the other end has got things like Boyle on Steam, The Scottish Boccaccio by D Cameron & such like. Stoker says we must use The Light Reader by Ivan Artov Stone. Mrs Ham suggests Bondage by Ann Fleming.[1] I can only think of The Liverpool Sound by Viscountess Mersey. So come on now. Something topical, politics, friends, anything?

Much love

    Debo

I *really* sympathise over the dog you're fond of. It is the worst thing in the world because you'll always have to be watching her and if she does disappear you'll worry till she gets back. Don't let anyone else shoot her, you know what I mean, they might do it ghoulishly.

1 An allusion to the sado-masochistic nature of Ann and Ian Fleming's relationship.

[February 1964]
Katounia
Limni, Euboea

My darling Debo,

Here are a few, most of them hopelessly feeble, but perhaps one might sift a grain or two out of so much chaff. I put them down helter skelter as they cropped up during the last few days.

Dipsomania	by Mustafa Swig
Canine Diet	Norah Bone
I Scream	Walls
In the Soup	A. Crouton
A Tommy in the Harem	Private Parts
Second Helpings	O. Twist
First Causes	F. Heckt
Weathering Heights	Nelson & Brontë
First Steps in Rubber	Wellington
Military Dilemmas	Major Crisis
Cease Fire!	General Strike
Flags of the Nations	Bunting (!)
Buy Me and Stop One	Home Dentist
William Locke	Robert Key
A Good Chap	Bacon
The Midnight Flit	A. Moss-Quito
Round the Bend	Harpic
Also Ran	Antrim
Dunking	by Ruskin
Will Yam Make Peace?	Thackeray
Plain or Ringlets	by Broccoli
Consenting Adults	Abel N. Willing

Trumpet Voluntary	Hornblower
Minor Rodents	Aygood-Mausser
Where the Hormones . . .	Christine Keeler
Venus Observed	I. Sawyer
Bridge Building	A. Belvoir
Last of his Line	Tom Cobley
Studies in Sentiment	E. Motion
Reduced to the Ranks	D. Motion
Intuition	Ivor Hunch
Weather in the Streets	Omega Losches
Stalks and Giants	by 'Jacobean'
Nancy Mitford & her Circle	Juno ffrench
Alien Corn	Dr Scholl
Rags & Tatters	by Ripon
March Days	A. Hare
Sideways through Derbyshire	Crabbe
A Bagman's Journal	Gladstone
Prominent Capes	Raglan
Crème de la Crème	Devonshire
K-K-Katie	by Kay Stammers
On the Spot	Leo Pard
Fireside Talks	P. Flinders
Modern Sheep Farming	B. Peep
Humble Pie	J. Horner
Theories on Investment	L. Locket etc etc
Bays and Bites	by An Old Sea Dog
Jellies & Blancmanges	Somerset
Famous Monuments	Patience
Room for One Inside	Pinecoffin
Shadow Cabinets	by A. Ghost Writer
Haute Cuisine	the Aga Khan
The Day After Gomorrah	Bishop of Sodor & Man
St Symeon Stylites	by A. Columnist
Lost Horizon	C. Connolly
Call Me X	Anon
Pardon Me	Belcher

DD, aged twenty, on her engagement to
Andrew Cavendish, 1940

PLF in uniform, 1944

DD on Grand National winner Royal Tan at Lismore Castle, Co. Waterford.
The horse was given to her by Prince Aly Khan after its racing career had ended

PLF (*left*) and Dirk Bogarde, 1957. The actor played PLF in the film *Ill Met by Moonlight* about the daring abduction, led by PLF, of General Heinrich Kreipe in Nazi-occupied Crete (*photograph Harry Gillard*)

Producer Darryl F. Zanuck and Juliette Gréco filming *The Roots of Heaven* (1958). PLF wrote the screenplay and spent several weeks on set in Maroua, Cameroon

DD in the dining room at Chatsworth, 1950 (*photograph Norman Parkinson*)

Daphne and Xan Fielding, Crete

Joan Leigh Fermor by PLF, 1946

PLF (*left*) and DD (*centre*) at El Rocio, Andalusia, 1958

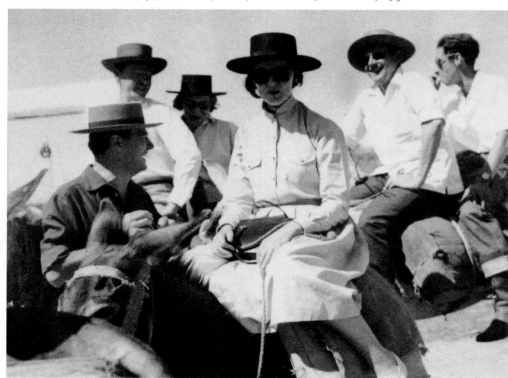

PLF and the actress Iris Tree in 1959
at Castello di Passerano, Lazio

The writer and historian Robert Kee

Princess Margaret (*centre*) and PLF (*on the gray*) dodging reporters on a ride in Tuscany.
Behind PLF is Judy Montagu and next to him champion horsewoman Natalie Perrone

Above: DD and Andrew (*back centre*) with their children: Sophia, Emma and Stoker. Prime Minister Harold Macmillan is seated next to DD's mother-in-law, Mary Devonshire. Chatsworth, 1960

Left: DD seated next to John F. Kennedy at the President's inaugural parade, January 1961 (*photograph* Life *magazine*)

Right: PLF and Nancy Mitford picnicking at Lismore, 1961

Below left: Joan Leigh Fermor with PLF (*standing back left*), Cyril Connolly (*back right*), Maurice Bowra (*centre*) and the historian Ernst Kantorowicz. Hydra, *c.*1958

Below right: DD and Eddy Sackville-West, 1964. The writer and music critic was a neighbour of the Devonshires at Lismore

PLF at home in Mani, *c.*1986 (*photograph Derry Moore*)

'Not a house in sight, nothing but the two rocky headlands, an island a quarter of a mile out to sea with a ruined chapel, and a vast expanse of glittering water, over which you see the sun setting till its last gasp. Homer's Greece, in fact.'

Melancholic	Will O'Waley
Knicknacks	Paddy Whack
The Battle of the Bulge	by Lord Slim

They're most of them pretty rotten, but one or two might do. None of them come up to the old-fashioned improper ones, which I have rather a soft spot for, though they're not your style, and of course, wouldn't do; to wit, The Babies Revenge (Norah Titsoff), The Cat's Revenge (Claude Balls), The Shaking Hand (Master Bates), The Ruined Honeymoon (Mary Fitzgerald & Gerald Fitzgeorge). Least said.

29 February 1964   Chatsworth
                                                             Bakewell

Darling Pad,

Oh how I have been meaning to write & thank you a MILLION times for the truly marvellous book titles.

E Motion & D Motion are two authors whose works I shall keenly follow from now on, ditto Major Crisis, General Strike & the rest. Thank you awfully. It must have taken hours & is deeply appreciated.

Much love & many thanks again from

Debo

23 March 1964   Chatsworth
                                                             Bakewell

Darling Pad,

It's agony, choosing 28 book titles from your list. I want them ALL.

I thought I might tell you the names of the key people here as, strangely enough, nearly all their names are meaningful words. Viz.

Link	gardener
Read	agent
Wragg	well we all know what he is[1]

Cherry	builder
Lord	gamekeeper
Fisher	controller (sorry, *comp*troller)
Child	his assistant
Bond	ex-comptroller
Stone	electrician
Hey	Bolton agent (a body to worship)

I had a nice few days in Paris with the Ancient Dame but one awful thing occurred. We (her, Stoker & me) were asked to a grand dinner & I sat next to one Pompidou[2] who turned out to be the local Lord Home and . . . *quelle horrible surprise* he can't speak English & we all know I can't do Frog if my life depends on it, so we wildly crumbled bread & stared straight ahead. It was murder. I also had the Brit Ambassador[3] whom I loathed so it was a dud dinner.

Do come to Liosmor.

Much love

Debo

---

[1] Tom Wragg, the librarian at Chatsworth, was the only one on the list whom PLF knew.

[2] Georges Pompidou (1911–74). Prime Minister of France under General de Gaulle 1962–8, and President from 1969 until his death in 1974.

[3] Pierson Dixon (1904–65). Ambassador in Paris 1960–5.

9 May 1964   c/o Mrs Denning
                                                    Church Farm
                                                    Branscombe
                                                    South Devon

Darling Debo,

I'm scribbling like mad in this farmhouse. Green hills all round, now crowned in tea cosies of mist, rain falling, gulls everywhere, also rooky woods; well-owled at night.

This letter is a bit disjointed because the farmer's three-year-old daughter, Dinah, v. pretty and comic, is booming up and down the flagged passage outside. A new apron has gone clean to her head and

I don't wonder. It's pink with a pattern of small blue bears carrying parasols and I would have pined for it were I the right age and gender.

It's true about Greece.[1] Don't tell anyone much (not that I can help it) but just you wait and see! The thing is to pitch a huge tent among the olives and help build a rambling peasant house and live happily in it ever after.

No more now, darling Debo, except tons of love from
     Paddy

1 PLF and Joan had decided to make their permanent home in Greece on the land described in PLF's letter of August 1962.

23 July 1964   Mani
                                                    Greece

Darling Debo,

My word, how difficult everything seems — it might be Chatsworth one was about to perpetrate, instead of a lowly cot. But the place is even more marvellous than I remembered.

Lovely lunch with Nancy in Paris, then left poor Joan there, in search of a nice pal to help drive that giant Peugeot, laden with tents, at least as far as Ancona, so that I could whizz here by air, to catch the eccentric man on whom all our future depends — i.e. the plot of land where the water is. Of course he isn't here. I prowl and mooch, trudging the rocky mile between the village and the *site*, to gloat all alone, stroke the rocks and the thistles, caress the olive trunks and dive off rocks into those warm depths. I slunk off there in the middle of last night, because of the full moon. Lots of phosphorus in the water, which was glittering on the surface with moonlight the further out I swam. It looked marvellous from the sea — all rocks and olives and cypresses, with great glimmering lunar mountains like ghosts in the background, a mythical scene. I slept under an olive tree and walked back after another bathe, just after dawn.

Please forgive any illegibility in this, I'm scribbling it in the village tavern by the distant beam of the tavern acetylene lamp, with the shadow on the wrong side, so that all this is invisible and illegible. Maniots loom and subside, hatchet-faced men; a Goya-esque chiaroscuro reigns.

I had a double-tailed mermaid tattooed on my left arm, above the elbow, just before leaving London, by a craftsman in Waterloo Road. I wonder if I was right.

No more, darling Debo, except hugs and tons of love from
      Paddy

11 November 1964   Chatsworth
                                                   Bakewell

Darling Paddy,

Andrew isn't minding being out of work ½ as much as I thought he would. He busies about with this & that, a lot of Fishmongering as he is getting near to being king of that strange outfit & it takes a lot of lunches & dinners. Then he's Shadowing his Commonwealth job in the H of Lords. The whole situation is so fascinating that it's almost a full-time job watching, & reading the mags.[1]

I hear through a sec at Downing St that the smell in The Cabinet Room is chronic. Six of them smoke pipes & none are clean.

Emma & Toby & Isabel[2] have been in the Argentine for a month. The one letter I have had sounds happy but hot, & they're living on culled cows. Shades of the cracked eggs & dead chickens from Lady Redesdale's Poultry Farm.[3]

The book titles you invented for the door in the library are being done by Sangorski[4] & out of extreme honesty the last one is called Book Titles by Patrick Leigh Fermor.

Ann Fleming is having a v rotten time because she is fearfully sad about Ian & is also broke.[5] Doesn't it seem mad that the lawyers didn't try & arrange things a bit better. It is a shame.

I do wonder how your house is getting on & if the drawing room cum hen house is taking shape? Do enlarge.

Much love & to Joan
      Debo

1 Macmillan resigned as Prime Minister in October 1963 and the Conservatives lost the 1964 election. Andrew Devonshire became a Liveryman of the Worshipful Company of Fishmongers, one of the livery companies of the City of London, in 1941 and was Prime Warden 1966–7.

2 DD's daughter Emma married Toby Tennant in 1963. Their first child, Isabel, was born the following year.

3 DD's mother kept a chicken farm and paid the wages of her children's governesses from its meagre profits. 'My sisters pretended that only cracked eggs, and hens that had died, came into our kitchen from my mother's poultry farm.' (DD)

4 The renowned London bookbinder, founded in 1901.

5 Ian Fleming had died leaving his estate tied up in complicated trusts.

Saturday December 1964   Mani, but only just

Darling Debo,

I *am* pleased about 'Book titles' by PLF. This means that at least one will still be on somebody's shelf – viz. your great grandson's – in 100 years time.

Things are coming to a temporary stop here – for two months, that is. Joan has already left for Blighty and I follow on Teusday, after folding things up here.

It *will* be lovely to have some proper food again. I look forward to caviar, sometime, the last roes of summer (Sturgeon's love song: *Go, lovely roes . . .*). One of the most exciting reasons for return is that *Holiday Magazine*, in America, have offered a huge sum, and all expenses, for a long article on the Danube,[1] which means a journey all down it, from Switzerland, through the Iron Curtain and all the way to the Delta on the Black Sea. I'm off as soon as I can get Iron Curtain visas. Rather fun?

This is a strange, rambling, jazz-vorticist flat over a taverna on the waterfront, overlooking the sea, caïques, tramp steamers and an avenue of jujube trees all a bit bleak under the winter sun and frequent clouds, early evenings and scarcely a soul about. I *do* hope you're about when I return next week. Little to tell, but lots to hear!

With tons of love,
     Paddy

1 'A Cave on the Black Sea', reprinted in Patrick Leigh Fermor, *Words of Mercury*, pp. 28–39.

25 January 1965   13 Chester Row, SW1

Darling Debo,

I've been scribbling here like a maniac ('Deadline Dick') to finish my wretched book[1] and make a beeline for the Danube; perhaps next week. (Any chance of you before then?) I am filled with excitement and misgiving about Rumania and, if it's not compromising or dangerous for them, seeing old friends and loves unglimpsed for TWENTY-SIX YEARS. I meant to talk to you about all this at Christmas, but, brutalized as I was with turkey and plum pudding, clean forgot. I look forward to Vienna tremendously.

Nothing much has been happening here. Joan and I went to Northumberland for a very funny weekend to see her little godson, H Harrod married to Lucy Lambton,[2] which was both very funny and great fun. I went to see Orson Welles' *The Trial* with Diana Cooper and Ricki Huston[3] (neighbours in Little Venice) three days ago. Towards the end Diana got up and said 'I think I'll wait in the car!' I thought she was bored stiff, but quicker witted Ricki jumped up and after her, then me, and just in time to catch her before collapsing in a faint. She came round in a chair in the foyer in a jiffy. The cinema people – girls, manager – were marvellous, and enslaved when Diana said 'You *have* been kind. Don't judge me by this ugly Mau Mau headgear I'm wearing' – a sort of black wool busby – 'I'm really a beautiful blonde', then 'I can't *think* why I fainted. Perhaps it was the sight of Orson Welles in bed.' (Furore.) She was absolutely alright again and we sat up drinking and gassing away till two.

Meanwhile tons of fond love and hugs from
    Paddy

---

[1] *Roumeli: Travels in Northern Greece* (1966).
[2] The writer and photographer Lady Lucinda Lambton (1943–) was married to Henry Harrod (1939–) from 1965 to 1973.
[3] Enrica (Ricki) Soma (1930–69). Beautiful Italian-American ballerina who became the fourth wife of the film director John Huston in 1950. Mother of the actress Anjelica Huston. 'Once in Naples we had had dinner in a *trattoria* when a tremendous wind-storm blew up the rubbish from the street and plastered it over the trees and telegraph poles. We pretended it was a surrealist exhibition or auction.

An evening newspaper, *Il Messaggero*, stretched on a wall was the best of the lot. I said, "I'll have that, even if it ruins me." Her eyes widened and she clutched me with desperation. "*DON'T TOUCH IT*," she whispered. "*IT'S A FAKE.*" (PLF)

17 August 1965   Bolton Abbey
                                                  Skipton
                                                  Yorkshire

Darling Paddy,

Sophy & I loom for a night in Athens on 10th Sept on our way to stay with Anne [Tree] in Spetsai. Any possible chance of you both being there, and having dinner with us?

It would be such a terrific treat to see you. We will be staying at The Great Britain (what a surprise).

Too stiff from much shooting to enlarge on anything.

Much love
    Debo

[1965]   Mani

Darling Debo,

How lovely you coming to Greece!

Joan, alas, has to go back to Blighty on the 8th, so I'll be here in solitary state, in a blue tent on the headland where the house is going up. You could either doss down in Joan's evacuated tent, or stay at the tiny hotel in the village (terrible loo but otherwise rather nice. No rot of that kind up here; we cut out the middleman and vanish into the middle distance with trowel and scroll). I might be in the absurd *art-nouveau* flat that we've got. I would be coming in every day to have a look at the building. My theory is, there must have been a time when Chatsworth was only holes in the ground. Actually, there's a bit more to show now, three beautiful arches, several walls, doors, window holes, but all open at the top still. One's quite liable to get ½ a ton of rubble on top of one's dome. But I *do long* for you to see the place, which is really lovely.

There's been some coming and going at the little hotel. Magouche with two beautiful daughters and Janetta with ditto & Julian Jebb,[1] then Barbara & Niko Ghika, with one Rothschild daughter Miranda[2] and her tiny Algerian daughter called Da'ad, aged three, tremendously tough, like a tiny little wire-haired weight lifter, very wild with her spoon at table, but no wilder than Maurice B[owra], who is also here now. He has gone deaf, but as ebullient & funny as ever.

Tons of love
    Paddy

---

[1] Julian Jebb (1934–84). Journalist and television producer.
[2] Miranda Rothschild (1940–). Daughter of Victor, 3rd Baron Rothschild, and his first wife, Barbara Hutchinson. Married Boudjemaa Boumaza in 1962.

29 November 1965   Chatsworth
                                                    Bakewell

Darling Paddy,

Such a lot of water etc since I last wrote.

The chief bit of water is that we had a monster shoot here on Sat, a record since the war, and one of the guns was Sybil Cholmondeley.[1] I can't tell you how really marvellous she was. I believe she's 71 but even not counting the shooting she was marvellous, down for brekker at 9 & ready for formal conversation – challenging sentences like 'I've been to Petworth twice & never seen anything in the least remarkable'.

I went to the Opening of Parliament, v pretty, but I'm sorry to say the Peeresses smelt, well, the Duchesses did anyway. Surely they couldn't have rolled.

Much love
    Debo

It's the French lady's birthday. She's 61, impossible to have a sister of that age surely.

---

[1] Sybil Sassoon (1894–1989). Married 5th Marquess of Cholmondeley in 1913.

2 May 1966   Lismore Castle
                                              Co. Waterford

Darling Paddy,

Thank you *so much* for sending your book. You really are a sport
& do you know I've practically decided to read it, as I note it is far
from stout & is peppered with snaps – all encouraging to one of 9.

Next day
The Dame has loomed and bought a house at Versailles[1] before she
came. What a step to take, it made her heart beat.

Andrew says we are ruined by the new taxes in the Budget, but
I've heard that before I think.

Ld Antrim & R Fedden are leading a lot of old women on a
National Trust cruise round Ireland & they are coming here next
week.

I think that's all for now. Thank you again 1000 times for *so kindly*
sending the vol. I am delighted to have it & v grateful.

Much love
   Debo

1 Nancy Mitford moved from Paris to the Rue d'Artois in Versailles at the beginning of 1967.

1 July 1966   Chatsworth
                                              Bakewell

Darling Paddy,

The two picture worms of Christie's David Carritt & Brian
Sewell[1] were here re-valuing the drawings for insurance.

I can tell you no cabaret has given such entertainment. We went
after dinner into the library & they opened the boxes & wrote
their idea of values down on bits of paper. Their faces & comments
were *so lovely*. Things that looked exactly the same to us were
marked up or down with such huge differences & names of what
sounded to us like Italian hairdressers were bandied about till we
were reeling.

I have become a sort of slave to a new passion which is the Shetland Ponies I have got. We have got three rather good ones & we show them – I can't tell you how exciting it is. We got a *2nd prize* at the Highland Show & it made my heart beat as if I'd nearly won the Derby. The other Shetland fans are fascinating like all specialists. The Royal[2] is our next outing on 8th July. Please pray.

   Much love
     Debo

---

1 David Carritt (1927–82), art historian and picture dealer; and Brian Sewell (1931–), outspoken art critic for the *Evening Standard*.
2 The Royal Smithfield Show, a livestock and farm machinery exhibition, of which DD was President 1972–4.

[1969]   Mani
[Visiting card]

During the war, Sir E Codrington is said to have put out an order which ran: –

The Coldstream Guards, in future, will shout 'Hoorah' and not 'Hooray!' when storming a redoubt.
Many Hooray Henries must have looked at each other sadly.
I wonder if Andrew ever shouted it when charging across southern Italy?[1]

I have worked out a mnemonic (way to remember) your postal code: 'DINNER EARLY FOR FIVE! 'IPP ('IPP 'OORAY')[2]

---

1 Andrew Devonshire, who served in the 3rd Battalion Coldstream Guards, saw active service in Italy 1943–4.
2 The Chatsworth postal code is DE45 1PP.

Fairly early July 1970   Mani

Darling Debo,

This is a fine time to be writing a bread-and-butter letter – in fact it's not one – too late – only that it encloses a 1000 thanks for that lovely weekend. You can't possibly imagine how fascinated I was by the trip to Newmarket, and seeing those two fine steeds do so well. I felt a bit like a debutante being led into some mythically wicked haunt in Paris by an expert old hand. You were good about stopping for drinks, don't think that the altruism goes unremembered!

Almost immediately after leaving Blighty, I flew to Athens, found Joan and Michael Stewart,[1] our glorious Ambassador here, & his v nice wife called Damaris, and we sped to Smyrna, where a Land Rover was waiting. Off we set for a Grand Tour of known and unknown classical sites in Southern Turkey: two and a half weeks in this amazing vehicle, changing places in the back where one lolled among brightly woven Caucasian rugs and saddlebags (mostly me). Sounds slight hell, but actually wonderful, owing to the niceness of the company, the jokes, the frequent pauses for drinks and picnics beside mountain streams, lolling under the poplars while the wine cooled in purling brooks. M Stewart is a perfect man, brilliant driver, excellent scholar, ex China expert at the V & A, slight limp from a polo fall. What was so astonishing about all the Ancient, Classical, Hellenistic (*ah, oui!*), Greco-Roman & Roman ruins was a) the enormous quantity (*oh lor*), (b) the comparative completeness, (c) the size, whole cities with temples, theatres, agoras, markets, stadia etc, (d) the absence of anyone else there: only a few nomads, with a score of camels or so grazing in the orchestra stalls. In lots of them, ploughed fields and wheat ran right in amongst the debris. The temples had false floors of bright-green waterweed; shallow quadrangles for millions of frogs – convolvulus & morning glory, & brambles twisted up the shafts of the columns, and on the capital of each of these was a stork's nest, full of young storks learning to clatter their bills like castanets while their parents glided and swooped about the wreckage after the frogs. Some of these cities were perched high up in the

Taurus Mountains, overgrown with jungle, like the ruins of Angkor or Mexico, others shot out into the sea, moles and quays sloping underwater, a maze for mullets. Masses of splendid bas-relief and marble moulding, all pitched headlong by old earthquakes and treasure-seekers dead for centuries.

The coastal mountains are cloaked with all this magnificent stuff; v tall mountains, too, appropriately culminating in Mt Climax – steep pine-forests with terrific gorges coiling down to bay after empty bay, nothing but goatherds and charcoal burners, every now and then a fast and deep green river with a mythological name. North, the other side of the Taurus Mountains, sweeps the Anatolian plateau, marvellous windswept pale skies, oceans of corn, flocks, oak woods, troops of half wild horses, mud-brick villages pronged with minarets (all fitted with loudspeakers, so that the idle muezzins, bawling into a mouthpiece at ground level can shirk their thrice-daily spirals). Rivers and storks again, cuckoos, hoopoes, bee-eaters, orioles and a billion larks. The Anatolian Turks are nice rough fellows; we dossed down in the unplumbed mysteries of their dwellings, mindful of the fact that kind hearts are more than *cabinets* . . .

There were magnificent old Seljuk bridges for caravans, and, every few leagues, an ancient khan or caravanserai, with accommodation for man and camel, hundreds of them, vast arched and gathered warrens of masonry, like Gothic cathedral architecture with knobs off, giant hollow fossils. In Konya, the capital of the old Seljuk (love that word) sultans, one is surrounded in the lanes by unfrocked whirling dervishes, forbidden to whirl in Atatürk's day, now sad grey-beards mooning about among the tombstones, or bubbling away morosely at their hookahs, and brooding on their fled youth when they were such splendid all-rounders. It seemed a bit of an anticlimax to be back among the sweat and the Sirens of Smyrna, just before coming back here. Nobody can do anything there in summer, it seems, except hunt for a cool place to snooze. The British Consul's son, half Greek, half Maltese, likes it, though. Bursting into French (*pause for response here*) he said: '*Comme c'est doux de ne rien faire toute la journée, et de se reposer après.*'[2]

No more now, darling Debo, except v v many thanks again and

do come. Do you want any more book titles? Annie wants some too, to make up for the void of Ian's strange collection;[3] would you mind if some were the same? Hands across the shires?

    With tons of fond love,
        Paddy

1 Michael Stewart (1911–94). Ambassador in Greece 1967–71. Married Damaris du Boulay in 1951. 'What a good, generous, warm-hearted man. The nicest ambassador we've ever had.' PLF to DD, 21 March 1985.
2 'How agreeable it is to do nothing all day and to rest afterwards.'
3 Ann Fleming had sold her husband's library, consisting mainly of books that had made a contribution to technical and intellectual progress – 'books that made things happen' – to the Lilly Library at Indiana University.

9 November 1970   Chatsworth
                                                   Bakewell

Darling Paddy,
    A quick thing to say if by ANY CHANCE you find yourself in England for Christmas DO come here.
    It will be incredibly dull, but you are needed, as per.
    Much love
        Debo

28 November 1970   Mani

Darling Debo,
    You've got no idea how braced I feel! After a few days rough stuff from the mountains – wind, rain etc – it's suddenly changed to golden September sunlight, no wind, not a cloud, smooth blue sea. Seeing was stripping, charging down the steps, diving in and soaring through the sapphire depths like a dolphin. Now here I am on the terrace all of a glow. Not bad when it's Dec. the day after tomorrow!
    I do wish I could come for Christmas but I don't seem to be coming back for ages. But *should* I, I'll be there swift as an arrow from the Tartar's bow (Wm Shakespeare). There would be an eerie

rattle on the streaming window as the wind hurled round the
building on Xmas Eve: –

> And if you ever hear drops
> Fall on your window pane,
> You'll know they're just my teardrops
> Falling for you like rai—in . . .
>   (Jack Smith, The Whispering Baritone, circa 1928)

Two days gap. Summoned away.
Well, now I actually *have* had a December bathe, and a thrill of
triumph runs through my frame.

The situation here is pretty rum. There are now twenty cats
stalking about the building. Oddly enough, they don't get in the
way at all, but it's v strange to see them at meal times, crowded
round their porringers, all those tails waving in unison. Joan hasn't
had the heart to chuck them in the briny, so here we are. *Must*
give some away. Now Aymer Maxwell has given us a puppy. I
brought it back, eight weeks old, from Euboea where he lives. He
created like anything in the car, but calmed down for a week in
Spetsai, where I took him to stay with Diana Cooper and her
circle, then drove to Patras to meet Joan returning from Finland.
We dreaded the encounter with the cats. The older ones all cut
him dead, but all the younger set worship him, gambolling and
embracing on the terrace all day, allowing themselves to be dragged
about by the scruff, lining up to snuggle into his basket when
shadows fall. He is more fan-ridden than Rudolf Valentino, and
wonderfully unspoilt. Name, Troilus. Breed, nondescript, but very
handsome, pale marmalade in colour with white spots and a bold
white flash that loses itself among Gladstonian wrinkles between
the ears when they are puckered in puzzlement, which is practically
the whole time. This brings the total of legs in the house –
including Joan & me, and the couple who look after us & two
sons, but not counting the mice or the centipedes (of course) – to
96. When A Maxwell comes on Saturday, 98. I wish you were
looming, to make 100 . . .

17 June 1971   Chatsworth
(Lady Mosley's *61st* birthday)   Bakewell

Darling Paddy,

It is truly ghoulish of me not to have written ages ago to thank
you & Joan for your vvv kind invitation for Sept.

The thing is I've been dallying & dallying because Ivan the
Terrible (Andrew. He is either Ivan the Terrible or Peter the Great
according to his mood) is *vaguely* thinking (did you know?) of
joining you in viewing the Fine Stands of Timber on your mystery
trip to Peru.[1]

Anyway, I suppose that's nothing to do with it but the bitter thing is
it doesn't look too good. Sophy goes back to Dread School around 13
Sept, then there's the Sheep Sale & the Jacob Flock Owners' Open Day
here on 18th & the next day I go to Austria for the 50th anniversary
celebrations of Organised Haflinger Breeding. I suppose you think the
foregoing are proofs of on-rushing daftness but I can't help it, it may be
my age of course but it's better than (a) taking to drink/drugs or (b)
bagging very young men for lovers, admit. I now prefer horse shows to
lovers & I've never liked drink – no doubt wd be a sucker for drugs
but have only tried when in extremis, viz. when I had a baby which
immediately died & the dr fainted & was found by Ivan stretched out
in the hall. But that was many & many a year ago.

So, Whack, ALAS, I must say no. Don't think you've finished with
me please, I mean sometime like March would be incredibly
pleasant, eh.

Emma & Toby have gone to live on their farm in Scotland for
good & are loving it. They've got a marvellous new baby called
Stella[2] who's got limpid blue eyes.

The Fr Lady Writer is far from fit, but she's back in Versailles.
She's seen twenty-two drs (including quacks) ranging from the
Queen's to an Indian osteopath & he was the only one who helped
at all, & none of them has (a) found out what is the matter with her
poor leg or (b) hit on a cure. Isn't it *foul*.[3]

Much love, & do keep in deepest. From
Debo

1 Andrew Devonshire joined PLF on a month-long expedition in Peru, setting off at the beginning of August 1971. 'We had been included, as minor amateurs, in a mountaineering expedition in the Andes: Andrew as a botanist in charge of plant specimens, and I as the guardian of the Primus stove.' (PLF)
2 Stella Tennant (1970–). DD's granddaughter became a supermodel in the 1990s.
3 Nancy Mitford had been operated on for liver cancer in 1969 and was suffering from Hodgkin's disease. Her condition remained undiagnosed until shortly before her death in 1973.

23 September 1971   Mani

Darling Debo,

I feel a bit lost here, quite alone at the moment, with nobody to boast to about all our Andean doings. I can't get over how creditably we did, bearing our earlier trepidations in mind. I hope Robin [Fedden] bore out all our vainglorious assertions.

I had a lovely few days before finally buzzing off, raging happily about the metropolis like a soldier on leave: saw two films, a sophisticated French one at the Curzon about a young shaver who goes to bed with his mother, among others:[1] and an endless, awful one called Bloody, Bloody Sunday:[2] endless close-ups of enlarged pores and lustfully quaking shoulder blades and empty bottles that left the viewers (Diana Cooper, Annie, old C.[3] and self) racked with gloom and tedium. But we cheered up over dinner at an old haunt of Annie's, but new to me, called Pastoria's, just south of Leicester Square – almost empty and terribly nice. The headwaiter asked Diana if she had a dog concealed within her drapery, she said 'No, a fox – a Mexican fox.' As the H. waiter was a Mexican, and they were thus compatriots, all was well. I expect you've heard that, a few weeks ago, his colleague at the Ritz said she couldn't have the dog in the restaurant, and she flummoxed him by saying, 'Call the police', and was allowed to finish her meal with the little blighter asleep in her lap. She really is first-rate officer material as far as initiative goes. She was in tip-top shape, I thought, and there was lots of carefree laughter.

I flew to Athens two days ago for the funeral of our old friend Geo. Seferis,[4] the poet. Joan, hot foot from Samarkand, Bokhara, Tashkent and Tiflis, arrives tomorrow with her bro Graham.

I'm still chewing away at our Andean past. Do tell Andrew I'll send a copy of my artless account of our adventure when typed, corrected, & re-typed – in about three weeks, I think, what with the *va-et-vient*, if you follow me.[5]

Many thanks again, darling Debo, and tons of love from
    Paddy

[1] Louis Malle, *Le Souffle au cœur* (1971).
[2] *Sunday Bloody Sunday* (1971). John Schlesinger's film about a triangular love affair starring Glenda Jackson, Peter Finch and Murray Head.
[3] Caspar Fleming (1952–75). The 'strange, gifted, unhappy son of Ian and Ann Fleming' (PLF) was named after Admiral Sir Caspar John, son of the painter Augustus John, whom Ian Fleming admired. He was known as 'Old Caspar' from Southey's poem 'After Blenheim' (1875).
[4] George Seferis (1900–71). Poet, essayist and diplomat. Greek ambassador in London 1957–62 and winner of the Nobel Prize for Literature in 1963.
[5] PLF circulated his account of the Andes expedition, based on letters he wrote to Joan, to his fellow participants and various friends. It was eventually published in 1991 by John Murray as *Three Letters from the Andes*.

27 November 1971   Chatsworth
                                                   Bakewell

Darling Paddy,

The news here is that Andrew went to hosp for over three weeks & he has come out a DIFFERENT PERSON. So much better, funny, clever & sympathetic – like he really is & not the Hyde of Jekyll and –. He has stopped refreshing drinks of alcohol[1] & lives on stuff called Schloer (apple juice) & Ribena (which looks dangerously like claret) & grapefruit juice (which is a first course at dinners in Chesterfield, so bitterly unfair). I can't tell you how well he's getting on on this strange diet. He was v poorly indeed when he went into hosp with ghoulish depression, a thing I never wish to see again.

We went to dinner with the Beits[2] to see Alf's cinema he took of friends between the wars. It was *riveting*. My bro[3] figured – I had completely forgotten how good looking he was. The Pagets[4] look just the same now. So does my sister Diana. The Droghedas[5] & Cecil Beaton are better now than then BUT the tragedies were Randolph

Churchill[6] (Adonis of 1st water), Bridget Parsons and Mamie Lygon[7] – almost unbearably sad to think what wrecks they are/were.

Three Pagets were at dinner & they made me sure it's better not to dye hair & do makeup now we're all old. Liz had a dress which somehow fell apart when she sat down & there were her old legs – what for I asked myself & looked away. Rose (whose face is lovely) had a black dress, the sort described as a *sheath* in the fashion mags, split up one side to her thigh & then, you see, she's forgotten she's got a hefty tummy & it doesn't do. Better not go in for that sort of thing, don't you think.

I've written an article about Haflingers for *Riding* & one about the goat I liked best for the *British Goat Society's Year Book*. Two publications which I feel you may not subscribe to.

Much love
Debo

---

1 Andrew Devonshire's stay in hospital was one of his periodic attempts to give up alcohol. He wrote in his memoirs that 'drink has run in the Cavendish family for generations'. *Accidents of Fortune*, p. 100.

2 Clementine Mitford (1915–2005). Posthumous daughter of DD's uncle Clement Mitford. Married Sir Alfred Beit in 1939.

3 Tom Mitford (1909–45). DD's only brother trained as a barrister and used to pay his sister Nancy a shilling an hour – a large sum in those days – to argue with him. 'He joined the Territorial Army, then the Queen's Own Westminsters, and served throughout the North African and Italian campaigns before transferring to the Devonshire Regiment when Germany capitulated. Because he had many German friends and affection for the country, he did not wish to participate in active service there and was sent to the Far East. He died of wounds in Burma, in March 1945. My parents revered his intelligence – he was the peacemaker in the family; they and my older sisters never got over his loss.' (DD)

4 Three of the five beautiful daughters of 6th Marquess of Anglesey: Caroline (1913–73), Elizabeth (1916–80) and Rose (1919–2005).

5 Garrett Moore, 11th Earl of Drogheda (1910–89). Newspaper proprietor and Chairman of the Royal Opera House, Covent Garden. Married Joan Carr in 1935.

6 Randolph Churchill (1911–68). The DNB entry for the son of the Prime Minister records that he was drinking double brandies at the age of eighteen – a habit that did not change over the years.

7 Lady Mary (Maimie) Lygon (1910–82). The most beautiful of 7th Earl Beauchamp's four daughters. Married to Prince Vsevolode Joannovitch of Russia 1939–56.

In the twenties, May 1972   Mani

Darling Debo,

Please forgive this hoggish delay! I was waiting to send you a copy of my *Lettres Peruviennes*, describing our adventures last year, but it won't be ready for a couple of days, so here goes.

I had an extraordinary experience three weeks ago: meeting General Kreipe[1] on a television programme, with all his Cretan captors, after 27 years. After the programme, all the Cretans – about 20 – the General & his wife (very nice), a niece of Field Marshal v. Rundstedt, and I had a huge banquet in a taverna. Lots of Cretan songs and dances, a few German folk songs sung by the General and me, after much wine had flowed. Some journalists got wind of it and broke in. One asked the General how I had treated him when he was my prisoner in the mountains and the Gen said – wait for it! – most energetically: '*Ritterlich! Wie ein Ritter*' ('*Chivalrously! Like a knight!*'). I felt a halo forming and it took me days to get back to normal. I took them out to all sorts of meals, and showered Frau Kreipe with roses when they left (she was extremely nice). She said: 'You're just like my husband told me you were all these years!' (Three cheers again! Forgive me retailing these dewdrops – but nobody else can, you do see.) It was somehow a wonderful rounding off to this ancient story. I've just got a charming joint letter from them!

The great thing of Spring 1972 is Robert's book![2] I only got it three days ago, and am already halfway. It's absolutely tip-top, and has that very special quality that only years of pain, toil and thought can instil: beautifully written, and fair and balanced to all sides, and, more than that, full of understanding, pity and sympathy for the almost insoluble ghastliness of the whole thing.

Gerald Brenan,[3] Carrington's erstwhile love, came and stayed a few days, he's 79, hares up the mountains like a buck in spring. He had a pretty and charming girl with him; love, but not concubinage, he told me. They are now wandering about the depths of Anatolia in a 2-seater.

[*incomplete*]

1 Heinrich Kreipe (1895–1976). The German commander of the occupying forces on Crete. He was abducted from the island in 1944 by a group of resistance fighters led by PLF.

2 Robert Kee, *The Green Flag: A History of Irish Nationalism* (1972).

3 Gerald Brenan (1894–1987). The British writer, who lived in Spain for much of his life, had an affair with Dora Carrington in the 1920s. After his wife Gamel's death in 1968 Brenan spent ten years with a young Englishwoman, Lynda Price.

[1972]

Darling Debo,

This is not really a letter, more an extremely rough travel diary of our adventures this year.

AN EXPEDITION TO THE PINDUS MOUNTAINS OF NORTHERN GREECE

Expedition Party:
Robin and Renée Fedden
Carl Natar[1]
Peter McCall[2]
Andrew Devonshire
PLF

Athens, 9 June 1972
We had bad news last night. We have been refused permission to climb in the Hakkiari Mountains in Turkish Kurdistan, so it's the Pindus for us.

I met the party at Athens airport, a joyful reunion. We dumped all our stuff at the Olympic Palace Hotel and had dinner at the Platanos in the Plaka and coffee among the reeds by the Tower of the Winds.

Yanina, 10 June
We got to Preveza from Yanina and drove out past the ruins of Nicópolis and a scattering of Vlach* huts. Then we drove up into the Louros gorge, through a forest of plane trees and on into the more

* Semi-nomad shepherds, speaking a Latin dialect.

open Dodóni country and into Yanina at last. It's been hideously
modernised since my last visit eight years ago, all the oriental nobility
has gone; but plenty of storks nest there still. We went to the Olympic
Hotel; an amusing and beautiful young couple run it. Then there was a
smashing dinner with Mr Nicolaïdis and two other mountaineers at
the Epirote Pavilion (*tzatzíki*, stuffed courgettes, and so on). I talked
Vlach – or rather Rumanian – to Mr Stergios; and wandered inside
the Kastro for an hour. Most of the old houses have gone; but I heard
some Ladino* through a shutter, then walked along the lakeshore
listening to the loudest and lewdest frogs I've ever heard croak.

Sunday 11 June
Out by car with Mr Nicolaïdis, the Yanina mountaineer, and Robin and
Renée to Kónitsa, and through Kalpáki to the Aoös River. We arranged
for Mr Tássos, an ex-schoolmaster and watchmaker, to be our guide.

   We went in the little steamer to the beautiful lake-island which was
full of Sunday crowds. Ancient plane trees surround the monasteries.
We visited the scene of Ali Pasha's death, then on through a corridor
of tall reeds to a marvellous feast of crayfish, frogs and trout, where
we were sent a bottle of wine by a party of Cretans (in my honour:
because of the TV programme with Gen Kreipe and his captors). We
dined in a taverna near the caves at the end of the lake, where more
wine was sent to us for the same splendid reason.

Monday 12 June
Renée, Robin and I bought stores all morning. Then after packing
and sorting, we went back for an even better luncheon of crayfish,
frog and trout, with croaking all round us. We drove to Dodóni, the
site of the ancient oracle, now lost in the oak woods: august and
severe in the heart of bleak hills with drifts of shale and rustling ilex
spinneys; mullein grows everywhere. We took our three mountaineer
friends and Mr Nicolaïdis's pretty wife to a return feast at the
Epirote place of our first night. Late to bed.

---

* Spanish dialect of the Jews who were expelled from Spain in 1492 by
Ferdinand and Isabella, and settled in the Levant, sheltered by the Sultan.

Tuesday 13 June
Up early this morning. Sending all our heavy stuff to Papigo in one
taxi, we headed for Kónitsa in another. (The policeman at the
beginning of the forbidden zone, close to the Albanian frontier, was a
Cretan from Alpha, near Réthymnon, who once brought me a
message to Prinés when he was a small boy.)

We found Mr Tásso Eythimíou and set off on foot from the
wonderful Turkish bridge which crosses the Aoös River like a
rainbow, then followed the spectacular gorge; and passed the ruins of
a Byzantine fort which the Turks captured by dressing up as
Orthodox monks. He told us that the mosque above the rainbow
bridge (once painted by Edward Lear) was said to have been ordered
by Suleiman the Magnificent.

Our path was an overhanging canyon of rock and forest, split up
into shade and sun by the early light. A green trout-laden brook
rushed through boulders beside an up-and-down switchback path
that led to the closed 18th-century monastery of Stómion, which had
been blown up by the Germans as a Zervas* guerrilla stronghold,
then roughly rebuilt. It stands on a rock above the river.

From here our way zigzagged uphill through thickening woods of
pine, walnut, sycamore, plane and chestnut, ever wider and taller, but
so steep we halted more and more frequently. Renée felt awful: I too.
It was much too much to take on for the first day. Suddenly Andrew
was smitten down, and had to rest every few yards, looking green
and ominous and feeling miserable. Carl and Robin helped him
along; not his fault, he had been shooting ahead in his best Peruvian
style till then. The forest grew steeper and higher. I had awful cramp,
legs like cast-iron drainpipes. There were long waits for the others to
catch up; a nightmare ascent for all. The heights of Smólikas and
Grámmos soar beyond the tree trunks. These mysterious woods full
of birds, the haunt of deer, wild goat, boar, bears and wolves.

One of our helpers got on all our nerves, especially by shouting a
bit hysterically when we were crossing drifts of snow. We cut steps with

*The right-wing resistance, EDES, was commanded by Napoleon Zervas.
The left-wing, ELAS, by 'Áris' Velouhiótis.

our picks, then spent ages crossing steep landslides where the whole
planet seemed to be on the move. At last we got to the longed-for
point where waterfalls came roaring down and an icy wind drove
through a steep funnel of the mountains. It was here that I suddenly
realised I had left my rucksack behind at one of our stops, and our
helper leapt back into favour by going back for it, a true benefactor: I
felt so tired it was nearly beyond me and Andrew arrived looking awful
and collapsed on the grass wishing the earth would swallow him.

In the end it was decided that Carl and Robin would stay the
night with him somewhere out of the wind where they could kindle
a fire, and catch us up tomorrow. We left them all our warm stuff
but were terribly worried.

A stiff climb followed, up a steep funnel of tumbled rock and
boulders with another snow-torrent rushing down it. We crossed it
many times, climbing hand-over-foot, slipping and starting landslides,
and falling in. It went on for an hour and a half, with night not far off.

But when at last we reached the top, we found Alpine meadows
and new ranges rearing up all round us like a gathering of castles.
They were Gamíla and Astrákas. There was a tinkling and a clanking
of flocks, a few scattered tarns, buttercups and lithospernum and
banks of snow streaking along the hollows.

Huge black-and-white dogs dashed at us barking fiercely. Then a
tall and fine-looking Sarakatsán* of the Tsouman clan turned up,
splendid in black hooded cloak and steel-hooked crook across his
shoulders. We hobnobbed for a while, sitting on the grass, his dogs
panting all round him; then trudged on over heartless tracts of shale
till we reached the Refuge just as it was getting dark. It is a beautifully
fitted-out hut of the Pindus Mountaineering Society, opened and
made ready by our pack-driver, who had arrived earlier from Papigo
with another eager young drover called Theodore and three horses,
our stuff and a few more young Sarakatsáns and their dogs. We told
him to take ropes and slings and pints of hot tea down the ghastly
giants' causeway tomorrow morning to help Carl, Robin and

---

* Greek nomad shepherds of the north, not on good terms with the
Vlachs.

Andrew. Renée cooked a delicious stew of bully beef and onions, preceded and followed by plenty of whisky. Mr Tássos seems much nicer all of a sudden. We went to bed in tiered bunks – it was rather like being in a four-poster – dog-tired and rather anxious.

One of the worst bits that afternoon was crossing a slanting acre of scree entirely covered with huge umbellifers and a six-foot-high forest of stinging nettles, only passable by holding our ice picks over our heads and laying about with them like battle-axes. Ah, the slipping on the pine needles and the steep grass underfoot! The solid-looking blocks we lurched across came loose and hurtled downhill in avalanches.

We saw three snakes, one brown, one green and a rather sinister one symmetrically speckled in a pattern of black and white. I started a pheasant and two ptarmigans rattled through the branches. Bright-coloured butterflies abound – including Red Admirals and Purple Emperors. There was a plant that looked like gunnera in the deeper canyons, and sudden bursts of hellebore and yellow marguerites scattered the meadows above, and crimson and purple anemones, and small flowers like forget-me-nots.

Wednesday 14 June

Tássos and Theodore went down with three horses, some Vitamin B pills, ropes, carabinas and flasks of hot tea wrapped up in newspaper. But after breakfast Carl arrived at the hut as cool as a cucumber; he and Robin had helped Andrew up that infernal path and traversed the meadows with the flocks, then taken the scree-path to this Refuge, all without seeing the horses; they must have missed each other on the opposite sides of a large intervening bluff. Then the other two appeared, Andrew looking much better. What a relief! Theodore came back two hours later. He had gone all the way down, found the remains of the fire, shouted for a while with no answer, climbed back again. An eager, nice, intelligent boy. How lovely to be among mountain people again!

They had spent a warm night in a sheltered nook of the rocks, keeping a fire going all night; Andrew had been enveloped in one of those silver emergency blankets that fold up to the size of a bar of chocolate.

This has been a day of rest and recuperation. Yesterday's 12-hour climb should have been seven at the outside. It was a wringing ordeal for the most hardened. We are on a ridge overlooking a wandering hollow of bright grass and we watch Egyptian vultures sailing past below us and settling beside the tarns with which the hollow is sprinkled. To the north lie the massifs of Smólikas and Grámmos, and the skyline is jagged with millions of pine trees; the other side of the now-invisible Aoös River, and to the east is Ploská, behind which lies the Gamíla massif and to the south are steep green overgrown landslides; and just in front soars the jagged Bastille of Astrákas: perpendicular limestone cliffs and needles that look totally unscalable, but which are nevertheless to be assailed.

To the west, between Astrákas and another great nearby bluff, an immense vista unfolds: range upon range, dominated to the north-west by the massif of Nemétzikas beyond which loom the peaks of Albania. They run on to Chimára and the Acroceraunian range and from the top of Astrákas, the Adriatic can be descried, with Corfu floating along the horizon in mid-air.

Most of this day of recovery is being spent lolling about the stone terraces outside the shelter, and chatting with the Sarakatsáns who gather every now and then; all belong to the Tsoumánides clan. Their flocks are scattered on many of the green levels and round the lakes; horses graze there as well and ply to and fro between the milking-fold and some cheese-huts about a mile away, beyond the bluff, laden with great tin milk-cans, flat on one side for lashing on wooden saddles. The nearest flocks are all sheep, except for the enormous black-and-white ram that leads them, and several smaller goats – NCOs – wearing heavier bells with a deeper note than the sheep's light chimes; all of them unite in a fluctuating chord that hovers in the air. We are well above the tree line and it's a magnificent scene, though rather a bleak one with its sweeps of grey shale, relieved by the blue tarns, the grazing horses and the flocks; great masses, like pinnacled cathedrals rise into a blazing sky, and beneath us a tremendous vista of mountain-ranges recedes, floating dim and far.

Renée and I remained alone in the shelter while the others scrambled to the top of the bluff to have a look round. To my consternation, a small caravan of laden horses appeared from the direction of Papigo. It was Mr Ioannidis, the mayor, and two brothers, Mr Christodoulou, and a local civil servant from Patmos. Renée went to break the news to Robin and the others. They had come for the night to see that we were all right and they turned out to be both delightful and helpful, and we had a great banquet. They lit flares with Butagaz cylinders to signal their achievement in getting here to doubting souls in the village below; then they packed snow into buckets to cool bottles of ouzo and fizzy wine from Zítza (where Byron and Hobhouse stayed for a night or two) and unloaded all sorts of good things – delicious fresh tomatoes, onions and garlic, excellent *tyrópites* and *alevrópites* (cheesecake and fritters), and two punnets of strawberries. It was a happy evening, full of friendly and jovial chat about the Battle of Actium, Cleopatra, Mark Antony, Augustus, King Pyrrhus, the Vlachs and the Sarakatsáns.

Thursday 15 June
Our guests – or hosts – left early, with promises of reunion in Papigo. After breakfast we set off down the steep approach path in the direction of Gamíla – grudging every inch of height lost – then through alternating layers of scree, rock and grass, climbing over stretches of snow and up the massive blocks and bands of rock beyond Ploská to the first of the rock-blades which jut into the void to the north; they form a fan of humps which gives the range the name of 'Camel', though it is more like a dromedary with many humps; and I remember peering up at them from leagues away on the Metsovo road ten years ago with Coote Lygon and Joan, never dreaming that one day I'd be in these terrific heights.

Gentians cluster in every fissure. Some of the rocky wastes we crossed resemble scores of wrinkled and interlocking polygons with clefts plunging all round them, jagged and pocked and spiked: ankle-breaking yataghan terrain of the kind that used to make Xan and me blaspheme in Crete. We made exciting descents of the snow-drifts later on, half ski-ing on our heels, as it were, and braking with our ice-axes. Robin and Carl were experts at this.

At one vantage point we watched a hawk pursuing a marten,

which took refuge under a rock while the hawk circled and swooped fiercely, but in vain. Rock-finches – grey when settled, black and white in flight – fluttered about the wilderness: in this treeless amphitheatre enormous grey mineral blocks were tumbled into galleries, buttresses, bands and pinnacles. It seemed all wind and sun.

We ate raisins, chocolate and almonds, sprawling beside a lake in a basin under the peaks from which, two days ago, we had looked down at the conifer-spiked watersheds we had threaded; and, over the now-invisible Aoös river, at the three eagle-nest villages, with their windows all gleaming, on the wooded flanks of Mt Smólikas. The frogs croaked in the lake, salamanders flickered about the shallows. (During the Occupation, SOE[3] used to make parachute drops of arms and stores in the hollow below.)

After a lake-side snooze, we went down by easy stages over snow and rock and grass, treading on lovely green lawns covered with flowers, and surrounded by rings of grey rock – glade on descending glade – until we were down again by the lake under our hut, where a score of hobbled Sarakatsán horses were grazing. Then – an unkind final touch – came the gruelling climb to our Refuge, with the sweat pouring off us. Andrew, to all our amazement, declared he was vexed by his lack of stamina the day before and immediately charged down to the bottom, then back to the top again, without drawing breath, in what seemed record time. An astonishing performance.

Delicious lentils for supper. We slept out, dozing off under millions of stars.

Friday 16 June
I awoke on the stone terrace, after a marvellous night, to see Carl, Renée and Robin rope-slung and axe-grasping, moving off to tackle the great hump of Astrákas. I followed them with binoculars for an hour or so. They were moving at high speed, up landslides, then across snowdrifts, till they disappeared in a fold, to re-appear much higher, later on, much smaller. Peter has his tripod camera geared to the summit, but we will probably miss them.

Andrew has set off with flower-presses under his arm to the regions we crossed yesterday to try and find some specimens. He has

been doing a lot of prep at Kew but, as it was with Kurdistan in
view, it may not be much help in the Pindus. He sounds dazzlingly
proficient to my untutored ear.

I'm writing this at the indoor table at the Refuge, and I have
looked up twice to find a tall Sarakatsán leaning on his crook,
peering down, and only exchanging greetings after I say something.
All the time, while we chat over a cigarette, his eyes flicker away to
all the elaborate photographic gear that litters the table. I feel a bit
ashamed to be surrounded by all this opulent stuff in front of these
austere men.

The Astrákas party, then Andrew, got back in the early afternoon,
both fully successful. It is swelteringly hot, and very misty in the
valleys.

At four, Theodore turned up with the mules. We had cleared up
the shelter and left it bright as a new pin.

Robin, Andrew and I started off downhill and the others followed
with the beasts. It was steep and shingly at first and dotted with small
pine trees. A scattered forest of juniper came next; then we were
sauntering down through park-like ledges of green with poplar and
hazel and tall, queerly lopped oaks, stopping to drink now and then at
charming springs. It was like Paradise, all the trees casting long shadows,
thousands of flowers, eglantine climbing everywhere: hellebore,
geranium, alyssum; down, down . . . We sat for a while by a spring
and a slate-roofed shrine to St Panteleimon under a plane tree where
an old crone came to fill the icon lamp. Then all at once we were in
the steep, slanting lanes and the massive walls of Papigo. We found
quarters at the inn of Cléarchos Starás, a fine old house where we sat
out and drank shandy gaff, our new passion, looking down on the
armadillo-roofs of the village while goats came down from the
mountains in clouds of dust, bells clanking. The church is a three-apsed
basilica in a gallery of squat pillars and with a free-standing belfry
among gigantic planes and ilexes. There are flocks everywhere.

Dinner under the plane trees. There were *lachanópita* (spinach
pasties) with much wine and lots of strawberries. Our mountain
friends of the other night all came and we sang for a while.
Mountain bastions towered overhead.

Saturday 17 June

Two cars from Yanina had arranged to pick up our stuff and meet us in Víkos.

We got up at dawn and set off, with Stratí quoting the Latin names of all the plants we passed; he had an active hunting bitch on a lead and loosed her on the mountains; she was off in a flash, yelping after hares or foxes. His conversation was all about Miss Devlin[4] being allowed to say what she likes: 'Lucky English! Lucky Bernadette, to belong to so great and civilised a country! Democracy in action! No wonder England is loved and respected!' He's very much against the present Colonels' regime here. Quite right.

We slanted down the steep northern bank of the Víkos gorge, past jagged pinnacles of rock like rotting tusks, descending into the plane-tree-shaded headwaters of the Voïdomátis River: they came roaring out of the rock and twisted away in a deep, right-angled and leaf-dappled zigzag, teeming with trout, under diving swallows, a nymph-haunted, nereid-struck place. We lolled here in the green shadows, then climbed across meadows with cows grazing and up the steep twists and turns of this extraordinary gorge to the sleepy and half-deserted village of Víkos, where we lay under another giant plane outside a handsome triapsidal church and watched the schoolmaster with ten little boys and girls, superintending the hoisting of the flag, then prayers and the singing of the National Anthem. Hopelessly tuneless mites.

Vassílis and Dimitri turned up with two taxis and off we rolled through the leafy and soporific blaze, back through Kalpáki, down to the plain (where I saw the Cretan gendarme again) then up into the Zagorochória, through Vítsi and Monodéndri. Stupendously beautiful. The houses might be in the Cotswolds, with honeycombed slices bevelled off the corners – all lived in by civilised villagers with fine manners. Then, on to the monastery of St Paraskeví. Eagles floated above the gorge where the monastery hangs like a disintegrating house-martin's nest. Both the cliff-sides are deep in clinging shrubs, creepers, ivy and cow-parsley. Echoes resound into the distance.

We found the cars and went on to Tsepélovo and met the kind mayor and the café-keeper, and lunched with some speleologists.

Here we found a Sarakatsán muleteer, Chrístos Karvoúnis. He has four animals at 150 drachmas a day. We clinched the deal at once, set off at teatime, and trudged for two hours through the magical forest of Tsepélovo, which is mostly pines, fir and beech. There were wild strawberries everywhere, which Andrew, being slightly colour-blind, has difficulty in spotting – 'Never mind! You've got the leaves!' – till we found a narrow glen above a stream. We feasted by the fire and slept in the open. There were many fireflies after dark.

Sunday 18 June
We woke at four, breakfasted and loaded up. Winding brackeny ascents led us through the forest to the ridge of the mountains deep in beech, hornbeam, pine and fir trees, some of them enormous. Sunlight fell through leafy beech saplings, dappling them like showers of gold. We went up hill and down dale, then dropping into the beautiful village of Makrinón, where we found some eggs. Robin was rather stern about our stopping for ouzo. All the roofs here are tin as the village was burnt down three times by the Germans in 1943 as a hotbed of Resistance. There was talk of a 'Captain Peter' and a 'Captain Charlie', SOE officers, both wounded in a fight here. The population is delightful. A dear old man with a *komboloi* – a lay rosary – and a sweeping white moustache led us down to the garth of the old deserted and slab-roofed monastery of the Dormition of the B.V.M., frescoed in 1792, and beyond a thick-pillared cloister filled with hay and a sheltered spring in a field with beech trees for shade and clumps of hazel for nuts. We snoozed here and then moved off in the late afternoon with the ridges of Mitzikéli and Ajúnca Rosía looming near – they must be Vlach names – with Peristéri in the distance. After crossing a rainbow-shaped Turkish bridge, we climbed through more forest and then up frightful slopes to a half-made road running from Elatochóri to Flambourári, where we drank shandy and hobnobbed with some Vlachs, greatly to the disapproval of Chrísto the muleteer: as a Sarakatsán, he hates them. Then on to a pine-girt clearing by a stream with grazing sheep and a Vlach shepherd with his Molossian hounds. There were long talks by firelight later on, and a blaze of stars overhead and nightingales

and a barn owl in the woods. All the shooting stars – they must be the Perseids falling – made it like trying to sleep in a planetarium. A sudden rush of dogs made us all zip up our sleeping bags and hope for the best. Peter said he heard wolves . . .

Monday 19 June
Most of the morning was an easy stroll under great trees talking with Andrew about Robert Kee's book on Ireland. Well worth waiting for. Then up on to the rolling plateau of Polistés: tree-stumps and dark beech-forests covered the ridges. Peter taught me some amusing and highly improper Sharpshooter songs, sung by his regiment during the war. Lots of Sarakatsán flocks, a few dilapidated shelters, no huts; then along a half-made road through terrible heat across unending nondescript country and out on to the blazing tarmac of the Kalabáka–Yanina road (the great Athens–Rome link of old): very tired, sleep-walking by now, we followed a goat-path down into Metsovo.

The awful staring red 'French' tiles, instead of the old dark roof slabs, the cast-iron railings and the cement, have nearly done for the town. But the Tositsas house – a fine old fortified Pindus house belonging to Evángelos Avéroff (later Minister of War) – hasn't changed. I stayed there years ago to write. The house and Apostolos, the old kilted caretaker, were as welcoming as ever. What luxury it seemed! We found a charming note from Vangeli Avéroff waiting for us and a big bottle of whisky.

Baths and sleep were followed by a visit to a Mr Bombas about mules for tomorrow. (Chrístos has already started back to Skamnéli.) We had drinks in a little cluster of booths where the Vlachs are still dressed in black serge kilts or jodhpurs, kalpaks and tufted brogues like plumed gondolas, and the women in old Pindus costume. Dinner in my ancient haunts gathered many old friends.

Tuesday 20 June
A morning of shopping, and then of writing, in the delightful old Epirote room where I wrote the 'Black Departers', i.e. the Sarakatsán chapter of *Roumeli*, eleven years ago. We trooped round the Epirote

museum that fills the rest of the house and all were delighted. We saw
Tatiana Avéroff for a moment, she's off to Athens; then, after lunch and
a nap, new mules turned up with two Vlach muleteers: Triandaphyllo –
'the Rose', as we thus call him, a gruff, amusing chap – and Yanni. We
loaded up, and, after farewells, our caravan moved out of Metsovo in
some state; along the road south, down into a valley and up a wooded
torrent-bed to Anthochóri. I talk Rumanian to the Rose and Yanni;
they answer in Vlach and there is great hilarity and much teasing and
banter between our fellows and the locals about the Roman Empire
and the Dorian invasion, as this is a purely Greek-speaking village. We
settled into a sweet-smelling Poussin-like meadow, new-mown, and
striped with wind-rows of cut hay and dotted with hay-cocks against a
Sèvres sky with a few white clouds – all sweeping up to a walled
grove of ilexes (*ilce* in Vlach), like a sacred wood. For a camp-fire, our
guides set fire to a whole dead tree, and the deep-noted bells of the
mules and the treble notes of the flocks are sounding all round us.
Excitement stops one going to sleep in this fascinating place. (Swiss
Carl is from the Engadine so his first language, like Giacometti's,[5] is
Romanche, which helps him catch the drift of the old Rose's Vlach.)
A final stroll under the stars led through a twinkling mythical world.
ET IN ARCADIA EGO. (We conjure up the Poussin picture.)

Wednesday 21 June, Khalíki
The last days were such a rush, I haven't kept up.
    We climbed an enormous mountainside – *stroúnga-stroúnga*, from
fold to fold – with flocks all the way and the only man we met was
an old Zervas guerrilla, Grigóris Goussiónis. Then Robin, Renée and
Carl headed for the peaks of Peristéri while Andrew, Peter, the mules
and I made a stiff ascent on our own, barked at by alarmingly fierce
dogs at every lonely fold. We smoked with three shepherd boys in
the Skafidhia Pass while choughs cawed and wheeled just above our
heads: the start of a whole new sequence of the Ágrapha range.*

---

* 'The Unwritten Mountains': very wild and remote and so-called
because, being unsafe for strangers, especially officials, they were never
subjected to a census, either Roman, Byzantine or Turkish.

Then downhill, and the minor drama of losing Andrew and a stiff re-ascent to the pass: a bit of a saga. Got back to the village of Khalíki at last to find the entire party reassembled. What joy! It had been baking, noonday-devil work. An old pom-pommed Vlach was holding forth in the village *plateía*. Renée found some trout here, and we slept on a lovely knoll, after cooking and eating them on the spot. Flocks poured past us all night, their bells tinkling while the Acheloös River sped through the boulders below.

Thursday 22 June
After an easy morning along a half-made forest road and a stream that must have been full of trout, we had a long midday pause, bathing, washing, reading, eating off rocks as flat as tables, and then sleeping beside the Acheloös while the horses grazed. We climbed into the hills to the Vlach-speaking hamlet of Agía Paraskeví, then to Gardíki higher still in the pine-woods, then dipped into the valley again and camped with a big fire by the river.

Friday 23 June
When we had made the sweaty climb to the landslide village of Messochóra, we followed a water-channel downhill. Tin roofs everywhere and concrete; then up, up, at midday, past the handful of houses at Spítia to a little plane tree that gave us a minimum of afternoon shade. Nice shepherds. On, and over the mountains to Platanákia we came on some cherry-gatherers, a schoolmaster and his class. They gave us some, and we followed the gorge to a charming village called Moschoplýtou. A doctor at the *kapheneíon* gave us a wonderful dinner. We are raven-fed, lucky travellers in *The Arabian Nights*. We slept in front of the café under the trees.

Saturday 24 June
Up early as usual, we passed through the village of Balkánion, crossed a steep ridge and sank into a new stretch of the Ágrapha, then to the village of Elliniká with a fine church under a spreading ilex. Then on through the bracken to Kalí Kómi and here we drank ouzo sitting on an iron bedstead out of doors in a shady yard. A killing noon-day climb lifted us to some plane trees where three little boys brought us a present

of eggs. A hellish slog to Petrotón came next. We settled there in a wild
garden. It is an eccentric, mad, inbred village. A huge bill was presented,
out of the blue, and the Old Black Rose was outraged by the utter
hopelessness of everyone. Insults flew, but all came right in the end.

Sunday 25 June
An appalling morning. They said we would have to cross the river
fourteen times. We crossed it at least fifty, up to our thighs in the
water, and slipping and squelching about with our heavy climbing
boots dragging like buckets. Robin took a wrong shortcut overland
but we all reassembled later on, totally exhausted, so we had a rest
under the trees of Kostí monastery. Up the right bank of the river, we
halted at a ramshackle *kapheneíon*, past the little village of
Koubourianá, and met an old Zervas guerrilla friend of Monty
Woodhouse.[6] Then, down to the bed of the Petridianá River again,
crossing it on bridges hanging as flimsily as cobwebs; we finally took
another wrong and premature turning to Foundotó. This is a hopeless,
tiny and de-populated hamlet among desolate crags but with kind
villagers; several girls were planning to migrate to Toronto. Hopeless.
All shale and slag and vegetation, every blade of it so precious there
was nowhere for the mules to graze. We slept under the church porch.

Monday 26 June, Trídendron
We got up at four and took a high road inland from the Petriá
River to Rósoi, which is opposite Petríla, then climbed down to a
ruined mill and up again to a hamlet inhabited by kind hags. There
is a queerly painted church there. We continued along a serpentine
path through woods of pine and fir that were being wrecked by an
inchoate new road like a gash of slag. Renée was loathing it. We
crossed the watershed and laboured down a heartless mountainside to
a clump of cherry trees. An old shepherd and two nippers shinned
up into the branches at once, broke off armfuls of laden twigs and
showered them down. Then the boys filled up their bucket for us
from a far-off spring and we gave them pocket-knives with pictures
of the Houses of Parliament on them. We went on to the delightful
village of Trídendron, in a small shower of rain, and shopped and
drank in the little *magazí*, where some Sarakatsáns gave us enormous

wedges of feta cheese, refusing all payment. A switchback path took us along the Ágrapha River. It was all forest and pine needles and towards dusk we dropped down to a fold beside another watermill where the friendly miller, called Theodore Parthénios, said our mules could graze to their hearts' content; one got lost, but we caught it again. Supping and talking round the bright logs, we built up preposterous fantasies about our destination tomorrow at Ágrapha village. We imagined it – or pretended to imagine it – as a town with a fine but over-restored castle, 'La Favorita', surrounded by baroque cathedrals, small palaces, picture-galleries, equestrian statues, kiosks with London papers on sale, cocktail bars, night-clubs, obelisks, roundabouts, dodgems, a museum, a zoo and a racecourse.

Meanwhile, there were nightingales, fireflies and heavy dew.

Tuesday 27 June
Next morning, our track pursued the western bank of the boulder-strewn riverbed. We had drinks at a little *magazí*. The mules went astray for an hour – or rather, we took the wrong path and they the right one – but it was a stroke of luck, for a landscape of the utmost beauty was suddenly all round us, the tremendous gorge with a river roaring or sighing below then a tributary full of trout flowing eastward through Salvador Rosa ilex-woods slanting with broken sunbeams, and wooded mountains towering like a theatrical backdrop. Headlands of ilex, plane and beech dovetailed along a second and ravishing canyon. *Le sublime*, indeed. A flimsy gossamer bridge was looped between plane trees and some tumbled and beetling rocks. Another of those Turkish rainbow bridges arched among clouds of leaves and we longed for this to go on for ever. A final zigzag led to the scattered and shady village of Ágrapha, which was delightful but quite unlike our fictional inventions last night.

One of the gendarmes here turned out to be a relative of my Cretan god-brother* Grigóris Khnarákis de Thrapsanó, one of our

---

* *Koumbáros* in Greek – *sýnteknos* in Cretan dialect, the name for someone who has been your best man at a wedding, or godfather at a baptism, a bond considered as close as a blood relationship.

comrades in the capture of General Kreipe, so we had a great welcome. There is no grazing, so we bought bales of provender for the animals, and slept under the ilexes in the churchyard. When we woke, village boys pointed out the place on the mountainside of a famous single-handed fight between Katsantónis and Velighékas, two heroic figures from Greek klephtic folklore, and there was talk of the great Karaïskákis.* It is *Klephtouriá* – the free world of the old patriotic outlaws, a Robin Hood scene transported. After our shady siesta, we trudged down to a water meadow where a spring rushed into the Ágrapha River. Water murmured under the leaves, and we built a big fire and cooked some lentils and slept. Lots of odd dreams, as usual. Woke up under the Great Bear, Pegasus and Cassiopeia. Bells, leaves, water, fireflies and the little owl – *ghióni* – sitting on a barn roof next to the stream.

Wednesday 28 June

The remoteness, the seclusion of these mountains! Huge watersheds, deep valleys, rushing rivers, nearly deserted villages, forest on forest, all *terra incognita*! No foreigners *ever*, no visitors – nothing to buy in the shops, never a tourist, *bobota* – maize bread – but utterly unpolluted by communications. No plastic, no petrol pumps, no Coca Cola or juke box, nothing but kindness and simplicity; it's Greece as I first knew it. The Old Vlach Rose and Yanni abominated it all, of course. Sophisticated Metsovites, they are as boastful and sanguine about progress as Kinglake's *Eothen* with the Pasha of Belgrade carrying on about the Industrial Revolution. The Rose says 'Why doesn't that cuckold, the President, bomb the lot of them? Curses on them! Why don't the wolves come and eat up the inhabitants? Anathema!'

We climbed sleepily all morning, though we are all resiliently run-in, now that our journey is ending, into a beautiful conifer forest past the shacks of some detribalised Sarakatsáns (Ah! Thank God I saw Sarakatsáns when they still *were* Sarakatsáns!) – where

* A local leader in the 1821 War of Independence against the Ottoman Empire.

we asked after yoghurt, but were unlucky. A nice woman asked us to stop for coffee, but we pressed on. High, high up a circular threshing floor gleamed, hinting that all the vestigial half-collapsed terraces round about, though scarcely visible now, once grew rye or some other rough crop. Great conifers surrounded us and the bald watersheds, when we reached them, commanded range on range of mountains, resembling troops of colossal fossilized wild animals, bare and ghostly. The forests themselves suggest Red Indians; a Fenimore Cooper world. Huge trees, many of them fallen and rotting, blocked the obliterated mule-tracks, but between their trunks, faraway vistas loomed, while the other side, down the impenetrable and wood-choked slopes, we were up to our armpits in bracken.

New ranges unfolded, then ankle-snapping landslides of shale and scree, and, far below us, a pyramid of mountain lifted the village of Márathos into the air, with its white church and its roof of dark slabs. We dropped down into deep brackeny woods where the trees had grown to great height and girth. One of them had been struck by lightning and all were covered in soft green moss. Sheep scuttled away through the fronds as we settled among this gathering of giants. Ominously, a bulldozer grinds away at the slope opposite and chain-saws are at work. It is the spearhead of the modern world invading *Klephtouriá*. Dynamite explodes and flying rocks echo down chasms and ravines.

Sudden clouds heralded a downpour and the Vlachs were immediately hooded like monks in their roomy homespun capes while we cowered for shelter as the thunder and lightning took over from the explosions. Then, in the beautiful aftermath of the storm, we climbed to the pyramid village and shopped and drank in the *plateía* of Márathos, emptied of its folk, like the village in the *Grecian Urn*.[7] There is a fine frescoed 14th-century church of the Archangels Gabriel and Michael, basilican, like most of them hereabouts, except for semi-circular apse-like transepts as non-functional as penguins' wings. The villages – the one or two souls still lingering – told us the frescoes were much damaged by ELAS camping and lighting fires inside. We are in Áris Velouhiótis country now and there are terrible tales in these villages of guerrilla conflicts and outrages. Our last night's camp was overshadowed by a rock, where, they told us, fifty nationalists had their throats cut by their political rivals and were then thrown in the ravine.

We returned to our camp. Black-and-white and silver-grey goats came stampeding downhill, halting in astonishment on the tips of rocks and then coming into our midst, nosing close and inquisitive. A little boy called Chrísto came running from the village to join us. Carl heaped up a blaze and there were fire-lit trunks and branches covered with moss all round. We stretch ourselves out on last year's leaves and go to sleep with the moon coming down on us through millions of this year's replacements.

We caught a truck to Karpenísi next day, spent the night there, then motored to Athens and feasted under the Acropolis. The Feddens, Peter and Carl flew to London, and Andrew and I motored to the Mani. It had been a marvellous mountain journey and it had lasted twenty days.

Please forgive this scrawl.

Tons of love from

  Paddy

1 Director of Cartier in London and a keen skier and mountaineer.
2 A friend of Robin Fedden; a passionate climber and veteran of the Sharpshooter Regiment, who worked in the City.
3 The Special Operations Executive (SOE) was a secret outfit established by the British Government to carry out clandestine sabotage and to support local resistance movements behind enemy lines. PLF was a major in SOE during the war.
4 Bernadette Devlin McAliskey (1947–). Firebrand political activist and Socialist MP for the Mid-Ulster constituency 1969–74.
5 Alberto Giacometti (1901–66). The Swiss sculptor, painter and draughtsman was born in Borgonovo, near the Italian border.
6 Christopher Montague Woodhouse, 5th Baron Terrington (1917–2001). As head of SOE in Crete, he played an important part in organising partisan resistance. Conservative MP 1959–66 and author of many books, mostly on Greek and British history.
7 'What little town by river or sea-shore, / Or mountain-built with peaceful citadel, / Is emptied of its folk, this pious morn?/ And, little town, thy streets for evermore / Will silent be; and not a soul, to tell / Why thou art desolate, can e'er return.' John Keats, 'Ode on a Grecian Urn' (1884).

20 May 1973   Lismore Castle
                                                       Co. Waterford

Darling Paddy,

I'm writing this in the aeroplane to Paris, where I'm hurrying to
because Diana is nearly at the end of her tether because poor
Nancy is so terribly bad, desperately ill and completely miserable. It
is *so awful*. Then one reads articles which say there is no need for a
cancer patient to suffer pain any more. Well, you try. She's not easy
to help I admit as she fights every yard of the way – I'd have given
in years ago wouldn't you. Incredibly brave I suppose, and I know
humans cling to life even when frightfully ill but I'm sure she is
exceptional.

Later, Frogland, 21 May
Well, Whack, the poor French lady is very poor. I'm sitting in her
nice light room, garden all lilac & moon daisies, but what's the good
of that when she feels so foul.

There is a school hard by, & sitting all day in the window I am
deafened by the screams of the beastly scholars. As soon as they are
let out by their unfortunate teachers there is a noise like the
Heythrop bitches leaving Redesdale's Gorse on a breast-high scent.
They take a lot of stopping, bells ring time & again before they are
persuaded indoors & a merciful silence comes.

Much love
    Debo

P.S. Eddie Tennant, my grandson, aged just six, said Granny I had a
dream last night of BARE WOMEN, tits & bums Granny, bums &
tits. Granny *did you hear*, BARE WOMEN TITS & BUMS . . . What
would Lady Redesdale have made of that.

25 July 1973   Chatsworth
                                                      Bakewell

Darling Paddy & Joan,

Thanks vv much for your incredibly nice letters, & t. gram.[1]

It has all been so supremely FOUL for poor Nancy. 4½ years of
pain without a let-up, 23 doctors all charming to talk to & quite
hopeless at doing anything for her.

Some of the funniness will live in the books, won't it, but we
shall miss her dreadfully – the instigator of jokes. My father was the
same & when those two were together all those years ago it was the
acme of entertainment. How deeply unfair it is that she should have
had this ghastly illness when she had always taken such care & lived
a strictly disciplined life.

The funeral at Swinbrook was strange in that it seemed absolutely
normal for her to be buried there when most of her real life had
been in France.

Please keep in deepest touch.

Much love to you both from
    Debo

[1] Nancy Mitford had died on 30 June.

5 April 1974   Chatsworth
                                                      Bakewell

Darling Whack,

EUREKA! I've found yr classic re Somerset Maugham & the
sheets. Do you need it? Shall I get it photo-ed & send it? RSVP.

It was in the maw of letters of yours, Xan's, Diana's, Woman's,
Emma's, Stoker's, Sophy's, my mother's, Wife's, Andrew's, Aly Khan's, Ann
Fleming's, Daphne's, Uncle Harold's, Evie Waugh's, J Kennedy's, Decca's
& so on & forth, all higgledy piggledy unsorted & muddled to death.

H Acton[1] is here. He & I are in despair, all the French Lady's
letters are there of course but completely muddled with the aforesaid
heaps. Oh me.

Luckily ALL hers to Mark Grant have landed back here, a vast pile from 1930 on. Good. Poor Harold is so fuddled by the nicknames, but we can sort them out. Two sisters come tonight thank God & our after dinner game will be sorting. The sad thing is the weather is so beautiful & one longs to be out.

Now it's the 9th of April, sorry.
The sisters came & went. Harold goes today. He is taking with him a suitcase of *sort of* bombs, letter bombs. Of course the Lady never wrote one without a monster barb somewhere but they are so good & so funny.

I found Evie Waugh's re the full pot by his bed – he went on to Renishaw & faithfully didn't tell Osbert[2] about 'the strange Trove of Edensor – they wot not of the pot'.[3] Did you see C Connolly sold one of those *Bridesheads*, on nice paper & numbered, for £800? How MAD.

Sophy is going to Florence in Sept so we will all go & torture Harold in his lair, which I've never seen – I suppose you have.

He is a dear old soul, but taking him for a walk is a bit unnerving. He is tipped forward all the way & one waits for the crash. Andrew loves him. He is in v good spirits, except worried by the budget & says we may have to leave here.

I've put a room as a Shrine to Nancy – all her books, furniture, pictures. It looks quite nice & people make a bottleneck studying the manuscripts. What would she think.

Eddie Tennant has been here without a keeper, completely wild & v v nice but oh children are tiring. They always want to DO something & when the food comes they don't want to eat because they just have (chocs, you know), then wolf something, then sick it up in the lift. I love him & he is Lady Glenconner[4] to the life, face I mean.

Much love & to Joan
    Debo

---

1 Harold Acton (1904–94). The historian and novelist, a close friend of the Mitford sisters, was beginning research on a biography of Nancy Mitford, published in 1975.
2 Sir Osbert Sitwell (1892–1969). The writer lived at Renishaw Hall in Derbyshire and was a neighbour of the Devonshires.

3 Evelyn Waugh's letter to DD, in which he reassured her that no one at Renishaw had shown any curiosity about the unemptied chamber pot, is reprinted in *The Letters of Evelyn Waugh*, edited by Mark Amory (Weidenfeld & Nicolson, 1980), p. 493.
4 Elizabeth Powell (1914–). Eddie Tennant's paternal grandmother married Christopher Tennant, 2nd Baron Glenconner, as his second wife, in 1935.

10 May 1974   San Stefano
                                                       Corfu

Darling Debo,

You *are* a marvel, finding that letter (and I'm lower than the dust answering so late, and will spare you the watertight complexity of my excuses).

Poor Graham, Joan's bro, stayed three weeks, and there were only three sunny days the whole time. He left last week and we came here to stay with Barbara and Niko Ghika, where it's pretty rainy too – thank God in a way, otherwise it might have seemed like a private punishment reserved for us. It's a charming house, built by Jaime, our old companion of Andalusia days, for Jacob Rothschild;[1] he only comes for three weeks every summer, so the Ghikas squat there whenever they want – she's done marvels furnishing it, and Niko enlarging the buildings where necessary – and having friends to stay. The only other person here is someone I've heard of for years and always longed to meet, viz. Dadie Rylands[2] – is that a name to you? Cambridge's answer to Maurice Bowra? You'd love him – not necessarily *only* because he's such an authority on W Shakespeare, but because of the natural ebullience, high spirits, enterprise, & unexpectedness. He's 72, never out of the sea, even in wind and rain, and walks so fast and far – actually *running* sometimes – over these damp mountains that all pant behind him. He was a great beauty when young, and I can well imagine that those blue eyes conquered all (Lytton Strachey, chief victim).

Barbara's dog charges into my bedroom every morning, jumps on the bed and curls up, and is then turfed off, always on the stroke of eight. It is known as the Ceremony of the Fleas.

Tons of fond love,
    Paddy

1 Jacob, 4th Baron Rothschild (1936–). Elder son of 3rd Baron Rothschild and Barbara Hutchinson (who married, thirdly, the Greek painter Nikos Ghika). Financier, philanthropist and lover of the arts; first chairman of the National Heritage Memorial Fund 1992–8, chairman of the National Gallery 1985–91. Married Serena Dunn in 1961.
2 George (Dadie) Rylands (1902–99). Literary scholar, theatre director and legendary don at King's College, Cambridge.

28 May 1974   Chatsworth
                                                          Bakewell

Darling Paddy,

Ireland was lovely. I do wish you had been there to study it all.

Andrew has TWO police cars wherever he goes,[1] one in front & one behind. The one behind pretends not to be one at all as the fellows are in (very) plain clothes.

I had a jolly day with a burly team of woodmen, who were doing some clearing. We got to some thick ivy & stuff & I said look out, there might be some birds' nests in that. The foreman said 'Oh of course you have that commitment as well.' Do admit.

Now I'm back to the grindstone here. Well it's a sort of grindstone.

I dread this book of David Pryce-Jones about my sister Bobo.[2] He seems to be set on doing it. It *can't* be any good because we don't want it so aren't giving any of the letters etc which are so brill & give an insight to her amazing character AND he didn't know her. The only person who could possibly do it wd be Diana, who is the best writer and the best at everything out of our lot. It will be a great pest. He has interviewed everyone who knew her who submitted to an interview. I can now divide sheep from goats, viz. those who ring up & say What do you all think about it – shall I see him? And those who see him without so much as are we for it. Top of sheep is Penelope Dudley Ward[3] (who I haven't seen for 25 years) & she FAITHFULLY phoned to say should she or shouldn't she & immediately said of course she wouldn't if we aren't for the book.

Top of the goats (so odd of the Bible to make goats into bad things when one thinks how one worships their bodies) is my sister Decca who, oddly, is for it. She took David PJ round old gov, ancient (92) parlourmaid etc etc. Can't see the point. And there is a strong rumour the book is to be about MISFITS & that the Amery who was hanged as a spy[4] is one of the subjects.

Well Bobo *wasn't* a misfit. She was a round peg in a round hole & was a casualty of the foul war like millions of others. He could never see or possibly describe how *funny* she was.

Bother it all – how I HATE books. The marvellous thing about yours is that they never appear, such a good thing. And if by any chance one does (a) read & (b) like a book it's so awful when it's finished.

Well, there we are Whack. I wish you were here.

Much love

Debo

[1] After Andrew Devonshire became a minister in the 1960s, and up until 1995, the Irish Government required that he have a strong police guard whenever he was at Lismore. Following the assassination of Lord Mountbatten by the IRA in 1979, the protection was extended to DD.

[2] David Pryce-Jones's biography, *Unity Mitford: A Quest*, was published in 1976.

[3] Penelope Dudley Ward (1914–82). Actress and friend of DD's brother, Tom. She was in Munich in the 1930s at the same time as Unity Mitford.

[4] John Amery (1912–45). The son of a cabinet minister, he attempted to recruit British prisoners of war to fight with the Germans on the Russian front and was hanged for high treason.

8 June 1974   Mani

Darling Debo,

A propos of the great virtue of my books being their non-appearance – beware! The present one[1] is getting so long, Jock M[2] says it may have to be broken up into vols – so you can't count on it.

Iris's Friedrich [Ledebur] turns up here in two weeks time, with two strapping boys by a later bed, as Frogs say. Do you know him? I love him, he's like a splendid old stag out of the Tyrolese forests. Last time I saw him, he peered for a minute at the bridge of my nose,

then said, in his cavernous voice: '*Dat is good!* You have Attila's Bow!'
'What's that, Friedrich?' 'Eyebrows dat vant to meet in the middle!
Ven de Spartans had a baby, dey looked at de eyebrows. If dey had
no Attila's Bow, *no good*! Dey just *TREW DEM AVAY.*'

    Heaps of love,
        Paddy

  1 *A Time of Gifts, On Foot to Constantinople: from the Hook of Holland to the Middle Danube* covers the first stage of PLF's voyage and took a decade to write. It was published in 1977 by John Murray (as were all of his books) thirty-four years after he set out on his walk.
  2 John (Jock) Murray (1909–93). Congenial and enterprising head of the dynastic publishing house. 'A nimble and efficient tree surgeon and delightful company.' (PLF)

14 July 1975   Chatsworth
                                              Bakewell

Darling Whack,

    No news, except bumpkin stuff. The Council of the Royal
Smithfield Club – top farmers & butchers from all over the British
Isles, every accent from Devon to Aberdeen via Wales & Norfolk –
met here on Thurs. Fifty of them. So the only room I could think of
was the nursery, & there they sat good as gold on hard chairs. I
offered the rocking horse, but they eschewed it, ditto high chairs &
Snakes & Ladders.

    I really love those men, & it's my last year as president. I shall
miss it & them.

    Then they had lunch, then the wives were let in (so typical of
England that they had to hang about till lunch was over) & of
course they wanted to see the house. I said 'I'll meet you at the end
of the tour.' The first butcher was out in six minutes. I reminded him
of Art Buchwald's lovely article on How To Do The LOUVRE in
six minutes[1] – but he'd never heard of Art Buchwald or the Louvre
so I chucked it & took him to see some cattle, which he had heard
of. A really good fellow.

    Much love
        Debo

1 One of the American humorist's best-known articles, written in 1950, was about a fictional American tourist who tried to win the 'Six-Minute Louvre' race, taking in 'the only three things worth seeing', the *Venus de Milo*, the *Mona Lisa* and the *Winged Victory*. Buchwald described how the tourist made good time 'under perfect conditions, with a smooth floor, excellent lighting, and no wind'.

1 August 1976   Chatsworth
                                                       Bakewell

Darling Paddy,

Just had a visit from Lady Bird Johnson & her daughter Lynda for two nights.[1] *Oh dear* they were nice. I was quite overcome by such extreme niceness. You would have adored the daughter, all lively & agog for whatever was next. They were ½ dead by the time they left having seen this dump, Hardwick, Haddon & much countryside to boot.

As they drove away I suggested Sudbury to which Lynda answered no we can't Mother is just about housed out. What I often feel like.

Much love
    Debo

1 Claudia (Lady Bird) Taylor (1912–2007). Married US President Lyndon B. Johnson in 1934. Their daughter Lynda was born in 1944. 'They stayed at Chatsworth in the unprecedented drought and heat of that summer. I was sad that they saw the park and the Peak District brown instead of green, Texas-coloured and un-English.' (DD)

6 August 1976   Mani

Darling Debo,

I'm beginning to feel rather excited about the Himalayas next month. (I wish Andrew were coming.) As Joan and her hermit-bro and I are going in Jan to stay with our marvellous friend whom I don't think you know, to wit Ian Whigham,[1] in a mangrove jungle in a Malayan creek, it suddenly occurred to me: why not hang about in India, instead of the vast expense of flying back and out again – and joining J and Graham as they pass through, taking wing for Malaya. I expect we'll be clambering about those glaciers till the end of Oct or early Nov – so why not settle and write for two months in, say,

Simla, and plum pudding in a residential hotel? I'm very excited about the idea. I do believe the hill station is deep in snow – the Hot Weather was the fashionable time. I love the idea of wandering through sheeted and dusty Government House, haunted by the tunes of Yip-i-yaddy and Tararaboomdeeay, and gazing across floors where my mum twirled when Rose of Simla.[2]

I read a book about Government Houses in India[3] last year. One v good looking ADC of yore was Capt Ld Something Thynne; he was in charge of getting the ballroom ready – there were shady sitting-out nooks of palms and similar everywhere. The Vicereine, pointing to the darkest of all, asked the Kansâmah what it was. His whispered answer was 'Lord Sahib's *Kissee-Kawasti*'. (Kawasti = place, in Hindi. No offence meant here.) Ran says such a nook was generally known as the *Kalajugga*, i.e. the Dark Place.

O the *kalajuggas* of the Soul . . .

Another snatch from the same book. (Fortunately you can't stop me if I've told it you before.) At a Viceregal Lodge dinner party, a v timid newly-arrived ADC at the end of the table was saying how quickly the dance tunes reached India from Blighty: the first tune the night before he'd only heard once in London. This remark chanced to coincide with a general silence, and the Vicereine called down the table and said 'And what tune was that, Captain Jones?'

Capt Jones: (paralysed with shyness) '"You'll remember my kisses", Your Excellency, "when I have forgotten your name".'

Enough of this. Strike up the fifes and drums! (Thackeray, *Rose and the Ring*)

Tons of love, darling Debo, and v many thanks again,

Paddy

---

1 'A delightful man, rather formal-looking, piercing blue eyes, a cheerful face. Extremely gifted for languages, drawing, painting and talking. He loved buying houses – Tuscany, Thailand, Malaysia – doing them up and selling them after a few years' sojourn. Much in our life as he was a great friend of Joan's brother, Graham.' (PLF)

2 PLF's mother, Muriel Eileen Ambler (1890–1977), came from a family with links with India. Married Lewis Leigh Fermor in 1909.

3 Mark Bence Jones, *Palaces of the Raj: Magnificence and Misery of the Lord Sahibs* (1973).

Christmas Day [1976]   Hotel Clarks
Benares   Varanasi
                                                        India

Darling Debo,

Well, we *did* have a time in the Himalayas, and as usual, I think it
was the greenhorn – viz. me – who enjoyed it most, and it would
have been perfect if poor Robin [Fedden] hadn't felt so rotten in the
middle of it. I expect you've heard all about our adventures by now;
anyway, I sent Joan enormously long letters – rather like the ones
from Peru – which I'll get done in several copies, and send you in
the fullness of time.[1] Please tell Andrew that I missed him *enormously*
– when together we managed to inject a frivolous note into things
which I didn't quite pull off on my own. We all broke up in
Delhi: Robin returned to England – Carl Natar and Peter Lloyd[2]
had already gone – and Renée and her newly arrived friend,
Rosemary Peto,[3] and Myles Hildyard[4] buzzed off to the south of
the subcontinent, bent on temples; and I returned to the hills
again, heading for Simla.

This was marvellous. I managed (on advice, and by help of, Penelope
Betjeman,[5] in a letter waiting there) to be allowed to stay in a seldom-
used Government guest house, which was the Hot Weather haunt of the
Governors of the Punjab – huge, rambling, half country-house, half
wooden-beamed cottage, flagpole on lawn, monkeys from Jakko Hill
overhead clattering all over the red corrugated-iron roof – I thought
they were gigantic rats, when I heard the noise on the first night – but
saw them trooping along the roof next morning holding each other's
tails like the Banderlog in *The Jungle Books*. There was a weeping
willow on the lawn, grown from a cutting from one over Napoleon
(Bonaparte's) tomb in St Helena.

My bedroom led off the gallery looking down into the ballroom.
The décor designed by R. Kipling's father – enormous beams,
chandeliers, displays of Afghan swords, spears, shields, helmets still on
the walls, the lances of disbanded Cavalry regiments with threadbare
pennants crossed – a very haunted place. The only other occupant
was a nice sad chap from Perth, Western Australia, called Stan

Hardisty, advising the Himalayan government about apple growing. We were dining together one night, talking about the faults of Indian fruit-tree planting and eating a blazing hot curry, when he put his fork down and said earnestly that they did not use enough spice, which seemed to me odd, as I was on fire. It took me some time to twig that he meant the Indians didn't plant their trees far enough apart. He had an odd experience last year, he told me. He was born with a hare lip (since operated, but just detectable), and so was his little son. They were going for a walk on Jakko Hill when a she-monkey started jumping up and down and screeching; *she had a hare lip too.* Making urgent signs for them to wait, she went trapezing up to the top of a deodar, and came hurtling down again, with a tiny monkey in her arms, *ALSO* with a hare lip, which she held up chattering joyfully.

The town — or village — half Surrey architecture, half baronial — goes on forever, along a sharp ridge, with roofs tumbling away into canyons on either side, dominated by Jakko Hill, with hundreds of mountain ranges whirling away in all directions like a half-created world rising from primordial smoke — then level layers of blue mist, a dazzling sky and on the N Horizon, the snowy peaks of Kulu, Spiti & Lahoul where we have just been climbing, all gleaming & flashing; and the mountains of the Chinese–Tibet border. Viceregal Lodge — now a seldom-used sort of Indian All Souls — rather impressive: four posters floating above the clouds . . . But never a European face in the lanes, everything rather run down — old eyes might well up. In former days, much revolved round amateur theatricals at the charming little Gaiety Theatre, where I found three photographs (1930) of my sister Vanessa[6] playing the lead in *The Constant Nymph*, still hanging on the wall of the dress circle, the names all neatly inscribed; and in *Simla Past and Present*[7] there are nice mentions of my mama on the same stage: 1917 *Two Sisters*, 'a wordless play in which . . . the beautiful Mrs Fermor held the audience breathless'. I like the wordless actresses and the breathless listeners . . . *and again*, in 1918, in a review called 'High Jinks' where Mrs F sang 'Oh, Johnny!' and 'The Kipling Walk'. I wrote about all this lingering fame to my ma. She *was* pleased.

There is one old Englishwoman called Hermione Montague –
one of four stayers-on from the Raj in Simla – who made *Simla Past*
seem very real. She's 86 – my mother's age – looks rather like Diana
Cooper, very funny, spry, and charming, a great beauty of yore and
still. Stan Hardisty and I asked her to dinner at our joint – candles &
blazing fire in the ex-Governor's huge dining room, bearers in smart
puggris. The electricity failed while we were having coffee, so we
wandered all over the building, candles in hand. In the ballroom, I
asked her: who were the best dancers in her heyday? She said, '*Well*,
there was Hamilton Thompson, in the Guides Cavalry – always
known as the Black Rabbit, I can't *think* why – and the other – the
other, my dear, was called Brocas Howell.' I *knew* she was going to say
that name a second before she uttered it, and chimed in simultaneously.
I'd heard lots about this tall, fair, heart breaker of late Edwardian,
early Georgian days, from my mother, who must have had a bit of a
soft spot for him. Mrs Montague admitted she very nearly eloped
with him from Jullanadar in 1913. 'He was such a charming fellow
. . .' She *WAS* surprised when I answered simultaneously, lots of
wonder and laughter in the shadowy ballroom! She lives in a
rambling house on Elysian Hill, full of pictures of dashing relations in
kilts and turbans, pig-sticking spears, snaps of herself grasping gymkhana
cups, five old Moslem servants, the curtains almost permanently
drawn. She gave me a charming watercolour of an officer being
carried in a palanquin, for my mother; and five other pictures of a
vanished India, for me. You'd have loved her. She was full of ancient
gossip straight out of *Plain Tales from the Hills*, by R. Kipling, a closed
book to you, alas.

I scribbled away happily in this mountain eyrie for a month and,
a few yards from the shady nook on the lawn where I had set up
my table, was a deodar tree with a gravestone at its foot, inscribed on
it was: 'the grave of / Coonah / the faithful dog / and affectionate
companion / of Lady Gomm / through 12 years / May 11, 1851'.
Six years before the Mutiny,

I descended from the hills, spent a night in the waiting room at
Amritsar, surrounded by sleeping figures like the sheeted dead, who
resurrected with me to catch the early train to Lahore, over the

Pakistan border, the old capital of the Punjab. The 1000 nights and 1 night! A mosque with the biggest courtyard in the world, a huge red Moghul fort, lanes and alleys of sinister romance, and 'Zam-Zammer' – the cannon beside which Kim met the Lama. Then to the Sikhs' golden temple at Amritsar, and on to Amballah. (I was roughly following the trail of Kim & the Lama, in fact, which has long been an obsession.) This was a haunted town, an overgrown ex-cantonment, full of old bikes and cars rotting and rusting in the sun. I spent hours in the English cemetery there, entered through a gothic octagon, rather like those gates near Lismore. All overgrown with fern and brambles, mynahs and parakeets in the peepal branches and creepers everywhere: 'Our darling Bertie, aged 6, 1842', 'Jack and Cissie Rigley, 1870', 'Willm Orlebar Harvey, 2nd Lieut. Royal Munster Fusiliers, Feb 1898, aged 22. Je n'oublierai jamais', 'Our darling Dody, infant son of Sgt & Mrs Duncan, Black Watch, 1903', 'Farrier Major Smith', 'Bugle Major Turner' – I was looking at the cracked and overgrown tomb of the last when an enormous hare jumped out, gave me a look, and loped off into the near-jungle, going to earth behind a tilted obelisk, commemorating the death by cholera of 17 officers, NCOs and men of the D of Albany's Highlanders in 1840. Meanwhile a troop of about 200 buffaloes was shuffling by beyond the railings in a vast dust cloud, attended by nearly naked drovers, v slowly!

Next, Dehra Dun, and back into the Himalayas at Mussoori, full of forests and the distant snows of Tibet, down through Meerut where one of Martyn Beckett's wives[8] once lived in the square, and so back to Delhi, to meet Joan, who had taken wing from Athens. We had a v nice lunch with Antonia Fraser's bro, Michael Pakenham,[9] then off to Gwalior where a marvellous fort scowls on a hilltop and the Maharajah has solid glass furniture, port decanters that circulate in a miniature silver train and a guest-house of the purest Oxford bags, Lalique and ukulele period. Then to the Buddhist remains of Sanchi, then by train to Lucknow, and wandered in the beautiful battered ruin of the Residency; then to Benares, viz. here. I couldn't resist the carol service in St Mary's Church this morning (a great change from the Burning Ghat yesterday). Congregation of

18, five of them Europeans: 'O Little Town of Bethlehem', 'We Three Kings' etc. As we came out, an elephant passed with a load of hay, stowed safely sternward out of trunk-reach of yoke fellows, followed by twelve camels similarly laden, but no myrrh or frankincense. There's a gala dinner tonight! Joan (who sends love) and I suspect it will begin with Father Krishna in a sledge drawn by white oxen.

No more for the moment, except Happy Christmas & New Year to one and all, and tons of fond love as ever from

Paddy

1 'Paradox in the Himalayas' appeared in the *London Magazine*, December 1979–January 1980, reprinted in *Words of Mercury*, pp. 73–82.

2 Peter Lloyd (1907–2003). Mountaineer and engineer. President of the Alpine Club 1977–80.

3 Rosemary Peto (1916–98). After being married to 10th Earl of Sandwich 1934–58, and producing seven children, her friendships were mostly with women. 'Rather splendid, great guts and dash, rather like an 18th-century admiral painted by Romney or Sir J. Reynolds.' PLF to DD, 1 February 1992.

4 Myles Hildyard (1914–2005). Keen amateur historian who lived at Flintham Hall in Nottinghamshire. He was awarded an MC in 1942 for his daring escape from a prisoner-of-war camp in Crete, described in *It Is Bliss Here: Letters Home 1939–1945* (2005).

5 Penelope Chetwode (1910–86). The writer and traveller, an old friend of Joan Leigh Fermor, had grown up in northern India and often returned to the subcontinent. Married the poet John Betjeman in 1933.

6 Vanessa Leigh Fermor, PLF's older sister, married Jack Fenton in 1931. They had two children, Francesca and Miles.

7 Edward John Buck, *Simla Past and Present* (1904).

8 Martyn Beckett often sang Rudyard Kipling's 'The Ladies' and accompanied himself on the piano.

9 Michael Pakenham (1943–). Diplomat who was at the British Embassy in New Delhi. Younger brother of the biographer Antonia Fraser (1932–).

22 April 1977   Mani

Darling Debo,

For some reason Joan has given up the Sunday Papers, and I *long* to see the reviews of Lady Mosley's book.[1] You couldn't *possibly* lend me any you happen to cut out – spare – to be returned at once. I enjoyed it enormously, and I must say your other sister's too.[2] I wish

you would write a book like everyone else, the abstention looks
rather ostentatious; and you wouldn't have to *read* it; someone else
(viz. one) would do that.

Tons of fond love
Paddy

1 Diana Mosley's memoirs, *A Life of Contrasts* (1977).
2 Jessica Mitford's second volume of autobiography, *A Fine Old Conflict* (1977).

16 May 1977   Lismore Castle
                                             Co. Waterford

Darling Paddy,

Re books, chiefly Mitford ones. The awful thing is I've thrown
away the reviews. I knew it was stupid at the time, sorry. Now there
is a new flood re Decca's effort. Not so rave as I expected, but good
enough I suppose.

It's too long to go into but I shall be thankful when the mags
have something else in them. One lovely thing was *Private Eye*, &
Twiggy[1] as 'Doreen Mitford' whose dazzling memoirs are about to
appear etc etc. She looks exactly like all my sisters rolled into one. So
funny because I saw her in the flesh at a film premiere which Cake
took us to, and said loudly to Andrew all that, so true.

I went to London *for the day* last week, Foyle's lunch for Diana.[2]
So really nice to see her fêted. I sat one off an actress called Phyllis
Calvert.[3] She leaned across our neighbour & said I know who you
are, you're Mrs Bruce. I had to say I wasn't in case she got further
into the mire, but DO ADMIT because Mrs Bruce is 83 & is famous
because she looped the loop last month in a weeny aeroplane.[4]

Later

I'm hurrying home for Martyn Beckett's Arabs – the bro of the
Ruler of Bahrain may want a palace & Martyn has designed a
winner, but to encourage him up M asked if he'd like to see a big
English house & good gracious he's said Yes & looms.

A telex came of likes & dislikes. We've got to welcome him with
Fruit Juice, Nuts & Toffees. Quaint. I must keep Collie's shadow off
his food, & only just stopped the new cook from putting a ham in
to soak. I don't want Martyn to have his head cut off.

Cowslips galore. Made friends with two County Council
workmen who are doing a marvellous job of opening up paths
round the lodges (for the *tourists*, oh pathos) & I asked them how
they get to work – 'We BOIK, under our own steam'. More people
ought to do that, & happiness might set in.

I quite see about not having to read my own book, but I may
have a shot at yours. What a wait.

Keep in deepest. Much love
    Debo

1 Lesley (Twiggy) Hornby (1949–). Like the Mitfords, the 1960s supermodel and
actress had blond hair and blue eyes.
2 A Foyle's Literary Luncheon was given for the publication of *A Life of
Contrasts*.
3 Phyllis Calvert (1915–2002). After a career in films, the actress starred mainly
on the stage and television.
4 Mildred Mary Petre (1895–1990). The world-record-breaking aviatrix and motor
racer had looped the loop in a two-seater De Havilland Chipmunk.

6 December 1977   Mani

Darling Debo,
    'Tis the pen of the sluggard! I wish I hadn't let all these days pile
up before writing. You *must* think I'm an ingrate; but I won't
compound my misconduct by burdening you with excuses – *all of
them tip-top, and absolutely watertight!* It *was* lovely coming to stay, and
culling those mushrooms and observing the tremendous progress made
by you and Collie. I could watch that performance for ever.[1] Also, you
were a true saint to appear at *both* those parties for one's book. I loved
them, and the last one, with all that noise, must have been very
surprising for the staff in the Ritz,[2] and very good for them, after
endless solemn banquets for the boards of city companies. All this, and
too kind words said and written about *A T. of G* turned the stay into a

glorious sojourn, *largely thanks to you*; and v many thanks, and with knobs on.

We had a lovely drive across France and Italy with Coote in her car – gazing at rose-windows and flying buttresses and eating our heads off at various serious and starry restaurants across Champagne and Burgundy. You've no idea how lovely those vineyards looked, with all the leaves russet and golden, clothing the hillsides for miles and miles as geometrically as designs on candlewick counterpanes. We stopped two nights in Grenoble, then crossed the Alps in a downpour after a draughty watershed night in Briançon, and coiled down into the Lombard plain, swallowing *pasta* by the furlong now, instead of chicken in half-mourning surrounded by button-mushrooms peeping through the beige. In Tuscany we stayed with Ian Whigham, who I don't think you know, except through my going on about him year after year. He's a glory, immensely funny and intensely nice. You'd love him. We had a rude shock in Brindisi; while we were having a pre-ferryboat supper in a trattoria, thieves made off with Coote's car. When we emerged, there it wasn't. It was found gutted of all its contents – had been up to the roof with things for the house, plus all one's garments assembled over the years – surrounded by odd socks scattered in the mud, letters whirled there in their haste by the robbers – on a rubbish dump on the outskirts. We hunted in the mire and brambles for hours, gazed on by the unhelpful louts of Brindisi . . . It was a blow. Endless hours were spent in different Carabinieri headquarters, while they typed with one finger. They are proverbially thick-witted. '*Do you know how to burn a carabiniere's ear?*' Italians ask each other. '*Ring him up when he's ironing his trousers.*' Anyway the car still *went*, so we came here, and marvellous it is (you know what I usually insert here. Take it as read, but *do* act on it). I'm hard at work on Vol II.[3] Chastening to think you'll never read it or its forerunner, but good for one I expect.

When I arrived here, a letter from my sister Vanessa told me that my mother had died suddenly and peacefully five days after I'd set out. Thank heavens I'd been down to Brighton frequently. She'd had two strokes, memory very faulty and another might have reduced her to vegetating, which she would have *loathed*. We'd had several laughs and she had managed to read my book *twice*, and was frightfully bucked by my mentioning her learning to fly, in the Introduction. She was nearly 88.

   Joan sends love, me too and fond hugs,
      Paddy

1 DD and her Border Collie were practising for a television programme. 'Her handling of sheep dogs is marvellous to watch; with short whistles and a few syllables she makes him guide, lead, head off, and then halt a flock of 20 sheep. It looks close to sorcery.' PLF, *Daily Telegraph*, 31 March 2000.
2 A party given by Ann Fleming to celebrate the publication of *A Time of Gifts*.
3 *Between the Woods and the Water: On Foot to Constantinople from the Hook of Holland: The Middle Danube to the Iron Gates* (1986). A sequel to *A Time of Gifts*, describing the second stage of PLF's walk.

15 March 1978   Chatsworth
                                                  Bakewell

Darling Paddy,

   There is frenzied activity going on here because the dump opens next week & so I've got a glorious team of saints setting out the shop[1] & thinking of numbers & doubling them when pricing the GOODS.

   Joanna Bigham, Jock Murray's daughter, is queen of calligraphy & puts the descriptions of the wares on tasteful cream-coloured paper & she has got a marvellous friend who waves her long thin hands over a stall which is covered by me with ghoulish SOUVENIRS & it immediately turns into Fortnum/Dior, *so clever*. I love shop keeping better than anything (except *perhaps* pedigree stock).

   The other thrill is that the BBC television has done me & Collie working sheep & it's coming on tonight. I rather dread it because of my awful voice, but the dog didn't do too badly.

   Much love
      Debo

1 DD had opened a gift shop in the Orangery at Chatsworth.

21 March 1978 Mani

Darling Debo,

I've just written to Andrew, the awful thing is, I thought I already had! I've sent it express, *jumping* at the Persian idea.[1]

Lots of kind letters from total strangers – or people not glimpsed for 50 years – keep on coming in about that book. I'm rather unspoilt about this sort of thing and glory in them. What's more, Jock writes that it *really is* selling well, so that's something to put in one's pipe and smoke.

It's pouring with rain here at the moment. Joan is in Athens, and the sea under the cliff makes a noise like angry lions at feeding time.

No more now, darling Debo, except *tons of love* from
    Paddy

[1] In the event, the Foreign Office dissuaded the party from walking in Iran because of the uprising against the Shah. Disappointed, they decided to head for the Pyrenees instead.

3 April 1978 Lismore Castle
Co. Waterford

Darling Paddy,

I had to be Alan[1] this year & bring the car & the luggage & the dogs. All went smoothly. It's years since I've done it & I note progress has been made since one drove up two planks at all angles to get on the foul boat to Mull. Lady Redesdale used to take a jerking rush. It was a miracle she didn't land in the deep. (And her car had a board out of the floor so one saw the road rushing by under one's feet.)

One jolly well knows one's in Ireland when the signposts say things like Two Mile Borris, Horse & Jockey, Galloping Green & Ovens. It doesn't smell like it used to. Dublin doesn't anyway. I suppose peat has been out for years. There are some TERRIBLE new buildings there. Nice ones with things like Liverpool Sack Hire Company written on them look as if they're for the high jump. How I hate change.

This place is much the same. Someone told me a woman had committed suicide by walking all the way to the river.

The *Irish Times* has got a new trick of saving everything by reprinting several pages of itself of 50 years ago, & except for a bit about Lindbergh & an inflammatory speech of W Churchill's it's v hard to tell when those pages end & 1978 begins.

Much love

Debo

No wonder people write to you about your book. I keep *glancing* & see their point.

---

[1] Alan Shimwell (1933–). A long-time chauffeur at Chatsworth who also loaded for DD out shooting.

14 July 1994[1]   Mani

Darling Debo,

Don't groan! The enclosed is just a tidier, slightly topped and tailed version of our Spanish journey, recently inflicted on Andrew. But I was so horrified, picking up a carbon copy of it – the loops, erasions, and general mess – that I sorted it out a bit, to make it more presentable. I don't know why, because it will only be scrutinised by some archivist in 100 years time; so do please *destroy* the first illegible screed, and replace it by this fairer copy, all for the sake of this greybeard yet unborn.

But *before* stowing it away, look at the passage marked*, for pathos.

Fond love,

Paddy

TRAVELS WITH ANDREW IN THE PYRENEES

Saturday 16 September 1978   Begun at Gavarnie
                                              Hautes Pyrénées

Darling Joan,

I caught the plane from Athens to Marseilles, arrived at three in the afternoon, wandered about the Vieux Port, caught the Toulouse train at 8 and dashed to the restaurant car full of hope and greed, only to find a cheerless cafeteria as bad as British Rail – cellophane snaquettes on a TV tray with elfin plastic cutlery – and munched miserably, the only mug in the place, complaining bitterly to the nice waiter, who hated it too.

Suddenly, between Arles and Tarascon, it started to get mysteriously dark: it wasn't only the cuisine that was awry: the moon over the Alpilles was vanishing fast until there was only a sliver of it left, and then none at all. '*Et la lune fout le camp, par-dessus le marché*,'[2] the waiter croaked in the dark. It was a total eclipse neither of us had heard anything about, and rather eerie.

After the Mani, Provence and Languedoc looked very green and beautiful in the recovered moonlight and I slumbered on until the kind waiter shook me awake at Toulouse – '*Vite! Vite! N'y a que quatre minutes!*'[3] We galloped to a faraway platform with all my stuff, I jumped in and snoozed till we hissed into Pau at 3.30. Found a taxi at last, which took me five miles beyond Pau to the frightful NOVOTEL which is worse even than its name, a hideous and heartless complex in a wasteland with nothing in sight except a giant supermarket, a clump of petrol-pumps and a flyover. (It was the RV Andrew had wired to Athens, in all innocence.) Slept till 10 a.m. and found an army of German businessmen arriving for an industrial fair. So I started the trudge to Pau – no taxis, and no buses on Sunday – but got a lift on a truck and spent a solitary and happy day mooching about the town. A lot of it whispers of Victorian and Edwardian villeggiatura and English libraries and a vanished foxhunt, all gone now except for winter steeplechases. But there is a handsome spiked and towered castle above the tree-shaded Cade de Pau (a tributary of the Adour) full of tapestries and armour and memories of Marguerite de Navarre, Jeanne d'Albret and, above all, of Henri IV, who was born in one of the castle rooms and rocked in a cradle made of half a turtle's shell trimmed with silver and gold, nestling now under a panoply of fleurs-de-lys. Bernadotte, the French revolutionary general, Napoleonic marshal and, finally, Charles XIV of Sweden, was born just down the lane.

For lunch I had one of the trout that abound in these mountains and a sort of cassoulet – very good – washed down with Jurançon, a delicious dry white wine from hereabouts, which has irrigated and illuminated all our travels; at night, red and roughish Corbières, from a hundred miles or so further east, takes over. Then to the Béarn museum – I tried dropping the final N of Béarn, like Madame de Guermantes,[4] but met only blank looks, as though I were a bit wanting – and pondered the stuffed bears there, which they say are extinct, and querns, flails, sickles and rakes; then moved on to the rather charming Musée des Beaux Arts. I made friends with the lady of the Roncevaux Hôtel (half the price of our miserable shelter) which I slunk back to after dinner and a Fernandel film. Spent more of Monday buying odds and ends – a compass, a *small* rucksack – then back just as Andrew burst into the NOVOTEL in tearing spirits, bringing the good news that Xan was arriving from Spain next morning. So we were at the station at 10 a.m., only to learn that part of the tunnel had fallen in (just missing Xan), and he only arrived at noon. We feasted joyfully and caught the late-afternoon train to Tarbes and Lourdes, then on to Luz-Saint-Sauveur.

In Pau the weather had been perfect, and has continued so, but a thin haze had veiled all the Pyrenees, an excellent omen; they say clarity presages rain. We were soon zooming along deep wooded gorges with spikes and beech-forests turning russet above streams and waterfalls, reaching the little town of Gavarnie as the sun was setting. (It seems the caricaturist Paul Gavarni took his sobriquet from here. It became our base on Renée's advice. It was the Feddens' HQ long ago, and she had given Andrew lots of old marked maps from the time when Robin was preparing *The Enchanted Mountains*.)[5] It's much more of a holiday resort than it was then, but it is pervaded just now by a valedictory *fin-de-saison* mood unnaturally prolonged by the miraculous weather. The only snag was the unobtainability of pack-animals. Troops of tourists amble and tittup up the valley and the beasts' owners charge the earth, so what hopes. The Cirque de Gavarnie is an amazing three-quarters of a circle piled on three rock-bands in succeeding tiers with wonderful echoes and a waterfall that beats Sumatra. My ice axe was pinched in five minutes. *Also*, that lovely spiral-ash-plant, bought at Kenilworth cattle show.[*]

We climbed up to the Cirque along the main valley next day, and back in a wide sweep through the forests; there was a slightly bolder march to the north next day and we got back in the gloaming. The third departure was upstream, threading valleys with a final haul over slippery acres of scree to the Pass of Boucharo where we had planned to spend the night, but missed the hut, so, down again and up next day as far as we could get by car to the same col. (I had meant to make a solitary higher loop through rocks and small glaciers to a famous upper pass called the Brèche de Roland, but the driver advised against it and I'm glad he did as night would have fallen, and it's rather dangerous.) From the col where the unmarked border runs, we plunged down the Spanish slope into the old Kingdom of Aragon: it was very exciting, scree at first, then zigzag paths, then green bowls of Alpine meadow, sometimes with cattle grazing and sometimes with chestnut horses; then through wonderful woods of pine and forests of beech going gold and red, and whitebeam, juniper and giant box, everywhere full of birds, choughs wheeling in the pass, eagles high overhead and, on a low rock, a huge goshawk perched, as in Japanese pictures. On a steep slope we ran into a cheerful Cockney chap from Uckfield in Sussex, covered in tattooing, studying birds, and heading north to pick grapes in the Bordeaux country for fifty quid a week, a bed and all found.

This breakneck descent brought us into an astonishing valley, the bed of the Ara River, crossed by an old rainbow-shaped bridge next to a ruined Romanesque church at Bujaruelo, and a rough inn with *chorizo*, black beans and wine like the purple ink my mother sometimes wrote in, and forest people with Aragonese smugglers' faces. We slept under the beech trees and set off downhill, dropping into the Ordesa Canyon, where huge mountains towered on either side. Below these overshadowing woods a deep gorge of green glacier-water rushed through troughs of twisting rock and deep cliffs and rapids. Then, suddenly, our path was full of turmoil; silver-grey cows with fawn and cream patches, furry cloven ears and sulky white muzzles, were all in an awkward muddle, lowing for strayed calves and climbing on each others' backs along the narrow path: massed mooing, horns clashing and bells clanking, goaded by hoarse drovers, the whole steep place was full of uproar and echoes.

They were coming down from their summer to their winter
pastures. We struggled through them and found a new set of drovers
hanging about round another old bridge called the Puente de los
Navarros: hollow-cheeked men padding about in espadrilles with flat
berets tilted over their eyes, and armed with long goads. '¿Had we
seen the herds?' they all shouted in chorus: '¿*Los ganados*?' The dust
and the noise emerging from the canyon soon unpuckered their
brows.

Beyond the bridge the country suddenly opened in a great
amphitheatre of mountains like the Bad Lands of Arizona and we
advanced through a dream-like late afternoon down a gentle valley
with haymakers raking and spreading the hay in newly-shorn water
meadows where the sun turned the poplars to flames. We came on a
wedding feast where all were blotto and were given wine under a
plane tree while we watched them dancing slow and ceremonious
jotas of great beauty.

We trudged on to Torla, which juts over trees and the river on a
buttress of rock. There was a grim windowless church with a tall
belfry in a maze of cobbled lanes. One or two arched doorways had
escutcheons over them, all the houses were roofed with slabs of
schist, as in Thrace, and everything smelt of hay, smoke and cows.
The herds we passed in the canyon soon flooded into the village,
houses and yards and fields filled up with them, and the rest bumped
on to the next day's fair at Broto, a few miles further down, to be
whisked off to Huesca and Saragossa. We slept at the small and only
hostel called the Ballarín in a room giving on a steep fall of stone
roofs and chimneys. The barkeeper had a very distinctively marked
dog, which he said was English like us. '¿What kind?' '¡It's called a
Bay-arg-lay!' he told us: a beagle . . .

In the morning we climbed about the steep left side of the Ara,
beginning with lovely fields and hazel-woods, then beech and pine-
forests with that tremendous circle of mountains to the east and the
gap above them – the Brèche de Roland – which I long to cross
one day. It was terrifically hot and we slept high in the woods for an
hour after eating the lunch we had brought in our pockets, plunging
down to the river in the late afternoon where another wonderfully

hoary rainbow bridge spanned a deep and reedy stream which, as it
was dammed a little further down with enormous boulders, was
quite still. I dived in, shot twenty feet to the bottom, then to the top
again, transformed into an ice-cube. We went back to the town with
the returning local herds, stuffing with blackberries all the way, then
to bed early with an alarm clock borrowed from the hotel people.
The Spaniards are marvellous with their directness, their manners,
their lack of graspingness and their concern.

We had to wake a butcher at 5.30. There was brilliant starlight
above the lanes and he drove us in his van up the valley in the dark
past the Bridge of Navarros to the little inn and the ruined church
at the head of the valley where we had had luncheon before. The
butcher – Señor Bun – woke his innkeeper brother, who lit a fire
under a giant horn chimney hung with sooty and cobwebbed hams,
and cooked us breakfast. It was only beginning to get light when we
crossed the bridge and started up through the woods. Andrew had a
moment of discouragement on the steep slope and thought of
returning in order not to delay us, but we cheered him up; spirits
revived, we reached the watershed at the Port de Boucharo, then
strolled back into France in a cloud of choughs. It was downhill all
the way through canyons and meadows and flocks and herds till the
Cirque de Gavarnie was all round us again. The little Hôtel Acazou
greeted us like homing prodigals. They were a charming lot; they said
they were much cheered by the high spirits, laughter and noise that
came from our table of three, compared to some of the gloomy
blighters they often got.

On the morrow we got a lift to Tarbes – stowaways almost – in a
charabanc full of hilarious Walloon pilgrims heading for Lourdes, all
of them pretty tight. They abandoned their language now and then
to crack improper jokes in French, making *The Canterbury Tales*
immediately real. Thence by train to Bagnères-de-Luchon. (We
started in Béarn at Pau, and at Gavarnie, went into Bigorre; then into
Aragon at Torla, and now I think we are in Comminges, not far
from the famous Abbey of St Bertrand, which I've always longed to
see. Alas, it's out of range.)

The little spa Luchon is now desultorily closing for the season

and we spent a delightful idle day. Unfortunately the mineral baths
were already shut, but we made friends with the nice scholarly fogey
who was curator of the museum and we planned the morrow's
assault over a giant relief-map. There were pictures of all the well-
known visitors since early last century and of the izzards, the wild
goats of the Pyrenees, and of ibexes looking very like Cretan *agrímia*;
bird-life too – not only stuffed eagles, lammergeiers, wrens, ospreys,
and reed-buntings, but Liane de Pougy, Émilienne d'Alençon, Cléo
de Mérode and La Belle Otéro, untinted and smiling oleographs, also
stuffed.

Luckily next day *la chasse à l'izzard* was forbidden – '*Ces gens-là
tirent sur tout ce qui bouge*',[6] the curator had warned us. We took a taxi
in the dark as far as we could to the beginning of the climb; to the
point, that is, where a landslide had recently tipped the road halfway
down the mountain, and crept round the top of the gap, flashing our
torches as it was still pitch dark; then followed the road for a few
miles to the Hospice de France, shut up now, but thriving until the
land slid: the lineal descendant of one of the chief staging points kept
by the Templars and the Hospitallers for medieval pilgrims crossing
the Pyrenees to Montserrat and St James of Compostela. It was
daylight when we got there, and an enormous barrier of mountain
loomed; meadows and woods at first, then steeper and steeper rocks
and shale and scree, ending in sharp saw-teeth, leaning crags and
sweeps of snow. We scaled this ascent, delighted to see how much
better acclimatized we were. Andrew, blessing his stars he hadn't
chucked at Bouchero, now treads the ling like a buck in spring.

All this was on the cold and shadowy side of the range: we were
among bracken and moss and wild grasses white with rime; and
blasts swept down through the gaps; and when we got to what
seemed the final ledge, a new, grey, forbidding and unravelled palisade
towered above. We wound and climbed through a chaos of rocks and
passed *les Boums du Port*: they are four deep tarns of dark water
reflecting almost sheer precipices; chimneys, landslides and white
streaks of waterfall followed, until a final interminable-seeming zigzag
carried us through a cleft about three yards wide between two
soaring massifs. Nearly blown off our feet, we ran through it into

blazing sunlight and Spain and flung ourselves down on the hot
rocks. Eating apples, we gazed down into a wilderness of forests and
rocks and meadows going down in layers and many brooks and out
across a great ravine to Mount Aneto, the highest peak in the
Pyrenees, a jagged spike above glittering snow-fields ribbed with
fragments which have rolled down into the chasms, gathering snow
like ammonites. They are the famous peaks of Maladeta and
Fourcanada and beyond them lay Robin's Encantats. The other side
of this barrier, which joins the Pic de la Mine *via* the Col del
Infierno, lay the mountains of Catalonia, which had been progressively
revealed on the way up, range jutting beyond range, row after row
threading south-east, showing pale and paper-thin and at last not to
be discerned from a ghostly film of cloud. (Somewhere beyond, to
the east, lie Montaillou and Monségur and the ghosts of hundreds of
Albigensians, and the shade of Esclarmonde de Foix, all burnt; and
the little state of Andorra.)

But our side of this palisade was still Aragon. We had broken into
it when we ran through that narrow slot, the Port de Bénasque –
Vénasque – and, on the other side of the valley, we could see
another religious outpost, the Refuge of Rencluse. Circular tarns were
scattered about this chaos, among them one of the seven sources of
the Garonne! The water comes out of a rock, gathers in a pool, then
goes underground. Someone discovered this by pouring in tons of
red liquid; everyone for miles was on the lookout for its re-emergence
and, after a long subterranean journey, it duly came out, far away, and
proved the link. Nothing but peaks were in sight, except the valley
winding below. We went down through steep grazing land with
autumn crocuses and harebells, then followed the valley of the Esera
through endless-seeming woods until we came to the little town of
Bénasque. The inhabitants talk a mixture of Aragonese Spanish and
Pyrenean French – 'Bigorrois' here, I think – and Catalan, a patois
which few strangers can follow. They were great smugglers once,
perhaps they still are. There's a lovely Romanesque church and some
rather fine hidalgo-ish houses with broken pediments and corner
towers. It had been a terrific day so we went to bed after masses of
garbanzos and jars of purple ink.

Again we were driven up a valley in the dark, did half of yesterday's journey backwards in record time, then dropped into the tremendous descent by defecting down a forest road from the Hospice, through huge beech woods with rushing streams; then, at last, after legging it nearly all the way to Luchon like three phantoms in a muck-sweat, we found a small wayside bistro and ate and drank ourselves to a standstill. That night we had a final trout and Jurançon, and lots of delicious Corbières. It was the last day of September, with a railway strike threatened the day after, so we had to make a break for it.

Andrew was to fly back to London next morning, just after Xan and I had pushed on into Spain by rail. He came to see us off and spotted a headline somebody was reading in the Pau Station Bar: '*Pope John-Paul dies in the night after a reign of only three weeks.*'

Bright pink from the sun, he waved his check cloth-cap as we pulled out and we flourished frantically back. He had enjoyed it tremendously and so had we. He took my big rucksack back to London and now I'm as light as Xan who sensibly had only a small knapsack for the whole fortnight.

It was now Sept 29. We went over the Somport Pass, changed to a bus because of the stove-in tunnel, crossed the Spanish frontier at Canfranc and headed west through some peculiar Meteora-like Aragonese mountains to Huesca, then on through the falling dusk with a Spanish middle-class family clattering as loud as ducks all the way to Saragossa. Here we found a tiny room with two beds of different heights, one almost *under* the other; and after eating some quails in a nice cellar, tried to sleep but failed, owing to a room next door full of almost non-stop gas-bags who all snored fortissimo when they weren't arguing, and left, long before dawn, with shrieks and laughter, lugging what sounded like kegs and firearms.

We flew to Madrid and spent a long morning in the Prado; drinks in the Café Jijón; then, after a vain search for your sucking-pig restaurant, we had a delicious luncheon in a vaulted place hard by. Doing a bust, we took sleepers – vital after last night – and our train crossed the whole of Spain, bringing us to Ronda at eight in the morning. We found a taxi and tiptoed in as Magouche was still asleep and so was Essie, her mother (they hadn't got Xan's message). The house is absolutely charming and totally run-in. It's only four years since we all inaugurated it. Essie is the very straight upright-sitting widow of an Admiral who must have been very pretty (not the A.), a little vague and confusing in conversation and extremely nice. Magouche is very kind to her. She (M) has a heart of gold and is awfully good with Xan's once-in-a-blue-moon snicketty-snaque utterances.

We went for a picnic and a very long walk in the hills under a blazing Mexican-looking sky that reminded me of Peru. We looked across the sea to the Pillars of Hercules and Gibraltar and the Atlas Mountains. Tomorrow to Málaga to see Essie off to Biarritz and a grand specialist, then New York. Our triune plan is to walk for a few days in the Gerald Brenan country, beyond Granada in the Alpujarras, before I go to Tramores just before Janetta gets back; then Blighty on the 23rd or 24th.

I've read lots of Xan's Wind-Book[7] and it's absolutely tip-top. He's totally *emballé* by it, charts are everywhere, and excitement reigns, which I beg him to let infectiously rip. I bet it'll be a great success.

Every night, when lamps are lit, green baize is spread on the table by the fire and out come the Word-Making-and-Word-Taking squares you cut out. They are marvellous and treasured, and all are loud in praise of your differentiations between M's and upside down W's and *particularly* by the *short line* along the top of the Z's, making it impossible to muddle them with N's lying on their sides.

Love from all here and lots more from me.

Paddy

1 Although out of sequence, PLF's letter to DD has been included at this point because of its enclosure: an account of the Pyrenean walk, which was based on a letter PLF wrote to his wife at the time.
2 'And the moon has buggered off on top of everything else.'
3 'Quick! Quick! You've got only four minutes!'
4 In *Remembrance of Things Past*, Proust's narrator was taught as a child that it was incorrect to pronounce the 'n' in 'Tarn' and 'Béarn'.
5 Robin Fedden, *The Enchanted Mountains: A Quest in the Pyrenees* (1962).
6 'Those people shoot at anything that moves.'
7 First published in German as *Das Buch der Winde* (1988), and in English as *Aeolus Displayed, A Book of the Winds* (1991). PLF considered it Fielding's best work.

13 January 1979   Mani
[Postcard]

Did you know that Miss Mitford (author of *Our Village*)[1] could write
and read at the age of three? Also that, at the age of ten, she won
£20,000 in a lottery, by insisting on the number 2224, which added
up to her age?
    A thought for the day.
        P.

1 Mary Russell Mitford, who descended from the same Northumberland family
as DD, published her sketches of village life between 1824 and 1832.

1 February 1979   c/o Heck[1]
                                                       Lockinge Manor
                                                       Wantage

Darling Paddy,
    Alright then, I did know about Miss Mitford's nice win on the
lottery. But I freely admit I didn't know why she chose the numbers.
So you ½ win.
    (Note. When the French Lady wrote *Highland Fling*[2] Lady
Redesdale suggested it should be called Our Vile Age (see?) but Evie
had just done *Vile Bodies* so it wasn't.)
    Andrew says he is going to you for a day or two at the start of
his walk.[3] My word, it would be a comfort if you set off with him,
even if you can only manage a fortnight.
    Julian Jebb plans to do a documentary film for telly on the Fr
Lady. I do wonder if it's a good plan. We've sort of said yes &
now I'm getting cold feet. The letters at home are DYNAMITE,
can't let anyone just dig in at them in case, you know, & I'm
too lazy & TOO BUSY to do them myself but I can see I shall
have to.
    Much love
        Debo

1 Hester (Heck) Loyd (1920–2001). An old friend of DD. Married Major Guy Knight in 1944.
2 Nancy Mitford's first novel, published in 1931.
3 Andrew Devonshire's plan to walk through southern France into Spain the following spring did not materialise.

22 February 1979   Mani

IN TEARING HASTE

Darling Debo,

I *do* wish I could kick off with Andrew for the first bit, but I don't see how on earth I can.

I've already put off going to Petra with Joan, which I had promised to do year after year; and I've just managed to get going on the bit of the book which my muse had been refusing for months, as a pony refuses a fence . . . But I *will* try and join him later on for a bit.

I've just got a boast-card from Daph, depicting a Cranach portrait of a cove called Duke Heinrich the Pious[1] – doesn't look very pious to *me* – a terrible ruffian in slashed doublet and hose, a feathered hat at a tilt, sword half drawn, a dreadful scowl and a lurcher crunching some ugly trove at his feet, which she says looks exactly like me. I'm very concerned . . .

Tons of love, darling Debo, and more later

Paddy

1 Daphne Fielding had sent PLF a postcard from the Old Masters Picture Gallery, Dresden, of a portrait by Cranach the Elder of Henry IV the Pious, Duke of Saxony (1473–1541).

21 February 1979   Chatsworth
                                                    Bakewell

Darling Paddy,
    What are:

            Heart of Oak
            Hue & Cry
            Dan's Mistake?

    What is:

            Tender & True
            Spartan Sleeper

    Now then. Your turn to be shown up. I shall be furioso if you
know.
    Much love
        Debo

24 February 1979   Mani

Darling Debo,
    Heart of Oak is our ship.
    Hue and Cry are our men (i.e. *either* the late Ld Sefton, *or* Prof.
Trevor-Roper in a famous hotel off Piccadilly).[1]
    Dan's Mistake was ever getting into that den in the first place.
    Tender and True is the sirloin that cannot tell a lie, even under
your piercing gaze in the shop.
    Spartan Sleeper is a yoga-practising Greek peacefully snoring on
his usual spike-mattress.
    Would *Ruff's Guide to the Turf* (easy to lose your way in a club
that size) have helped me to the right answers? Do tell. Joan and I
have been scratching our heads like mad.
    Tons of love,
        Paddy

[1] Both men's first name was Hugh. The famous hotel off Piccadilly was the
Criterion.

17 March 1979   Chatsworth
                                                   Bakewell

Darling Paddy,

Now then. I LOVED your answers to my questions. Very *clever*, but *wrong*, one & all.

Hue & Cry, Heart of Oak, Dan's Mistake AND Queen of the Nile (which I forgot to put) are all GOOSEBERRIES.

Spartan Sleeper is an ONION.

Tender & True is a PARSNIP. And no doubt you wot of an excellent spud called Pink Fir Apple.

Have you read a book about the Sitwells called *Façades* by one John Pearson?[1] It is completely fascinating. I read it on orders from Uncle Harold[2] who suggests that this Pearson does the history of the Cavendish family. So I'm going to meet him next week to see what he smells like. The only trouble is that he wrote the life of Ian Fleming & I remember Ann loathing him, or would she have loathed anyone who set about that? I haven't asked her, as I don't want to be put against him yet. You might think the history of the Cav family is dim in the extreme but the funny thing is it isn't. Every generation produced one or two amazing people, i.e. Henry Cavendish of laboratory fame couldn't order a suit except when the moon was in a certain state, & some of the dukes were extremely rum & noteworthy.

Mark Amory is nearing the end of editing Evie's letters,[3] really Nancy's to him are marvellously good. 'Now Evelyn I am not, repeat not, a communist. I am a Christian, early if you like.' And he ends one 'and if by bugger you mean de-camp' – almost *too* sharp, eh.

Much love
    Debo

I'm going to be 59 in a minute. How can I have lived so long. Sophy is 22 tomorrow. Emma will be 36 next week.

---

1 John Pearson (1930–). Author whose books include *Façades: Edith, Osbert and Sacheverell Sitwell* (1978), *The Life of Ian Fleming* (1966) and *The Profession of Violence: The Rise and Fall of the Kray Twins* (1972).
2 After retiring from politics in 1964, Harold Macmillan took up the chairmanship of his family's publishing house, Macmillan Publishers.
3 *The Letters of Evelyn Waugh.*

19 March 1979   Chatsworth
                                                 Bakewell

Darling Paddy,

Since I know you will see the point of the gooseberry names, I have discovered a book called *The Anatomy of Dessert*, most beautiful print on ditto paper, written by one Bunyard, limited edition of 1000 signed by the author, 1923. But do you think they sold 1000? OH DEAR, if not.

The chapter on gooseberries is CLASSIC. Apparently 'it owes its development to the Midland workers who raised new seedlings for competition and so was the Big Gooseberry born in Macclesfield & other industrial towns'. Lord Brougham, Lord Derby, Lord Eldon, Ranter, Bribery, Queen Caroline, Prince Regent (dull claret red, very large oval), Glenton Green, Ocean, Lander, White Swan (slightly hirsute), Mitre, Careless, Antagonist, and in the Hairy Yellow class, Criterion, Gunner & Caterina. Red and very hairy are Ironmonger & Beauty.

It says 'the Gooseberry is, of course, the fruit par excellence for ambulant consumption. Freedom of the bush should be given to all visitors.' Do admit.

This is really a gooseberry letter so will leave it at that.

Much love

Debo

THE INTERNATIONAL PRIMATE PROTECTION LEAGUE

This came, usual thing asking for money. Poor Archbishops, I thought, feeling the pinch. But it turned out to be monkeys.

Mayday 1979   Athens

WRITTEN WITH ONE FOOT IN THE STIRRUP

Darling Debo,

I'm so sorry being such a rotten correspondent, just when you've been such a faithful and funny one. I loved all the names.

This is written in a bit of a hurry, chez Barbara and Niko Ghika in Athens, on a sort of shady roof garden embowered with exotic plants and in the distance I can hear the rhythm of communist choruses, baying like a chorus of trained jackals about a mile away to celebrate their favourite day. Give me maypoles.

Last Sunday night – Easter Sunday in the Orthodox Church – our car was blown sky high with an explosive charge and a length of fuse, with a red poster with hammers and sickles. I think they'd got the feast confused with Ascension Day. I think it's all part of an attempt of ours to erect a modest bronze plaque to Fallen Comrades in Crete. It was to go up at a certain Abbey in the island. The Abbot and monks all consented, there was a feast to honour the decision, but a week later, it was withdrawn: four men in cars had turned up, Communists from Heraklion, and frightened and threatened the monks. The same thing happened at *another* monastery, where our submarines used to surface on the same coast. Then a splendid village said *they'd* have it, and shoot anyone who tried to disturb it; and a few days later, BANG! at our doorstep. There is quite a powerful Comm. Party in Eastern Crete. The west is all O.K.: shows what a minority can do. The amount of telephone calls and telegrams from Cretan pals and Greeks in general – indignation, sympathy, etc, has made it almost worthwhile. But not QUITE, as insurance pays nought for Malicious Acts. Bugger them all.

Tons of fond love from
Paddy

1979   Sevenhampton Place[1]
(as from White's)   Swindon

Darling Debo,

It has been an orgy of *dictionary game* here, with croquet by day, and I thought I was doing rather well, when up turns a young shaver called Bannister – son of Sir Roger Bannister the Miler[2] – six-foot-six tall, bashes them through the hoops almost without looking and strides on to the next with the pace of the Long-Legged Scissor Man, leaving one rather pensive and humbled.

    Tons of fond love from
        Paddy

---

[1] PLF was staying with Ann Fleming.
[2] Roger Bannister (1929–). The first man to run a mile in under four minutes.

11 September 1979   Chatsworth
                                         Bakewell

Darling Paddy,

Did I tell you I've been *commissioned* to write a book.[1] What madness, but I've gone & signed a contract so there we are. V trusting of the commissioners, they think because my sisters can write I can too. Ha ha. They will be sorry soon.

    Much love
        Debo

---

[1] *The House: A Portrait of Chatsworth.* An account of restoration work undertaken by the Devonshires, together with excerpts from the 6th Duke of Devonshire's *Handbook* (1844). 'For one heady week it topped the Best Seller List in the *Evening Standard*.' (DD)

2 October 1979 Mani

Darling Debo,

We've got two owls here, very close to the house, who hoot like anything just beyond the sort of arched gallery where we dine. I'm very jealous of Joan, because she's an ace at imitating them through clenched palms, as I bet you can too. I can't do it, like being unable to whistle, because of two front teeth being too far apart, I suppose. Anyway, when Joan breaks into their dialogue, there is an amazed or embarrassed silence, then bit by bit they answer, until an enthusiastic three-sided exchange begins, which it is hard to break off. I can hear them now (8.30 p.m.).

I wish I could whistle like you, you're the most skilful whistler I've ever met. I think of you at the wheel, driving medium fast, and whistling 'There may be trouble ahead, let's face the music and dance'. Miraculous.

No more now, darling Debo, except tons of fond love from
    Paddy

I *say*! Great news about the book. You'll do something that's a bloody marvel, mark my words.

18 January 1980 Chatsworth
Bakewell

Darling Paddy,

I was in foul London, dropped into WH Smith to buy the sort of mags which are my drug & there facing me on a shelf called BEST SELLERS was Shanks's Europe[1] in paperback. *Oh good*. I bought one (imagine) because it's so light & handy & you never know I might have a read. You would have been so pleased to see the *display*. What a thrill.

Last night I went to AN OPERA. The second in my life. It was a plan of Andrew's in aid of the Putney Hosp for Incurables & good Cake came & turned it into a gala. One forgets between seeing her what a star she is & what incredible & wicked charm she has got. The Swiss conductor panicked & struck up 'God Save The Queen' when she was still walking round the back to get to her box & I heard her say Oh God & she *flew* the last few steps dropping her old white fox cape & didn't turn round to see what would happen to it.

She does a wonderful sort of super shooting-lunch dinner, brought from Clarence House & handed round by her beautiful footmen in royal kit, between the acts; the cheeriest thing out. We were a bit stumped though because when she'd gone home we had to go to the Savoy & have a second grand dinner with the organisers. It was a bit of a test forcing down sole after Cake's richest choc mousse. It's tough at the top, I can tell you.

Now I shan't go away again for ages because I must sit & work. The Editor[2] came (you didn't know I'd got one did you, well I have) & looked over my prep & didn't throw it in the fire which I thought he certainly would but told me to get on with it so I must because it's haunting me.

What I can't think is how people start books so I looked at two when I was staying at the Wife's. One was Whyte-Melville & began something like 'That's a natty suit' & the other was a thriller which began 'The body lay face down on the track.' Won't do, do admit. So I looked at yours. 'A splendid afternoon to set out.' NO GOOD TO ME. Bother. Do send some suggestions.

Do you know about the museum in Austin, Texas?[3] Well, don't throw anything away, doesn't matter what, they'll have the lot. They've got all Evie's stuff, & Osbert [Sitwell]'s, & letters saying things like 'Arriving on the 2.14 on Saturday so much looking forward to seeing you' are put under glass and *revered*. I saw five big cardboard boxes with MITFORD written on them, asked to see, & they were Decca's notes for her two most boring books (*Trial of Dr Spock* and *Kind & Usual Punishment*), big sheets of foolscap saying Call Helen 8 a.m. Well, really. So when I talked to her I said I'd seen them. She said she was about to throw them when Austin offered her $10,000 dollars for the twaddle. Amazing, eh.

Much love
Debo

I've found some good quotes in the D of Portland's bumper book,[4] but the best is good old Hobbes who said 'Reading is a pernicious habit, it destroys all originality of thought.'

1 DD's name for *A Time of Gifts*, from the Scottish expression 'to use Shanks's mare' meaning to walk.
2 Richard Garnett (1923–). DD's editor at Macmillan.
3 The Harry Ransom Center at the University of Texas at Austin, which holds an important collection of manuscripts of twentieth-century British, American and French authors.
4 William Cavendish-Bentinck, 7th Duke of Portland, *Men, Women and Things* (1937). 'A too discreet memory of what must have been a very charming man, married to the famous Winnie, whom I saw aged ninety-something, dressed in pale pink tulle, smothered in jewels and made-up to the eyes, at a Court ball – a sight never to be forgotten.' (DD)

[February 1980]   Mani

Darling Debo,

Here's a beginning. 'Chap I. Our crest is a mouldywarp and you may well ask what that is as I did, well, it's a mole and a more unsuitable emblem for my sisters and me it would be hard to hit on.'[1] I'll do better in my next.

Thank you so much for your letter, it's just what I needed, packed with splendid stuff and many laughs, so you've nothing whatever to bother about, re the book, I mean. Just let it rip. Now. If you want a pal to go through the thing during or afterwards, I'm your man. You probably want nothing of the sort; but I always let a stern though friendly eye peer through it, usually Joan's, sometimes several, just to get the full works. The thing is, they've got to be fond of one, know what one likes and give one a touch on the shoulder or elbow when one inadvertently puts something down one would regret rather. I get so close to the stuff (my own, I mean) that my eye and ear get a bit out and a detached loved one can be a godsend. I don't mean grammar or style or syntax because the publishers will do all that and, anyway, in your case, the less it's mucked about with the better.

The great thing about our Spanish trip was the actual journeys in late December. Xan and Magouche met us at Madrid, and we drove to the Escurial, and stayed there in the bracing cold. Have you seen it? Bleak and splendid is the word, half palace, half monastery, all granite, full of dead kings, with a bell that goes on vibrating half a minute after each toll. Next night at Ávila, the coldest town in Spain (but marvellous), it looks like one's childhood idea of Troy: a city entirely girdled by a battlemented city wall, the green hill now white under snow, with seven great gates and 88 towers. We huddled rugged-up over the charcoal brazier of our inn, sipping toddy and reading out loud. Then a swoop south to the huge Abbey of Guadeloupe, where a Black Virgin is enthroned above a high altar which is a haunt of smells and lace. Their abode above Ronda has become delightful, with thick walls, blazing fires, mountains all round, twenty minutes' walk to the amazing town, where a wonder-bridge spans a deep chasm full of swallows. One day we climbed up into some mountains and looked down on Gibraltar and the Mediterranean & the Atlantic hanging in space, with Jebel Musa, the *other* pillar of Hercules, on the Moroccan side; then the Riff Mountains; then the faraway glitter of the Atlas . . .

In mid-Jan, we set off for Portugal, driving through the cork woods of Estremadura where black swine rootled everywhere, dossing down at Évora; we made a dash to the Atlantic coast at Setúbal (where the B.V. Mary rides on an elephant on one of the church walls), and across the Tagus into stately Lisbon. Next stops, Cascais, Cintra and Nazaré (back on the coast) eating prawns by the bucketful and crabs encased in shells so huge and hard they give you weighty mallets to break in like a burglar. The beautiful old city of Coimbra next, with beautiful baroque library, on through castles and abbeys – especially Alcobaça, where a trout-stream dashes bubbling through the gigantic kitchen, and Batalha, where a Plantagenet Princess Philippa, daughter of John of Gaunt and mother of Henry the Navigator, lies in a splendid tomb. From Oporto we wandered upstream beside the Douro, sipping at many romantic quintas; then plunged on north, through Braga, and over the Spanish border again into the Galician mountains, to Santiago de Compostela, a maze of cathedrals, monasteries and lanes, filled, on the feast of St James the Apostle, who ended up here, with swarms of pilgrims. The place is

then wreathed in smoke from a censer several yards wide, which is
perilously swung by teams on the great Feast Days.

We broke up here, after a wonder trip. They drove on to León,
and Salamanca and then south. Joan and I flew to Madrid and
stopped a night in Barcelona, one of my favourite towns in the
world.

There's a grand hotel here called the Oriente, where they gave us
an enormous suite rather cheap. We soon saw why: no lights were
plugged in, rooms were choked with half-a-dozen towel-horses and
hat stands, the corners of the vast bedrooms were dark with cobwebs
and mousetraps ready-set, and crumbled biscuit. We ended a lovely
exploring day with a feast on the Ramblas (the main street), and I
saw Joan back and decided to continue my research, so had a brandy
and water in a lane in which every house was a bar. The kind host
stood me this. My next port of call was an Andalusian joint – I was
drawn in by the sound of clapping, and ordered a beer at the bar,
watching a party of twenty at another table, some of them gipsies,
strumming guitars, singing, clapping in rhythm, and occasionally
getting up to twirl and stamp out a *seguidilla, malagueña* or similar
dance; then shouting for more drink. What a nice way to spend an
evening, I thought. I was the only other customer. The host, a rather
seedy, smooth and bald figure, asked what I was. *Inglés* I said, and he
patted me on the back and pointed to an enormous moth-eaten
stuffed bull's head on the wall, over crossed banderillas. 'You see that
bull?' he said. 'I killed him in the ring in Valencia thirty years ago.
They don't have horns like that now.' 'What? You're a matador?' I
said. 'You've cut your pigtail?' (*Cortar la coleta,* cribbed from
Hemingway, means 'to resign from the ring'.) More slaps on the
back, then he left me. After half an hour I thought I'd move on
somewhere else, plonked down on the bar the equivalent of a quid
to pay for the beer I'd drunk and waited for the change. '£5 – in
pesetas,' the barman said. I said, 'What rot.' He burst into a frenzy
and all of a sudden I was surrounded by all the twenty from the
table, screaming and shaking their fists, closing in. I shouted 'Where's
the gentleman who was a matador?' – I could see him skulking in
the background – and there was a moment's silence. '¿What

matador?' they all cried. '¡Him!' I said, pointing, 'who killed that bull up there in Valencia thirty years ago!' They all turned on him at this: he'd never been in a bullring in his life, except in the 7/6ds. But they soon turned back on me, including the 'matador'. I remembered a useful phrase and cried '¿Where's your Castilian sense of honour?' '¿Donde esta su honor castellano?' This gave them another moment's pause, but only a moment. The barman, inside his rampart, stooped down and straightened up brandishing a club, three feet long, came out and started whirling it round his head, and towards me, all the others still shouting. I managed to get another moment's silence by pointing to the club, then to the top of my dome and saying '¡This gentleman desires to strike me with that piece of wood (didn't know "club") on top of my head! ¡Este señor quiere tocarme con esta pieza de leño *aqui* sobre mi *cabeza*.'; '¡Si! Si!' he cried, his eyes rolling round and round, breaking into a war dance. With really wonderful coolness (non-swanks) I smote the bar and said '*¡Not a peseta more!*' and walked firmly and quite slowly to the door.

Two of the party followed me into the street, not to clock me, but to reason with me, as my last exclamation had been '*¡Verguenza!*' viz. '¡Shame!' – perhaps fearing a complaint. I strode off in a seething fury, found three uniformed policemen coming down a side lane, and urged them to return to the bar, which they did. The people all came out into the street, rather cowed now; but apparently this particular brand of police weren't allowed inside premises, they were only for keeping order in the streets. They advised me to go to the police station, so off I set, feeling a bit milder, and suddenly thought, 'What the hell!', started laughing, and headed for the Ramblas, and was soon having a beer for about 2/6 at an amazing drugstore, full of all the low life of Barcelona. Lots of male and female tarts. As I finally left – about 4 a.m. now – you know Spanish hours – a marvellous-looking tart, eyelashes a foot long, standing between two queer pals, one tough, the other willowy, tapped me on the shoulder and said, '¿Which of them do you want? ¿Him? or ¿*Him*?' pointing at both of them in turn; then at herself, '¿Or perhaps *me*?'

Well, I mean to say . . .

When I got up to the suite, Joan was fumbling her way like a sleepwalker through the jungle of towel-horses to the bathroom, so I told her the whole saga, and our laughter must have put the wind up the mice in the wainscoting. I felt very set up by the whole evening.

No more now, I've gone on too long, and less legibly every second. Do send another smashing letter soon; and

Tons of fond love, as ever from
    Paddy

1 The Mitford family emblem is a mole.

13 March 1980   Chatsworth
(My Dad's birthday, he'd have been 103)   Bakewell

Darling Paddy,

Now then. What are Hoary Morning, Bedfordshire Foundling, Seek No Further, Dutch Minion, Hanwell Souring, Striped Monstrous, Reinette and Hall Door?[1] RSVP pronto. If you get the answer I will give you a prize, not quite sure what.

Woman is the undoubted star of J Jebb's film on the Ancient Dame of France. She is amazing. There's a good scene of her sitting on a tree stump on the banks of the Windrush reading the Chubb Fuddler.[2]

I am exactly like a headmistress about to retire, terribly boring & matter of fact & awful to look at.

Much love
    Debo

1 Varieties of apple.
2 In *Nancy Mitford: A Portrait by her Sisters*, a television documentary by Julian Jebb, Pamela Jackson read out a passage from Nancy Mitford's *Love in a Cold Climate* (1949) describing Uncle Matthew's annual treat: the arrival of the Chubb Fuddler, who sowed some 'magic seed' on the river, which brought the fish to the surface, 'flapping, swooning, fainting, choking, thoroughly and undoubtedly fuddled'.

9 April 1980   Mani

Darling Debo,

Back two or three days ago after your Uncle Harold's prize-collecting[1] visit to Athens. He was *glorious*. Such a relief to hear his short, funny, scholarly, charming and deeply moving speech – ex tempore, except for what looked like half a sheet of crumpled lav. paper which he peered at only once – after the booming of Madame Simone Veil,[2] foghorned from *twelve pages* of typescript, one predictable cliché after another. There were lots of banquets, pretty boring ones, including a solemn feast with the President of the Republic, which was nicer than it sounds, as his wife is the sister of our dead poet friend, George Seferis. All sorts of jaunts were involved. Last Monday we were all flown to Olympia, which Joan and Michael Stewart and I wandered round in the wake of Mr MacM., all of us nipping off into the pine trees for secret swigs of ouzo when the bearleading archaeologists weren't looking. Nice grandson Adam.[3] The next day, this small party were piled into a beautiful yacht, and sailed to Salamis – where Mr M. recited yards of Æschylus – then to the temple of Aphaia on Aegina where we had a glorious banquet of lobster and John Dory under the plane trees' shade.

A visit to Marathon followed next day and another feast, all great fun, organised by Michael Stewart and, a bit, me. The hero was a wonder throughout, v funny, *particularly* good on the Blunt scandal breaking the day your catalogue appeared in the Exhibition – 'sold out and reprinted same day!'[4] He also stimulated everyone by explaining that the war of Troy was nothing whatever to do with 'Helen', who was getting rather long in the tooth anyway, but all about a beautiful young mare that the Trojans had pinched from the Greeks – 'Can't you see her, being trotted past those old Trojans, a beautiful chestnut with four white socks and a blaze, and a flowing mane and tail? They wanted to improve their bloodstock! The Greeks came to get her back and that Wooden Horse business was just a horsebox!'

I do envy you all at Lismore.

Tons of love from

Paddy

1 Harold Macmillan, Chairman of the British Acropolis Appeal Committee, had been awarded the Onassis International Prize.

2 Simone Veil (1927–). French lawyer and politician, elected first female President of the European Parliament in 1979.

3 Adam Macmillan (1948–). Son of Harold Macmillan's only son, Maurice.

4 'I was in Fort Worth for the opening of the exhibition *Treasures from Chatsworth: The Devonshire Inheritance* at the Kimbell Art Museum in November 1979. The scholarly catalogue was written by Sir Anthony Blunt, Surveyor of the Queen's Pictures, who stayed at Chatsworth several times when working on it. I was often alone with him at meals and thought him cold, distant and uncommunicative. I turned on the television at dawn on the day of the grand opening party to see Blunt's angular face and the sensational news of his exposure as a Soviet spy. There were hurried discussions as to whether the catalogue should be withdrawn. It was not and it sold like hot cakes.' (DD)

29 July 1980   Chatsworth
                                                       Bakewell

Darling Paddy,

Will you do a *v* kind thing, write just how that tale goes re Derek Jackson[1] at a conference. Please. I know it's a pest, but I can't remember how it went.

No news. 6000 Scouts & Guides are camping in the park. Goodness knows what happens when darkness sets in.

Much love
    Debo

1 Derek Jackson (1906–82). The distinguished physicist, amateur jockey and heir to the *News of the World* married, as his second wife, DD's sister Pamela 1936–51. He subsequently remarried four times.

6 August 1980   Mani

Darling Debo,

Scene A Roman palace where an international congress on nuclear physics is taking place.

Time During a morning recess between lectures, a number of years ago.

Dramatis Personae Derek Jackson and another English delegate. They are strolling under the arcades during the break.

Other English Delegate 'I'm told we've got an extraordinary fellow delegate on this congress. English, too.'

Derek Jackson 'Really? Who?'

O. English Delegate 'Well, he's not only a brilliant nuclear physicist, but he was a famous pilot during the [war] – covered with decorations, and all that – and rode three times in the Grand National and dashed nearly won it. It seems he's one of two identical twins and got married to one of those Mitford girls, you know.'

Derek Jackson 'I say, before you go any further, I think I ought to tell you that I'm the chap in question.'

O. English Delegate 'Oh, really? I'm so sorry, I didn't quite catch what you were called when we were introduced.'

Derek Jackson 'Derek Jackson.'

O. English Delegate (after a pause) 'No, that wasn't the name.'

I'm in my outdoor study, which is a sort of shady bower, on one of the lower olive-terraces, viz., a criss-cross of laths on four uprights, covered with branches and creeping plants, cool and slightly dappled underneath. Two terraces down, two mules are audibly munching, and I see them swishing their tails. We're taking them up into the mountains for a picnic tomorrow. (Where the mules munch, there munch I.) Rock nuthatches hop about in the olive branches, and I find their name rather difficult to say. Why not rack nothutches, hitch nuckrackies, nockratch hickies etc.

No more now, as I see you're urgent, so off to the pillar-box.

Tons of love

Paddy

I'll address this envelope to Bolton, and wish I could climb in.

25 January 198[1]   Mani

Darling Debo,

Back to base again, and rather worried because absolutely no
news of Annie. Do, *like a saint*, sit down in a few seconds and
scribble *all*, as being in the dark makes one anxious.

Joan and I are just back from Syria, where we went with our old
travelling companions, Xan and his bride, Magouche. We took wing
to Damascus, a vast Oriental slum really, but marvellous all the same,
with the biggest and most beautiful mosque I've ever seen. One
simply sat at the foot of tremendous pillars, at the heart of hushed
acres of carpet, and mooned two hours blissfully away. Then across
the desert to Palmyra, a knockout, and on to the Euphrates, back
to Homs, and Hamah, a warren of souks with scores of giant
waterwheels turned by the green Euphrates. Then to the tangled
lanes and caravanserais, sunsets in the desert:

> But when the deep red eye of day
> is level with the lone highway,
> And some to Mecca turn to pray,
> and I toward thy bed, Yasmin,
>
> . . .
>
> Shine down thy love, O burning bright!
> for one night or the other night
> Will come the Gardener in white,
> and gather'd flowers are dead, Yasmin!*

Yes. Huge crusader castles, Krak des Chevaliers, tremendous
Greco-Roman theatres (Bosra), the fortress of the Jebel Druse. Xan
and I went to the Hammam in Aleppo, a great domed building put
up in 1200 AD by Nur-ed-Din el Shāhed el Mansūr, Saladin's
brother.[1] We were pounded to a pulp in the steam by brawny
Moslems, then wrapped in towels and gold hemmed robes, set on
divans with cardamom coffee and hookahs, where we reclined,
listening to the muezzins wailing next door, and sallied out into the
gloaming, the cleanest men East of Suez and north of the Hejaz, and

* From James Elroy Flecker's marvellous 'Hassan'.

the Bedouins of the souks followed our fragrant and disembodied progress with black and blazing eyes.

Now we're back here among the cats and the owls, cold as hell, but clear and starry.

No more now, darling Debo, except heaps of love from
    Paddy

---

1 PLF had been misinformed about the history of the building. The only Nur-ed-Din bath in Syria being in Damascus, it is likely he bathed in the thirteenth-century Hammam al-Nahasin, built by Saladin's son.

6 February 1981   Lismore Castle
                                           Co. Waterford

Darling Paddy,

Look where I am, at an unaccustomed time of year. Andrew came as per for the fishing & had a sort of frightening collapse, temp of 103, unable to walk, delirious. He's *much better* now, mending fast in that amazing way he has, extraordinary one for being really ill & very soon pretty well alright.

He's had many major worries lately. Chatsworth is being made into a charitable trust & the Poussin *Holy Family* is to be sold in April to underpin the trust & you can imagine the heart searching & thought & meetings & discussions & all which led up to the decision to do this.[1]

Enough of us, now to Ann.[2] I rang several times, the last time I got her as she had just got back from N Ireland, & was tired of course after the journey but the fact she was able to go there shows she's not too bad, eh.

The trouble was a twisted gut as far as I can make out which can easily be a killer & she damn nearly died. When I get back to England I'll have a proper talk to her & will write again.

Diana is in London for Feb. She's being marvellously good but misses him dreadfully. They'd been as one for nearly 50 years. Many a publisher is after her but she doesn't feel like work. (Perhaps you don't know Sir O [Mosley] died in Dec.)

Your outing sounds awful. You are lucky to like that sort of thing. (I KNOW Flecker, you needn't put it, FOOL.)

There is a musical called *The Mitford Girls*[3] coming on at Chichester in the summer. Really & truly what next. I've noted the script & it's perfectly alright, I mean nothing objectionable, so I don't mind. The man kindly spouted it out to me & Woman & Diana & the fellow who plays the piano is IT. He played for Noël Coward the last two years of N.C.'s life.[4] The tunes will do you in, the *theme song* is 'It Looks Like Trouble Ahead', & things like 'Ukulele Lady' loom large. I wish *you'd* been there.

I'm going to the rehearsals to try & get the voice & pronunciation right. It was *disastrous* in the telly of *Love in a CC*.[5]

I do wonder who'll be me. They'll have a job to get Diana right, & Woman for that matter.

I must stop & get ready for the Dr (who is an Irish Dr in a play, arrives with pills in his hot hand, flies out in a hurry because it's Clonmel Races shouting Give him two sleeping pills AND TAKE ONE YOURSELF).

Much love

Debo

1 The painting was sold at Christie's on 10 April 1981 and fetched £1,165,000.
2 Ann Fleming had cancer, initially diagnosed as a twisted gut.
3 By Caryl Brahms and Ned Sherrin (1981).
4 Peter Greenwell (1929–2006). The composer and pianist was Noël Coward's accompanist during the last decade of the Master's life.
5 An eight-part ITV adaptation by Simon Raven of Nancy Mitford's novels *The Pursuit of Love* (1945) and *Love in a Cold Climate* (1949). 'Hideous children who swallowed their words, a Hons' Cupboard with NO LINEN in it, *oh dear.*' DD to PLF, 4 November 1980.

29 March 1981   Chatsworth
                                                         Bakewell

Darling Paddy,

Any chance of you looming? I go to Lismore on 2 April till 30th. COME.

The editor has been. Richard Garnett, son of David,[1] that's all.
Do be impressed. The terror of it. But he was v v nice & we
sat with scissors & paste & chopped up a photo-ed copy of the
Bachelor Duke's *Handbook* & stuck the bits we like above my bits
describing the same bits of house. Good sport. Now I've got to look
sharp & finish it, the outside & some more boring details. What a
business it all is.

Lismore, 3 April.
Somehow got stuck, & now I'm here. Oh, Whack, the beauty of this
place, & suddenly it's fine & WARM (well, sort of) & everything
two weeks early & busting out all over.

I jolly well knew I was in Ireland when the first garage I came to
in Wexford had OPEN & CLOSED signs both up. A bit further on I
asked someone how far to Waterford. Eight miles he said. His mate
said it's 28. First man said 'I knew there was an eight in it somewhere,
God Bless.' All in one sentence.

I do love them but I do wish they'd stop shooting people's knees.
It's such a *horrid* trick.

Much love,
Debo

---

[1] David Garnett (1892–1981). Bloomsbury author whose books include *Lady into
Fox* (1922) and *Aspects of Love* (1955). Became Duncan Grant's lover in 1914; married
to Ray Marshall 1923–40. After his wife's death, he married Angelica Bell, the
daughter of Duncan Grant and Vanessa Bell.

7 April 1981   Mani

Darling Debo,

I would have loved to come to Lismore, but I *can't*. I'm getting a
move on with this wretched book[1] at last, after dragging my feet as
usual. I long for it all to be finished, and me free. I was an idiot to
leave it all so long. It seems to be all right, thank goodness. I'm a bit
nervous, after everyone being so nice about Vol. I.

The frogs are making a terrible noise. A curlew should be imposed.

I wish you would come here sometime. I think, quite apart from anything else, one ought to know *how* and *where* one's friends live, then one can imagine what's going on. Otherwise they disappear into a sort of void until you see them again.

Tons of love

Paddy

Library book-title: 'WILD OATS, A cereal story' . . .

1 *Between the Woods and the Water.*

7 June 1981   Chatsworth
                                               Bakewell

Darling Paddy,

I went to lunch with Ann at Sevenhampton three days ago, & hasten to write & tell you what I expect you know, that she is very ill.

Once you have got over the shock of her poor twisted face everything appears to be normal. Alas it is not.

She was in bed so I did not see her walk but I know it is a struggle & she has one of those things to lean on to help her along. She is blind in one eye & I noticed someone has brought her books printed in a v big type so presumably the remaining eye is not perfect.

The word *lumbago* which she speaks of reminded me of Nancy, who used to think the awful pain in her back was that. The truth is the wretched thing is all over her. No one knows how fast it will choose to move. It may be more or less static for some weeks, but it may not. At the moment she is a bit better, seeing people & apparently quite pleased to do so. Her d in law told me they have taken her off the drugs which made her feel so awful, so that is why she is sort of brighter.

I am very sorry to write like this but I know she is one of your greatest friends, & I guess you're coming to England soon?? DO let me know your plans. I will be here nearly all the time except for a

few days in early July when I go to my good Wife for the preview
& the first night of *The Mitford Girls* at Chichester, what a lark. I
have got to go & tell them how to speak, to say 'orphan' for 'often',
'frorst, corf & orf', & try & make them resist host*ess*. What a hope.

Much love
Debo

17 June 1981   from Corfu

IN HASTE

Darling Debo,

How miserable about Annie. I had heard roughly the same just a
few days before from Pat Trevor-Roper,[1] who came to stay for a few
days. He, too, thinks that things are uncertain, and may end abruptly;
so I plan to come to London early in July, and will make a sign at
once.

Saddest news last night, about Philip Toynbee's[2] very sudden death
from the same beastly thing.

I went to Crete for the 40th anniversary of the battle, which was
marked by all sorts of ceremonies, lots of v nice Aussie, N.Z. and
British veterans, Scots Guards pipers in plaids and silver and feather
bonnets, Maoris blowing 'The Last Post' till one's hair stood on end.
Lots of old Cretan hands were there. I wish Xan had been, and
would have urged him more if I'd realized the scale of the thing.

I had to make an address[3] in Greek at the unveiling of an SOE
monument at Heraklion, to which we had all contributed. Pat T-R
had told me exactly what to do, to overcome nerves: a double
whiskey quarter of an hour before, no more no less. I had it in a
little bottle in my pocket, and threw it down the red lane in the loo
of the Defence Minister's private bomber, just before we landed at
Heraklion. It did the trick! There were lots of troops in hollow
square, masses of archbishops and incense, thousands of old friends,
rolling drums, crashing arms etc. When Avéroff, the Def. Minister was
summoned to unveil the monument, he unexpectedly shouted for

me, and we paced across the square together, each pulled a string and down flopped the British and Greek flags. He made a short address, then led me to the mike, and Pat's formula must have been just right as I got through it in ringing tones with *not a single mistake*! It seems to have been a success, and when the public ropes were down, old whiskered pals broke through, and one was mobbed pretty well black-and-blue with hugs. No dry eyes anywhere, all a-clank with medals, full-size ones for the first, and probably last, time in one's life. It was very moving.

Joan and I motored here a few days ago, where we found the Ghikas and Jacob & Serena Rothschild. They buggered off two days ago, and have been replaced by Stephen Spender,[4] hot foot from China where he has been travelling all over the place with David Hockney.[5] He doesn't look awfully well but is as nice as ever. His wife Natasha rolls up this evening. I forgot to mention that the great point of our coming was the presence of Dadie Rylands, in order to be here with him. He's a glory and I bet you would love him, 82, swims like a fish, pink cheeked, blue eyed and enchanting. He's the most wonderful reader-aloud in the world. It has been a new Trollope novel every year – *Phineas Redux* this year, but I won't go into that – and he does all the voices marvellously – Phineas, Dss of Omnium, Ld Cantrip, Mr Chaffanbrass the barrister, Ly Laura – last night we had twenty pages of a marvellous murder trial scene at the Old Bailey, full of surprises and sensations. We wait for reading time of an evening exactly like children.

Home in a few days time, taking the Spenders with us.

No more now, Debo darling, except see you soon and tons of love from

Paddy

---

1 Patrick Trevor-Roper (1916–2004). Quiet-voiced, bookish and learned eye surgeon, author of *The World Through Blunted Sight: An Inquiry into the Influence of Defective Vision on Art and Character* (1970).
2 Philip Toynbee (1916–81). PLF and the writer were both in the Intelligence Corps during the war. Their shared interest in literature, history and late-night parties created an enduring friendship.

3 PLF enclosed a copy of his address with this letter.
4 Stephen Spender (1909–95). The poet and novelist married Natasha Litvin (1919–), a concert pianist, in 1941.
5 David Hockney (1937–). The painter and Stephen Spender recorded their travels in *China Diary* (1982), illustrated by Hockney with photographs by Spender.

24 June 1981   Chatsworth
                                               Bakewell

Darling Paddy,

Your speech is a wonder. V brave to have the whiskey, think if it had made you sort of different, like it would have me. It must have been v moving, floods all round.

If you come do come to *The Mitford Girls* at Chichester.

I've found a book in the library here I long to show you.

Much love
    Debo

[July 1981]   Mani

Darling Debo,

After *three days* of trying to get through to Pat Trevor-Roper (and he to me) to find out whether Annie would be up to seeing me – or anyone – we have just got through. He tells me that when he went there on Sunday, she was in a coma and under deep sedation and could hardly recognise him, and that the whole thing is only a question of a few days.[1] Things being so, he strongly advised against my coming back, rather indicating that it would be hopeless under the present circumstances, and, very possibly, too late . . .

You can imagine how one feels, as you must too. I can't get over the idea that I'll never see her again. I wish I'd simply dashed back, as you suggested, but she was very down when Pat was here, and he said wait; then not a word for days and days, during which she had a brief recovery, when she saw Robert and John Wells.[2] I wish I too.

You've been marvellous keeping me informed of things. Do try and ring or send a telegram if there's any change, as they say.

　　Lots of love,
　　　　Paddy

1 Ann Fleming died on Sunday 12 July.
2 John Wells (1936–98). Actor, satirist and founder member of *Private Eye* who appeared as Q's assistant in the film of *Casino Royale* (1967).

19 July 1981   Chatsworth
                                            Bakewell

Darling Paddy,

　　I found your letter today, when I got back from Ann's funeral.

　　OH DEAR. What is there to say, except how she will be missed & what a hole there will be where she was.

　　The funeral was awful. There is nothing like a country churchyard for killing the mourners. I drove down from here & got there very early & sat in the car & then in the church. Oh dear. The flowers, & the churchyard flowers & the people all looking anxious & no one knowing where to sit. Her sister arrived, ridiculously smart in a hard black shiny straw hat, she's gone *tiny* & looked like a wretched ill bird of the crow family, not my favourite.[1] When you think how they didn't like each other I thought how daft *form* is.

　　No one in the congregation were CHURCH GO-ERS so didn't know when to stand, & the clergyman had to tell them – *honestly*. How she would have taken in all that.

　　The burial part seemed to be done very quickly & was over by the time I got to it, thank goodness. We all went to the house for lunch. It made me think of what Robert said about Philip Toynbee's funeral, & how he kept expecting him to come in & thought he'd just been left behind in the churchyard by mistake.

　　I always thought Sevenhampton a very sad house, but really yesterday it was hauntingly so. After a bit people started talking & laughing like one has to. Brainstorm[2] was very tight & said he has

decided to buy a house in Derbyshire so I rushed to the car &
fetched the *Derbyshire Times* & we looked at the For Sales & I think
he's rather decided against it. *Raving.*

Goodman[3] looked huge but drained, hunched up in a chair too
small for him.

The curious thing was there was a service for Philip in London at
the same time. So Robert didn't come. The other notable absentees
were Pat T-R & Lucian. Perhaps Pat had to do some ghoulish
operation & Lucian sort of wouldn't be there, would he.

It's no good going on but oh what a gap. And as I looked at the
people there I thought how I should never see any of them again
because it was Ann who gathered them all up. I hope Mark Amory
& Jacob[4] & one or two others will be exceptions.

Decca went to Philip's service. It is v v sad for her because he
was really the only friend left in England. She went to *The Mitford
Girls*. I went to the 1st night and a preview. It's dotty of course,
spindly actresses being us, & getting everything just wrong. How
could they be expected to get anything right.

It seems to be an extraordinary success & got a standing ovation
on the royal 1st night charity perf. They talk of it going to London.
Too odd for words. I looked first at the floor & then at my watch,
so did P Jebb. The good thing to be said for it is that there is
nothing unpleasant, just STOOPID.

Richard Garnett (editor) has taken my book, a v odd feeling
which you must know all too well (or all too little as we know how
your books hang about when it comes to *finishing*). I suppose he'll
come back saying he wants it all different. Never mind, it's like the
theatre, we never need go again.

Much love
Debo

---

1 Laura Charteris (1915–90). Ann Fleming's younger sister. Married to Viscount
Long 1933–42, to 3rd Earl of Dudley 1943–54, to Michael Canfield 1960–9 and
to 10th Duke of Marlborough in 1972. 'She seemed to me to be hard and a bit
too smart, but with hindsight this may have been unfair.' (DD)
2 Raymond Carr (1919–). Historian and Fellow of St Antony's College, Oxford.
'When my daughter Emma was up at Oxford in the early 1960s, she nicknamed

her popular tutor "Professor Brainstorm", after the "Beachcomber" character in the *Daily Express* "By the Way" column.' (DD)

3 Arnold Goodman (1913–95). After Ian Fleming's death, the large and powerful solicitor helped his widow sort out her husband's financial affairs and had become a close friend.

4 'Thankfully I did not lose Jacob Rothschild. Instead, he and Serena have become great friends of mine. When Chairman of the National Heritage Memorial Fund, he often came to Chatsworth to oversee the regeneration of Buxton, which was a grateful beneficiary of the fund. His own achievements at Spencer House and Waddesdon are a lesson to anyone in charge of a family legacy – but to me the garden of The Pavilion, where they live, is the all-time treat.' (DD)

3 August 1981   Chatsworth
                                                      Bakewell

Darling Paddy,

Here are the last pages of my BOOK, finished & gone. I KNOW you want to see how it worked. Well, anyway, here it is. Too late to say it's all wrong.

I must say I'd rather write a book than read one any day. Not so sure about the victims who are supposed to read mine. Can't help that, I never would have done it if it hadn't been ordered by Uncle Harold.

You would have loved the Buckingham Palace party[1] on Mon night. All trad to begin with, a huge crowd of people, got two OMs at once viz. Freddie Ashton[2] & Solly Zuckerman,[3] all kinds of freaks like Harold Wilson[4] with his garter stitched on to a sort of blazer like house colours for a cricket match, Sybil Cholmondeley queen of all she surveyed, the Queen ditto, the Bride v fascinating-looking & so on & forth. Come 1.30 & Andrew insisted on leaving so I didn't see the scrum of dowagers fighting for blue & silver balloons with Prince of Wales feathers painted on them. Emma said it was like a Brixton riot only the rioters were *white*-haired ancients fighting for grandchildren & gt grand children at home. Lovely.

Much love
     Debo

1 To celebrate the wedding of the Prince of Wales and Lady Diana Spencer.
2 Frederick Ashton (1904–88). The dancer and choreographer was awarded the Order of Merit in 1977. 'He was the best company imaginable and a brilliant mimic – he practically turned into the Queen Mother when acting her arrival at Covent Garden, as he did Queen Victoria, seated in Andrew's grandfather's Bath chair in the garden at Edensor House.' (DD)
3 Solly Zuckerman (1904–93). Scientist and public servant, President of the London Zoo 1977–84, awarded the OM in 1968.
4 The former Prime Minister was made a Knight of the Garter after his retirement in 1976. He was suffering from symptoms of Alzheimer's disease although his condition was not yet publicly known.

15 April 1982   Lismore Castle
                                                   Co. Waterford

Darling Paddy,

I've got a new friend. Met him at Ann Fleming's once. He used to be keeper of drawings & manuscripts at the BM, retired of course like everyone (who isn't dead as well) called John Gere.[1] He really is a good egg, came to Chatsworth to look for some Raphaels or something or other & we ended up going on mystery trips to the Tram Museum (shut) & such places. He found some dire mistakes in my book. One in a Latin inscription which you can imagine yours truly had somehow overlooked, just in time to get the damned things put right. He's got a wife, never invited by Ann, but she & Lady Abdy[2] got up an exhibition re the Souls which might have been jolly had one been in London & able to tear oneself away from Peter Jones.

This place is as beautiful and odd as ever. The town is a bit sad, more shops shut, no tourists (longed for by all) because of the fantastic prices & the fact that people think the south of Ireland is the same as the north. Inflation is 23%. You get fewer than four stamps for a £1. It's 26p each, even for a letter to the next village. Goodness knows how people with big families feed their children. It must be as difficult now as it was when the wages were 30/– a week. And so on.

No word of R Kee, but I was sitting in the beautiful new

hairdresser's salon (The Golden Scissors) in Main St above Crotty's
Bar Best Drinks, wireless full on as per, & a man started on about his
book[3] & how we must all buy it pronto, well of course.

Emma has been made head of all the National Trust gardens, a
great compliment, eh. Ld Antrim would have been pleased. She's got
120 head gardeners to deal with. Rather her than me.

Much love
Debo

I said to the gardener here It all looks very nice. Ah he said When
it's open in the summer *people of all nationalities are charmed with it.*

1 John Gere (1921–95). Curator at the British Museum Department of Prints
and Drawings 1946–81. Married art historian Charlotte Douie in 1958.
2 Jane Noble; art dealer and co-author with Charlotte Gere of *The Souls: An
Elite in English Society 1885–1930* (1984). Married Sir Robert Abdy in 1962.
3 Robert Kee, *Ireland: A History* (1980).

5 May 1982   Mani

ONE FOOT IN THE STIRRUP

Darling Debo,

There was a bit – v. nice – about you and the book in *The Times*
the other day. *I do pine for it.* It read gloriously I thought.

We went to Athens for all sorts of splendid ceremonies for the
award of the Onassis Prizes[1] (I'm on the committee, heaven knows
why. I seldom open my mouth), presidential luncheons etc. Then
back with fellow committee member Michael Stewart & Ghikas.
Now I'm off – tomorrow – to Budapest (a) to see an old Hungarian
pal, and (b) go through a brief refresher course in a hired car across
the Great Hungarian Plain, then over the Rumanian border into
Transylvania, so to Bucharest, where I'll see Balasha's sister.[2] I'm very
excited about this. My memories of the *middle-distance* were getting a
bit blurred. One remembers skylines – chimneys, steeples, mountains,
forests – and foregrounds – prams, elephants, trams, wheelbarrows –
but the in-between past dissolves in a kind of haze.

I'm so glad you cleave to J Gere. We became great pals chez Annie. I hope I was enthusiastically remembered by you both. You cruelly never mentioned it.

Do please send lots more news. I'll be back here in a fortnight.

Meanwhile, tons of love,

Paddy

---

1 Awarded for contributions to Greek 'culture, environment and social achievement'.

2 Princess Elena (Pomme) Cantacuzène (1900–83). Married Constantin Donici, a Moldavian boyar, in 1924.

28 May 1982   Mani

Darling Debo,

I've just had such an odd time. Feeling I wanted to have another look at my 1934 itinerary for Vol II of *A Time of Gifts*, I flew to Hungary a fortnight ago. There was no room in any hotel, so the Tourist people, in a way they have in Budapest, billeted me on a private citizen, a frightfully pretty fair-haired one called Aggy – short for Agatha – who turned out to be a great pal of your wonderful Bill [Stirling], and of P Stirling.[1] We peered at her album of snaps of the Highlands and stags and kilts. Wasn't that rum?

I drove 1000 kilometres in E Hungary, in a hired Volvo, all over the Gr. Hung. Plain, over which I'd trudged – and ridden – as a stripling, and the Hortobágy, with its troops of semi-wild horses, then to north, where I sat with chance acquaintances drinking delicious red wine in a maze of caves dug out of the mountain. Most of my halts were at places I had stayed at of old, a series of minor Bridesheads really, but with all the Grafs fled long ago, except one, called Hansi Meran[2] who I last saw when he was 12, and I 19, staying with his parents. He had been arrested when returning from the war in the East by some Russians, who sent him to Siberia for 10 years, on no charge at all. On his return he married a v nice village girl, settled in the village in a cottage outside the rambling baroque Schloss at Körösladány, and worked in the commandeered

fields. He was enormously tall when I saw him now, Marie
Antoinette's biggest gt. gt. gt. gt. nephew, grizzled and weather-beaten,
rather shy with v nice blue eyes. He remembers my visit in April '34
perfectly. A Biedermeier table had been salvaged from the Schloss
(also a portrait of gr, gr etc grandma Empress Maria Theresa) and he
said 'You used to sit at that all day writing away in a green book.'
(Diary. I've got it by my side today.) A visiting sister called Marcsi,[3]
who lives in Vienna, was there – thirteen, when last glimpsed 48
years ago, now a great-grandmother. We talked about their parents –
his mother was a great beauty called Ilona Almásy, and their v nice
governess, a coz called Christine Esterházy.

I lurked round two other places – now roadmenders' storages –
then slipped over the wall of a vast place called Okígyós, where I had
played bike-polo of old. A school now, but with all the box-hedges
neatly trimmed, vast trees, millions of doves, tulip trees and Magnolia
grandiflora, lakes, reeds, old Slovak gardeners who talked fondly of the
old Wenckheim incumbents, when I dared to tackle them in German.

Then back to Budapest and my nice landlady, and took wing for
Bucharest, hired another car, and drove to where Balasha's sister
Pomme lives and teaches English & French to commissars' offspring,
near the Carpathians. Stayed 24 hours, talking night and day; then on
to Transylvania, which is where I had gone after the Hungarian
Plain.

This was another series of Bridesheads: they had all been the
dwellings of Hungarian landowners who had stayed on when
sovereignty was transferred after the First World War. (All gone now,
of course.) I slunk round *seven* of these, one or two pretty Palladian
ones, but nearly all loony bins now, with wild-eyed figures mopping
and mowing among the tree trunks and up and down the
balustraded steps. One of these had been the setting of a short
romance and I felt very queer. The last one was a big, late medieval
place with giant chestnuts, pink and white candles, whose owner,
Elemér[4] (85 now) I'd seen in his Budapest tenement a few days
before. It's now an experimental nursery for bamboo and similar
plants, inhabited by v nice peasants. In all those places the locals were
thrilled to learn I had been a pal of the old folks. These ones said,

'Have some baratzk made out of Mr Elemér's plums. Please give him our respects. We feel guilty living in a stolen house, but it's not our fault.' Unlike Hungary, the repression in Rumania is fiendish. I gave lifts to dozens of workmen & peasants. *All* complained bitterly *if they were alone* but sickly in praise if there were more than one. I couldn't bear the idea of returning to Baleni in Moldavia, the home of Balasha and half her family. You know all about that . . .

Tons of love from
Paddy

[1] Peter Stirling (1913–94). Brother of David and William Stirling.
[2] Count Johann (Hansi) Meran (1921–94). Married Ilona Farkas in 1960.
[3] Countess Maria Meran (1920–92). Married Béla Rudnay de Rudnó et Divék-Ujfalu in 1944 and had ten children.
[4] Elemér von Klobusiçky (1899–1986). Married Juliana Apponyi de Nagy-Apponyi in 1943.

16 July 1982   Mani

Darling Debo,
    A week after I got back from Hungary and Rumania, Joan and I suddenly decided to go to Crete, taking the car to the west end of the island by a ferry. I can't tell you how moving it was. We went to countless villages that were our haunts. Hugs, whiskers, tears! Many are oldsters now, and many dead; but it really was glorious. The only trouble was having to have 15 meals a day. *Every single house* in a village had to be visited, bread broken, meat carved, wine poured, lest the owners pined away. Some of the people in the west I hadn't seen for nearly half a century, in remote villages perched like eagles' nests, said: 'O dear, how *thin* you've got.' Others in the east a week later said: 'You *have* filled out, oh dear, oh dear . . .' Presents galore, the boot of the car was filled with delicious cheeses the size of cartwheels, demijohns of marvellously pure and heavenly wine, red and white, wicker-covered gallons of mulberry raki, baskets of raisins, walnuts and almonds, two shepherd's crooks. Most of us stood godfathers to Cretan friends' children. All my goddaughters are now forty-something,

with vast broods of their own. (We mostly stood godfather to little girls, as in the Orthodox Church children with the same godparent are not allowed to marry each other. The god-relationship is thought more binding than blood, and the idea of such a marriage worse than incest.) We both felt re-born by the whole trip.

I've just been sorting out Annie's letters for Mark Amory,[1] only holding back ones that are terribly wicked about people, so damaging – oddly enough, there were not as many of those as I feared. I know quite a lot are missing, and will probably turn up as bookmarks. Early ones I probably threw away, worst luck, not realising then that it's a great shame to throw some people's away. My word, they are good and funny, aren't they, the quickest and most direct form of communication I've ever seen, all of them surprising, all of them brilliant, several of them rather sad, none of them with a flicker of self-pity. I wonder if you've been on the same task.

Just before the Hung. Rumanian journey, a Persian singer called Shusha[2] – very nice, known years ago – turned up here to take notes for an *Observer* profile of yours truly (due in Sept). I bet it'll be a bit embarrassing. *Can't wait.*

Finally and most important. Please write.

With tons of love from
    Paddy

1 *The Letters of Ann Fleming*, edited by Mark Amory.
2 Shusha Guppy (1940–2008). Iranian-born writer and folk singer.

1 August 1982   Chatsworth
                                                  Bakewell

Darling Paddy,

Thanks v much for yours. Oh, what has happened to the wretched TOME. I sent it in June.

It was published last Thurs, 29 July. All that week I was *frenzied*, all of a frenzy, pushed from BBC to ITV, to British Forces Network to Radio London, Radio Reading, man from *Daily Express*, another from Liverpool Something, *Irish Times* man never turned up, Radio

Yet Another, John Dunn prog, *Round Midnight* prog . . . RAVING, but the all-time ego trip, people *taking one seriously* (well, almost), Foyle's Lunch, a Phone-In radio prog . . . I kept thinking the French Lady wouldn't have done this but of course it was terrific fun & v bad for the character.

The first was something called *Start the Week* with Richard Baker, 9 a.m. on Mon. Four interviewers for four victims. Idiotic, because the interviewers, all pros who worship the sound of their own voices or they wouldn't be pros, took over & talked over one another. One was a psychiatrist with all the maddening patter of his trade, one read a long typed paper pretending he wasn't reading with a lot of clever quotes & one was a sharp woman who liked scoring off the victims.

Signed at *Boots in Chesterfield* on Sat & don't laugh but there was a queue & I signed away for an hour & bang went 248 books, all their stock. Terrific fun because we've got heaps of friends in Chesterfield and they all turned up.

Now to Sheffield for Radio Sheffield, thence to Nottingham for Radio Trent. What a very strange life.

Anyway all this boasting is for your eyes only because I know you understand & I also know you understand how terrifically unfair it is because think of the professors who are busy writing real books & just because of my daft name & address mine whizzes. Oh well, that's life but it IS unfair.

As for Ann Fleming's letters, mine from her are v v good & exactly her talking but unpublishable. They wd cause offence & worse to all & sundry. Too soon?

Diana is v well indeed thank God, when you think that last Sept she was paralysed, couldn't feed herself or anything.[1] She is a dr's triumph. Rare bird I know but as one only hears the rotten things done in hosps one jolly well ought to laud a success like her. She looks v beautiful & her shaved hair has come back curly, so odd, never been that in her 72 years.

WHEN ARE YOU COMING THIS WAY?

Much love

Debo

Have boldly put a couple of reviews. Please excuse all this boasting. *It's gone to my head.*

1 Diana Mosley had been successfully operated on for a brain tumour.

17 November 1982   Mani

Darling Debo,

I've just come across the following in a letter of July 28th 1931, from Carrington to L. Strachey. I expect you know it, so this·is just in case.

'. . . I went with Julia [Strachey] to lunch with Diana [Guinness] today. There we found 3 sisters and Mama Redesdale. The little sisters were ravishingly beautiful, and another of 16 very marvellous and grecian. I thought the mother was rather remarkable, very sensible and no upper classes graces.

We were half an hour late . . . Mercifully lunch was late as they had only just come back from Stonehenge.

The little sister was a great botanist, and completely won me by her high spirits and charm.'[1]

All right, eh?

Love,

Paddy

1 *Carrington: Letters and Extracts from her Diaries*, edited by David Garnett (Jonathan Cape, 1970), p. 473. Lytton Strachey and Carrington at Ham Spray were neighbours of DD's sister Diana and her first husband, Bryan Guinness, when they lived at Biddesden Manor in Wiltshire.

15 January 1983   Chatsworth
                                                          Bakewell

Darling Paddy,

I'm going to Houghton[1] tomorrow, to shoot on Monday. Sybil is 89 this month. I haven't seen her for *two years*. How mad when in the nature of things she can't go on forever. One ought to make monthly appointments with people like her.

John Pearson's history of the Cavendish family is very bad.[2] Isn't
it a waste of a good subject. Journalese I think it's called, sarcastic,
generally *narky*. It reads as if he hated writing it, a schoolboy forced
to do a boring essay. *What a pity*. He is so nice. I can't think why he
had to write it like that.

Must stop & get my hair done for Sybil.

Much love

    Debo

[1] Houghton Hall; the Marquess of Cholmondeley's Palladian house in Norfolk.

[2] *Stags and Serpents: A History of the Cavendish Family and the Dukes of Devonshire*
(1983) was generally well-received.

? February 1983   c/o Wife, Bignor Park

Darling Paddy,

Do note the enclosed.[1] He is obviously a terrific fan of yours.

I wrote to say how I'd loved the comp. & how you were panting
for the results.

Now I want him to have a comp. inspired by Decca cheating the
American telephone people out of paying, it goes like this: –

If you put a personal call in America & the fellow you want
isn't available you don't pay. Right. She was in New York. Bob
[Treuhaft] was in Calif. Their dog, Coco, went missing. She was
worried to death till the phone rang & the operator said 'I have a
person to person call for Mr Coco Isback.' 'Sorry he's out & can't
take the call,' she said but happiness set in & all for nothing. Of
course it's easier in America where outlandish names are normal. I
mean what a hope of persuading an English tel operator of a Coco
Isback.

Much love

    Debo

[1] The enclosed letter has not been found.

18 March 1983   Mani

IN FEARFUL HASTE

Darling Andrew,

This is just a brief note to say I'm putting together a book of odds and ends – including our Peruvian Adventure[1] – and I'm going to dedicate it to you and Debo. I wanted to dedicate one to each of you, sometime. But then I may be run over by an Athenian tram, or topple over a cliff, with the thing dedicated to no one, so this is better than that.

All the best, dear Andrew,
Yours ever
Paddy

1 *Three Letters from the Andes.*

10 April 1983   Chatsworth
                                                 Bakewell

Darling Paddy,

Well, a book dedicated to Andrew & me. *What a wonder.* Never heard of such a thing, & never was more flattered, pleased, proud, boastish, anything. Can't wait.

I might learn to read in honour of the honour.

I can't get over it, & await the day of publication as keenly as good old Jock Murray.

Decca & Bob land in London next week. Lucky them, going to you. She's got an attack of nerves re her P Toynbee[1] so do soothe it down. Very unlike her, she usually bulldozes along I should have thought. I bet it's good.

Diana's chapter on Carrington & Strachey[2] is IT. Quite a different view of them to any one has ever read before.

Jim Lees–Milne[3] is writing a life of Ld Esher, the one who was Sec to the 8th Duke of Devonshire. He has turned up some rich tales of that marvellous man.

Much love & so many thanks for being on the 1st page of yr
Book. What an excitement. From
    Debo

[1] Jessica Mitford was writing a memoir of Philip Toynbee, published as *Faces of
Philip* in 1984.
[2] Diana Mosley included a chapter on Dora Carrington and Lytton Strachey in
Loved Ones: Pen Portraits (1985).
[3] James Lees-Milne (1908–97). Architectural historian, biographer and diarist, who
was 'now and then exaggeration prone'. (PLF) Author of *The Enigmatic Edwardian*
(1986), a life of Viscount Esher, writer and politician, who had a fondness for
adolescent boys. Married Alvilde Chaplin in 1951.

20 June 1983   Mani

Darling Debo,

    I set off for New York with my old Cretan guide and pal, Manoli
Paterakis,[1] a glorious chap with eagle-brows and blazing eyes and very
funny, who rarely leaves his goat-folds high up in the mountains of
Western Crete, a man in a million. The pilot turned out to be an old
friend too, so we were spirited into the super-luxury class and given
masses of champagne, caviar and foie gras. Lots of Cretans met us at
Kennedy Airport, and we were whisked off to a distant green corner
of Long Island almost exclusively inhabited by them, and made a
tremendous fuss of. We stayed with our old head of intelligence in
Heraklion, a brilliant student then, now a successful inventor:[2] he's
perfecting an internal combustion engine which will reduce fuel
consumption to 10% of its present amount, so he'll probably be a
billionaire. The whole thing was to mark the 42nd anniversary of the
Battle of Crete, and M and I were the guests of honour.

    Endless interviews and TV broadcasts culminated, the first Sunday,
in a great gathering in a vast hall called the Crystal Palace on
Broadway, where we were on a dais with an Orthodox bishop and
other celebrities, and all made speeches, including me (not a dry eye)
and Manoli, who rambled on splendidly about shooting parachutists
among the rocks. Feasting followed, and marvellous Cretan dancing,
the leaders twirling in mid-air, smacking their boots thrice before

landing, to the strains of the lyra and other Cretan instruments; marvellous costumes. It all sounds as if it might have been hell, but it wasn't, because of the warmth, kindness and enthusiasm of all concerned. V moving in fact. (By the end, we were laden with engraved gold and bronze plaques, and framed documents like those above psychiatrists' couches in the *New Yorker*, explaining how we had each won the war single-handed, and lots of other lovely presents.) The next weekend, the whole troop flew to Toronto, where the same happened. We were seized and hugged by the son of Father John Alevizakis[3] (see Joan's pictures in *Cretan Runner*,[4] if handy – also of Manoli), fed and housed by him and driven to Niagara, where we gazed marvelling through the spray. Managed to slip away to the centre of New York for several days, and put up at a rather nice shabby-genteel place called the Royalton, on W 44th Street, bang opposite the much grander and more famous Algonquin, which was used for breakfast and last drinks; but we had to chuck this, as the waiters were from Macedonia and Samos and, knowing our mugs from the local Greek press, we weren't allowed to pay for drinks, and finally slunk off elsewhere for fear of ruining them. How nice to devote almost an entire letter to boasting. We got back after a fortnight, tired but happy.

I enjoyed goatherd Manoli's calm acceptance of skyscrapers etc. (His only other absence from his native ranges was ten years ago. We were flown to Paris for a TV Resistance programme, and they put us up in a charming place called l'Hôtel Château Frontenac, near the Étoile. M's suite had three thicknesses of lace curtain, panels of green pleated watered silk like your study, pastel-colour reproductions of Boucher and Fragonard – *Le Baiser à la dérobée*, *l'Escarpolette* etc – great brass beds and taps like golden swans' necks. I asked him what he thought of it and he said 'Very nice.')

No more now, darling Debo, except tons of love (and news, please,) from

     Paddy

---

1 Cretan resistance fighter and a chief participator in the abduction of General Kreipe in 1944.

2 George J. Doundoulakis (1921–2007). Second World War espionage hero and physicist.

3 The village priest of Alones, a small village in south-west Crete, where PLF set up a wireless station during the war. His son, George Alevizakis, served in the Royal Hellenic Air Force before moving to Toronto after the war.

4 George Psychoundakis, *The Cretan Runner: His Story of the German Occupation* (1955). PLF translated and wrote an introduction to the book, which included over a dozen photographs of the participants by Joan Leigh Fermor.

11 August 1983   Bolton Abbey
                                                    Skipton

Darling Paddy,

Spent two days filming with a wonder called Penelope Keith.[1] Did you ever see her on the telly, *To The Manor Born, The Good Life* etc, no acting necessary, she's exactly like she is & perfect with an even more exaggerated voice than all Mitfords put together.

The subject of her interview was v unexpected – Capability Brown. The director had to tell us to stop laughing once or twice, that's never happened before. It's usually stop yawning. Anyway I spoke my mind about how he buggered up our garden & how thankful I was he hadn't stopped up the river to make a soggy old lake (a miracle he didn't, now I come to think of it, a favourite trick of his), so I hope it won't be too dull. Couldn't be with her. Her hubby is v Lancashire & talks same, he's a copper on the beat in Chichester. Next time I stay with the Wife I shall Break & Enter there in the hopes of being apprehended by him. He's lovely.

Now it's a spot of sport, no grouse because of ghoul wet & cold in April & May, so we'll pay attention to the picnics instead & Prince Philip is coming next week. What a shame he's hit a dud year after last year's bonanza.

The wedding of Catherine Guinness to Ld Neidpath[2] was too lovely, at Biddesden, all glowing pink brick on a boiling evening, a dance after, all out of doors, so rare not to be frozen at night.

My Diana hadn't been in the house since she left 50 years ago & nor has a housemaid by the looks of it, but oh the beauty of the bones of the place.

An aged American fell in love with Diana & followed her about

& I heard his wife say 'I might as well take to drink & go back to New York.' She'd done the first alright. I WISH Ann had been there, she ought to have come out of wherever she is for the night.

Andrew is *wonderfully* well, ne'ery a refresher, consequently in marvellous form & the best of all companions.

V much love & to Joan

    Debo

1 Penelope Keith (1940–). Actress famous for roles in television series and a keen gardener. Married to Rodney Timson in 1978.

2 DD's great-niece was married to James Neidpath 1983–8.

(DD)

In February, I wrote a harrowing letter to Paddy about an incident which pre-cipitated the inevitable physical crisis in Andrew, brought on by his alcoholism. It was after the annual journey to Lismore for the opening of the salmon-fishing season on the Blackwater.

Even this traumatic experience failed to persuade him to take action. Not until the end of June did he seek treatment as a way out of the desperate afflic-tion that affects not just the sufferers but so many people around them. With this help and a huge effort of will Andrew remained sober for the rest of his life.

It was not his first attempt at giving up. In his memoirs he wrote, 'I made periodic attempts to give up alcohol for varying lengths of time, from a few months to a time in the '70s when I gave up for two years, as the result of some drastic electric treatment.' This did not have the hoped-for effect and it was not until this year that he conquered what he called the 'old enemy'.

6 February 1984   Chatsworth
                                                   Bakewell

Darling Paddy,

I've had two excitements. The first was being asked to shoot at Sandringham[1] & studying the house for the first time, & the second was Sybil Cholmondeley's 90th birthday party.

Sandringham was built about the same time as Batsford[2] & smells

just like it, it NEEDS palms & glut but has been cleared of same.*
It's got a wonderful atmosphere & makes one feel dangerously at
home straight away.

My bathroom had three marble basins with letters engraved
into them. The first said HEAD & FACE ONLY, the next
HANDS, & good heavens the last was blank so what can it have
been for.

I picked up a hoof, off Andrew's writing table, with Persimmon
(Derby winner FOOL) written on it, turned it over to see if it had a
golden shoe & an awful rare liquid poured out all over EVERYTHING
– ink. How could I guess. I wrecked Andrew's sponge trying to wash
the carpet & had to give up as the horrible beige thing was turning
blacker & bluer every minute so I rang for the maid & fled. Two
hours later there was no sign of the dread accident, aren't those sort
of professionals amazing?

Then back to Norfolk a week later, to Houghton for Sybil's 90th
birthday. I was so *honoured* to be asked, the other two non family
staying in the house were Sir Steven Runciman[3] & Gp Captain
Cheshire VC,[4] a bit more distinguished than yours truly, plus two
non favourites of mine Elie & Liliane Rothschild.[5] The last
communication I had with her was to write an incredibly rude letter
about Pryce-Jones' foul book, I can't quite remember why I wrote it,
must have been provoked but can't remember what by. More than
just the book no doubt.

Part of the fun was arriving the day before the great dinner &
watching it coming to without a speck of responsibility. Lavinia[6] &
Nini[7] (do you know her, Sybil's daughter, polio when young, lame,
charming, probation officer) were doing the names for the tables.
Six tables of eight. I heard them muttering Give me the Dss of
Kent. No that won't do, where's Pss Alexandra? The result was a
triumph, everyone pleased with their place, even though I had Elie,
famous for rudeness, but tamed by the awesome fact of the whole
of the royal family being dangerously near so he was positively
polite.

* Even Queen Mary's Fabergé stuff has gone to London.

You simply can't imagine the beauty of it all. That staggering Stone Hall set up for such an entertainment made me think I should never see anything so beautiful again, gold plate dug from the cellar by D Rocksavage,[8] orchids on every shelf because the present-givers mostly plumped for flowers & somehow Sybil IS orchids, daffs wouldn't do, Sèvres china and the room itself, decorated & yet hardly because of it all being one colour viz. stone. Oh heavens it was wonderful.

All their old servants came out of cotton wool to do the job & do it they did most wonderfully.

Cake wore something shimmering as per, Pss Alexandra a terrific tartan thing in silk with huge sleeves, Dss of Kent came dressed as a clergyman – black silk with white collar & cuffs – we all made a monster effort, jewels galore &, a rare thing, there was exactly the right number of people.

Surrounded by the Oudry *White Duck*, many a Gainsborough, Sybil's mater by Sargent, the Holbein of a squirrel & '*my brother Philip's Things*'[9] positively gaudy among the indigenous Kent kit, French clocks surrounded by sort of diamonds, eastern this & that, all one size too small but adding a lot, the royal people, seven minutes of block busting non-stop fireworks seen through the fat glazing bars & the old glass which is full of swirls & distortions, fires & flowers everywhere. Oh do try & picture the scene. SHE wore a pink cut-velvet & satin dress made for her mother in 1901.

The Duke of Grafton said some good words after dinner, & she, swearing after that she had no inkling anyone was going to do that, answered most brilliantly. She quoted from Horace Walpole something about dowagers being as common as flounders[10] ('What are these flounders?' Elie asked) – nothing could have been better.

The fact that the Queen & all the rest of her push were there made the dreamlike feeling more so. Those rooms were made for all that & so was Sybil. I kept thinking how lucky I was to be there. I WISH you had been & all other appreciators of such rare fare.

Two sad funerals this week to bring one down to earth as it were. Our v.v. loved lawyer Tim Burrows only 56 & irreplaceable, & Sir

Arthur Armitage, trustee of this dump & such a good fellow, ex vice Chancellor of Manchester University etc etc.

Then to the Wife where we stay for Uncle Harold's 90th birthday party. I expect that will be the v. opposite of Sybil's, it's lunch in a tent.

I'm sure there are 1000 other items but I *must* stop & get to work on a terrifying speech I've got to make on the thrilling subject of Redundant Farm Buildings (just your subject I know) to the Royal Soc. of Chartered Surveyors, terrifying because they are all pros. Why did I say I'd do it. Mad.

Much love

Debo

1 DD was a guest of the Queen and the Duke of Edinburgh on their Norfolk estate.

2 Batsford Park in Gloucestershire was rebuilt by DD's grandfather, Bertram Mitford, 1st Baron Redesdale, in the late nineteenth century. DD's brother and older sisters lived there as children until it was sold to Lord Dulverton, Chairman of W. D. & H. O. Wills Tobacco, in 1919.

3 Steven Runciman (1903–2000). After an early falling out over PLF's nocturnal excesses in Athens after the war, when Runciman was British Council representative and PLF was Deputy Director of the British Institute, they became lifelong friends. PLF greatly admired his books on the Crusades: 'the skill of the writing, the vast range of his scholarship – even, here and there, the witty asides and brackets – called the name of Gibbon to many minds.' *Spectator*, 13 January 2001.

4 Leonard Cheshire (1917–92). Air Force officer and founder of the Cheshire Homes for the disabled.

5 Liliane Fould-Springer (1916–2003). Art collector and philanthropist. Married Baron Elie de Rothschild, by proxy, in 1942. An aunt of David Pryce-Jones.

6 Lavinia Leslie (1921–). Married 6th Marquess of Cholmondeley in 1947.

7 Lady Aline Cholmondeley (1916–). Only daughter of 5th Marquess of Cholmondeley.

8 David Rocksavage, 7th Marquess of Cholmondeley (1960–). Hereditary Lord Great Chamberlain since 1990 and director of the film adaptation (1997) of Truman Capote's first novel, *Other Voices, Other Rooms* (1948).

9 'When showing people around Houghton, Sybil Cholmondeley used to point out paintings, furniture and decorative works of art, sometimes exotic and often with an Eastern influence, collected by Sir Philip Sassoon, saying, in her precise clipped tones, "These are my brother Philip's things – the best of their kind."' (DD)

10 In a letter to a friend, Horace Walpole wrote that 'Dowagers as plenty as flounders' lived around Strawberry Hill, his house on the River Thames.

26 March 1984   Mani

Darling Debo,

What a spanking description of those Proustian birthday celebrations at Houghton! I've read it again and again, and aloud to gaping listeners, all agog at those wonders by proxy.

I had a very bracing letter from your Emma, full of kind words about 'Das Herz von Douglas',[1] which I had inflicted on all friends at Yuletide. Somebody sent a copy of it to an 87-year-old Gräfin Strachwitz, who is the gr. gr. niece of the poet who wrote it. Apparently, her relation is also her life's passion, and she has sent me an enormous book she has written about him, the first of three vols, all arriving in due course. It's full of pictures of spiky Schlosses in Silesia and Bohemia, and pictures of splendid old grafs that Nancy would have liked when swotting on *Frederick the Great*[2] – all epaulettes and sabres and a criss-cross of fencing scars, ending up with a picture of herself, unscarred, but otherwise the image of Field Marshal von Bock[3] in a picture hat. Rather like O. Sitwell's remark about Dame Ethel Smyth: 'Ethel would be the dead spit of Wagner if only she were more feminine.'[4]

Must now write to D Cooper.

Tons of love,
    Paddy

1 PLF had sent Emma Tennant his translation of 'The Heart of Douglas' by the Silesian poet Moritz, Graf Strachwitz (1822–47).
2 Nancy Mitford's last book, a life of Frederick II of Prussia, published in 1970.
3 Fedor von Bock (1880–1945). The commander of Hitler's failed attempt to capture Moscow had a thin, hatchet-like face.
4 Ethel Smyth (1858–1944). Composer, militant suffragette and prolific author. At the age of seventy-one she fell in love with Virginia Woolf who described her as 'an indomitable old crag'.

6 April 1984   Chatsworth
                                               Bakewell

Darling Paddy,
    Hoorah re you looming. COME TO IRELAND.
    We'll be there 16–28 April. You would be WELCOME any or all
of that time.
    Much love
        Debo

16 May 1984   White's
                                               St James's
                                               London SW1

Darling Debo,
    I'm still living in an afterglow of those lovely days at Lismore. It
was more marvellous than ever, even than that glorious first sojourn,
twenty-eight unbelievable years ago. *Why* I'm so late in writing to
say all this is a mystery I can't fathom; but 1000 thanks, and to
Andrew. It *was* bracing to see him fit and well again.
    I've been enjoying my minor season – or Greece dweller's
equivalent of a Mediterranean seaside holiday – and, the weekend
after my return, went first to Coote Lygon's cottage, then to the Mad
Boy's[1] for two nights. He's considerably slowed up, walks rather
laboriously on a stick, legs swivelling along rather like a pair of
dividers, so my long walks were solitary trudges across green Berkshire,
and I wish we had been on the march instead along the Blackwater
with an escort of unjacketed Garda a couple of fields behind. Poor
Robert had a fall and a sort of stroke three days later, but Coote says
he is better now. I fear they will be more and more frequent.
    Well, *next* weekend – to continue *Jennifer's Diary*[2] – was at Daph's
(she had telephoned to Diana Cooper while I was hobnobbing with
her as she lay abed and when she suggested it, I couldn't resist). Well,
her quarters in the Old Laundry[3] are simply glorious and she seemed
very happy and settled and surrounded by loving souls. We went to
the v nice house David & Caroline Somerset, now Beaufort,[4] live in,

full of gigantic grandchildren of Daph and lots of guests, and I got her nice intellectual granddaughter[5] who had just written a book. The last morning I went for a tremendous walk before brekker in that park, where two simply tremendous herds of deer were on the move looking v romantic, and was overtaken by David on a glorious steed, accompanied by two Springer spaniels. He told me that two evenings before Master, your Leic Sq pick-up,[6] died, he (Master) was given rather a turn by seeing three foxes sitting on his father's grave, giving him a serious look. The day before, Daph and I came out of the house, and his stooping rather absent-minded relict was ambling down towards the moorhens with a companion, and, spotting Daph, asked her if she lived near. Daph said Yes, here in the laundry, and the Dss said 'I expect you have lots of fun with the milkmaids', suggesting nameless high jinks among the churns and the mob caps. Then she asked David, ever in blue jeans, where he lived and he said 'I live here too, don't you remember me' and she then said to Daph 'They won't like him like the other feller who was here'.

Drinks with Jim and Alvilde [Lees-Milne], also quartered nearby. He said Joan's brother Graham had been the terror of all the surrounding nurseries and schoolrooms when young, and got so cross with Jim's sister once that he smashed his tennis racquet over her head so hard that all the strings broke and her head came through.

Many, many thanks again, darling Debo,

and tons of love from

Paddy

1 Robert Heber-Percy (1911–87). Known as 'the Mad Boy' because of his wild behaviour. Married twice, to Jennifer Fry 1942–7, and to Lady Dorothy Lygon in 1985, but his liaisons were mostly with men.

2 The social column by Betty Kenwood (1906–2000), chronicling the activities of the English upper classes, ran for more than half a century in *Tatler* and *Harper's & Queen*.

3 Daphne Fielding moved to the house on her son-in-law's estate after her divorce from Xan Fielding.

4 David Somerset, 11th Duke of Beaufort (1928–). Married Lady Caroline Thynne, Daphne Fielding's daughter, in 1950.

5 Lady Anne Somerset (1955–). Historian, whose first book, *Ladies-In-Waiting: From the Tudors to the Present Day*, was published in 1984.

6 Henry Somerset, 10th Duke of Beaufort (1900–84). Master of the Horse, 1936–78, to three British Sovereigns. Known as 'Master' because of his long service as Master of the Beaufort Hounds. 'A few years previously, Debo and I had been to see a film in Leicester Square called *The Belstone Fox*. We were the only people there, except for a very tall silhouette in the front row. It was the late Duke of Beaufort. Afterwards, on the pavement, he looked sad. "What did you think of it, Master?" Debo asked. "O, I didn't like those hounds being run over by a train," he replied. "Don't worry, Master," Debo reassured him, "scenes like that are always faked." He cheered up a lot and was driven off in his big beflagged Master of the Horse Daimler. "He's very short-sighted," Debo said, "I bet he thought I was a street-walker."' (PLF)

19 August 1984   Bolton Abbey
[Postcard]   Skipton

I thought you'd like this P.C.[1] Got permission from Ld Oxford as you note above.

I took Stella Tennant to the S of France for a few days. Asked her what she was going to do when grown up & without a moment's hesitation she said Oh I'm going to be a coroner.[2]

Much love
Debo

1 A postcard printed with an extract from a letter from Raymond Asquith to Katherine Horner, written from Chatsworth in 1906, 'How you would loathe this place! It crushes one by its size and is full of smart shrivelled up people . . . there is only *one* bathroom in the house which is kept for the King.'
2 DD's fourteen-year-old granddaughter was to become a famous model.

18 December 1984   Mani

Darling Debo,

Joan and I met Xan and Magouche in Salonika towards the end of September. The Hotel Mediterranean Palace, where I had appointed the rendezvous, had been pulled down ten years ago, but I found them mooching about in a café hard by, and we set off for Turkey next morning, through Thrace and Macedonia, and finally reached Constantinople, & dossed down at the Pera Palace, which used to be charming, now gone to pot. Here we sight-saw, gaping at all the marvels I hadn't properly gazed at for half a century, and in the evenings, hobnobbed and ate deliciously with various exalted Turks who lived in romantic wooden palaces in bosky gardens on the edge of the Bosphorus. I'd forgotten how *simply delicious* the food is: have you ever been there?

From here we struck south, to Bursa, and climbed Bithynian Olympus. Then came to a score of ancient sites of incredible beauty lost among mountains and woods and wilderness – Sardis, Aphrodisia, Priene, the Meander Valley, Ephesus, Didymus, Smyrna, and on up the Aegean coast, bathing by full moonlight in creeks and coves, till we got to Troy. A tremendous jumble but it made one's heart thump all the same, standing on those crumbly grass-grown battlements with the wind driving cloud-shadows across the Scamander valley . . .

Well, next day we got to Channakalé – the 'Channack' of the Dardanelles, where the Hellespont is about a mile across, steep ridges of Asia on our side, and of Europe on the other. I'd *always* longed to have a try swimming across, and, suddenly confronted, couldn't very well wriggle out. I'd been given the name of a boatman who might show me the way, and finally found one, and next morning, with Ahmad, a nice deep-sea fisherman, brother of the Channack Hotel owner, Joan and I set off up the Asian coast to Abydos. We weren't allowed to land because it was a military zone, so we almost ran the skiff aground and I dived in, not far from where HMS *Goliath* was sunk in 1915 (the whole straits are full of sunk men o' war from the Gallipoli campaign). I slogged along after the skiff, Joan and Sevki shouting encouragement and instructions across the stern. One *has* to cross either in the early morning or in the evening, as a wind blows up in the late morning and at noon and makes rough waves. It should take just about an hour. It was 9.50 a.m.

It seemed quite easy at first, the landmarks – lighthouses, mountains, minarets, forts etc – changed places with heartening speed, and the dreaded current didn't seem too strong. A huge Russian tanker, *Bogomiloff*, loomed from the north leaving a strong wash behind it which kept lifting me up and dropping me again. Then the *Gooriah* from Tunis, next the *Dâmbovitzà* from Constantza, a Rumanian liner, and from then on there was always a ship or two and often several. Ahmed stuck a red Turkish flag with the crescent in the stern slot and, when we looked like being run down, waved another one.

Only when I thought we were halfway did I start to feel the dread current. The water suddenly became choppy and ruffled, and hard to make headway in. Joan and Sevki of the hotel kept sending encouraging cries: 'Only ten minutes *fast* now and you'll be through!', so I toiled on but could see, by the speed of the scene-changes on shore, that the current was beginning to carry me downstream. Two or three miles away, the ridge on the Ægean was Gaba Tepe, the 'Anzac Cove' of 1915.

I was swimming sidestroke and began to notice a strange fluctuating hiss, a very eerie sound, like an echo in a vast dark room, under my submerged left ear and I thought it must be the grinding of pebbles and silt at the bottom of the sea. The *surface* current flows S.W., but, *under* this current, another one flows the opposite way, and I thought the noise – brought about by the narrowing of the channel at the Dardanelles a mile downstream – might be the shock of the two currents colliding. (A few days later, in one of those wooden palaces on the Bosphorus, I mentioned this to Nuri Birgi, the nice Turkish ex-ambassador to London. 'Don't you believe it,' he said. 'It's Russian submarines. I often hear them here at Scutari. They're supposed to surface, but they don't – or only one in every 30 or 40!') So here I was, about a mile S.W. from Leander's and Ld B's crossing places, a mile N.W. of Xerxes' and Alexander's boat-bridges, on the track of the Argo on the way back with the Golden Fleece and next to Troy; but too concerned about the current to think of all this, except in fitful snatches. A vast castle was advancing from the S.W., with great round bastions with crescent flags; and two mosques – one of them with a minaret topped with a green spike, sliding upstream as well. It was Kilid Bahr, much battered – but all in vain – by our naval guns in 1915; immediately opposite Channack at the narrowest point of the whole Channel.

Joan kept shouting 'Are you all right?', and smiled cheerfully; and I *was*, though getting rather tired. I felt she might be sitting on her hands to avoid wringing them.

I churned away like mad, the fort and the mosques vanished, but it still looked a discouraging distance to the European shore: the Asian one, meanwhile, my kick-off point, had faded into the distance. The current took me past a row of bathing huts, followed by a derelict hotel, then there was nothing ahead but open country and sea — sheep, hillsides, pine woods and dried-up torrent beds; and, infuriatingly, with the sudden widening after the narrows, it all seemed to be sliding away westward and out-of-reach and I had grim visions of being whirled out between Cape Helles and Kum Kale. For this bit, the chart says — or I think it does, it's a bit indistinct: 'Current 4 knots at times', and, all of a sudden, there was a strong counter-current *upstream*, indicated on the chart by minute arrows. But it was no help.

I tried swimming on my back, but what with the clash of currents, the steamers' wash, and, by now, the midday waves, I couldn't keep direction, so thrashed on as before. I was very tired, but I must have made some headway at last; things began to look up when Ahmed cut off the skiff's engine to avoid running aground. There were pebbles underfoot, and Joan shouting 'You've done it!', and soon I was stumbling ashore among slippery boulders and green seaweed, a couple of hundred yards upstream from a wooded headland and a ravine full of poplars.

I sloshed back into the water again with a gravelly handful of Europe, and was hauled aboard with joyful cries, feeling exhausted but jubilant; dressed in the little cabin, drank some tea brewed by Ahmed, then followed by a slug of whiskey brought by Joan, and we headed back full tilt to Channack and Asia, where Xan and Magouche were waiting with a bottle of champagne; they had followed our course with binoculars from the hotel balcony, like Zeus and Hera from the clouds above Tenedos.

I had got to the other side at 12.45 a.m. after swimming for exactly 2 hours and 55 minutes. I'm still not quite sure how far it was but I *think* 3–4 miles. Sevki of the hotel said I got out at a place called Havuzlar ('pools: Avuzlar' on the chart); but I think it was further down, about a mile, at the mouth of a stream called 'Suyandere' or Soğan dere – 'Onion Valley', also famous from the Gallipoli battles.

Too tired to eat any luncheon, and Joan ditto psychologically, we slept like logs, telephoned for tea and toast, and up came delicious Welsh Rabbits instead. But my limbs had turned to stone, so I slunk creakily off to a charming hammam and lay on the marble slab dissolving and watching, on the other side of the perforations in the dome, the daylight fading and then turning black, while a burly masseur was taking me apart and then reassembling me by trampling up and down my spine like an elephant; and I emerged into the dusk feeling light as a feather and strolled to the end of the lane and smoked a thoughtful hookah there in a café, half an hour of total felicity, watching the twinkling lights and reflections in the narrows, and thinking that, tho' I was only the most recent in a long list of copycats, I was certain I had beaten all records for slowness and length of immersion; a wreath no future swimmer is likely to snatch at.

Well there we are, Debo, what a rigmarole to inflict, put together from what I put down next day. Do you mind if I crib it for an article?[1]

I do hope this gets to you in time for Yule at Dingley Dell[2] – it brings all fond wishes for Christmas to you, and to Andrew, and all you and yours, *ed il vecchio zio Cobley e tutti quanti*,[3] and tons of fond love from

     Paddy

I feel a bit out of breath after all the above and I bet you do too.

[1] PLF published an account of his feat in the *Independent*, 7 March 1999.
[2] PLF spent many Christmases at Chatsworth, which he called 'Dingley Dell' after 'the abode of Mr Wardle in *The Pickwick Papers* by Charles Dickens, famous for its Yuletide feasting and fun'. PLF to DD, 28 November 2002.
[3] 'Old Uncle Tom Cobley and all'. PLF translated into Italian the English folk song 'Widdecombe Fair', and enjoyed regaling friends with his rendition (see p. xvi).

30 January 1985 Mani

[Why no gnus?]

12 February 1985 London

Darling Paddy,

Yes, Sorry, HOPELESS not to have written (a) re Hellespont &
now (b) yr very old birthday.[1]

Pressure of Business is the reason, & having had to do a piffling
little piece on Bolton Abbey for some artist lads at Bradford (a mag).
It came between me & everything for ages. Now it's done & posted
thank goodness, & very bad as well.

Business is Pleasure of course but takes nonetheless time for that.

Anyway the Hellespont & the above & below currents, Joan in the boat & the time it took & the success of the whole boiling & now you're *70*, just too extraordinary for words. So *congrats* on that & don't do it again, eh.

Before I get on, a few questions.

If you saw a notice saying DIM PARCIO what country wd you be in & what does it mean?

Olives. You know how when you buy them they are green or black? Well, are they the same kind treated differently? What happens? RSVP (Or are they Cox's Orange Pippins & Beauty of Bath?)

David Harlech's death in a motor accident is the FOUL news here. You simply can't imagine how awful the funeral was. In a little cold dark chapel on a hill near Glyn (Harlech, where they lived). The churchyard full of people as the chapel was wee. Those poor children going through it all again as their mother was killed in like manner. And now the children's children, heaving backs in grey suits sobbing & clinging to each other & the raggle taggle but completely charming mothers & the unmarried one called Alice with brilliant yellow dyed hair, Mary & Lees[2] & her vast untidy sons & Jackie Onassis & Teddy Kennedy,[3] she just the same as ever, he stout & broad as Henry VIII, scarlet face, thin aeroplane sort of suit completely filled by his body, not a patch on his bros I'm afraid.

Andrew is in Ireland, fishing & loving it because there are some fish this year. But the real reason he's enjoying it is because he is so well. No refreshing drinks for some months & he is cheerful & even fishing himself (which he hasn't done for years, just watched the others). So isn't that GOOD.

When they were all fishing I had some Loved Ones for a weekend at Chatsworth – Nicko Henderson & his excellent wife,[4] R Kee, the Mlinarics[5] & blessed Arthur Marshall.[6] I do love Nicko Henderson. He's a new friend. We meet on the board of Tarmac, can you imagine.

The other day we gave a dinner (Tarmac I mean) & Nicko & I asked the guests & the idea is to get top politicians & one or two industrialists & some of the Tarmac pros to talk to each other about the State of Things.

What wd Lady Redesdale say, asking a lot of people to dinner who I've never met. No women except me & when you've eaten a bit someone taps on a glass & says now we'll hear what you all think & everyone (except me of course, too stupid) spouts out a lot of tosh about dollars & exchange rates & employment & unemployment & some of them talk in that new language which is incomprehensible but it is FASCINATING, a new world to me as you can imagine. (A paper belched out by their office about some huge scheme said something was a *revolving evergreen facility*. Well, what is it?)

So I asked Mr Thatcher,[7] & he came, imagine. He kissed my hand & talked to me about You Aristocrats so I said I wasn't one & he had a G & T & all was well with the world.

Uncle Harold came. I wd have given much for a camera when U Harold, D Thatcher & the Chairman of Tarmac were squeezed on a ridiculous little sofa (private room at Claridge's). U Harold oiled up to Mr T like anything to make up for going for his wife in the H of Lords.

Nicko & I are going to America with our employers in April. What a thrill.

I shall think of 1000 other things when this has gone, but there we are.

Much love
Debo

1 PLF celebrated his birthday on 11 February.
2 Mary Ormsby Gore, Lord Harlech's older sister, and her husband (Alexander) Lees Mayall (1915–92), ambassador to Venezuela and Vice-Marshal of the diplomatic corps 1965–72. 'When Lees was serving at our embassy in Paris, he left me with an abiding memory. Aly Khan gave a big dinner at the Pré Catalan after Longchamp races and at 2 a.m., when nearly everyone had left, Lees was still dancing, alone, with his eyes shut, holding a single delphinium at arm's length.' (DD)

3 Edward Kennedy (1932–). Elected to the US Senate in 1962, filling the seat vacated by his brother when JFK became President.

4 Nicholas (Nicko) Henderson (1919–). Diplomat and writer. Following his retirement in 1982 as ambassador to the United States, he was appointed a director of Tarmac, the leading supplier of building material. Married Greek-born Mary Cawadias in 1951.

5 David Mlinaric (1939–). Interior designer, decorator and friend of the Devonshire family. Married Martha Laycock in 1969.

6 Arthur Marshall (1910–89). Humorist, writer and broadcaster best known for being on the BBC panel show *Call My Bluff*. 'At Chatsworth one day, he and I walked across the lawn, heavily populated with people listening to the Sunday band. Someone spotted Arty, then at the height of his TV fame, "*Look*, it's Arthur Marshall. It *can't* be. It *IS!*", and rushed up for an autograph and chat, so delighted to meet the man who made everybody laugh.' (DD)

7 Denis Thatcher (1915–2003). DD once asked the Prime Minister's husband how he kept up with his wife. He replied, 'Love and loyalty my dear.' *The Mitfords: Letters between Six Sisters*, edited by Charlotte Mosley (Fourth Estate, 2007), p. 781.

19 February 1985   Chatsworth
                                                                   Bakewell

Darling Paddy,

A headline in *The Lady* re theatres:

NEW PLAYS
A MIDSUMMER NIGHT'S DREAM

Well, even I know that's not a new play.
And a headline in the *Farmers Weekly*:

BIEN VENUE – A GOOD RAPE

I think that's all for now.
Much love
    Debo

21 March 1985   Mani

Darling Debo,

About DIM PARCIO, I give up. Do explain.

Olives. There are between 50 and 100 different kinds, black, deep purple, dark green, pale green, and some – never seen them – almost white. ALL the ones down here (the best in the world) are purply black, not very big, but marvellous. After picking (Joan, Léla and some village women, with Petro, our Léla's hubby, sawing and pruning in the branches) they are loaded in sacks, the teams of donkeys take them to the old press in the village, a terrific grinding and clatter, then out streams – first trickling, then a gush – the jade green oil, which we dip bread in and munch in ecstasy. It tastes bitter at first, but perfect in a few days; then it comes back to the house (clippety-clop) in things like flat-sided milk cans and is poured into a vast metal circular tank, which lasts us for a year, and plenty to give away. The rest we sell. Léla splits some of them and marinades them in brine, for hors-d'oeuvres for a week or two. Table olives are much bigger, beautiful smooth ovals, kept in their own oil, which lasts forever. These are obtained by grafting, which also changes the shape of the leaves – much longer and floppier.

I love your description of the Tarmac PR luncheon. Revolving evergreen facility, indeed.

We've got a fellow-writer called Bruce Chatwin[1] staying, v nice, tremendous know-all, reminds me of a couplet by O Goldsmith:

> 'And still they gazed and still the wonder grew,
> That one small head could carry all he knew.'[2]

He's a great pal of Jackie Onassis.

Please keep in touch, and tons of love from

Paddy

1 Bruce Chatwin (1940–89). The writer, who had been a friend of PLF since 1970, spent seven months in a hotel in Kalamata writing *The Songlines* (1987). After his death, his ashes were brought to Greece by his wife Elizabeth and buried near PLF's house in the ruins of a Byzantine chapel that he had always loved. He had become Orthodox at the end of his life.

2 'The Village Schoolmaster', from Oliver Goldsmith's poem *The Deserted Village* (1770).

2 April 1985   Lismore Castle
                                                    Co. Waterford

Darling Paddy,

All v jolly here & exactly as ever. We've been coming 38 years & lots of things are unchanged, various patches of damp & such like I mean.

Americans take it in the summer & it seems they aren't too keen on holes in the carpets so we've got to explain that it's *smart* to have them. Uphill work.

Clodagh[1] is still afloat, & Mrs Farquhar,[2] 83 & 86 now. One has lost a bit of a vocal cord & the other has had a stroke but goes on the same as ever & said furiously when you're 90 they take away your driving licence. I rather wish they'd done that at 86. She can't see a thing & is all over the shop.

I've been asked to review the newly republished (paperback) of the D of Bedford's killing book called *How to Run a Stately Home*.[3] He is a *card*. I'm enjoying doing it.*

     Much love
          Debo

* For the *Field* not the *Times Lit Sup*. Surprised?

DIM PARCIO = NO PARKING in Welsh. Rich, isn't it.

I'm going to America with Tarmac. We're looking at quarries, sandpits & concrete blocks. Imagine what a help I shall be to them. The wonderful thing is having Nicko Henderson on the board, a boon companion if ever there was one.

---

[1] Lady Clodagh Anson (1902–92). A spinster neighbour of the Devonshires at Lismore. 'Andrew's Granny Evie and Clodagh's mother were connected by marriage. She was the only person I knew of Anglo-Irish background who was accepted by the inhabitants of Lismore and beyond as one of themselves. She kept unusual hours and did not wake till lunchtime. She loved her garden, but it was often dark before she was ready to start work, so she gardened by the headlights of her ancient car and when the battery failed she wore a miner's lamp so as to be able to go on weeding late into the night. She was a regular churchgoer to the magnificent Church of Ireland cathedral in Lismore. When the service started at 10.30 she was

always half an hour late and came in with a clatter of banged doors and dropped books. It was decided to start the service at 11, to give her a chance. She made the same noisy entrance at 11.30. The service wasn't delayed any further or the congregation would have missed lunch.' (DD)

2 Elizabeth Farquhar; an outspoken neighbour of the Devonshires.

3 Reprinted in *Counting My Chickens, and Other Home Thoughts* (Long Barn Books, 2001), pp. 150–2.

4 April 1985   Lismore Castle
                                                              Co. Waterford

Darling Paddy,

Bruce Chatwin. OH how unfair you knowing him. He wrote a book (if it's the fellow I think it is) which I so adored I've never really felt like another.[1] You know what I mean, like my Dad & *White Fang*.[2]

How ghoul if he's a know-all, but I wd like just to see & smell him to see for myself. Or is it like meeting royal people & actors, better not? Have you always known him?

I've got my Deity here, John Smith,[3] the genius of the Landmark Trust, & his well-named wife Christian. We've done the rounds in a day, the Lodges, Youghal, church, deanery & Sir W Raleigh's dump, Ballynatray, & home via Dromana.

Cheered to see smoke coming out of a chimney at Ballynatray but oh the sadness of the little church. You know the one where they had to dig up one grave to plant another body & there used to be bones all over the place. It's an impenetrable thicket of laurels, brambles & sycamores now, no bones to note, & they've taken the roof off the church (it used to have a fireplace with a brass surround, do you remember?) & filled the doorways with concrete blocks, really dog in the manger behaviour, just because THEY don't want to get in doesn't mean ONE doesn't.

The Garda lads (three of them who go everywhere even with me now) looked at it amazed & said Sure t'would be easy to restore, well it wouldn't but no English policeman would say that wd they.

Clodagh came to lunch. J Smith was suitably riveted. J Smith VERY IMPRESSED at me knowing you.

Anyway it's Chatwin I want to know about & of course your arrival in England & coming to Chatsworth.

Much love
    Debo

---

1 *On the Black Hill* (1982), winner of the James Tait Black Memorial Prize and Whitbread First Novel of the Year Award.
2 DD's father, Lord Redesdale, like his fictional alter ego Uncle Matthew in Nancy Mitford's novels, was said to have read only one book in his life, Jack London's *White Fang*, which was so good that he had never wanted to read another.
3 John Smith (1923–2007). Financier and philanthropist who founded the Landmark Trust in 1965 to preserve unusual historic buildings, which are then let out as holiday homes to the public. Married Christian Carnegy in 1952.

24 June 1985   As from White's or
                                               Mani I suppose

Darling Debo,

Jock [Murray], fearful of my slipping between his fingers, keeps on thinking of new and vital things to be done, so I'm *STILL* not off; but I'm going to try and make a break for it, back home by the weekend. I feel smitten down by a sort of melancholia, rather a rare thing with me, and for no specific reason, except everything seeming gloomy and hopeless – I dare say subconsciously banks, hostages and *rain* have something to do with it. But I long to slink off.

No more now except lots of love and thanks to you both from
    Paddy

27 August 1985   Mani

Darling Debo,

When we got back, there was a *disco* opening at the top of our road 400 yards away and, as our valley acts like a megaphone, the mad jittery racket after sunset was hell unloosed, and we thought we were going mad. Well, it continued for a fortnight, during which *not a soul went there*, and suddenly there was silence; and now they are gone. We thought we might have to draw stumps forever. It was a close shave.

Two or three weeks ago the telephone rang, and it was Coote Lygon, shyly announcing that she and the Mad Boy had decided to get married.[1] It's the best news one has heard for a long time. Hip hooray! I can't think of a better presiding spirit for Faringdon. The only thing is, I hope Rosa[2] doesn't slip strychnine into her soup.

Scarcely anyone has been here, and I must say, I don't blame them in August. But tomorrow John Julius and his Mollie[3] appear for a week, which we are looking forward to in our rustic isolation; then a dribble of guests all through September, and on 1st October we meet Xan and Magouche for a tremendous sight-seeing ramble of baroque towns, churches, Schlosses, and so on, in S Germany and Austria, which I love. I *slightly* dread one aspect of this trip: while in Blighty, *probably* through guzzling so at Dingley Dell, I put on five kilos, as I discovered to my dismay stepping on the scales when I got back. Well by dint of abstinence, clean living and swimming about a mile a day, I've managed to drop *eight*, and it's still going down. I emerge svelter and browner from the waves each day. But what will Germany do to all this? With the terrible example of everyone all round one wolfing it down like ogres?

I've just been reading *Loved Ones* and enjoying it very much; but was rather mortified to see that the Derek story, 'No, that wasn't the name', didn't come in.[4]

One of the cats killed a snake last night, quite long, with orange, black and white spots. It looked terribly dangerous but the book says it's a harmless rat-snake, and indeed, halfway along was a huge bulge, which must have been a rat. It resembled those pictures of pythons or boa constrictors digesting bison in *The Wonder Book of Nature*.

Do send news; tons of love from

Paddy

Joan *did* enjoy her stay with you.

In the Introduction to my new book – the 'thanks' part – I'm thinking of putting '– also to the proprietors of the Stag Parlour near Bakewell, for revision'.[5] That'll make them scratch.

1 Robert Heber-Percy and Lady Dorothy Lygon married when they were both aged seventy-three and parted a year later.

2 The cook at Faringdon, the house that Robert Heber–Percy inherited from Lord Berners after they had lived there together for eighteen years.

3 John Julius Cooper, 2nd Viscount Norwich (1929–). Historian, only son of Duff and Diana Cooper, married Mary (Mollie) Philipps as his second wife in 1989.

4 See PLF to DD, 6 August 1980. Diana Mosley's pen portraits of friends included a chapter on her former brother-in-law Derek Jackson.

5 PLF worked in a downstairs room at Chatsworth, known as the Stag Parlour, 'for fevered sessions' of revision on *Between the Woods and the Water*.

7 December 1985   Mani

Darling Debo,

Now. (a) What did you think of the Annie book?[1] I thought Mark made a very good job of it, though I would have left out the harrowing letters, especially Ian's, when things started going wrong. What about you? (b) How did the Nancy book[2] go?

(c) How are you? More later.

(d) About two months ago, Joan and I flew to Frankfurt, where Xan and Magouche were waiting, in order to start a giant baroque journey next day, so settled in a smiling hamlet on the banks of the Rhine in a huge castle called Johannisberg where dwells a marvellous Russian Pss Metternich,[3] a pal of Magouche's. The most fabulous Hock in the world is made there, and most of next morning was spent in catacombs scooped out of the castle rock; there were spacious halls here and there, with tables and candles and rows of gleaming glasses and bottles, a sort of competition was afoot, where we sat and sipped various nectars beyond compare, then sped down the Rhine to another Schloss, inhabited by a frightfully nice Scotch Pss of Hesse that her familiars call 'Peg',[4] you probably know her, very funny and welcoming. She was in a bit of a wax about Tony Lambton's book,[5] thinking it inaccurately rotted all her people-by-marriage ('and why did Stinker Lambton say I was like only a *rather* jolly vicar's wife, instead of just a jolly one?') After this castle-life, we went seriously to work, scouring the Rhineland, Württemburg, Swabia, Franconia, Bavaria and Saxony for these extraordinary churches, which I still haven't entirely taken in, tho' I gaze at their pictures non-stop. The trompe l'œil ceiling paintings are perfectly summed up by a pre-war French song ('*Quand notre cœur fait boum!*')[6] of which some of the last lines are:

Et le bon Dieu dit BOUM
Dans son fauteuil de nuages.[7]

These gave cricks in the neck in uncounted staggering intervals.

Well, it was a wonder. We darted into the Tyrol and out again, slept in a lorry drivers' hotel in Salzburg (no others available), then back to wonderful Passau, where two other rivers – the Ilz and the Inn – join the Danube from either side, under flatiron-quays piled high with architectural wonders, and turn the river for a mile or two into a tricolour with their differently hued currents. I love the Danube, and feel bound up in it since my early days, a sort of honorary merman.

We followed it slowly downstream to Vienna, where those Lippizaner horses were only *exercising* in the Hofburg (they had just got back from a visit to Blighty – did you go and see them?) instead of going through their fascinating and neurotic paces at home. We went and had delicious coffee and squashy cakes at Demel: that Regency Rumpelmeyer's in the Kohlmarkt next door.

We broke up here, the Fieldings back to Spain, Joan to Blighty, me to Hungary, after an unflawed month. I went to Budapest,* to see old pals, and one especially. Do you remember my reading aloud to you and Andrew a bit about swimming with a pal down a river in Transylvania, being taunted by two pretty reapers on the shore, and our jumping out and giving chase over the stubble? He – Elemér von Klobusiçky, called 'István' in the book – plays a tremendous part in vol 2 of Shanks's Europe.

Well, I wanted to show him the relevant bits of the book and find out if he approved; also hoped for a laugh or two. He lives in a sort of workmen's tenement block of flats on the E outskirts of Pest. I telephoned again and again with no answer, so took a taxi for miles in the pouring rain. Monoglot taxi had no idea of the district

* Crossing the Burgenland where you frolicked of old.[8]

(called Centenarium), but I managed to spot it in the end from a former visit, pretty bleak in the pouring rain, a semi-skyscraper on a bombsite with an old laundry, rubbish, graffiti and prams without wheels. Found his door, with two new names, and his, faded and illegible, on a peeling strip of adhesive tape. But no banging produced any results, the whole area was abandoned. An old crone pottered along in the end. '*Uncle Elemér bácsi?*' She made signs of his having bust his leg months ago, being in hospital. I left a telephone number, and slunk back in the gloaming to my dismal hotel. Called to the telephone, there, on the other end was the rather pretty girl, head of the Communist cell for Elemér's former block, who, in spite of E's 85-year-old ultra reactionary stance, had rather a crush on him (I took them both out to lunch three years ago). She told me he smashed his leg in August, since when he had been in a military hospital W of Buda (as an ex-hussar from the Great War, I suppose!).

So next day I got a friend, Dagmar, wife of my Hungarian writer pal Rudi Fischer,[9] to drive me there, in some rather nice leafy hills. But, when we arrived, a gaggle of nurses told me he'd left that morning for an old folks' home in Pest. So back we went – still pouring and many miles now – to a pretty grim, prison-like building outside but not too bad indoors, where I found Elemér's quarters at last, a room with five other old boys, rather nice. It was dark again and I had difficulty spotting which he was. He was asleep, tired after all the moving. When I woke him and the lights went on, he looked v drawn, top teeth out, white stubble, but still recognisably good-looking, aquiline, & pink cheeked. The sad thing was he couldn't recognise *me*! When I said 'I'm on the way to Greece' he said, again and again, 'In Greece lives my old friend Leigh Fermor. Greet him from me.' (We've been in constant touch, till three months ago.) 'But, Elemér, it's *me*!' 'No, no, you are too young. Give him my love.' Dagmar had stolen off by now. We talked a long time – he still only a *quarter* convinced it was me, still using the third person, as though I were absent. I'd brought him lots of whiskey, tea, coffee, books etc from Vienna, but don't think he twigged they were for him. I asked about his sister Ilona, who lives in Transylvania – he'd

forgotten her married name and address, also his son's, who lives in
Düsseldorf. This good-looking chap, Miklos,[10] hadn't been for a bit,
but his daughter-in-law, a Frog Pss Caroline Murat, had, twice. He
really wasn't taking in much, so I had to tear myself away at last, as I
felt I was tiring him. I buggered off, feeling very wrung by it all.
Eclipse of a Honvéd Hussar! I've a terrible fear he won't emerge, or
last very long . . . But I'm glad I saw him. I've found everyone's
addresses and have written. He was a tremendous friend. You'd have
loved him in palmier days – he was so funny. The nurses were very
nice and all adored him, even the Bolshevik matron. The place was
miles from anywhere, it was pouring cats and dogs, no taxis
anywhere, pitch dark, so I slumbered in a wicker chair in the porter's
lodge for an hour, till a doctor gave me a lift to the middle of town.

I flew to Sofia next day and found it horrible. The intervening
51 years had changed the cheery little Balkan capital into the HQ
of a dim and remote Soviet province with huge scarlet hoardings
everywhere displaying the faces of the leaders in frames the size of
tennis courts. I had meant to explore the whole of Bulgaria in a
hired car as a refresher for Vol III, but caught a bus to Salonika
instead (three sodden hours at the Bulgarian-Greek customs while
oafs fumbled through one's effects like slow-motion rag-and-bone
men), then over the Greek frontier to Mount Athos. Paradise.

Joan, Graham, Michael Stewart and I all arrived here (in the
Mani) on the same day, then Artemis Cooper[11] turned up in search
of details about wartime Cairo. The next day I had horrible news
from Crete about Manoli Paterakis – see Joan's post-war photo in
The Cretan Runner. He was my guide and closest Cretan friend in
the island, hand in glove in all sorts of risky junctures, a man in a
million, two years older than me, v. funny with a hawk nose, piercing
eyes, and vast knowledge of the mountains. His was a goat-herding
family. He had fallen and been killed. I dashed to Athens, caught a
plane to Canea, and drove with two old friends to Koustogérako, one
of the highest-perched villages in Crete. The whole of the Resistance
Movement seemed to have gathered on the stone steps, and there
was poor Manoli in his open coffin (one embraces the brow of the
dead here, cold as the clay). His wife and children absolutely swollen

with weeping. After the burial, his brothers took me under a walnut tree and told me what had happened. Some of the young chaps in the village had teased him, in a friendly way, 'Eh, Uncle Manoli, you can't hunt ibex any more like you used to!' (They are very shy rare animals – forbidden to hunters now – and M was the best ibex shot in Crete.) Next day, before dawn, he dashed up the White Mountains, very high. Other, later climbers, lost sight of him but heard a shot at dusk, and went down again. When he didn't appear next day, a search party climbed up, and at last found a large shot ibex on a ledge. Peering down a precipice, they saw Manoli's body 300 feet below, and totally inaccessible. He must have been hoisting the ibex on his shoulder – slipped and fallen into the chasm.

Among other adventures (including General Kreipe) we had tried to sink two tankers in Heraklion harbour. The plan was to swim out to them, stick magnetic explosive 'limpets' on their sides, press a button, swim away again, and buzz off. We were hiding among some wreckage in the harbour, getting ready to disrobe when a patrol of two Germans approached, with one torch. They stopped, didn't move for a few seconds, then quietly moved on, and we hastened stealthily away, blessing our stars that at least we were dressed. They must have seen us, we thought. But no alarms were raised. We slunk off to the hills next day, tails between legs.

A few years ago, when we were invited to New York as guests of the Cretan Union of America, on the last evening they took us up the Empire State Building with the 5 o'clock traffic thundering below. I saw a pensive look on Manoli's face, and asked him what he was thinking of, and he said 'I'm just thinking that back in Crete it would be just about time to go up the folds and feed the ewes.'

Christmas draws nigh, and I hope it's a happy one for you, darling Debo, and tons of fond love from

　　　Paddy

1　*The Letters of Ann Fleming*, edited by Mark Amory.
2　Selina Hastings, *Nancy Mitford, A Biography* (1985).
3　Princess Tatiana Vassiltchikov (1915–2006). Married Prince Paul Alfons, last Prince Metternich-Winneburg, in 1941. Schloss Johannisberg was almost totally

destroyed by bombs in 1942. After the war the Metternichs rebuilt the greater part of the castle and made it their permanent home.

4 Margaret (Peg) Geddes (1913–97). Married Prince Ludwig of Hesse and the Rhine in 1937. Their house at Wolfsgarten was a centre of entertainment and culture after the war.

5 Antony Lambton, *Elizabeth and Alexandra* (1985). An account of the Grand Duke of Hesse's two daughters who married, respectively, the Grand Duke Serge, brother of Tsar Alexander III, and Nicholas II, last of the Romanov Tsars.

6 'When our heart goes boom.'

7 'And the good Lord says boom / In his throne of clouds.' Charles Trenet, 'Boum' (1938).

8 In 1937, DD drove with her mother and sister Unity through Austria to stay with Janos von Almásy at Bernstein Castle in the Austrian province of Burgenland.

9 Rudolf Fischer; language editor of the *Hungarian Quarterly*, guide, philosopher and friend to PLF for many years. In *Between the Woods and the Water*, PLF acknowledged his debt to Fischer's 'omniscient range of knowledge and an enthusiasm tempered with astringency'.

10 Miklos von Klobusiçky (1946–). Married Princess Caroline Murat in 1967.

11 Artemis Cooper (1953–). Granddaughter of Duff and Diana Cooper. Author of a forthcoming biography of PLF, of *Cairo in the War 1939–1945* (1989) and, with her husband, historian Antony Beevor, of *Paris After the Liberation 1944–1949* (1994).

23 January 1986   Mani

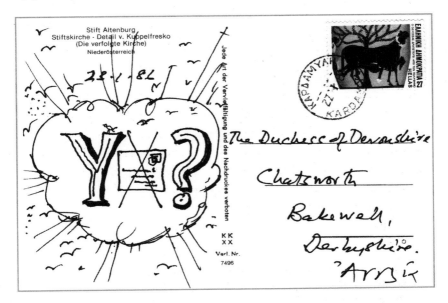

18 February 1986   Chatsworth
                                                        Bakewell

Darling Paddy,

Yes I know, HOPELESS, specially as I got such a fat one from you. I was haunted by that man you hunted from pillar to hospital & didn't know you but knew your name. OH old age, the foulness of it.

Anyway thanks for that & the rest in that letter. It was a treat.

The trouble is I'm trying to start a new book.[1] I can't think of anything else but I can't do it, so the result is NOTHING. Nothing done which ought to be done & everything left undone.

The first sentence is very trying, you'll admit. Famous Authors (that fraudulent thing in America which explains how to be one) says write 'the' on a bit of paper (well what else could it be on) & then put down some more words. I ask you. Then I thought *'well'*, as all interviewees on the wireless begin. No good. And 'like', and 'it came to pass.' No good either. So I looked at a few ghoul vols, no help. I think it will be 'if', like Kipling, but the nub of the ensuing sentence is Dutch to nearly everyone, not to you because you know everything & not to my editor (R Garnett) because he knows everything, but to 99% of the fools who read books.

It's going to go like this: 'If you live in the same place for a long time you become hefted to your hill like an old sheep. The surroundings slowly but surely take hold & become part of you, the known familiar earth & water, trees & buildings, their shapes, colours & smells . . .' and so on.

Hefted . . . well of course *you* know. Do you think The Dear Reader will like louping ill, orf, yellowces, scrapie, fluke, foot rot, worms & udder clap (udder falls off)?[2]

And what will they make of earblight, brown rust, eyespot &, worse, SHARP eyespot, septoria, take all, yellow rust, net blotch, snow rot, rhynchosporium, loose smut, glume bloth and bunt?[3] Do you think they'll chuck it?

The trouble is the subject is so huge & has been on the go

since 1550 that it could make many books but it is NOW I want
to write about because I don't think anyone has, much. An *estate* I
mean.

Anyway it's taking up the slack with knobs on & I squirm about
trying to do it & not succeeding.

J Murray's list came with 'the impatiently awaited . . .' Didn't have
to pay much attention to know what that would be.

My m in law doesn't die, nor I'm glad to say, does Sybil
Cholmondeley, now 92. You could say the same for poor old Diana
Cooper I suppose & I know she is longing to.

Much love
    Debo

1 *The Estate: A View from Chatsworth* (1990).
2 Diseases in sheep and goats.
3 Cereal crop diseases.

28 February 1986   Mani

Darling Debo,

'Wheat-ears covered the furniture, and one of the Swedes, well-
versed in the English terminology of his passion, explained as we
strolled from specimen to specimen the differences between turgid
ears and the common bearded kind; then we surveyed the Polish
variety and appraised the spikelets and the awns, the median florets
and the glumes.' Who wrote that, and in what book? Answer inside
envelope.[1]

Smashing first sentence, don't change a thing, apart from removing
either 'known' or 'familiar' as they are both doing the same job.
Otherwise, tip-top. But don't remove a single one of the earblight,
brown rust list, down to udder clap. One nearly swoons away with
the magic of the language.

Well that was a nice letter. I was beginning to pine a bit, as so
many of the people who once used to write to me are dead or
dying. When I got back from Kalamata this evening, Joan told me

my Hungarian pal Rudi Fischer had rung up from Budapest to say that my *other* old Hungarian friend Elemér – the one I hunted down in the Old Folks' Home – died three days ago, after a fall and pneumonia, but kindly looked after and *not* Dickensian, as one would dread in an Iron Curtain country. I wish he could have read all I've written about him in the forthcoming vol, he *would* have laughed.

Now. Have your copy of *Time of Gifts* handy. I remember seeing it in the bookcase behind where you sit, so reach back, and look up page 95, bottom two paragraphs, and overleaf.[2] Then read the following sheet, which is copied from a P.C. I got the day before. It's all so queer. I got it Xeroxed this afternoon to send to two or three. The rucksack had been Mark Ogilvie-Grant's.

A lovely week in Athens with Barbara and Niko, with a party for – can you beat it? – my 71st birthday. *Do* write some more, it cheers one up.

Tons of fond love,
    Paddy

(Postcard – franked in England – Hounslow, 10 Feb. 1986.
Verso of P.C.: 'Cheers! From the Pubs of London')

Herrn Patrick Leigh Fermor

Kind Sir! I was thrice fortunate on my trip to the erstwhile capital of the BRITISH EMPIRE. I discovered the velvety smoothness of Guinness, the exquisite taste of gourmet steak and kidney pudding and your magnificent magnum opus, *A Time of Gifts*. You will perhaps be surprised to hear that my late maternal grandfather Alois Schoissbauer figures in it. Indeed, he was none other than the pimply youth who 'borrowed' your rucksack rife with manna in Munich. He is clearly recognisable for he often told me the tale. You will no doubt be interested to know that it (the rucksack) later concealed all his belongings when he fled across the Alps from Tyrol to Switzerland when the Nazis wished to incarcerate him in a KONZENTRATIONSLAGER, not as a Jew[*]

[*] which he was not, being a Bavarian and a Roman Catholic.

but as an anti-social element. I later inherited the Rucksack and carried it all the way across Asia to Peshawar where it was stolen by an Australian hippie, at least so I have been led to believe.

Respectfully your obedient servant,

Dr Franz Xaver Hinterwälder,

Professor of Farsi and Pashtoo, Firdausi School of Oriental Languages,

Kirchstetten, Nether Austria

As an attentive reader I was able to discover from *A Time of Gifts* that your LXXI birthday is approaching next Tuesday. Permit me to take the occasion to wish you the compliments of the season.[3]

---

1 From *Between the Woods and the Water*, p. 109.
2 The passage describes how, in early 1934, PLF's rucksack, containing his passport and travel journal, was stolen from a Munich youth hostel.
3 The writer of this hoax card has not been identified.

25 September 1986   Mani

IN HASTE

Darling Debo,

When the Kalamata earthquake happened, I was having a quiet ouzo up in the mountains with Desmond Shawe-Taylor[1] and Chloë Obolensky,[2] and noticed nothing. Joan was down at the house, playing chess outside with Dimitri O,[3] when the chessmen started moving about on the board, with a sort of subterranean rumble below. Kalamata is badly stricken, much of the population living in tents, poor souls, and at least half the houses with big red crosses on the door, meaning 'uninhabitable: to be pulled down', some of them *look* all right, but are chaos inside, others have tumbled down completely. It's all right now, with the mild autumn weather; but what about winter? People in the seismological know forecast more shocks round the corner.

An Italian skin-diver disappeared last week and was found days later stuck in a cave, with his face eaten away by fish. In the little pool, by the chapel a hundred yards from here, a v rare and v small turtle has appeared; black with yellow spots, and a long spiny tail. No mate, so a spinster or a bachelor. I saw him half an hour ago, nibbling a floating fig dropped from the overshadowing tree.

    Tons of love,
        Paddy

---

[1] Desmond Shawe-Taylor (1907–95). Chief music critic on the *New Statesman* 1945–58 and *Sunday Times* 1958–83.
[2] Chloë Georgakis (1942–). Theatre costume and set designer. Married to Leonid Obolensky 1964–80.
[3] Prince Dimitri Obolensky (1918–2001). Professor of Russian and Balkan History at the University of Oxford. 'He was an enchanting companion on the hills of Euboea, in the meadows near Oxford, or in the foothills of the Mani in the southern Peloponnese.' PLF, *The Times*, 7 January 2002.

1 October 1986   Chatsworth
                                                  Bakewell

Darling Paddy,

That earthquake. What a rotten thing. The shaking chessmen, how terrifying. And the poor Kalamata-ites, such frightening pictures on the telly.

So, WELCOME for the Book Party.[1] I'm hoping like anything to come to it & so is Andrew.

    Much love
        Debo

---

[1] Given by John Murray for the publication of *Between the Woods and the Water*.

2 January 1987   Chatsworth
Andrew's 67th birthday   Bakewell

Darling Paddy,

The most unexpected thing over Christmas was my sister Woman,
even a nonner reader than me, sat glued to your effort, sometimes
both the books (sort of) in her hands at once.* Do be pleased. Now
she's blazed the trail I might have a go.

A mag called *Derbyshire Countryside* says it believes on GOOD
AUTHORITY that the proprietors of the Stag Parlour near
Bakewell are Andrew & me. A good bit of detective work, eh.

Now I must take Richard [Garnett] to look at things like a gate
post I'm very fond of. I wonder if he'll see the point, he doesn't
always, he's so logical & that particular gate post isn't. Then we're
going to the site of the National Hedging & Walling Competition
which took place on a farm near here in Oct '85. Hedgers & wallers
came from all over. They had to do a chain each. Well, I thought, a
cut & laid hedge was a beautiful thing but just a cut & laid hedge. I
had no idea of the different *styles*, for instance Welsh is totally unlike
Northamptonshire. They're for keeping in (or out) different animals,
see; steers & sheep & all the variants of them, v local like the breeds,
some sheep being more escapist than others. So the result is like
knitting patterns, same idea of making a bit of stuff but gone about
in a different way. Or basket work. So clever it defies description.

Anyway 15 months have passed since these geniuses have done
their work & we're going to see what the hedges look like now.

I expect you're yawning with boredom by now so I'll spare you a
descripo after we've seen them.

Andrew has gone to Constantinople with Anne [Tree] & one of
her daus. I have been in two or more minds as to whether to ring
him up & tell him Uncle Harold has conked, to get a telephone call
there wd make him in a fever of nerves. Anyway I have cleverly
made them have the funeral on Mon instead of today which is what
was threatened, so he'll be back as planned.

The Macmillans are all at war with one another, the saddest thing

---

* Like shooting with two guns without a loader, quite a feat.

that can happen to a family I think. Much non-speaking & jealousies, some are drunk, some have been drunk & aren't any more, some have a glimmer of charm, but most none. When you think of Aunt Dorothy, & the old boy for that matter, it's odd. She WAS charm.

GOOD NEWS. Jim is going to do the Bachelor Duke.[1] Apparently he's long thought of it & we never dreamed he would but have stalled over others who wanted to do it. So now I'm pleased, no one is more suited to the job, do admit.

I bet you haven't read all this. Now to the Gate Post.

Happy New Year.

Much love to you both

 Debo

We're doing terrific clearing in the garden, the impenetrable thickets of self-sown yew, holly, sycamore & foul Rhododendron ponticum, so you can see things a bit. Lo & behold we discovered a statue I had never seen before. Knocked from its plinth, engulfed in rhodies. So I rushed for the Bach D's *Handbook* & there I found it, an *Athenian altar*, that's the plinth for the statue which obviously never belonged to it. The altar is 4th or 5th-cent BC, he says, & has got a *civic* (according to the BD's *Handbook*) inscription. Oh do come & explain it. A bit of a thrill, finding it.

---

[1] James Lees-Milne's life of the 6th Duke of Devonshire was published as *The Bachelor Duke* (1991).

[Undated]   Dumbleton

Darling Debo,

Do you remember when I came to Dingley Dell to stay, when Uncle Harold and Sybil Cholmondeley were the only others, except you and Andrew. Andrew went off to inspect some young people, I can't remember where, only that he had got a badly torn shirt, which caused worry. Mr Macmillan and I went off for a walk, and, after a few moments, a pheasant flew across the path, and I said, 'What a lovely pheasant!' Mr Macmillan said, 'Yes. And we're very lucky to have them.' I asked him why, and he said, in that slightly cavernous voice, 'It's entirely due to the Roman occupation of Britain. The junior officers were very fond of them, and collected them in large numbers. I believe there was a certain amount of rivalry about which centurions had the most or the handsomest birds. It went on for centuries. In the end, of course, in 410 A.D., in the reign of the Emperor Honorius, the order came for all the legions to be recalled to Rome, but they weren't allowed to take their birds with them, so, very reluctantly, all the centurions let their birds go. There must have been thousands of them. Anyway, they survived the Picts and the Scots, and the Saxons' invasion.'

He had a wonderful knack of delivery, half-solemn, half light-hearted.
Tons of love from
Paddy

16 March 1987

As from Flat 2, 51 Lennox Gdns, SW3
Or messages left midday at White's Club.
Keep in touch!

Darling Debo,

Two weeks ago a nice man rang up and said 'Sir Something Greening here. The Queen was wondering whether you and your wife could dine at Windsor on April the 7th and stay the night?' Joan, having picked up the phone in her bedroom, said '*I* can't. I'll be in *hospital*,[1] but *he* can,' so threw in one. I *was* surprised, and wondered if you and Andrew could have had a hand in it – or Deacon? I long to meet beforehand, and learn about the reefs and shoals.

Tons of love,
Paddy

Here's a snatch of imaginary overheard conversation from notebook.
'He has no scruples at all.'
'Oh really? I just thought his voice hadn't broken . . .'

---

1 For a hip operation.

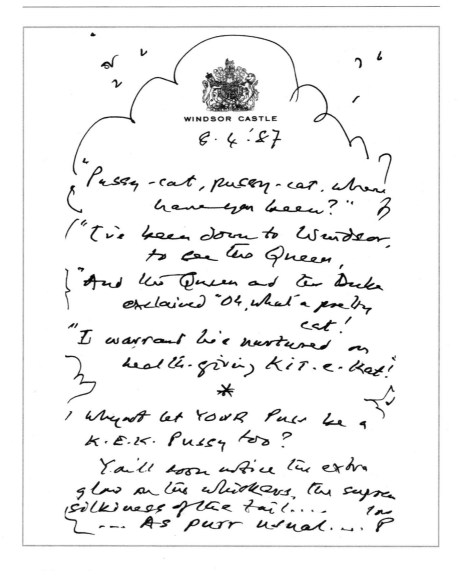

WINDSOR CASTLE
6.4.'87

"Pussy-cat, pussy-cat, where
    have you been?"
"I've been down to Windsor,
    to see the Queen,
"And the Queen and the Duke
    exclaimed "Oh, what a pretty
                    cat!
"I warrant he's nurtured on
    health-giving KIT.e.Kat!
                    *
Why not let YOUR Puss be a
K.E.K. Pussy too?
    You'll soon notice the extra
glow on the whiskers, the supreme
silkiness of the tail....   In
    ... As purr usual... P

22 May 1987   Mani

Darling Debo,

  WHERE IS YOUR PRIMROSE McCONNELL NOW? And
what is it? A kind of gardening tool, a cattle breeder's handbook, a
classified list of subspecies of potatoes, a pneumatic jack for tractors?
A kind of effervescent hairwash?[1] The only McConnell in the DNB is

William McC (1833–1867) an illustrator, who did pictures for various publications, viz. *The Months* and *Upside Down; or, Turnover Traits.* Could he have been her father? Is it a picture or a BOOK? The latter doesn't sound very like you . . . But there's no mention in the *Oxford Companion to Literature*, and the only McC in the *Encyclopaedia Britannica* is a small town in Illinois. Admittedly our *Enc. Brit.* is the 11th edition, published early in the century.

You see what I've been reading. C Russell says it might end in the Chatsworth library unless Debo has it buried with her. Is it a heart-shaped locket with a spring and a faded curl inside? I'm counting on a P.C. pretty soon, to put me out of my agony.

I *am* enjoying these letters. You and Daph get a marvellous set of dewdrops, and Diana [Cooper] a deluge. One gets a pretty clear picture of what he was like, but do tell about him a bit.

It's suddenly summer here. Masses of swallows, but not a single tourist yet. Joan hobbles further and further every day and in a month or two will fling away her ashplant (one of the twisted ones from the Kenilworth rare-cattle show) like a Lourdes pilgrim. She is busy clipping a rosemary hedge with heavy shears at this very moment, so all goes well.

What news?

Lots of love,

Paddy

---

1 PLF was reviewing *Letters of Conrad Russell*, edited by Georgiana Blakiston (1987). The 5th Earl Russell (1878–1947) had willed to DD his copy of *The Agricultural Notebook*, a standard work of reference for farmers, first compiled by Primrose McConnell in 1883.

7 June 1987   Lockinge Manor
                                                        Wantage

Darling Paddy,

It has SORT OF ended up in the Chatsworth library, if you count the few books I like & have in my sitting room or bedroom. I was amazed when it turned up after dear old Conrad died. Inside is written After my death this book is to be given to Debo With love Conrad Russell, XII night 1947.

Oh how IGNORANT you are, you who I thought knew everything.

P McConnell BSc FGS, Yeoman Farmer, North Wycke, Southminster, Essex, made the 9th edition in 1919, revised & enlarged & dedicated to Captain Primrose McConnell MC who of course was killed in action on the Salonika front in 1918. 1st edition 1883. It contains EVERYTHING & how to do EVERYTHING from explaining Gunter's Chain to how much stoking a man can do in a day (poor man, an awful lot), Ville's Dominant Ingredients of Manure, the classification of Wheats, Germination Data, points of the Kerry Cow, diseases of sheep (sturdy, braxy, scab etc. I expect you know how to deal with these).

So you see why I preferred it to jewels.[1] Of course I was too stupid to take him in properly. I knew I loved him but didn't know why. He was IT. Daph darned his tweed hat of sheep colour with bright red wool & he was so pleased. Don't you love the snap of him sewing up his cheese.

I'm trying to *get on* with my book & have boldly sent the bits on the Game Department & Agric Shows to R Garnett & await his fiercely critical comments in terror because if he says it's hopeless I CAN'T begin again. Now for 'Woods & Farms', squeezed between Tarmac AGM & some queer Social Events like a dance at Cliveden on election night given by J Goldsmith,[2] & tons of people to stay including the American Amb & ten attendants. Nicko is coming here in a minute & we buzz up to Chatsworth to have six American concrete people to lunch tomorrow, Tarmac-induced. The head concrete man has got a piano in his aeroplane & he plays 'My Way' to the sky as he floats around his quarries. Do admit one gets hold of some odd people in Life's Rich Tapestry.

Much love

Debo

---

[1] Conrad Russell had asked DD whether she would prefer to be left jewels rather than the handbook.

2 James Goldsmith (1933–97). The billionaire businessman gave a dinner before the dance at which DD found herself sitting between her host and a media man, who, 'in the way of such people, didn't turn up until the pudding – MURDOCH. Goldsmith had blue, eagle eyes that bored into you. They were one of the weapons that contributed to his presence and charm.' (DD)

17 September 1987   Chatsworth
                                                      Bakewell

Darling Paddy,

I've been in Pittsburgh, setting off yet another exhib of drawings from here. I boldly addressed 600 grown ups in a tent & rattled on for ¾ of an hour. Poor them. But you know how polite they are, they never stirred.

I was killed by kindness & am home ½ dead but re-amazed by their interest in things like this old dump.

Everything pounding along here v nicely. The Pss of Wales comes on Sunday to see to a thing to do with National Parks. What shall we feed her on, always a worry as she prefers the fridge to the table I'm told.

Much love
Debo

27 September 1987   Mani

Darling Debo,

I was horror-struck when shown that *Daily Mail* interview, done six months ago, and forgotten. The maddening thing is, it's mostly my fault, viz. given after luncheon and *a great deal too much to drink*. The interviewing lady wanted to hear all about parachutes, generals, Crete, etc. I said I couldn't go on about that, as it's such stale news, so we drifted off into embarrassing things about childhood years etc. The interviewing lady was perfectly nice, and wanted to *be* nice, so the fault for all that hugely embarrassing stuff is *one's*, more's the pity. A sharp lesson.[1]

The day after it appeared, someone rang up whom I last saw

when we were both nine. (N.B. Break off at this point, and, though it's against all your principles, read one page – p.4, and ½ p.5 – in the Introduction, letter to Xan, in *A Time of Gifts*. I think it's high up on the right hand wall of Andrew's Englishman's room. One always spots one's stuff, like a cow with a lost calf, fields away.) Well, as I was saying, the chap on the phone was a fellow juvenile delinquent or semi-loony in Maj Truthful's School at Salsham-le-Sallows – really Maj Faithfull's at Walsham-le-Willows – in Suffolk. It was fascinating, all the details he remembered about that extraordinary place. I was deeply in love with the gardener's daughter (aged 10), called Eileen Fairweather. He said she was fearfully pretty, so that's nice. But he finished by saying 'We have another remote link. I've moved back to Suffolk recently to be on the spot for our first grandchild, Kate Heywood-Lonsdale, Amanda's[2] niece.' He must have gathered that you and I are pals. I can't remember him at all.

    Tons of love,
        Paddy

---

[1] PLF, interviewed by Lynda Lee-Potter, revealed that he had run wild as a boy. 'When people first met me I made an excellent impression . . . It was only bit by bit they realised they had a fiend on their hands. At home I was always allowed absolute freedom. I always had total confidence based on nothing whatsoever. I was never diffident, and not being frightened of things is frightfully important.' *Daily Mail*, 9 September 1987.

[2] Amanda Heywood-Lonsdale (1944–). Married DD's son, Peregrine, 12th Duke of Devonshire, in 1967.

---

31 October 1987   Chatsworth
                                                       Bakewell

Darling Paddy,

    Hope you're OK. It was FOUL not seeing you when you were in the land of the living. Actually the living are fast dying. R Heber-Percy, and now my Benefactress of Swinbrook[1] & lo & behold she has left me the Mill Cottage, so wills are thrills & mills there's no doubt.

    It needs Seeing To. I went down there last week & reminded

myself of the olden days, same apple tree thank goodness, & I measured my bedroom, 7′ x 8′, just the right size.

I'm struggling with my book. I'm on the farms now & enclose the bit about the sheep sale for your editorial eye. Throw away.

My dear Wife is here. She has been knocked about by the gale. Her woods are a sad sight she says & the noble garden cedars have curtsied & are in heaps on the ground. Unscathed here.

I've been in America with Nicko Henderson. A better travelling companion you couldn't find, ne'ery a cross word in spite of days spent at cement works & hovering over quarries in a helicopter. The door burst open three times, you can imagine my screams. Then dinner with the cement-ers. Quite testing.

Roy & Jennifer Jenkins[2] are staying here. She is head of the National Trust & their AGM is in Buxton. He has become head of Oxford & had to make heaps of speeches in Latin, well you know all that. I think they've made him a lord & she is certainly a dame & so it goes on.

Emma is here. Her rugs were a huge success at Chelsea Crafts Fair, no wonder I say.[3]

Much love

Debo

Really & truly the captions in F Partridge's book of photos[4] are v embarrassing. How could she fall for that.

---

1 Marion Buckland; a friend of DD's aunt Dorothy Mitford, and a keen member of the Girl Guides. 'Apparently she had no dependants. She left me the Mill Cottage and the adjacent Mill, with the option to buy the Swan Inn from her executors, because she thought I loved the place and its associations more than anyone else.' (DD)

2 Roy Jenkins (1920–2003). Bon viveur statesman and political biographer – a combination rare in public life – who, according to his friend Sir Nicholas Henderson, depended greatly on the support of his wife, Jennifer, whose judgement and quiet charm brought her a successful career in the public and private sectors. Created a life peer in 1987, in the same year that he was elected Chancellor of the University of Oxford.

3 Emma Tennant made and sold hooked rugs.

4 Frances Partridge, *Friends in Focus: A Life in Photographs* (1987). The caption to photograph 179 reads: 'The Duchess of Devonshire gracing Ham Spray with her company during a bottling session of some Spanish wine.'

16 November 1987   Mani

Darling Debo,

I don't expect you've read any of that book[1] yet. I *do* wish you would; what's the good of writing them? I promise that there are lots of jokes you'd like. Take a leaf out of your sister Pam's book!

I can't tell you what a heap of letters was waiting, and it keeps on growing, all to be answered. This one doesn't count, as there was none from you (nor expected: *only later*), and it's all the result of publication.

It's marvellous bright autumn weather here. I charge about the mountains every afternoon. They are covered with cyclamen and crocuses. There is a bit of sensation here at the moment. Some human remains — quite recent ones — have been discovered in a bag of fertilizer under a bridge near a mountain village, but only a *third* of a person. A baker disappeared from a nearby hamlet four years ago. The rather sinister *boulangère* said he just walked out on her one night and never came back, so speculation abounds.

Tons of love from
     Paddy

1 *Between the Woods and the Water.*

28 November 1987   Mani

Darling Debo,

Tip-top, your page about the sheep sale! Lots of pace and *brio*. You are clever. I wondered whether the last bit, about Botticelli etc, was a bit Philistine;[1] but I *think* it's OK, we don't want you travelling under false colours if you know what I mean. The rest is spanking. Do send some more.

When your letter arrived, I had just finished writing one to Mark Amory, oiling out of reviewing Frances Partridge's book, because I'm v. fond of her, but wouldn't have known what to say about the captions. Gracing the bottling party was pretty rotten.

I am alone here and I wish my third vol. of Shanks's Europe was spinning along like yours.

Keep in touch, and tons of love

Paddy

1 DD ended her description of a sheep auction with, 'I would give a lot to see [the auctioneer] on the rostrum at Christie's. He would make the Bond Street dealers sit up and look sharp or the Rembrandts would walk away, here come the Botticellis, sound in reed and udder, change the tup and you'll get a van Gogh . . .' *The Estate, A View from Chatsworth*, p. 48.

28 January 1988   Mani

Darling Debo,

We went to stay for ten days with Janetta and Jaime over *les fêtes*, in a warm and spacious borrowed house between Arles and Les Baux. It was lovely and I listened to the carols in Provençal that I was wild about half a century ago.[1] An enormous ram drew a wicker cart up the aisle full of *bondieuseries* followed by twenty thoroughly shaggy shepherds in scratchy cloaks, each with a kid or a lamb in his arms, till the whole place was full of baa-ing and bleating. It was all a *glorious change*. I walked for miles and miles in the Alpilles, then trudged round the Palace of the Popes at Avignon. We ate till we could hardly move at that marvellous restaurant in Les Baux – the Oustau de Baumanière – ❀❀❀ but no more expensive than that beastly lunch at the Ritz. I sat in cafés, watching others buy delicious things for dinner at the market stalls, lulled by the clink of *boules* as I sipped a drone's Pernod . . .

Love from

Paddy

1 '"Pastre dei mountagno," etc. sung with Guy Branch and Balasha Cantacuzène before the war.' (PLF)

29 June 1988   Chatsworth
                                                     Bakewell

How did the telly week go?[1] RSVP.
  All v good here, no other news, which is good news.
  Much love
    Debo

---

[1] PLF was being interviewed by Melvyn Bragg for *The South Bank Show*, broadcast on 28 January 1989.

8 July 1988   Mani

Darling Debo,
  Well it's all over! The TV visitation, I mean. A team of three
came out for two days first, cased the joint, hired quarters,
commandeered transport etc, then there was a bit of a lull till the
Director[1] came back again. He stayed with us up here. The only
thing was he was terribly tight a lot of the time, after having been
a Double First, loved and then cast off (because of the demon D).
He played chess a lot with Joan, and *very well*; but when later the
others arrived and occasionally rode over him roughshod, he would
weep on her shoulder: 'They all hate me so.' He was far the nicest
and most gifted. Eventually all *eight* were assembled in the village.
We gave them a feast up here, and made them as happy as we
could with wines, spirits and grub (they were v grateful. Apparently
some of their 'subjects' treat them like dirt. The US Celebrity, John
Updike,[2] during a week gave them neither bite nor sup. They had
to send miles for a cup of Nescafé). Melvyn Bragg came out for
2½ days, to do the 'key interview'. He seemed much nicer than
in London. The 'interviewing' went on all over the house, on
mountain tops, in grottoes and caves, Byzantine churches, some in a
caïque in search of the entrance to Hades. George Psychoundakis[3]
came over for three days from Crete. Anyway, it seems they shot
and taped enough for several hours, and were constantly patting
one on the back. They even got *Joan* to appear for a few seconds

(she *hates* it). We strolled across the terrace, then down an avenue of
cypress and rosemary hedges . . . Well, it was all so cheery and
congenial in the end that we all felt rather abandoned when they
buggered.

Tons of love, dearest Debo, from
Paddy

1 David Cheshire (1944–92). Television director and producer.
2 John Updike (1932–). The *South Bank Show* interview with the American
novelist was broadcast on 28 October 1990.
3 George Psychoundakis (1920–2006). Cretan resistance fighter who served as a
dispatch runner for SOE. Author of *The Cretan Runner*.

27 May 1989   Mani

Darling Debo,

We had a marvellous journey in the Yemen for much of last
month, and the beginning of this, with Xan and Magouche, flying
from Cyprus in the evening, leaving the sunset over Taurus
Mountains to the north, then darkness falling over the desert, with
first Medina, then Mecca twinkling below. I hadn't quite realized
that the country is *all* mountains, with spectacular fortress villages
like Bastilles, standing in the Empty Quarter and Thesiger-land.
The inhabitants are the nicest imaginable, full of jokes and
kindness – they *must* be nice, as their very pretty children are
without fear, dash up and shake hands or simply slip theirs into
yours to lead you about and show you things, and never beg, but
they do murmur '*Kalam!*' (Arabic for 'pen') in a pleading chorus.
Forearmed, we distributed them by the dozen and won all hearts.
The only trouble was *Ramadan*. We hadn't reckoned with it, they
snooze all day, but when the sunset-gun goes, and all the muezzins
in all the minarets start wailing together, everyone makes
whoopee all night. They wait for the bang with all spoons poised
over plates of delicious soup; then chew a mild hallucinogen
called *kat* all night (which puffs out their cheeks like Derbyshire
Neck) and smoke hookahs till daybreak. I got unpopular by

halting the hired Range Rover in villages to buy headdresses to
be turned into tablecloths, and Xan to buy melons. I urged that
textiles last longer, Xan replied, 'Yes, but they don't taste as
nice.'

    Lots of love,
      Paddy

18 December 1989   Mani

Darling Debo,

    A little while ago, John Julius Norwich sent me the marvellous
alphabetical verses which he and I have both been after for years. I
knew only the first two lines, *An Austrian army awfully arranged /
Boldly, by battery, besieged Belgrade.* They are early 19th century, and
the author is unknown. I tried to do something similar, but
starting with Z, backwards, in a style which is much freer in
every sense of the word; it takes a rather racy turn, here and there,
as one was more at the mercy of alliteration than meaning. It was
worse, but I've bowdlerized it here and there with that lovely
BLANCO fluid. Anyway, I send it with all greetings for the
Winter Solstice – it's too late for Christmas, and too un-Yule
like.

    I've got a lovely suggestion for twin vols for your false door in
the library, not mine, alas, but in a glorious book called *Remainders*,
by Eric Korn:

> *J'accuse* by Emile Zola
> *Emile Zola* by Jack Hughes.

(Nancy would have liked that, with her passion for the Dreyfus case.)
He also suggests *Morgan Forced Her* by Howard Zend.

    It's a wonderful December here. Joan and I went on a picnic
today under the olive trees. (We've just finished our harvest. Not up
to much. No rain for months.) In spite of the rainlessness, it was
billiard table green under the branches, with a flock of snow-white
goats grazing, a vast sweep of blazing sea below, and a single cloud. I

hope it stays; for Christmas, poor old Niko Ghika is coming, with John Craxton[1] to hold his hand, and Niko's Portuguese maid to help.

    Tons of love,

        Paddy

[1] John Craxton (1922–). Distinguished British artist, member of the Royal Academy, who illustrated the dust jackets of PLF's books and who settled in Crete in the early 1970s.

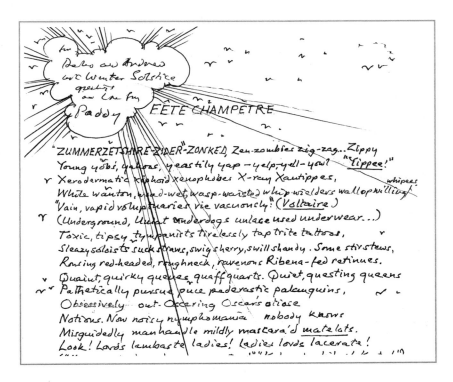

FÊTE CHAMPÊTRE

'ZUMMERZETSHIRE ZIDER' – ZONKED, Zen-zombies zig-zag . . . Zippy

Young yobs, yahoos, yeastily yap – yelp – yell – yowl '*Yippee!*'

Xerodermatic xiphoid xenophobes X-ray Xantippes,

While wanton, woad-wet, wasp-waisted whip-wielders wallop willing whipees.

'Vain, vapid voluptuaries vie vacuously' (*Voltaire*)
(Underground, Uniate underdogs unlace used underwear . . .)
Toxic, tipsy, tympanists tirelessly tap trite tattoos,
Sleazy soloists suck straws, swig sherry, swill shandy. Some stir stews,
Rousing red-headed, roughneck, ravenous Ribena-fed retinues.
Quaint, quirky queues quaff quarts. Quiet, questing queens
Pathetically pursue puce pederastic palanquins,
Obsessively out-Oscaring Oscar's otiose
Notions. Now noisy nymphomaniacs nobody knows
Misguidedly manhandle mildly mascara'd *matelots*.
Look! Lords lambaste ladies! Ladies lords lacerate!
('Kossacks kidnap Kappelmeister!' 'Kalmucks kibosh Kate!')
Jeep jangles jeep, Jehu jolts Jezebel, Jack jostles Jill,
Idle idiots imbibe ideas idler imbeciles instil.
Harmless homosexual hedonists hold heterodox heyday,
Gracious gay gadabouts gather, gracefully going grey.
Furtive fops follow fleetingly-flaked-out fairies' feuds,
Eager ears eavesdrop. Every eye extrudes.
'Dentist deflowers dons, dairymaids, duchesses, dingos, dudes . . .'
(*Cling close! Clasp cobber! Cool! Clap clear clinch concludes . . . !*)
Bogomils* broach bashful burglars, but bent buglers bungle blast,
And all, after acid's acrid aftermath, abscond aghast.

Inam 9891.01.32   *Romref Ghiel Kcirtap*

---

* Bulgarian heretics. They gave up marriage and giving in marriage, and turned towards their own sex. They are the originals of the old English 'Buggers', who were here, till blanco'd out and replaced in the cause of propriety.

2 January 1990   Chatsworth
                                                            Bakewell

Darling Paddy,

   I was just thinking, AGES since I heard from you & somehow we didn't coincide in August so I was v v pleased to get yours.

The reaper has been at work over Xmas. First Stanley Olsen,[1] then both Droghedas &, worst of all, Sybil [Cholmondeley].

She spent Christmas Day with gt grandchildren, decided to stay in bed a bit on Boxing Day & the person who took her lunch up found her propped with pillows, specs on nose, book in hands, dead. About to be 96. Oh how I loved her.

I'm going to Houghton in two weeks, can't imagine how odd it will seem without her presence. Or perhaps she will be so strongly there one will only be aware of her & the others will be the non-existent ones.

We had all the children & grandchildren for Xmas except beloved Stella Tennant who has gone to Chile to stay with Lucía Santa Cruz[2] for a few months.

Isabel Tennant, Celina & Jasmine Cavendish,[3] all sort of grown up now, are incredibly nice. Isabel & Celina are lovely but the fashion is to make the very worst of your looks. They sit at dinner with hair & face in the soup, hooped backs, & someone cleverly said they (and their peers) are heaps of wool. But they are SO nice. William Burlington[4] has got shoulder blond hair & he wears a mac two sizes too small which he bought 2nd hand some years ago. He's called the Apparition. Also incredibly nice but you wouldn't give him a lift however hard it was raining.

My book is finished & has gone off to Macmillans. What a wonderful feeling. A year late.

LONGING to see you. Please enlarge on London dates. I shall have to come to London sometime re illustrations for my stupid book. Jim [Lees-Milne] says he can't read it, it's *above his head*.

Much love
Debo

I LOVE the Bulgarian heretics being buggers & *J'accuse* & Jack Hughes.

---

1 Stanley Olsen (1947–89). Anglophile American author of *John Singer Sargent: His Portrait* (1986). 'He bicycled round London with a Cocker Spaniel in a basket on the handlebars. Having lunch with him on a wintry day, I was impressed by a big bowl of Iris reticulata on the table – typical of his unusual style.' (DD)

2 Lucía Santa Cruz (1943–). Historian. Daughter of a former, very popular, Chilean ambassador to Britain. Stella Tennant's godmother.

3 Lady Celina (1971–) and Lady Jasmine (1973–) Cavendish. The daughters of
DD's son, Peregrine.
4 Earl of Burlington (1969–). DD's photographer grandson married Laura Montagu,
née Roundell, in 2007.

13 January 1990   Mani

Darling Debo

Your letter's just come – ½ an hour ago – and the airport taxi is
waiting under the olives. Dinner in Athens tonight. Paris next day.

Marvellous description of Sybil Ch's death. The spectacles set the
scene.

I'm writing crampedly because I've drawn a riddle the other side.
The answer, perhaps stale – is in looking-glass writing below.

Love

Paddy

['Name of W. Stickers?' 'Yes.' 'You are under arrest.'

Question: What will tomorrow's headline be?

Answer: Bill Stickers will be prosecuted.]

3 April 1990   Chatsworth
                                                               Bakewell

Darling Paddy,

A typical thing. When we moved here in 1959 I had a
wallpaper made for the Centre Dressing Room, a v complicated
affair copied from a fragment I found in a cupboard. Cole's of
Mortimer St did it.

D[avid] Mlinaric asked if he could have ditto for a client. Yes of
course. Where are the blocks? Cole's have got them I said. Cole's said
No, they're at Chatsworth. Never seen them, I said. Oh said Mr Hall
(who runs the wondrous factory with clattering man-handled
machines, health hazards all) you MUST know where they are. *I sent
them myself in February 1958* — two heavy packing cases. Oh Mr Hall
you come & look for them, I said — he doesn't know this place &
the needle in haystack style.

Any chance of Nancy's letters to you?[1] I would be forever
grateful if you would let me photo them & I would faithfully send
back, no mislaying of them I promise.

So what to do? Michael Pearman[2] had an inspiration. Jesse
Grafton, long retired carpenter, lives next to him, the only living
fellow in that dept who goes back to 1958. Oh yes he said they're in
the Plunge Bath. *And sure enough they were.* So do look in your
Plunge Bath & you never know what you might find.

Much love
    Debo

1 For the collection of Nancy Mitford's letters, *Love from Nancy*, edited by
Charlotte Mosley (1993).
2 The librarian at Chatsworth.

17 April 1990   Mani

Darling Debo,

1,000,000 apologies for being such a sluggard with the pen. It was
'flu first, then the utter and total torment of beginning, writing and
finishing those *Daily Telegraph* articles,[1] the hardest thing I've ever

done, oddly enough, and I'm afraid not very good. *Anyway*, I've faxed them off on the day I said I would and can breathe again.

Now, first things first, Nancy's letters. I've had a tremendous search, and can't find them alas alas! We were *never* terrific correspondents. I wish we had been, because we were sister-souls talking. I should say 10–15 at the outside. I'll have another great hunt the moment this is finished.

Lots of love
Paddy

1 'Travels in a Land before Darkness Fell', *Daily Telegraph* Weekend Magazine, 12 May 1990, reprinted in *Words of Mercury*, pp. 40–50, and 'Ghosts That Haunt the New Dawn', *Daily Telegraph* Weekend Magazine, 19 May 1990. PLF had been sent to Romania by the editor of the *Daily Telegraph*, Max Hastings, to report on the aftermath of the fall of the Ceaușescu regime.

10 May 1990   Chatsworth
(My mother's birthday, 110)   Bakewell
Train to London for 1 night

Darling Paddy,

Any hope of you for the dance (7 July)?[1]

So excited re your articles in *D Tel*.

I wonder if I shall manage them. There is a v good best seller by my bed, called *Woods & Water* or some such name. I'm going to read that one day.

Much love
Debo

1 A ball held at Chatsworth to celebrate William Burlington's coming of age.

26 July 1990   Mani

Darling Debo,

I still haven't quite come round from that amazing thing on the 7th! It was a marvellous grand arrival there – the expanse of empty

Above: DD shooting at Bolton Abbey, Yorkshire. 'Describing a shoot to a non-participant is as bad as going over games of golf or bridge, so I spared Paddy the bother of reading about it'

Right: DD in her sitting room at Chatsworth

Ann Fleming in the blue drawing room,
Chatsworth, 1966

Diana Cooper

Philip Toynbee and Jessica Mitford, 1966

Andrew Devonshire and PLF in Peru, 1971. 'We had been included, as minor amateurs, in a mountaineering expedition in the Andes'

Jacket design by John Craxton for *A Time of Gifts* (1977)

Niko Ghika and PLF in Corfu with a tabletop painted by PLF showing Greek and Latin names for the winds

PLF at Dumbleton

Joan Leigh Fermor at Tramores, Andalusia, staying with Janetta and Jaime Parladé

Right: DD and her working sheepdog, Collie

Below left: HRH the Prince of Wales and Sybil Cholmondeley on her ninetieth birthday, 1984

Below right: DD with her sisters Diana Mosley (*centre*) and Pamela Jackson (*left*), 1980s

PLF and Xan Fielding at the fiftieth anniversary of the Battle of Crete, 1991

Joan Leigh Fermor in the Mani

Elisabeth Frink (*left*) and DD at the installation of Frink's *War Horse*, April 1992

Above: DD with her granddaughter Stella Tennant, Chatsworth, 2006 (*photograph Mario Testino*)

Right: From DD's letter to PLF, 23 September 2006

Stella came. We had to be together in a photo for Vogue's 90th birthday come Christmas. So one Mario Testino, famous photograph came in a helicopter with a crew of make-up, hairdresser "fashion editor" etc from London

I've got a really beautiful dress, grand evening, given me by Oscar de la Renta so that was my kit.

They bound Stella's legs up to where they join her body, in tartan. A union jack flag hung from her waist & her top & was what my father would have called meaningless.

Hair skewbald/piebald, all colours & stuck up in bits. THEN they produced "shoes" with 6 inch heels. More

DD and PLF. Edensor, February 2008 (*photograph Bridget Flemming*)

black-and-white check floor, then the great swoop of scarlet stairs, with your solitary triumvirate welcomingly halted half way up . . . It was as if the whole house had transformed into a different element, half familiar and half unknown, like a fair, or an aquarium full of resplendent creatures and any number of friendly faces, starting with Henry's.[1] The tented acreage – those steps and the normally outdoors reclining statue and dog being *indoors* gave a real through-the-looking-glass feeling. The whole thing, that array of people looking after us, everything being marvellous and *on time*, as though being painlessly managed with a magic wand – there were so many openings for things being held up, or going wrong. None did and, for me, the whole thing dissolved into one of those golden Turner radiances. I know you weren't too keen on the Masque, but it was lovely it being from an Inigo Jones drawing in the Library, *and as for* that thunderous Beethoven accompaniment to the fireworks, words spring so abundantly to the nib that I'll spare.

The great thing was that you and Andrew spread such a feeling of enjoyment and warmth and fun, that it seemed to affect everything else. It was only later that it occurred to me that I had told my entire life story to Madame de Vogüé[2] last time, the only one, I'd sat next to her, but it didn't seem to matter. Part of the previously golden Turneresque mist was that I lost touch with all nearest and dearest – couldn't find you or Robert, sat and had long chats with Coote and Billa.[3] What was strange was that it seemed simultaneously to last for ever and to be over almost at once. Like Wellington's battle comparison. It all looked fantastic, driving away, looking back on bridge and river, the big tent, the full moon high up, a few decorative alabaster clouds floating discreetly, some people strolling under oak trees, and dawn beginning to break. It was still total glory. I'll never see anything like it again, nor will anyone, and many many thanks to you and Andrew,

    And tons of love from

      Paddy

1 Henry Coleman (1947–). Butler to the Devonshire family since 1963.
2 Maria Cristina Colonna (1941–). Married in 1966 Count Patrice de Vogüé, owner of Vaux-le-Vicomte, the seventeenth-century chateau outside Paris that inspired Versailles.

3 Wilhelmine (Billa) Cresswell (1911–2005). Architectural conservationist. Married the economist Roy Harrod in 1938. 'For many years she and Roy were an important part of university life at Oxford. After she was widowed and returned to her native Norfolk, she made a big impact on the tide of interest in the preservation of the best buildings as founder of the Norfolk Churches Trust. Thanks to her, and her friend the Prince of Wales, this organisation flourishes.' (DD)

30 July 1990   Mani

Darling Debo,

JJ Norwich's daughter Artemis and her husband Antony Beevor have just left. He's writing a book about wartime Crete,[1] so is doing a round of old hands. Both are extremely nice. He described his very reserved Wykehamist father and equally reserved mother trudging back from the polling station on election day:

He 'By the way, what did you vote?'

She 'Labour. What about you?'

He 'Conservative.' (Pause) 'I say, we needn't have gone!'

Tons of love,

    Paddy

1 *Crete: The Battle and the Resistance* (1991). Winner of the Runciman Prize.

14 September 1990   Chatsworth
                                                         Bakewell

Darling Paddy,

Wife has found a frightful mistake in *The Estate*. It wasn't Mrs Pettitoes who was a Berkshire, but Pig-wig.[1] The result of pure laziness on my part in not checking. I am horror-struck. I expect it is full of such slips.

The next two weeks are going to bore everyone stiff, the hullabaloo arranged by Macmillan for pushing it under the noses of all. They'll be sick of my ugly mug & worse voice by 27 Sept when it's supposed to burst on an unsuspecting world which will have had enough already.

Someone has sent us a video of the fireworks at the ball, amateur, &

taken from over the river. He & his friend did a lot of talking which comes over better than Beethoven, they said things like I bet this cost a bit WHAT? I BET THIS COST A BIT & such-like prime comments.

Andrew says (he is a news-on-telly addict) that some American soldiers in Arabia have applied for danger money. Do you think you & Xan & Andrew & everyone we know could ask for some back-dated ditto? My word you'd be rich.

 Much love
  Debo

1 Two characters in Beatrix Potter's *The Tale of Pigling Bland*.

23 October 1990   Mani

Darling Debo,

The bad news, of course, is about Xan, the dread disease running riot, everywhere, when thought to be only what's called a spot. He went into hospital in Paris day before yesterday, for some preliminary treatment, and came out two hours ago (just been on telephone). He *sounds* v cheery and high-spirited; Magouche, when alone on the blower much less so, naturally enough. It really is a bugger. They've got hold of a lovely flat, in the Place des Pyramides, where Joan of Arc, all gold, waves a flag on horseback ¾ of the way down the Rue de Rivoli. We've just been talking about it. It's bang opposite the Hôtel Regina, where I spent the first night in my life abroad with mother & sister, aged nine, a marvellous palace it seemed to me, with lav paper with pictures on and a serial story, so one *had* to read on. Each sequence took about 10 sheets which must have entailed a huge turnover.

 Please keep in touch, and tons of love from
  Paddy

I've come across this, in an old notebook: –

Nurse (to Iris Tree, when v ill) Lady Diana [Cooper] is here. Do you want to see her?
Iris Not in the least. But I want her to see me.

31 October 1990   Chatsworth
As from, but really c/o Wife at Bignor   Bakewell

Darling Paddy,

Thanks so much for yours. *OH XAN. It is foul beyond words.* I never thought of him as a cancer person, somehow one can imagine some people getting it & others as non-qualifiers, but one forgets the indiscriminating way it strikes. YOU YOU & YOU, taking no note of age, sex, upbringing, mode of life, profession, where you live. It is like 'Oranges & Lemons', down it comes & there you are. I keep thinking about him & only hope 'they' don't allow it to hurt. Ghoulish for you & Magouche & all who love him. Oh bother everything to do with bodies when they go wrong.

Home via Woman, lunch in the pub at Swinbrook to view my kingdom, & then next day DON'T LAUGH a Lit Lunch in Leamington Spa for my stupid book at which I have to speak to the unlucky audience for ¼ of an hour. So do a Chinese cook (written a book on his art), Lady Donaldson on P. G. Wodehouse & Michael Holroyd on Shaw.[1] Do admit the terror. I kick off I think (they always start with the worst & end with the star) & I'm going to say BOOKS how I hate them – as an avid non-reader it is awful to have added to their number etc etc. The trouble is a bookseller is giving the lunch so I do hope he/she/it won't mind. Wouldn't be asked again so it doesn't matter much.

Then I dig in at home for a bit to struggle with a children's book about farm animals[2] which a publisher wants *very soon*, wouldn't suit you.

Much love
Debo

---

[1] Frances Donaldson's life of P. G. Wodehouse was published in 1982, and the second volume of Michael Holroyd's life of George Bernard Shaw, *The Pursuit of Power, 1898–1918*, in 1989.
[2] *Farm Animals* (1991).

22 December 1990   Mani

Darling Debo,

The Xan news isn't cheering. They both sound very chipper on the telephone, but that's as expected. Janetta says Xan is a bit better, as they've knocked off the wretched chemical treatment temporarily, but it can only be temporary. We are going to Paris in January, I do hope it's the right thing to do; if one's feeling rotten, visitors can be a fearful burden. A very minor worry at the moment is that the *Daily Telegraph* rang the other day and said, would I do a pre-emptive piece about Xan, and I'm finding it unexpectedly hard – he's very difficult to pin down, a strange and rare specimen. I remember about 15 years ago, Xan telling me *The Times* had asked him to do one about me and he let me have a look; 'Any criticisms or suggestions?' I don't think there were any, as it was a corker – '*Can't wait!*' I remember saying – lots of bad taste hilarity.

I know you never read, but did you see the bit about *The Estate* in the *Spectator*? I'm afraid the pen rather ran away with me about tupping and drenching, couldn't resist it.[1]

Tons of love from
    Paddy

I've just come across this in an old notebook: –

> The operas of Benjamin Britten
> Should never be actually written
> In ink, or sung loud
> But inscribed on a cloud
> With the tail of a Siamese kitten.

[1] In PLF's 'Books of the Year' choice, he wrote, 'The Duchess of Devonshire carries us helter-skelter through innumerable acres, fells and woods, into byres, auction-tents and timber-yards, up into lofts and down drains. It is full of deep rustic addiction, comedy and barnyard lore, with no dearth of tupping and drenching. A week back I knew nothing of orf, scrapie, swayback, blackleg, rattle-belly, pine, scad or scald but I'm older and wiser now.' *Spectator*, 24 November 1990.

6 January 1991   Mani

Debo –

    Happy New Year to one and all, and tons of love from
      Paddy

A song against dropping in, obviously inspired by a Victorian muse.

VOIX D'OUTRETOMBE

I dropped in at my neighbour's house
At six o'clock one morning;
I thought no shame to knock him up
Just as the day was dawning.

I found him reading by the fire
After a light refection.
'Come into my den,' he said,
'I'll show you my collection.

'This little gun is fired by steam
And shoots a silver button.
I call on sheep when day is done
And turn them into mutton.

'This chopper's handy on a stroll
At the turning of the leaf;
I track young bullocks to their byre
And change them all to beef.

'This garotte's for domestic fowls
When days are long and sultry;
In record time the noisiest coop's
A heap of silent poultry.

'That Sheffield poleaxe on the wall
Is sprung with tensile steel;
I waylay calves in summertime
And, suddenly, they're veal.

'Now this electric crossbow here
Is proving a real benison;
Its bolts convert the antlered ones
Like lightning, into venison.

'This "Circe" razor's just the thing
Upon a country walk
– Nothing to touch it, in a sty,
For turning swine to pork!'

'And what's that cleaver in your hand,
So sharp and bright and bare?'
I asked him, as, with nonchalance,
He strolled towards my chair.

'Don't rise,' he said, 'this one's my joy!
Just the right length and weight!
It's kept for early birds like you.
It makes them all "The late"!

'One application does the trick –
Just watch!' – the chamber shook;
He put the cleaver in the sink
And went back to his book.

P.S. I append some sketches which attempt to catch the feeling of
the period.

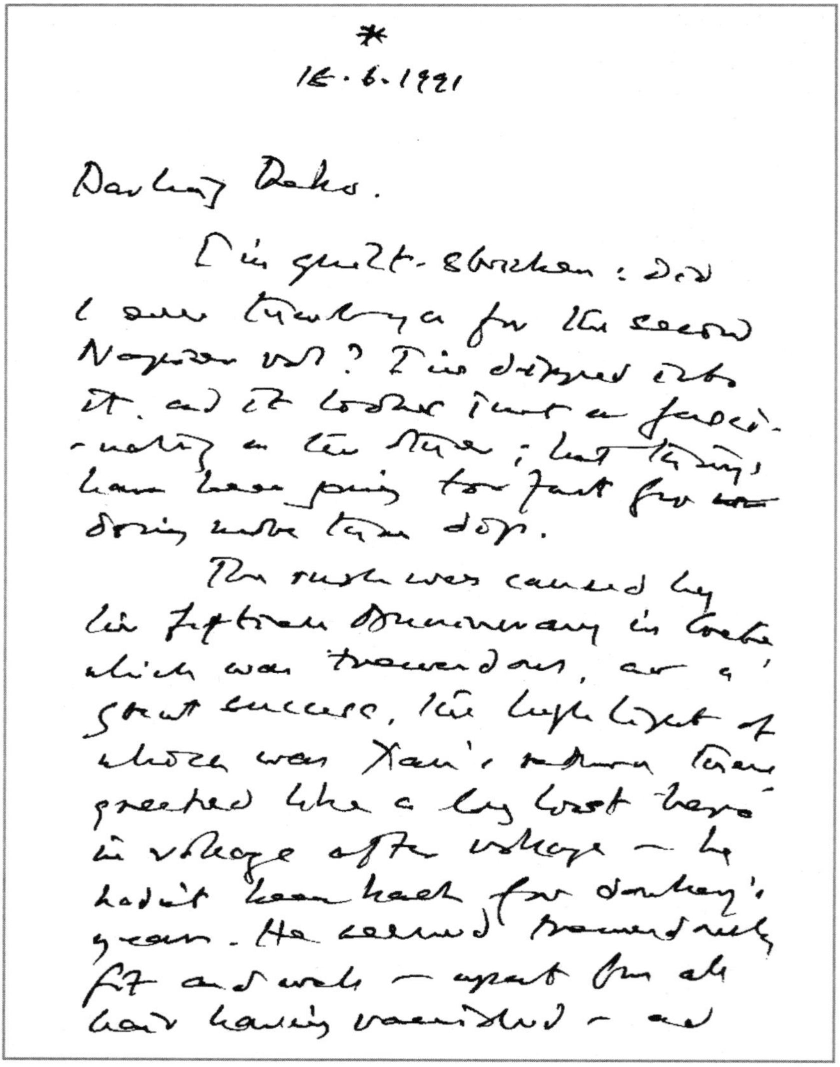

*

18.6.1991

Darling Debo,

[handwritten letter text]

---

18 June 1991   Mani

Darling Debo,

I'm guilt-stricken: did I ever thank you for the second Napier
vol?[1] I've dipped into it, and it looks just as fascinating as the other;
but things have been going too fast for me for doing more than dip.

The rush was caused by the fiftieth anniversary in Crete, which was tremendous, and a great success, the highlight of which was Xan's return there, greeted like a long lost hero in village after village – he hadn't been back for donkey's years. He seemed tremendously fit and well – apart from all hair having vanished – and it was a glorious success. We – Geo. Jellicoe,[2] Xan, David Sutherland[3] (ex-commander of SBS), Nick Hammond[4] and I were given a special parade of Marines for the presentation of medals – not to be *worn*, alas; only stroked from time to time; and sort of blue velvet hollow marshals' batons containing scrolls saying we were marvellous. I had to address hundreds of splendid N.Z., Aus, and British Veterans about the Cretan share in the Battle. They were dry-eyed at the end of it, but only just.

I've got to return to Blighty for a bit from the 24th onwards for 2–3 weeks (being allowed to doss down at Janetta's), and will be in touch, so we must have a lovely feast. *Why* I'm coming back is to be made a D Litt by the University of Kent. I'm v excited as the Hood – what colour, I wonder? – is slipped over one's head in the chancel of Canterbury Cathedral, only a stone's throw from the place I got the sack from 1000 years ago.[5] We stop for 4 days in Paris on the way back, to see Xan and his mate.

Tons of love
Paddy

1 Priscilla Napier, *Raven Castle: Charles Napier in India, 1844–1851* (1991). PLF wrote of the first volume, *I Have Sind, Charles Napier in India, 1841–1844* (1990), 'I love the dashing style of the author, and the no nonsense absence of humbug, and the humour.' PLF to DD, 2 September 1990.

2 George Jellicoe, 2nd Earl Jellicoe (1918–2007). PLF had been friends with the diplomat, politician and businessman ever since they had invisibly passed each other in pitch darkness, soon after midnight, in a cove off southern Crete in 1942. Jellicoe, who had been on a raid that blew up some twenty German aircraft, was boarding; PLF, who spent the next fifteen months dwelling in caves, was landing.

3 Colonel David Sutherland (1920–2006). Wartime commander of the Special Boat Service and deputy commander of the SAS 1967–72.

4 Nicholas Hammond (1907–2001). Distinguished classical scholar recruited to SOE who helped to organise Cretan wartime resistance. Published a memoir of his war service, *Venture into Greece: With the Guerillas, 1943–1944* (1983).

5 PLF spent three years at The King's School, Canterbury, the oldest school in

England, and sometime haunt of Christopher Marlowe and Somerset Maugham, where he was thought, probably rightly, 'a dangerous mixture of sophistication and recklessness'. He was expelled, aged sixteen, after being caught holding hands with the local greengrocer's beautiful daughter.

27 July 1991   Mani

Darling Debo,

I must have been cracked to make a putative date for lunch on the very day I was going through those extraordinary doings in Canterbury. I'm so sorry – thank heavens you *couldn't* come. I ought to be locked up.

The whole thing was marvellous. I went down with Jock & Diana [Murray], and all guests and graduands were given luncheon in the main Dining Hall of my old school, and it made me feel like the Prodigal Son. We put on marvellous scarlet robes in the Treasury of the Cathedral and floppy Holbein hats, and did a slow march up the nave behind a man with a mace – the sort of thing Andrew has had to do dozens of times. Then, at the top of the nave-chancel steps the Chancellor (rather a dasher, head of BP, called Robert Horton)[1] and the other bigwigs in green and gold robes designed by the first Chancellor (viz. Marina, Dss of Kent) sat in a formidable array. The only other Dr to be made that afternoon was a nice American, Barbara Burn (DCL)[2] then three hundred BAs. Marvellous dewdrops about us followed. I would have liked it to have gone on forever, and must get a copy to read when feeling depressed. Then I had to answer – less than five minutes. A lovely *Barchester*-like day, tea under a shady copper-beech in the Archdeacon's garden, ending with a great banquet at the University. A heavenly day and everyone going out full-tilt to be kind and welcoming.

Lots of love
Paddy

[1] Robert Horton (1939–). The British businessman was Chancellor of the University of Kent 1990–5.
[2] Barbara Burn (d. 2002). Doctor of Civil Law and prominent leader in international education.

22 August 1991   Chatsworth
                                                           Bakewell

Darling Paddy,

Xan. Oh what a paragon he was. *How* you will miss him, your
best Wife and everything else. Reading the obits brought back
the amazing career, & '*je déteste les robes du soir*'[1] came through
strong.

I expect he was quieter by the time I knew him, all savagery
gone, like my Dad told my Wife when she said 'I imagined you'd be
so frightening, Lord Redesdale.'

I'm reviewing (don't laugh) *The National Trust Manual of
Housekeeping* for a mag with the smallest circulation in the world.[2]
It is good sport. You can't imagine the horrors that go on in
houses — moth, rust, carpet beetle, Byne's disease which attacks
mother-of-pearl, humidity, mould . . . I bet you've never heard
of the infamous Bacon Beetle. Denied his favourite food (bacon,
fool) because there's no breakfast in Nat Trust houses, he goes
for a blob of fat from the belly of your best stuffed-fish.
Surprised?

Another cheery thing. I was in the garden talking to a friend, too
loud I expect as per, when a man came up & said Excuse me I've
read about a 1930s voice but I've never *heard* one, do keep on talking,
please. So I did, lorst and gorn forever & he was doubled up and so
was I & in the end he said well I'll give you one thing, you haven't
got a stiff upper lip.

Much love
    Debo

1 Xan Fielding, who died on 19 August, aged seventy-two, was fiercely bohemian.
Invited once to a 'little reception' in evening dress, he replied angrily, 'I *hate*
evening dress.' 'The phrase stuck to him. He got reconciled to them later on . . .'
(PLF)
2 DD reviewed the manual for *Historic House*, the magazine of the Historic Houses
Association, Winter 1991. Reprinted in *Counting My Chickens*, pp. 146–9.

9 September 1991   Mani

Darling Debo,

It was marvellous the spread newspapers gave to poor old Xan, tho' some of them made it look as though he'd won the war single-handed, with me as his loader. But I *was* pleased, for his sake and all his pals, not to vanish un-sung. I don't know what one will do without him, though we only met a few times a year, owing to remote abodes. I wrote my bit about him two years ago, but when Magouche rang up with the awful news, got on to the head of that department in the *D Telegraph*, to add the bit about the final visit to Crete, and what a miracle it was. The head of obits. is a chap called Hugh M-Massingberd,[1] whom I've only met once but he was tremendously helpful, and said they had added a lot of stuff, to precede my bit, would I like to hear it? So he read it all out. There was quite a lot about Daph's and Henry's (first secret) wedding:[2] were they some freak kind of bigamists. Was D's and X's marriage valid etc? Terrible gossip column stuff, all of which he had taken out when I blew up; also, at the end of 'writer, soldier, traveller, etc', they had stuck 'adventurer', which means a sort of crook, which is just what Xan wasn't – a paragon of correctness! – so that came out too, and several other dark jams, some of them due to people no longer knowing what words mean.

I'm so glad the dedication has given pleasure.[3] I often think it means more to the writer than the dedicatee. You come first on the page as Andrew is up front all through, and you very slowly glitter for a second in the wings. I wish the vol. was a bit less slim, but I'm such a slow coach with the longer ones, and may get run over before the current one is ready to be dedicated to anyone.

All greetings to Andrew, and lots of love from
    Paddy

---

[1] Hugh Montgomery-Massingberd (1946–2007). Obituaries editor of the *Daily Telegraph* 1986–94, who introduced a new, less reverential style to the paper's necrological column.

[2] Daphne and Henry Bath faced parental opposition when they announced that they wanted to marry and the ceremony took place privately in 1926. They then

had a public wedding in 1927. Their divorce in 1953 covered only their second marriage and in 1955, when they were both remarried, they sought an appeal to the High Court to get the annulment extended to their first.

3 The dedication to DD and Andrew in *Three Letters from the Andes*, which had just been published.

18 September 1991   Bolton Abbey
                                                              Skipton

Darling Paddy,

I loved you being Xan's loader in the war – page more likely, like Good King Wenceslas.

HASTE, back to the grouse, MILLIONS of them.

Much love
     Debo

10 November 1991   Mani

Darling Debo,

The last weekend before leaving, Joan and I went to stay with Myles Hildyard at his strange and rather marvellous house called Flintham in Notts. It's got a tall Paxtonian greenhouse, with tree-ferns etc, two stories high, jutting straight out of an equally tall library, full of splendid vols. But the point is the *total niceness* of Myles – do you remember he came over to lunch? The only other guest was Ken Davison,[1] whom I hadn't seen for years. The atmosphere in the house is like Leach illustrations to Surtees, marvellous rambling stables where we went to see two pensioned donkeys of great charm. Endless walled gardens with crumbling statues. Fascinating to *me* was lunch 20 miles away at a house called Aubourne, of which the point was that the inhabitant, Henry Nevile,[2] was staying at Baleni – my Rumanian hangout – when war broke out, and we came back in Sept 1939 together, seen off by my pals and Lady Hoare (Bill Bentinck's sister and the Bucharest ambassadress),[3] who equipped us with sweets and toys, and a tied-on label for Henry, as she was not quite clear about our ages: 24 for me, 18 for Henry, who had just left

Ampleforth. We went over all our adventures on the way − 5 days −
halting at Venice, before both heading for the Guards' Depot in
Caterham, he later than me. I hadn't seen him for 52 years. Lots of
snaps and albums. He's now Ld Lieutenant of Lincolnshire, hard to
link with the pink-cheeked blue-eyed nipper of yore, but v. nice.

After that we saw Lincoln Cathedral, on tiptoe because of Evensong;
then Ld Byron's abode, Newstead, but too late, it was closed, as shadows
had fallen. Myles said, 'Slip in, and have a look at his dog Bo'sun's
monument, we'll keep cave (KV)', so I slithered through a hedge, and
zig-zagged through the rhodies rather furtively, but thought this is no
way to trespass: the only thing is to walk slowly, pausing for the view, if
possible finishing a cigar, as tho' taking a pre-bath breath of fresh-air.
The monument is very moving. I gazed unapprehended.

Lots of love

Paddy

[1] Kensington Davison, 3rd Baron Broughshane (1914–2006). Opera administrator
and critic.
[2] Henry Nevile (1920–96). Served in the Scots Guards. Lord Lieutenant of
Lincolnshire 1975–95.
[3] Lucy Cavendish-Bentinck (d. 1971). Married in 1922 Sir Reginald Hoare, British
minister-plenipotentiary in Bucharest 1935–41.

27 November 1991   Chatsworth
                                                      Bakewell

Darling Paddy,

Can't think of any news. Births, marriages or deaths are the
headings for my other abroad-dwelling correspondent viz. Decca but
all seems quiet in those departments just now.

Smithfield[1] looms, Cake to lunch there, much raising of glasses &
toasts to Tom Dick & Harry, any excuse really. I love going in her
wake through the crowds, she has an extraordinary effect on the
populace, the faces when she's passed unexpectedly are v revealing,
giggles, amazement, cameras too late, only getting backs of people
like me. Worth seeing.

We have MUTTON & caper sauce for lunch. It's trad now, used

to be lamb, she asked for mutton, almost unobtainable unless you keep a sheep specially, for more months than usual, till Mother Nature turns it from lamb to mutton.

Tonight wonderful Dame Elis Frink & husband[2] (surprisingly to do with racing, an ex-starter I think) come for the night & a look round tomorrow, then to Manchester where she is to give a lecture & I'M GOING. Wonders will never . . . but it's only because she's so fascinating. Then the Prince of Wales comes, in the middle of the night from a dinner in London. I must put a trail of breadcrumbs to his room. Can't wait up, too sleepy.

Much love
Debo

1 The Royal Smithfield Show.
2 Elisabeth Frink (1930–93). The sculptor and printmaker married in 1974, as her third husband, Count Alex Csáky.

6 December 1991   Mani

Darling Debo

I loved your Cake-walk description. I adore your letters, but wish they hadn't got such *RARITY* value, as all my other correspondents have conked out.

Florence Nightingale had a passion for really good mutton, as distinct from lamb. It was the mainstay of her luncheon parties near you in Curzon St in the evening of her life.

Lots of love
Paddy

4 January 1992   Chatsworth
                                                 Bakewell

Darling Paddy,

Christmas was a full house, 16. Very jolly. Followed by a week of pure luxury, viz. no one, so I could moon about the garden and do exactly what I fancied. Those dead days between Xmas & New Year are really good, post-less, no one where they're meant to be & totally calm.

One evening *White Mischief*[1] was on the telly. *Did you see it when it was a film?* I didn't, but MY WORD I was fascinated by it & can still think of 0 else. My poor old eyes have suffered from a close study of the Red Book, trying to work out who was who, from Lady Idina[2] on. What an incredible affair − the only one I ever saw − can't say *knew* − was Ly Delamere[3] who used to come to Frank More O'Ferrall's[4] Derby night dinners, & I was struck by her beauty even when pretty old, extraordinary eyes & smothered in square 1930s jewels. I wish I'd studied her properly.

Diana [Mosley] is coming soon. I do hope she'll remember some of them. Erroll was too lovely in the film.[5] I suppose he really was. Bother not knowing him. The sort of hopeless cad I love.

We went to the dinner for the deification of the Sainsbury bros at Downing St to note the new bit of the Nat Gallery.[6]

I fell, hook line & sinker, for Mr Major.[7] Norma was somewhere else so he was alone saying How do you do. He said that, & then said How very nice to see you again, which was very nice because I'd never seen him before. He exudes GOODNESS, unheard of in a politician, eh.

I sat between old Lord Sainsbury[8] & Tim, MP. Old Ld S has always been a socialist & he said You know I'm very radical. So I said Oh yes & he went on about how when he bought a house in Suffolk in the early 30s the gardener had never had a holiday. Well I suppose ours never had, nor our groom whom I adored & spent my childhood with. If he'd had a holiday I would have had a nervous breakdown.

Anyway he was a dear old soul, 90 this year, & I gladly cut up the tough pheasant for him. He doesn't seem to mind being very rich.

The speeches, John Sainsbury & the PM, were short & perfect. John had a slight go at Venturi the architect (who wasn't there). I believe there had been *monumental* rows but all he said was that, after a slight disagreement, Venturi was heard to say Lord Sainsbury doesn't seem to realise I'm a genius.

So that was the highlight of the autumn.

I'm back to 2nd childhood in the chicken line. I look after them myself & the intense pleasure of watching them at work & play is something I have missed, I suppose since the war.

I'm SWAMPED in eggs, so asked the farm manager for the regulations re selling them in the Farm Shop.[9] You simply can't imagine how wild they are. It seems you have to have doctors & vets in white coats who do unspeakable indignities to the poor hens. Then you have to post away, to some laboratory, their messes — sorry, faeces. But before you consign them to the post you must check with the PO the regs re posting chicken's messes.

When this pantomime is completed you have to grade the eggs, mustn't be a millimetre out in guaranteed size. Then you get a Packing Station number but they don't tell you how to do that. Then, MOST IMPORTANT, you must wash your hands before *and after* collecting the eggs. In my case it's quite a trek to the chicken house, so what happens if it is cold & I put on gloves? Mightn't there be an infection in one of the fingers?

Oh Whack what madness when ½ the world is starving & would be quite pleased to see my beautiful eggs.

I'll keep you informed of the progress towards selling them, even if you aren't in the least interested.

Much love

Debo

1 The film about the infamous murder of 22nd Earl of Erroll in Kenya in 1941, based on a book by James Fox (1982), was released in 1987.

2 Lady Idina Sackville (1893–1955). An inspiration for Nancy Mitford's character, The Bolter. Lady Idina's third (of five) husbands was the murdered Lord Erroll, to whom she was married 1923–30. Her first husband was Captain Euan Wallace, with whom she had two sons.

3 Diana Caldwell (1913–87). Married, in 1955, 4th Baron Delamere as his third wife and her fourth husband. Her second husband was Sir John (Jock) Delves Broughton who was tried, and acquitted, for the murder of Lord Erroll, with whom she had been having an affair.

4 Frank More O'Ferrall (1904–76). One of three Irish brothers who ran the successful Anglo-Irish Bloodstock Agency. He and his wife, Angela, were great friends of the Devonshires.

5 Lord Erroll was played by the British actor Charles Dance.

6 The three Sainsbury brothers, John, Simon and Timothy, funded an extension to the National Gallery, designed by the post-modernist architect Robert Venturi at a cost of some £50 million.

7 John Major (1943–). The Conservative Prime Minister had been in office for just over a year. Married Norma Johnson in 1970.

8 Alan John Sainsbury (1902–98). The father of the three brothers, Life President of the supermarket chain, was created a life peer in 1962.

9 In 1977, DD opened a shop in Pilsley, a village on the Chatsworth estate, to sell high-quality British produce.

31 January 1992   Mani

Darling Debo,

Marvellous letter about the PM and the banquet for the Sainsburys and their table talk. Cyril Connolly, during a reception for Gen. de Gaulle at the Fr. Embassy, and as his turn came in the queue, Gen de Gaulle, shaking hands, said *Très heureux de vous revoir*,[1] and C.C. was delighted (never met before). So it must be a Head of State secret device. C.C. had been given a modest form of the Légion d'honneur a month or two earlier, was wearing it for the first time on his lapel, 'When what should I see but John Lehmann, with something the size of a *pineapple* round his neck on a ribbon! Evening ruined, of course.'[2] I expect he was loved because of Mme Massigli's[3] fondness for Lehmann. I couldn't bear him.

There's a storm on, howling winds outside, and no light here or in the village, so this is being scribbled by candlelight.

How fascinating about *White Mischief*. I didn't care for the book, or the film, because in both Idina – Dina to me – seemed such a travesty. We must go back a bit.

When, in summer 1937, Balasha Cantacuzène (whom I adored as you know, twelve years older) and I were living in the top bit of a watermill in a steep forest of orange groves opposite the island of Poros, in the top of the Peloponnese, we saw three figures approaching under the vine leaves, one well-known, and a frequent visitor, an amusing queer Greek diplomat called Aleko Matsas (perhaps you knew him), a slim, long-legged woman in a green top, green shorts, sandals and dark glasses, and a tall rather willowy chap of my age (viz. 20) in rust-coloured sailcloth trousers. B said to me, 'Who can Aleko have brought? She reminds me of Dina Wallace.' Of course it *was*. She and her bro Buck D. L.[4] had been v kind to B (being brought out in London soon after the end of WWI by her worldly mother). Great embracements ensued. The tall young man was her son David Wallace,[5] whom she had met – for the first time since he was a baby – shortly before. He must just have come of age. All contact with Dina had been forbidden after she had buzzed off with (?) Gordon (?) Erroll? (She was called Haldeman then.) They had all three met in Athens. They stayed with us ten days including a *three-day* peasant feast at the mill. There was something absolutely charming about her, very pretty, light-boned, slight recession of chin, v funny and appealing too, totally unlike the bitch in the film, much better and lighter style. She was leaving in a week for Prague to meet 'somebody I'm a bit potty about, I'm afraid, a sea-dog called Ponsonby'. I wonder why Prague, so far from the briny. She had a passion for taking snaps. I wondered what happened to them, there must have been 100, but her daughter, married to Ilk,[6] couldn't find them when I asked her years ago.

David, who had just been sharing rooms at Oxford with Guy Branch[7] and Jeremy Hutchinson,[8] I saw a lot of later. He was dropped into Northern Greece and killed in a guerrilla skirmish with Germans, while rescuing somebody wounded. Billy W[9] was the only one to survive of them.

I've got to dash to the post. Lots of love,
　　Paddy

---

1 'So pleased to see you again.'

2 John Lehmann (1907–87), the poet, writer and publisher, was made an Officer of the Legion of Honour in 1958. Connolly was awarded the lesser rank of Knight in 1947. Their meeting at the French embassy took place in 1960, when Connolly was 'much impressed by "Bonny Johnny" Lehmann's chestful of medals'. Jeremy Lewis, *Cyril Connolly, A Life* (Jonathan Cape, 1997), p. 503.

3 Odette Boissier; wife of René Massigli, French ambassador in London 1944–55. The ambassador in London during General de Gaulle's 1960 visit was Jean Chauvel (1897–1979), a diplomat and – like Lehmann – a poet.

4 Herbrand Sackville, 9th Earl De La Warr (1900–76). Labour politician.

5 David Wallace (1914–44). Lady Idina's elder son died in action on 17 August 1944. Her younger son, Gerard, was killed in action on 20 August 1943.

6 Sir Iain Moncreiffe of that Ilk (1919–85). Genealogist, writer and friend of PLF since they trained together at the Guards' Depot, Caterham, in 1939. Married in 1946 Diana Hay, daughter of 22nd Earl of Erroll. 'Iain had a delightfully romantic cast of mind: he looked at life through a Baroness Orczy–John Buchan–Dornford Yates prism.' PLF, Afterword to *Ill Met by Moonlight,* Folio Society, 2001.

7 Guy Rawstron Branch (1913–40). Read English at Balliol College then worked for the British Council before joining up as a Flying Officer in the RAF. Killed in the Battle of Britain. Married Lady Prudence Pelham in 1939. 'Guy was much admired by Maurice Bowra and Isaiah Berlin. The sort of person that everyone fell in love with.' (PLF)

8 Jeremy Hutchinson (1915–). 'A brilliant QC and one famous for his skill, balance and witty enjoyment of life.' (PLF) Brother of Barbara Ghika. Created a life peer in 1978.

9 William (Billy) Wallace (1927–77). Captain Euan Wallace's youngest son by his second marriage to Barbara Lutyens. His two older brothers, John (1922–46) and Edward (1923–44), were both killed in action.

22 January 1992   Chatsworth
                                                            Bakewell

Darling Paddy,

A quick line to say the P of Wales was here (as per) earlier this week & he plans a wk-end at Sandringham (which he borrows from time to time) on 10 April. He is asking the non-shooting types, some painters I've never heard of, dear good Angela Conner[1] etc. He kindly includes me, can't think why. I know he's going to ask you (blind date? Can't remember if you know him). Anyway the house will be choc a bloc & IF you can come (you will, won't you) you will be in my dressing room, we must squeeze in together. I told him that's nothing new, I have slept head to tail with you & nine Spanish gardeners before now.[2]

I've done that wk-end twice. We tool round the wondrous

Norfolk churches in the freezing April cold & this year he thinks he might get us into Holkham.[3] Just think how jolly.

So, if & when the invitation comes kindly accept & take an anti snoring pill as we'll be cheek by . . .

Haste for post.

Much love

Debo

Fancy you knowing Ly Idina & giving her such a good reference. Of course she must have had huge charm & that did not come through in book or film. It was the *story* which I found so gripping.

1 Angela Conner (1935–). The sculptress, a friend of the Devonshires since 1964, made portrait busts of several members of the family and designed a water sculpture, *Revelation*, for the garden at Chatsworth.

2 'In 1958, I went with Paddy and others to see the Whitsun parade in El Rocio, Andalusia. There was no room at the inn, so we slept head to toe on the stone floor of a shed already occupied by some Spanish gardeners. Quite an odd night.' (DD)

3 Prince Charles arranged a private visit for his party to Holkham Hall, seat of the Earl of Leicester.

1? February 1992   Mani

Darling Debo,

Your letter about Sandringham. You write IF you come: can a duck swim? I suspected your kind guiding hand in all this a few days earlier. A terribly nice secretary rang and said would wife and I come for the weekend? I said, after a quick 'aside' confabulation, that alas, it would mean only me, as wife couldn't, and she said, 'Well, we've got *one* of you, anyway.' So there we are. You know what a hermit Joan is – longs to be a fly on the wall, to hear what's said and, above all, to learn what was eaten, which I never can remember. Thank heavens I did remember to trouser the menus on the only former occasion.

It's very decent of you to let me doss down in your dressing room, and reminds me, *in a way*, of that Spanish pilgrimage to Our Lady of the Dew, 1000 years ago.

Lots of love from

Paddy

9 February 1992   Chatsworth
                                                   Bakewell

Darling Paddy,

I've just got back from several days in the Soft Under Belly of SW Wilts, in other words staying with Sophy.[1]

Do you know that country? Driving to Crichel[2] for lunch we passed four cars in 16 miles, the narrowest lanes you ever saw, no humans & steep ups & downs of downs & then wet valleys, so beautiful, secret & real country. I believe it all belongs to two people therefore isn't covered with this & that foul buildings. I'd never seen that part of England before. If I was rootless & deciding where to live I'd have no doubt.

Sophy's bit has far the best woods I've ever seen. One is enormous, 1500 acres. There was a lawn meet of the S & W Wilts at Fonthill House, where the ancient grandad Margadale lives.

Diana [Mosley] & I were early, as per, so the old boy asked us in & showed us his pictures & all of that, then said I'll go out of the kitchen & let you out of the other door. He went out, forgot we existed & there we were, fatally locked in, while horses & hounds loomed. In the end a henchman saw us at a window & let us out. V comical.

On the way home I spent a morning at a rare breed chicken & ducks place, looking for amazing ones for the Prince, who fancies some. The owner is one of those specialists I love, blinkered interest in old poultry.

Let's go together to our famous wk-end.

Much love

    Debo

---

[1] DD's daughter Sophy was married to Alastair Morrison, later 3rd Baron Margadale; they were living at Fonthill, near Tisbury in Wiltshire.

[2] DD was on her way to lunch with Toby and Mary Anna Marten in Dorset.

11 March 1992   Chatsworth
                                                          Bakewell

Darling Paddy,

Sandringham looms. I expect you've had a letter telling you to
look sharp for 7 p.m. on Fri 10th & to wear a hat at church (no,
that's me now I come to think of it). Shall we somehow go
together? Will you come here the night before – election night I
hear now – and we'll tool along by car? *DO.*

Everyone frantic here, getting ready for the house to open.

Do you know Elisabeth Frink? She's a wonder & has become
rather a friend. I went to see her new work, a life-size heavy horse,
sort of Percheron type, Géricault-like bottom, & tail wound round
with rope. Bronze. I have a great longing for it for the garden here
. . . It's not the sort of thing you rush out & buy after breakfast but I
hope Stoker will try & persuade the dear old trustees to dig deep. I
HATE her Easter-Island type heads but oh the animals are
wonderful. And she is wonderful. Army bred. Her ma is the dau of a
Skinner's Horse officer. She's 82 and very beautiful. Never saw her
parents between the age of 5 & 16 except *once* & was shunted from
boarding schools to aunts all those years. How did people survive all
that & WHAT FOR in the end. I wish she was coming to
Sandringham.

63 eggs yesterday.
Much love.
LONGING to see you
    Debo

(DD)

Lis Frink's bronze War Horse, 1991–2, *was bought by the Chatsworth
House Trust, and she and her husband Alex stayed at Chatsworth in April
1992 to oversee the installation. She liked the place I chose – at the end of
the canal – where we positioned him with his back to the house looking
across the Old Park. He travelled from the foundry in a horsebox, and was
decanted into the bucket of our JCB and driven across the garden with*

supreme care and precision by Brian Gilbert. The horse's ears are back, he is
about to strike and bite at the same time. You are in danger if you stand in
front of him. We watched in the rain. A group of prep-school boys watched
with us. I begged them to remember meeting the famous sculptress and that
they had seen an historic moment for Chatsworth, the War Horse *being the*
first important sculpture bought for the garden for 150 years.

Lis Frink was once seen, never forgotten: gardener, poultry keeper, home-
giver to her mother and mother-in-law, and, to my mind, the unrivalled
sculptor of horses and dogs.

26 March 1992   Mani
[Postcard]

Debo

'Sing a song of Saxons
in the wapentake of Rye,
Four and twenty eoldermen,
Too eold to die.'

Just seen this in *The Times* 'word watching'. A wapentake is a
Saxon land measurement. I thought the rhyme rather up your
street.
    Love
        Paddy

10 June 1992   Chatsworth
                                                              Bakewell

Darling Paddy,
    I'm EXHAUSTED. Telly crew here doing a sort of documentary
on this old dump, inside and out. I had forgotten how one always
has to do everything three times. There is something wrong – light,
sound, one's own stupidity, etc etc – each time so the poor old
wooden actress has to start again.

Your book-backs figure. I said, re Abel N Willing, it sounds a bit old-fashioned now as everyone is abel n willing for everything but it was all the rage once. True, you'll agree.

I went to France for two glorious days with the Prince of Wales last week. A magic carpet, Queen's Flight, no passports, no airport buildings, no nothing tiresome. We started at Vaux, then Courances[1] for the night & a long stare at the green alleys with the tallest oaks going, next day Chartres (where the English Nanny so rightly said it was a bad light for sewing). I can't manage a religious feeling in that crowded dirty building, shuffling Japs by the thousand & that French trick of chairs instead of pews. Give me Swinbrook, or one of those magic Norfolk churches where Billa [Harrod] prays away like mad for the prince.

    Much love
      Debo

---

[1] The chateaux of Vaux-le-Vicomte and Courances owned, respectively, by the Vogüé and Ganay families.

14 June 199   Chatsworth
                                               Bakewell

Darling Paddy,

    I forgot two things. Ludo Kennedy is writing a book on Scotland.[1] When in Edinburgh he asked the guide at the Castle what the most usual question from American tourists is. He said 'What time do they fire the one o'clock gun?'

    The other thing is a dozen and a half of what vegetables are gold?

    18 carrots.

    That's it for now.

    Much love
      Debo

Elis Frink has been made Companion of Honour. *For Services to Reggie*, I suppose. He is (was) a Maran cock who was poorly after a fight with a Light Sussex & she took him to the vet every day for a week till, alas, he conked. Do admit. It conjures up a good picture. Distinguished sculptress queuing in the vet's surgery with a huge ill Maran on her lap. That's what I love about her, she adores her chickens.

[1] Ludovic Kennedy, *In Bed with an Elephant: A Journey through Scotland Past and Present* (1995).

30 July 1992   Mani

Darling Debo,

I still can't get over that awful stuff in the *Sunday Times* about the marriage of our marvellous Norfolk host.[1] Apart from the impertinence and disloyalty, and almost worse than both, was the sanctimonious, mock-sorrowful tone. I feel terribly sorry for *both* parties, but I've never even seen her, and the Prince of Wales only at that lovely weekend.

A second cause of vexation was the rotten obituary of Henry Bath in the same wretched paper, underlining what a duffer he was at school and how slovenly dressed, always mistaken for a gardener or something similar. Not a hint of the splendid looks, the originality and fun and the *unexpectedness* of his conversation. I saw him so seldom in recent years, and nearly always in Clubland, and always with delight, where he looked like a stag among a herd of Belted Angus.

Just before leaving England, I had a message, through Margaret, Janetta's housekeeper, saying she also did for Dirk Bogarde, who lived just round the corner in Cadogan Gardens, and that he'd love a visit, and that he had had a stroke (only physical) and had been knighted. So I did go and see him, nicer than ever, in his bachelor flat right up at the top. His great pal Tony Forward died last year and he feels v. hopeless and bereaved, and works like mad at very well-put-together novels, since retiring from stage and screen.

No more, darling Debo, except lots of love from
Paddy

[1] *Diana: Her True Story* by Andrew Morton, which revealed that the Princess of Wales had been unhappy for most of her married life, was being serialised in the *Sunday Times*.

10 August 1992   Chatsworth
                                                  Bakewell

Darling Paddy,

I was on the points (as Wonderful John's[1] dairy man says when a
cow is about to calve) of writing to you when your lovely letter
came.

I know, the papers are more than foul about the good prince.
Rights & wrongs in both directions, I *expect*, but I *know* nothing,
only guess a good deal. He has been so dignified, never one word
from him. She is truly a wonder at work, she has a power of
healing, King's Evil type, and leaves people weak at the knees but
strong in whatever was wrong. I've seen that & it is extraordinary. I
don't know her in everyday life but all say she is not easy. So, who
knows.

Gill Coleridge[2] is keen on me doing an anthology of this old
dump. Gt fun to find refs, from Bess of Hardwick to you in the
Stag Parlour. I'm looking in any life, letters I can lay hands on.[3]
An unexpected find is Sir Alan Lascelles, assistant sec to the P of
Wales, b 1887. On 27 Aug 1912 he came over here & writes 'there
are some beautiful drawings & a lot of rather tiresome Grinling
Gibbons carving.* As a house it is not so fine as Harewood & far
less liveable in. The children's schoolroom is hung with Sargent
portraits, God help them.' Good stuff eh.

Do look for any more of the same, please.

Much love
    Debo

* There isn't any, but never mind.

1 Lieut.-Col. Silcock; the land agent at Lismore.
2 Gill Coleridge (1948–). DD's literary agent, a director of Rogers, Coleridge &
White Ltd.
3 This book project never materialised.

14 August 1992   Chatsworth
                                                      Bakewell

Darling Paddy,
      FORGOT
      BELTED ANGUS re Henry Bath being a stag among . . .
      Well, Whack, this breed is a figment of your fertile . . .
      Belted *GALLOWAY* please. On the Rare Breeds list but still
afloat, just. ABERDEEN Angus. Oh when will you ever learn. (D
Devonshire, Vice President, Rare Breeds Survival Trust.)
      A young American came to interview me re Decca for an IN
DEPTH article in *New Yorker*.[1] Have you ever heard of an article
being SHALLOW END but that's how they usually end up.
      All the usual questions like 'and you were determined to marry a
duke, I believe'. It really is a waste of time as they know what
they're going to put before they come.
      Talk about names of things being changed, an international
committee, how made up God knows, has decided that grouse are to
be called Willow Ptarmigan. Beat that if you can.
      Much love. DO COME back soon
      Debo

      [1] The journalist Arthur Lubow was assigned by Tina Brown, editor of *Vanity Fair*
1984–92, to write the article about Jessica Mitford. When Brown left to become
editor of the *New Yorker* she took Lubow's article with her, assuring Jessica that it
would be published in her first issue of the *New Yorker*. In the event, Brown decided
that it 'wasn't right' for the magazine and the article never appeared.

30 September 1992   Mani

                        IN TEARING HASTE

Darling Debo,
      We are setting off, this very second, to Antibes to collect a
marvellous literary prize called *Le Grand Prix Jacques Audiberti de la
Ville d'Antibes*, for *A Time of Gifts* in French – (beautifully translated
by Guillaume Villeneuve. Nobody will read the English version any

more . . .) I'd never heard of it, I confess, but it's 50,000 francs and trails glory, they say, so we're feeling very cock a hoop. We meet Janetta there, but not Jaime, as his mother has been taken ill in Madrid. Visions of lobster and bouillabaisse float before the mind's eye, only corrected by remembering the Chinese saying: 'When you see a crossbow, don't always expect roast duck.' Then to Paris and further feasting, followed by Prague with Coote, unseen by me since March 1934 magical and sparkling with snow.

Finally a few days in London, when I'll be in touch almost at once. Please forgive haste.

Tons of love,

Paddy

6 November 1992   Mani

Darling Debo,

The night before we left, we had dinner with Magouche in Bruton St. Joan had to go early, so I stayed and gassed away, then decided to walk home; across Berkeley Square, into Curzon St, through Shepherd Market – my old haunt when young[1] – and into Market Mews, heading for the Sloane world. I had only gone a few paces when, on a wide black surface on the left side, I saw a strange message in huge letters in white:

> '*OPRIG*', it said,
> and, underneath,
> '*GAGINONANUS*'

What could it portend? It looked simultaneously insulting, enigmatic and vaguely improper, especially the message below. Could it be a reassuring message to the neighbours after a visit by the Soc. for the Abatement of Noise? When I got closer, all was revealed, as illustrated in the enclosed sketch fig. (1), and only when I was standing bang in front. In case you don't get it absolutely at once, all is revealed in fig. (2), not to be unfolded until after a look at fig. (1). I noted it down on the back of an envelope, and have been struggling with the spacing of the letters ever since.[2] If on leaving your front door, passing the Curzon Cinema, and turning right into the Mews, you'll [see it]. I hope the owner will have gone for a spin, leaving the concertina doors ajar, so that you see it as I did.

No more now, but please send news.

Lots of love,

Paddy

[1] As a young man, PLF lived at 43 Market Street, Mayfair.
[2] PLF sent copies of these drawings to several friends.

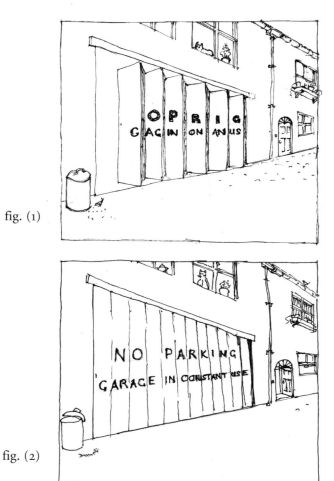

fig. (1)

fig. (2)

GAGINONANUS SPEAKS
by John Wells[1]

Before the earliest burning light
Before the world that once was his
Hung turning day to turning night
Gaginonanus was and is

Gaginonanus, mightiest Lord,
Whom all the Seven Kings obey,
At whose high uncreated word
Preadamites were prone to pray

Great God of Gods, all nature's grail,
The inward soul of every thing
Behind the Maya's rainbow veil
Withdrawn, within, inhabiting

New gods and false as empires rise
Are worshipped, spires fall and climb,
All-seeing and with placid eyes
Gaginonanus bides His time

Like leaves the centuries are born
Like leaves are born to bud and die.
Gaginonanus smiles to scorn
The drifting aeons as they fly

Ignored, unknown, forgotten still
Gaginonanus sees their play,
The awful working of His Will
Until His dreadful Judgement Day

★

But now, O Prig! O Lax! O Loose!
That hour is come! O sunk in crime!
Your garages in constant use,
You dare not park at any time

His awful Name is manifest!
No cloud-etched letters skyward burn
The Blessed Ones who love Him best
Know their Great God will soon return

Behold, in these condemned last days,
Gaginonanus, Lord of All!
As saints and sages dumbly gaze
His Name is written on the Wall.

₁ Inspired by his drawing of the garage doors, John Wells sent PLF this poem.

28 January 1993   Chatsworth
                                                           Bakewell

Darling Paddy,

It was so lovely having a quick talk the other day. I'm so old-fashioned I'm still amazed that you can do that in two secs just pressing those knobs & there you are. A bit disconcerting when you answered in Greek but never mind.

My dear Wife is here. Oh Paddy she is suddenly 1000, *diminished* in every way. The rot started with an operation for cataract and glaucoma on one eye. It went wrong & she's as good as blind in that one & the other one isn't perfect. So she walks with little steps, very slowly, bent because she's looking at the ground. Can't read, at least she can for a few minutes & then it goes fuzzy. But the worst thing is she won't try & be helped. There are all sorts of gadgets, magnifying glasses with a light attached & such like but any excuse not to give the thing a proper try, too cumbersome she says. Anyway that's what unnerves me, the WILL has gone. V hard to make her laugh, you just can but not like of yore. Well that's old age I suppose but it is horrid to see.

Masses more but for my next . . .

Much love

Debo

29 April 1993   Mani

Darling Debo,

I was *so sorry* to see about Elisabeth Frink[1] and rang you up, but
you were at Lismore.

Love

Paddy

1 The sculptress died of cancer on 18 April, aged sixty-two. Her husband pre-
deceased her by a few months.

24 May 1993   Long Crichel House
                                                      Wimborne
                                                      Dorset

Darling Debo

Here, embedded in the leaves and cow parsley with the nearby
click of croquet balls and cuckoos in the middle distance, takes some
beating. Carrington was right, in her letters, to say that cuckoos here
and there give a great feeling of dimension to a landscape, and I see
exactly what she meant. They've now gone to bed in their far-flung
usurped nests.

One of the most tiresome aspects of medical matters is the
hanging about. They can't have me in Sister Agnes till tomorrow
week.[1]

I'll keep in touch.
Tons of love to you and all from
    Paddy

I went to see a film called *Indecent Proposal*[2] last week. Don't miss it.
I've been brooding on it ever since.

1 PLF was going into King Edward VII's Hospital, Sister Agnes, for a back operation.
2 Starring Demi Moore as a married woman who agrees to sleep with a billionaire,
Robert Redford, for $1,000,000.

SUNDAY [June 1993]   White's
Stolen stationery   37 St James's St, SWI
Sister Agnes really

Darling Debo,
    Hooray! This morning I've been in the underground swimming
pool for the *second morning running*, while a beautiful physiotherapist
gyrated among the patients – three of them – telling them when to
twiddle their legs and shake their hips, as though training tadpoles;
and, *what's more*, my stitches were taken out ¼ of an hour ago, all
27. Not stitches at all of course, but just like paper staples. They
come out with a slight but transitory sting, and now twinkle on
the pad at my side. All this means that departure impends – next
Teusday morn, when this Golden Coach turns back into a
pumpkin. Then, crawling about London for a few days. Weekend
recuperating chez George Jellicoe. I've got to be in Athens on the
25th, to be made a doctor of Humane Letters, with Niko Ghika.
Finally, home.
    The point is, will you be down here at all? If so what about a
feast, or a drink, or 200 slow yards in Hyde Park?
    Fond love,
        Paddy

28 November 1993 Mani

Darling Debo,

It's all very odd here. After months and months of drought, reducing all the olive-growers in the Mani to despair – there's nothing else, only a few fishermen – the heavens suddenly opened a fortnight ago and swept the road that comes down from the main one to our bit of sea, clean away! Nothing but rubble and mud and enormous boulders and tomb-like holes ten feet deep, and acres of silt spreading into the sea at the bottom of each canyon and torrent-bed, like ogres' ping-pong bats. Our motor-car is safely perched on our headland, thank heavens, but can't *go* anywhere. We can only get to the village by muddy trudges across fields and up lanes, otherwise we're completely cut off. But we've got lots to eat and drink, plenty to read and masses of logs for the fire, so, in a way, it's rather nice.

It was my name day (Michael, here in Greece, as 'Patrick' always turns into 'Petro') – 8th Nov, the day after we got back, and, after church at the tiny chapel of SS Michael & Gabriel two fields away, half the village came here for food and drink and then music and dancing, all morning, wonderful black-coiffed crones skipping along like flappers round the drawing room, then out onto the terrace and round the fountain in a double chain, interweaving like oranges and lemons. They *love* it, and so do we after the initial anxiety.

What a fascinating and memorable man Canon (?) Beddoes[1] is! It's such a rare name, I'm sure he must be a relation, or descendant, of the poet Thomas Lovell Beddoes (1803–1849), just looked him up in the *DNB*. When he was still at school, he wrote a play, never published, called *Cynthio and Bugboo*. He was best known for a long poem called *Death's Jest Book*, which was the one I'd vaguely heard of. He died at Bâle, and sounds a riveting and very strange character.

I loved our visit, too, and thank you so much. It was marvellous seeing Andrew moving about so featly, wielding his crutch like a field-marshal's baton.[2]

Tons of love,
Paddy

P.S. I've reopened this, because they've just telephoned – i.e. this morning – from Dumbleton, to say that poor Graham has died in bed from heart failure. It's a shock but *of course* a relief. He would have hated to go on vegetating, if he had realised (and he *did* in a sort of way) and was bewildered and depressed by it. We'll both come back for the funeral next week – Wednesday I think – driving straight there from Heathrow and stay two days at Dumbleton, and then back here, I think. It's a beautiful old church there, and they will certainly sing 'Fight the Good Fight', written by Joan's and Graham's great uncle, a canon of Worcester, and a favourite character of J Betjeman.[3]

1 The Very Rev. Ron Beddoes (1912–2000), Provost of Derby Cathedral 1953–80 and semi-retired vicar of Beeley and Edensor 1980–97. 'He was a compelling preacher who often fixed his blue eyes on you and made a questioning sound "Hm?" to sharpen your attention.' (DD)
2 Andrew Devonshire had had a hip replacement.
3 John Betjeman (1906–84). The Poet Laureate, a friend of Joan Leigh Fermor since the 1930s, admired the hymns of John S. B. Monsell (1811–75).

16 April 1994   Mani

Darling Debo,

I don't know what's happening to the Greek posts, your letter took a *fortnight* to get here, then we had to go to Athens to see a specialist – Joan had a false-alarm heart irregularity, all over now, but anxious for a moment: cardiogram first like a row of Salisbury Cathedrals, and now like a well-tended country hedgerow.

About the Nancy–Evelyn letters,[1] I'm all for. Both are tip-top, Evelyn's always amusing and intelligent, only spoilt now and then when he seems to assume a slightly tiresome role as backwoodsman stickler. Nancy is eerily wise, always funny, often learned, or fascinated by the scent she is following, never affected or showing off. I treasure the vol. you gave and have just been dipping here and there. They are like a shot in the arm.

I must dash for the last post before the weekend.

Lots of love

Paddy

1 *The Letters of Nancy Mitford and Evelyn Waugh*, edited by Charlotte Mosley (1996).

17 July 1994   Chatsworth
                                                Bakewell

Darling Paddy,

Lunch for Daph's 90th birthday at Longleat ('in my new penthouse
suite' said Ld Bath,[1] viz. part of that wonderful library under the roof).
It was odd beyond everything. Everyone except grandchildren pretty
ancient to go with the 90 yr old and by gum there was a STEEL
BAND which made such a racket you couldn't hear yourself, let alone
anyone else, which in my case was dear good Dirk Bogarde who I
hadn't seen for YEARS & Jim [Lees-Milne].

Daph was the other side of Dirk & Andrew was on her left. She
was best at hearing of anyone. Coote arrived late, I didn't hear why,
& was dressed like Daph, nice snap, same *robe* I mean. Caroline
[Beaufort], thinner, nice as ever, & a little old person with straight
white hair, children's socks in bedroom slippers. She said 'Are you
Debo?' 'Yes.' 'I'm Oonagh.'[2] Oh I did think of R Kee & the source
of his Irish love. 'Do you ever see him?' 'No.' She has gone back to
live in Ireland but can hardly bear the climate. So an ancient who
has been with her for 40 years comes in with the brekker & every
morning says the same words about the weather, 'raining & blowing
again.' Poor Oonagh gets doured by it & her & no wonder. She said
'I've got Alzheimer's. I packed my best skirt & then thought why
have I done that, I shan't want it, took it out, & of course I did want
it for this lunch & look what I've got on.' 'Lovely,' I said. Oh dear
me.

We got a kind welcome from mad Bath & a mouthful of beard &
other extra hair.

His son looks normal & charming.

Much love

    Debo

1 Alexander Weymouth, 7th Marquess of Bath (1932–). Daphne Fielding's eldest
son, the hirsute, bohemian owner of Longleat House in Wiltshire.
2 Oonagh Guinness (1910–95). One of the three blonde sisters, known as the
'Golden Guinness Girls', married in 1936, as her second husband, 4th Baron
Oranmore and Browne. Famous for her wild parties at Luggala in County Wicklow
and for her many lovers, who included Robert Kee.

7 December 1994   Mani

Darling Debo,

I got a letter yesterday, from friends and neighbours of the sweet Northamptonshire folk I was farmed out with in WW1. She writes in a prim rustic hand, though migrated to Greenwich: 'Please sign the enclosed book for my father as he knew you when you were a small boy. He is now 92 but saw you last when he was 16 and you were three. His name is Philip Redwood and he lived with his mother and his sister Gladys and his aunt Nellie Barker just near the Martins (brewery people who looked after me), when you lived there while your parents were in India. My father thinks you came to live there when you were one. He remembers the first time he saw you, you were sitting up in Mrs Martin's arms. He remembers you being called Paddy Mike by them. *He says you were a dear little mite, a joy to have around.* He remembers clearly one evening when it was still light, hearing you call: "I don't want to go to bed!" The last time he saw you was the day the family moved to Woolaston, where my grandmother was a nurse. He remembers you helping him to tie up some garden tools on the garden path, and you put your finger on the knot for him to stop it slipping . . . Priscilla B. Hedly.'

I've just sent the book off: *T of Gifts*, containing a description of Kaiser Bill and Little Willy being burnt on the fire celebrating peace day, carried on Margaret Martin's shoulder – and being rushed home piggyback, because a boy, dancing around with a Roman candle in his mouth for a lark, swallowed it and died in agony spitting stars.

But it's all fascinating and makes me come all over queer. My word, they were all nice.

Lots of love,
Paddy

Orthodox Easter [10 April] 1995   Mani

Darling Debo,

Easter morning, before everyone is up.

Just before Good Friday, a chimney expert came to alter a smoky chimney, and started by throwing petrol up it, and setting it on fire, very exciting. At the same moment, a terrific noise came up from the olive groves below the house: 100 sheep came bounding about, baa-ing in every key, and fighting for room, all with huge curly horns. They had been brought to eat up the long grass which had choked the whole place, so tore away at it for three days, then buzzed off. They were four-legged scythes, really, bleating lawnmowers. It was living in a whirl.

Tons of love,
Paddy

23 September 1995   Chatsworth
Bakewell

Darling Paddy,

Now many serious questions re Charlotte Mosley's editing of Nancy/Evelyn letters. She's sent me the typescript. Oh dear me I sit & laugh & laugh again. Her intros aren't there yet. Anyway, to help her with her notes I'm HOPING you'll kindly answer the following:

What did Rose Macaulay look like?

Do you agree – or don't you – re Chagford (and name of hotel please) that it was 'an establishment run expressly to suit the needs of writers where Evelyn had retired to work on *Brideshead*'? Enlarge please.

Do you know who the love of Richard Hillary's[1] life was?

Thanks in advance for answers to all above tiresome questions.

I haven't finished it by the way, so I'm sure I'll have more questions, real life intervenes as you can picture. Evie WAS odd, wasn't he.

Much love & to Joan.

Debo

---

1 Richard Hillary (1919–43). Battle of Britain hero whose face and hands were badly burnt when his aircraft was shot down in 1940. He endured months of surgery in an attempt to repair the damage and wrote about his experiences in *The Last Enemy* (1942), a wartime bestseller. He returned to active service and was killed in a night training operation, aged twenty-three.

[October 1995]   Mani

Darling Debo,

I'm sorry being so slow! Now. Here we go.

What was Rose Macaulay like? I've had a shot at drawing her, but the trouble is, it's nothing like (see fig. attached). The thing is that she was nearly transparent, like wax, you could see a candle through her and the shape of the skull round the eye sockets, hollow temples, and features of great delicacy and distinction, Roman nose, I think, and an expression of intense interest and humour, a bit sad in repose. Didn't worry much about clothes, a sort of shallow cloche with bronze-coloured leaves all round it is what sticks in the mind. She was lovely in conversation, quick and unexpected, lots of laughter, hands on knees. She may have looked frail, but the first time we met I was taken to lunch by her at the Lansdowne Club. When the lift came up to the fourth floor, Joan and Patrick[1] got in, and she said 'We'll walk!' When they had disappeared, she said '*Let's race them!*' and started off down, helter skelter like a pony. We got there first, and when the others got out she said 'Did you have any trouble? Lift break down, or something?' Talking, her head had a very slight tremor, as tho' she were 'worrying' her interlocutor. She lived in Hinde Street – books heaped up on all furniture – in order to go to early Mass at All Saints Margaret St every morning. (If she had heard your father grumbling about smells and lace, she would have said 'Just right for me, can't have enough of it.') Then she would bicycle to the Serpentine, come rain come shine, and after 100 or 200 strokes, bike back to brekker and then to work. She scarcely drank anything, but loved parties, day's work done. You'd have loved her.

Diana [Cooper] and she were on the same cruise ship to Russia, and quizzes were organised. One of them was 'Which would you choose, death or dishonour?' Everyone fumbled, but when Rose's turn came she said, 'Oh, dishonour, every time!' and, to the question 'What is your most secret wish?' she said, 'Oh, power! Absolute power!' Then laughter. In one of her last books, *The Towers of Trebizond*, a character says: 'I never had a more social time than staying with Paddy and Joan on Hydra, but I like that.' One was honoured! Apart from all that she was brilliant, like all people called M.

heas too big.

There went
be one in
the National
Portrait
Gallery.

All wrong.
She was
much
slighter
and
lighter.
Boniness in
right.

Eeg.

Chagford. Run by Mrs Carolyn Postlethwaite Cobb, an almost spherical v good style New England American, daughter of the chaplain at West Point. She ran this charming hotel on the edge of Dartmoor with Norman Webb, a nice Devonshire chap she had opened a home for lame donkeys with in Morocco. I think Alec Waugh[2] first discovered it, then Evelyn and Patrick Kinross. I went there with Patrick, to write *The Traveller's Tree*, he to write a novel, *Beloved Innocent?*, about his ex-wife Angela Culme-Seymour, Janetta's half-sister, and I often went, using the magical centre room with a blazing fire, hunting three times a week, then drinks with Carolyn at 7, she being bedridden in latter days, something to do with asthma. When she died and I went down to the funeral, Norman and Evelyn and Laura [Waugh] were almost the only others there, in Chagford churchyard. I went once again when it was run by some awful people, and wish I hadn't. Carolyn was very funny, v kind, as good as gold, loved Evelyn. She adored having writers there, and was a true friend.

Richard Hillary. There was a love affair with Anne Mackenzie (who Xan and I were a bit keen on at different times), but she couldn't bear to face him after being so mangled. His true love and comforter after his awful burns was Mary Booker − did you know her? − prematurely white hair, v beautiful, kind, intelligent, charming. I remember staying up dancing at the 400 until it closed, then talking to her − end of war sort of time − and thought she was wonderful. When Hillary died she married Micky Burn[3] (captured at St Nazaire raid. Colditz. Then *Times* correspondent all over E Europe). Haven't seen her since. I think lots of people fell for her because of her beauty, quietness, niceness and sympathy.

Magouche arrives this evening, then we fly to Crete to put Xan's ashes under a tree up in the mountains.

Now for a dash to the post.

Lots of love,

Paddy

[1] Patrick Balfour, 3rd Baron Kinross (1904−76). Traveller, writer and journalist, best known for his life of Kemal Mustafa Atatürk. His novel, *The Innocents at Home*, was published in 1959. Married to Angela Culme-Seymour 1938−42.

[2] Alec Waugh (1898−1981). Evelyn's older brother wrote his novel *Thirteen Such Years* (1932) at the Easton Court Hotel in Chagford.

[3] Michael Burn (1912−). The author and journalist wrote about the love affair between Richard Hillary and Mary Booker (whom Burn married in 1947) in *Mary and Richard* (1988). DD had known Burn, a friend of her sisters Unity and Jessica, since he used to stay at Swinbrook House in the 1930s.

23 October 1995   Mani

Darling Debo,

One detail I'd forgotten about Rose Macaulay. She had a very battered old car, which she drove fast and dangerously. It came into a long thing in rhyme that I published in the *Statesman* when the *literary* part was respectable, 40 years ago − of which two lines were (I think)

> 'Edith and Sachie and both Osberts and Vita
> All packed into Rose's four seater.'

Nice about the weight of the Queen's tiara, and you hiding yours,[1] like sneaking one's tie off when nobody else is wearing one.

Ages ago, I went to a party given by Brig. West. Everyone was tightish. Daph, still Bath, was curled up in a ball next to a chair where Duff C[ooper] was sitting, covered in medals and decorations. Daph was wearing a tiara, as they'd all been to a Court ball. Daph was so rapt in talk and laughter that she didn't even notice or pause when Henry [Bath], on the point of buzzing off with Virginia, said, 'I think I'd better take that', neatly uncoiled the bauble from Daph's hair, and slipped it into the pocket in the tail of his tail coat, and stalked away. Daph was amazed a bit later by its absence, until we reassured her. I thought for a moment that it might have been later on the same night when I came and collected you from a ball at the Savoy, and took you on to another in Chelsea – whose? – a lovely evening.

No more for the moment.

Lots of love

    Paddy

Was the ball at the Savoy given by someone called Christie-Miller? A yearly event? One year, they say, David Cecil[2] was hastening to it along the Strand, when a tart stopped him and said, 'Would you like to come home with me, dear?' and he answered, 'I can't possibly. I'm going to the Christie-Millers'.'

---

1 The Devonshire diamond tiara, a large and imposing piece, was made in 1893 for the 8th Duke's wife. 'My grandmother-in-law, Evelyn, Duchess of Devonshire, was Mistress of the Robes to Queen Mary for 43 years. Together she and Queen Mary weathered long hours of tiara-ed evenings. After one particularly lengthy engagement, Granny was heard to say, "The Queen has been complaining about the weight of her tiara . . . the Queen doesn't *know* what a heavy tiara is." I once wore this tiara to a dance at Windsor and realised when I arrived that I was the only one so bedecked. As soon as I could, I took it off and shoved it under a sofa.' (DD)

2 Lord David Cecil (1902–86). Scholar, biographer and Professor of English Literature at Oxford.

1 May 1996   Mani

Darling Debo,

Talk about Fermor's echo being silenced through too much water, the whole landscape here has changed because of the winter-long deluge. It's turned into what Xan called I.J.S. ('I.J.S.? What's that?' *Impenetrable jungle, Sir!*' It always worked.) Wild grasses and flowers and weed have shot up a yard, the branches droop laden with leaves and blossom, so one stoops through a foot-wide space between the two. The cats have gone mad tearing about the I.J.S., ambushing and pouncing on each other, thinking they are lions. I must say, they look just like them, though smaller, of course.

There are sudden woods of wild *glads* of a poignant hue, also tortoises are coming out and courting each other, sounding through the glades like guests in horn-rimmed spectacles embracing at a cocktail party.

Joan and I have decided to give this place to a wonderful institution called the Benaki Museum,[1] who long for it, one lives in it for as long as one of us, still surviving, is still on the scene, then they take it over and look after it forever. They are terribly nice – well they must be, to hanker for such an odd place.

I got made a *Chevalier des Arts et Lettres*,[2] which I must say I'd never heard of, but it means one can slip a minute rosette, I believe purple, into one's buttonhole before tripping down the gangplank at Orly.

Now. Five minutes to the post leaving. Keep in touch.

Love
       Paddy

[1] The museum in Athens was founded in 1930 to house Greek works of art from prehistoric to modern times.
[2] PLF was made a Chevalier de l'Ordre National du Mérite in 1992 and Officier de l'Ordre des Arts et Lettres in 2002.

[July 1996]   Mani

IN A FEVER TO CATCH THE POST

Darling Debo,

This is only a rushed line to say how dreadfully upset I am for you – and for me, in a different degree – by the sad sudden news of Decca's death, and I'm dashing down these lines of commiseration, against time.

The other day I came on a bulging folder, absolutely crammed with her letters, and mine too, diligently typed out – from when she was getting ready her Philip Toynbee book. They read hilariously, and I suddenly wished the correspondence hadn't petered out when it was all over. My last glimpse of her, I think, was when you and she were singing 'Grace Darling' to the amazed Bruce Chatwin in that Thai Restaurant in Passionate Brompton.

Anyway, tons of commiseration, darling Debo, and love from
    Paddy

Wednesday 9.15   Mani
[1996]

IN UNBELIEVABLE HASTE

Darling Debo,

Could you really bear us for Christmas? It's not only a marvellous idea, but solves all. Please don't have second thoughts.

My thought in bed this morning was: –

Q. *How can people vote with their behinds?*

A. *By remaining seated during a standing ovation.*

Your review of Jim's book[1] was tip-top.

I've got to break off now, as a rock nuthatch has got into the studio and is flying round and round and banging against the panes and hovering desperately in ceiling corners. Ladders and a blanket needed.

    Love
    Paddy

Late Special. Got him! He's up and away and it's a lovely sunny morning.

1 James Lees-Milne, *Fourteen Friends* (1996). DD wrote that Lees-Milne's portraits of friends were 'compulsive reading . . . He notes the faults as well as the virtues of his mates, but he does not criticise, and loves them in spite of all. Lucky people.' *Counting My Chickens*, pp. 135–6.

10 December 1996   Mani

Darling Debo,

How lovely, being one of your pin-ups in the Oldie![1] What a shame you weren't there for J Betjeman's welcome to Poets' Corner. I loved it (all except the speech-making part, which had me rather rattled).[2]

Last week, during a lull after a morning of intermittent thunder, there was suddenly a blinding flash and the loudest double report or explosion I've ever heard, so dashed over from the studio to the house to find Joan and Ritsa[3] gazing across the valley in wild surmise, where a cloud of leaves, dust and smoke was swirling out to sea. All the lights had gone off (it was an overcast morning), telephone off, and all the street lamps along the road. Then a downpour, real buckets, set in, and lasted for 24 hours. It was a sort of thunderbolt about 200 yards away, and very shaking but nothing has been found. It seemed very eerie that night, deluge outside, the glimmer of candles within, like a stranded ark, containing nothing but us two bipeds and four puzzled cats stalking about the shadows.

Longing for Christmas!

Tons of love,

Paddy

1 Along with PLF ('the best company I know, the cleverest and the funniest. They say he is a very good writer'), DD's other pin-ups were the 6th 'Bachelor' Duke of Devonshire (1790–1858); her sister Diana; Flanagan & Allen and the Crazy Gang; Sybil Cholmondeley; Screaming Lord Sutch; and Elvis Presley, 'the greatest entertainer of all time. He made opera singers sound hopeless.' *The Oldie*, 1 December 1996.
2 PLF gave the address at the unveiling of a memorial to John Betjeman at Poets' Corner in Westminster Abbey on 11 November.
3 PLF's cook and housekeeper.

2 January 1997   Dumbleton

Darling Debo,

That *was* a lovely Christmas. I loved the carol singing, my only worry being that *nobody* now ever sings my favourite, viz. 'The Holly and the Ivy'.

I'm sitting in this house, looking out at the snowflakes tumbling into the orchard below, where fifty sheep graze on frost-bitten tussocks of grass. Beyond it stands the old mill this house is named after, the broken wheel, iced solid, and the millstream iced over. Only a thin ribbon of water survives in motion, the rest is locked under a lid of ice. Two hundred pigeons live in the top part of the mill, and flutter out and in. *Beyond* the stream, which is called the Isborne (the only river in the kingdom, it seems, which flows due south to due north), in a field, stands a neighbour's sturdy horse, rugged up – one rug yesterday, but two today, I note: also grazing. But what about water? The Isborne is wired off, and the two troughs are frozen solid. Joan says they melt it by licking it with their warm tongues, then lap it up. How odd it is that horses never seem to lie down for forty winks, but just stand there come wind come weather, doing a Frink . . . Beyond it, the Cotswolds fade away into cotton wool.

How nice Sophy's little group was! Alastair marvellous and two dream children.[1] I am wearing your handsome Yuletide tie, and long black stockings you sent two years ago. We had lovely walks, as usual, in the woods about the Ho. – Jim [Lees-Milne], Pat [Trevor-Roper] and I, revelling in the wintry beauty of it all. I remember doing the same with Nancy years ago, and saying the woods must have been pretty well the same when they were the edge of Sherwood Forest: no change from what Gurth and Wamba, the (two Saxon shepherds in *Ivanhoe*) gazed down on, and she cried, 'Oh, surely not the *Rhodies*, Whack?'[2]

Well, there we are, darling Debo, and thank you and Andrew very, very much and tons of love from
      Paddy

And also from Joan.

---

1 DD's grandchildren Declan Morrison (1993–) and his sister Nancy (1995–).
2 Rhododendrons did not become popular on English country estates until Victorian times.

Leap Year 1997   Mani

Darling Debo,

Coote's barn party was lovely[1] – a hundred people there, and more, and deafening noise when we arrived, the whole of the West Country really, Coote presiding splendidly and roundly at the top table.

I had a long chat with Daphne's Christopher,[2] who said Daph was fine (and so she sounded when I rang her up), but Joan got him at one of the place-shifts, and had an extraordinary conversation with him. He said he'd gone to see Daph a few days earlier, and asked her what she did in the evenings, and D. said 'Oh, the three R's, you know.' 'What, Reading, Writing and Arithmetic?' and she said, '*No*, darling. Reading and R–r–remembering rogering!' Rather fast.

It's been very cold here, and raining too, but now glorious, billiard table green on all the olive terraces, so brief and precious to us, scattered with scarlet, purple and mauve flowers, Adam's Blood, and snowdrifts of daisies.

I'm in the studio. Three cormorants looking somehow very disreputable, have just flown past, and out to sea. No fish for us.

One feels a bit out of things, so please write.

Tons of love,
     Paddy

I've got a marvellous new hearing aid, recommended by Deacon, called Hidden Hearing. I'm surrounded by ticking clocks, crashing seas and deafening blackbirds which have been in eclipse for ages.

---

[1] Dorothy Lygon celebrated her eighty-fifth birthday in March 1997, a non-leap year.
[2] Lord Christopher Thynne (1934–). Daphne Fielding's son married Antonia Palmer in 1968.

10 July 1997   Mani

Darling Debo,

A few days ago Joan bumped and slightly split a rib against something. It's getting better, but agony if she makes a sudden movement. She won't see a local doctor, but has long chats with Christian Carritt[1] on the telephone, so we have bedside games of Beggar-my-Neighbour and Word-Making-and-Word-Taking (an old-fashioned and much better Scrabble). I go for long wonderful swims in the cool of the evening, and stride about the oak-woods up the mountainside. No flowers now till the first cyclamen and Autumn Croakers, but the withered grass is a golden, lion-coloured hue, marvellous with evergreen ilex and olive branches, especially from afar, giving the landscape a legendary, rather biblical look. Last night I stalked across a treeless slanting plateau and the setting sun sent my shadow across it for about a mile. It felt very queer. Nothing but tortoises about, dashing for cover like speed-kings at my approach.

I not only didn't see you, but nobody while in Blighty, but got on with some work. The evening before we left I was buying a paper at that stall on the south side of Sloane Square when an Irish piper struck up in the middle and a small crowd was assembled there round a veiled statue gesticulating like a madwoman under the tarpaulin, so hastened across and found Christopher Thynne, as per, snapping everyone. He said the figure on the plinth was Sir Hans Sloane (Hans Place, Sloane St, etc), a famous collector, benefactor and botanist; it was removed (I think) from the Physic Garden. The gathering were all descendants or fans, and I did twig from the jerseys and the pearls that they were all more or less Sloane Rangers. C. pointed to a group by the flower-seller's shed – all Sloanes of riper years. Their MP, Alan Clark,[2] was going to unveil it and say a few words, but I had to hurry off. I'd like to have seen that, as I don't know what he's like. I caught a glimpse of Andrew at Pratt's looking rather old fashioned and formal in an old school tie. Then away next morning.

Tons of love,
Paddy

---

1 Christian Carritt (1927–). 'A selfless, funny and charming London GP loved and relied upon by all her patients, many of whom became her great friends.' (DD)
2 Alan Clark (1928–99). Diarist and Conservative politician, MP for Kensington & Chelsea from 1997 until his death in 1999.

28 July 1997   Mani

Darling Debo,

I've just been going through all the books here in search of Ly Longford's wonderful 2-vol life of the D of Wellington, but hunted in vain. What I wanted to find was a passage where Wellington says, thank god all his generals – Peninsula, Waterloo etc – were all out-and-out hunting men, and it was their skill, dash, eye for country and spirit that brought all the victories, saved Europe, and laid Boney low. It was in the light of England's military debt to hunting in the past that made the MOD's veto of hunting on vast expanses of age-old hunting country seem so ungrateful, shocking and lacking in historical sense.[1] Ranksborough and the Wissendine Brook etc could now give way to a Govt vehicle and a team of white-coated vermin operatives padding across the sward with hoses and gas-canisters . . .

Here's something I found in Lemprière's wonderful *Classical Dictionary*. (Conjure up in your mind's eye *The Rape of the Sabine Women* by David & people like that – undraped ladies being carted off, and bickered over, shoulder-high, by undraped but helmeted Romans.)

'According to Varro, Talassius was a young Roman who carried off a Sabine virgin, crying out "Talassio!", meaning that she was now for Talassius. It is more probable that the cry "Talassio", used at a Roman wedding, is like our "Tally-ho!", used at a fox-hunt; and that the primary meaning of both words is unknown.'

Rush for post.

Lots of love,

Paddy

---

[1] The Ministry of Defence's veto was one of the Labour Government's first steps towards a wholesale ban on foxhunting with dogs, which came into effect in 2005.

Monday [May 1998]   Dumbleton

Debo,

ALL IS REVEALED! I mean those enigmatic symmetrical swirls
across the landscape you sent me, those puzzling pictures of a few
months ago.[1]

How do I know? At six p.m. yesterday evening we went up in
a balloon with seven other people, setting off from Aston
Somerville, on the way to Evesham, full of calmly grazing sheep,
and drifted south, spotting the Mill House, Dumbleton Hall,
Overbury, then many a meadow and stately house between the
Cotswolds and the Malvern Hills, with our small river, the
Isborne, glittering in its serpentine and willow-shaded bed. We
drifted along till nearly sunset, leaving a deep band of smog
underneath us – although it looked pure blue from ground level –
which reached higher than the Cotswolds, and so thick that our
huge balloon, 160 feet from basket to summit – cast a giant
ghostly shadow on what looked like a hanging screen of smoke,
like an ogre's shuttlecock (not flat, like the trees and steeples
below, but bolt upright), seemingly half a mile away. Then we were
above it in pure pale purged ozone. All this is caused by factories
and motor-cars alone, awful to think of. The promoters of these
balloon trips are anti-smog fanatics, and urged it in mid-air most
compellingly.

But, as we descended in a vast field near Tewkesbury, there below
were spread field after field patterned *just like your photos*, I suppose
left by some reaping or sowing farm appliance: twin tracks, with a
wide arm stretching several yards, so needing very wide arcs to turn
and making those wonderful symmetrical designs – not as perfect or
as complicated as yours, but jolly nearly. Did you know all about it
all along? Do send any further elucidation.

We subsided in the quiet eventide, drifting along tree-tops and
nests and landing among buttercups and daisies and black-and-white
bullocks that first scattered then recovered and came crowding back
with nasty looks while we folded up and packed the vast collapsed
multicoloured carcass in its tarpaulin jacket. The two farm girls who

showed us the way out were very excited by the invasion, and lots of snaps were taken, then the sun set and we tooled back in the dark. *End of bulletin.*

  Love
    Paddy

All is by no means revealed, hence this reopening. It is witheringly upheld that the patterns in the fields observed yesterday are far too complex for any farm machinery to have wrought. Furthermore, it is urged, the fields observed from the balloon are just flat grass, whereas the patterns in your album are cut in standing crops, and, what's more, there are no exit or entry marks for farm machines, or, indeed, for cunning topiarists with sickles, or shears or nail-scissors, unless they were hovering with small personalized balloons.

  Do, please, shed light!

1 DD had sent PLF a calendar with photographs of corn circles.

1 September 1998   Dumbleton

Darling Debo,

  Many thanks for those mystery cornfield photographs. One of my difficulties about them is: how could visitors from outer space know so much about Art Deco? Answer me that!

  I'm ¾ of the way through Frances Partridge's *Life Regained,*[1] and feel simultaneously impressed and depressed by it.

  It's looking lovely here, much better than last year, thanks to the absence of rape (by Joan's request) which made the whole landscape look like Lord Lonsdale's waistcoat.[2]

  Love
    Paddy

1 *Life Regained, Diaries 1970–71* (1998), Frances Partridge's fifth volume of diaries.
2 5th Earl of Lonsdale (1857–1944). Known as the Yellow Earl because of his fondness for the colour.

[January 2000]   Dumbleton

Darling Debo,
    Blake once wrote a poem which begins:

> 'A robin redbreast in a cage
> Puts all Heaven in a rage.'

I've just discovered an unfinished continuation of it I scribbled in a
notebook long ago. It goes as follows: –

> 'Blackbirds fluttering from a pie
> Cause four-and-twenty cheers on high
>
> When a pig wanders from its pound
> The angels call for drinks all round
>
> An egg falls from the curate's spoon
> And cherubim with rapture swoon
>
> The bed bug snug, the nibbling louse
> Delight the angel of the house
>
> When moths make holes in coats & things
> The cherubs beat their tiny wings
>
> When rodents eat the Stilton up
> The Heavenly Hosts on nectar sup
>
> A death-watch egg is hatched in teak
> And there's ambrosia for a week
>
> When weevils raid the biscuit box
> Jehovah's brow at once unlocks
>
> And lawns wrecked by the burrowing mole
> Make heaven shine bright from pole to pole
>
> Uncleanly Fido in the hall
> Spells archangelic bacchanal.' etc etc

The above very clumsy lines apply to the film about Chatsworth and
its parasites that we saw a few days ago on TV.[1]

    Love

        Paddy

[1] Channel 4 was showing a six-part documentary about life and work on the
Chatsworth estate which included a segment on the damage that insects cause to
textiles and artefacts.

Orthodox Easter Sunday   Mani
End of April [17 April 2000]
[Postcard]

Debo,

    Sarah, Dss of Marlborough,[1] hated her grand-daughter, Ly Anne
Egerton and got hold of a portrait of her, blacked the face, and
hung it up in her room, with the inscription: '*She is much blacker
within.*'

    Love

        Paddy

[1] Sarah Jennings (1660–1744). Quarrelsome wife of 1st Duke of Marlborough and
confidante of Queen Anne.

26 or 27 April 2000 or both.   Chatsworth
Sto's birthday. 55 wd you believe it.   Bakewell

Darling Paddy,

    I'm in the dentist's waiting room in London, soon I hope to St
Pancras & HOME.

    Just had lunch with Nicko because OUR FARM SHOP in Eliz
St opened TODAY.[1] A great excitement, you can imagine. The last
lap has been a monster push for the shop staff but there we are it's
open & an Eaton Sq dweller has already ordered her dinner for
tonight for 8 people & our chef rushed round with it, all excited.

Can they keep it up? Eccles Cakes going to all ex-pat northerners who exclaimed when they saw them. What good sport.

The telly are doing an hour on Nancy and her books.[2] Would you take part, be interviewed?

My sister Diana is havering & wavering, says she's too old & wrinkled – I say don't be so vain. Coote is going to see him. There aren't many left who knew her well, dash it all.

Mary H[enderson] brought a picture of a cow & showed it to the butcher saying the bit she wanted. It reminded me of Woman, and Charles de Noailles' amazement, when she slapped her thigh saying 'Il faut le couper LÀ'[3] re some pig meat.

Much love
Debo

Did you know Napier Alington?[4] Did Joan? Do ENLARGE if you remember him.

[1] DD had opened a London branch of the Chatsworth Farm Shop in Belgravia.
[2] 'Nancy Mitford, The Big Tease', a BBC *Omnibus* documentary, broadcast in 2001.
[3] 'You must cut it HERE.'
[4] Napier Sturt, 3rd Baron Alington (1896–1940). Son of Humphrey Sturt, 2nd Baron Alington, and Lady Feodorovna Yorke.

5 August 2000   Mani

Darling Debo,

I can't tell you what a time I've had trying to find a marvellous letter from you that was waiting for me here. I wanted to write a proper answer to several questions on it, so put it off for a couple of days and then it got itself lost – i.e. wriggled its way into the awful hayrick of papers that stand at both sides of my desk like rival towers of Pisa.

The only question I can remember was about Napier Alington. Of course, you're just too young to have come into the hobnobbing zone, but I wasn't. I met him first in Athens, pretty soon after I'd got there in May 1935, and had just taken up with the beautiful Rumanian I loved, who was an old friend of Napier's (he said he liked being called that rather than Naps). He had just come from Egypt, staying with the Loraines,[1] and was travelling with Rosie Kerr,[2] who doted on him, like everyone else. We got on terribly well from the start, and it was a lovely time in Athens, packed with glamour and fun, of which Napier somehow seemed to be the centre. We went on lovely trips to Sunium, peeked at Byron's graffito, and to Delphi. You know what he looked like from the Augustus John picture, which gets him to a T. He had a slightly *lifted* tone of voice, the sort that Douglas Byng[3] imitated, or aspired to, and was unbelievably funny and warm. He was a mixture of *grand seigneur* and, in a way, of clown, in the sense of seeing comedy whoever it was and contributing to it. As far as segs,* he was what Maurice Bowra called 'stroked all round the wicket'. He wasn't quite sure who his dad was – he thought perhaps an Italian, perhaps Jewish.[4] He was tricked into entering a lift shaft in a palazzo in Rome, and fell three storeys, and was broken up rather, but it didn't show. (His host thought he was carrying on with his marchesa.) Do look him up in Bunny Garnett's *Letters of Carrington*. There's a nice description of him and Ph. Hardwicke (brother-in-law, I think) going over to Ham Spray.[5] He adored his mother, who he called Feo. His elder brother was killed in the Great War. When Napier heard the news, he very eccentrically took a gun, went for a walk in the woods, and shot his fourth left finger off which he masked by keeping the two next fingers together in a sort of point, wearing a ring with a blue stone in on his little finger. I went there (Crichel) a couple of times, it was the last weekend before I went abroad in 1940 (soon after we met at the ball). Three young girls were staying in the same room, and, fairly late, he thought it would be fun to haunt them with sheets over our heads, creeping in with loud moans (Mary Anna, Libby Hardinge and another girl called Farquharson,[6] all about 10). They adored it, sitting up and shrieking with arms clasped round their knees.

   Not much solid stuff in all this rot, I'm afraid. You would have loved him. He was sent out to Egypt in the RAF – not able to fly,

---

* My new spelling for sex – such a dull word, it would keep it out of all newspaper headlines instead of obsessing them. Xan (Gsan) owed a lot of his success to it.

because so knocked about – but by the time I got to Cairo, he was already dead, having been tenderly looked after by Momo Marriott.[7]

This letter is so disjointed because of the tremendous heat. I'm scribbling away in a shuttered room, waiting for sunset to go for a long cool swim, as I did last night, watching the sun disappear on the way out, and swimming back under a crescent moon. Bliss.

Tons of love,

Paddy

1 Sir Percy Loraine (1880–1961). High Commissioner in Cairo 1926–9. Married Louise Stuart-Wortley in 1924.

2 Rosemary Kerr (1908–85). Unmarried daughter of Admiral Mark Kerr, Naval Attaché in Italy, Austria, Turkey, and Commander-in-Chief, Greek Navy, under King Constantine 1913–15.

3 Douglas Byng (1893–1988). The cabaret star, famous for his female impersonations, often accompanied his own camp songs on the piano at the Café de Paris in the 1930s.

4 Napier Alington's biological father was reputed to be Prince Marcantonio Colonna (1844–1912), assistant to the Pontifical Throne, the highest lay dignitary in the Roman Catholic Church.

5 Dora Carrington described Napier Alington and his cousin Philip Yorke, 9th Earl of Hardwicke (1906–74), arriving at Augustus John's house, Fryern, 'both half naked in vests and a ravishing female beauty a cousin of Nap's . . . They had been swimming at Kimmeridge.' D. Garnett (ed.), *Carrington, Letters & Extracts from her Diaries*, p. 417.

6 Napier Alington's daughter, Mary Anna Sturt, her cousin Elizabeth Hardinge and Zoë, daughter of Robin d'Erlanger and Myrtle Farquharson.

7 Maud (Momo) Kahn (1897–1960). Daughter of Otto Kahn, the wealthy American financier. Married General Sir John Marriott in 1920.

19 November 2000　　　　　　　　　　　　　　　Chatsworth
　　　　　　　　　　　　　　　　　　　　　　　Bakewell

Darling Paddy,

The enclosed, one page in real life but two in the photo, turned up in a drawer at Lismore, spotted by Stoker. He thought it was Betjeman & sent it to Deacon. She saw your writing & sent it to me . . . BUT the beginning is missing. Do you remember it? Can you do it again? OH DO. Mad of me not to know it by heart, but I don't . . .

We've had a series of lectures here. Last night Archives by a
wonderful old gent who has burrowed deep & found such curiosities as
the second-ever map of Ireland, a contemp copy of Bess of Hardwick's
will, a seal of King John re some long-lost estate & a letter from
George VI to my father in law on Billy & Kick's engagement[1] saying
what an awful fellow old Mr Kennedy was when Amb here. What an
extraordinary house this is. I'd never seen any of those.

The blessed Spanish amb. & wife[2] came for a weekend. What a
good pair. All strangers (except Kees) in the drawing room when
they arrived. I lost my head and introduced her as Mrs Thing. I'd
better give up asking people to stay. She is such a sport, ended her
b&b letter 'Love from Thing'.

The stuff from the Hermitage has landed at Somerset Ho & we're
going to the opening on Mon. I guess Jayne Wrightsman[3] will be
crowned Empress of All the Russias because I have a feeling she has
paid for it AND she's enabled them to do up three derelict rooms at
the Hermitage itself.

Much love
Debo

1 Both sets of parents had been against the engagement of Andrew Devonshire's
older brother, William (Billy) Cavendish, Marquis of Hartington (1917–44), to Kathleen Kennedy, sister of the future President. The Devonshires were firm Protestants
and the Kennedys entrenched Catholics.
2 Santiago de Mora-Figueroa y Williams, Marqués de Tamarón (1941–), ambassador in London 1999–2004, and his wife, Isabella.
3 Jayne Larkin (1919–). Art patron and munificent benefactor of, among other
institutions, New York's Metropolitan Museum, the Hermitage Museum in St
Petersburg and Somerset House in London. Married Standard Oil mogul Charles
Wrightsman in 1944.

29 November 2000   Mani

Darling Debo,

Here's the poem, if you can call it that. We were staying at Long
Crichel, and somebody wondered what the surnames of the inhabitants
might represent, on the analogy of 'Wellington' and 'Sandwich'.

Raymond Mortimer,[1] it was thought, might be a kind of hat, and
Eardley Knollys[2] a new kind of footwear (it was before Pat Trevor-
Roper had succeeded to his place) and Desmond Shawe-Taylor
would be a kind of harness ('got a short tail, see?'). But what about
Eddy Sackville-West, so gentle and sensitive and willowy? Desmond
came out with a brilliant suggestion, 'It would be a brand-new kind
of boxing-glove.' Applause was general, and it gave immediate rise to
the attached verses.

   Tons of love,
      Paddy

THE LAY OF THE SACKWILLE GLOVE

I

'Twas a summer's day at Long Crichel
And Phoebus vas shining bright,
And the 'ole of the Dorset Fancy
Vas gathered to see the fight.

II

Shawe-Taylor vas there on 'is bobtail mare
In the flashest of nankeen suits,
And Mortimer, too, in 'is beaver 'at,
And Knollys in 'is Blucher boots.

III

There vas many a bang-up Corinthian,
And many a milling cove,
But the gamest of all vas *SACKWILLE-VEST*,
As inwented ve *SACKWILLE GLOVE*!

IV

They pitched the ring on the welwet lawn,
And the gemmen vas crowding thick,
For BATTLING BEN from Blandford
Vas meeting the VIMBORNE CHICK.

V

'*Up vith yer dukes!*' cries SACKWILLE-VEST,
And their maulies met vith a bang –
And down goes the CHICK, as the BATTLER'S right
Connected 'is neb vith a clang.

VI

Now this clang vas caused by a doorknob
Concealed in the BATTLER'S right,
But nobody spies it, and everyone cries:
The BATTLER AS VUN THE FIGHT!

VII

But over the ropes jumps SACKWILLE-VEST
Vith 'is right 'eld be'ind 'is back,
And 'is left up'eld in preclusive spar,
Vot prowokes th'impending vhack.

VIII

'Is long, left daddle vas 'eld on 'igh,
Manoowering in the air
Clad in a newly-fangled mitt,
MADE OF LEVVER AND 'ORSE'S 'AIR!

IX

Forty-two rounds they milled and slogged
Like the pugs of 'oom poets sing
At the Var of Troy, and their slammin' dukes
Fair made the Velkin ring.

X

Ben's proboscis vas 'ammered flat
Vith many a vell-aimed stroke;
Both 'is peepers vas black and shut,
And 'alf of 'is ribs vas broke.

XI

'Is ears svole up like cauliflowers,
'is gnashers vas down 'is froat,
'Is claret vas tapped like a stove-in keg
At the wreck of a wintner's boat.

XII

They carried BEN off on a five-bar gate,
And round the 'ERO pressed
All the covies, bawlin' fit to bust:
'*THE WICTOR IS SACKWILLE-VEST!*'

XIII

So fill up your glasses, gemmen all,
And all you milling coves,
And drink long life to *SACKWILLE-VEST*,
As inwented the *SACKWILLE GLOVE*!

XIV

So fill up the blushin' bumpers
And empty ve flowin' bowl
To *SACKWILLE, VE SEVENOAKS BRUISER!*
To bashin' VEST, from KNOWLE!

PATRICIUS PRATUS AGRICOLA

(Written at Long Crichel, donkey's years ago. Found incomplete at
Lismore and written in full 29.XI.2000.)

1 Raymond Mortimer (1895–1980). Critic and literary editor of *New Statesman*,
joined the 'Bachelors', as the inhabitants of Long Crichel House were known, as
their fourth member.
2 Eardley Knollys (1902–91). Painter who, with Eddy Sackville-West and Desmond
Shawe-Taylor, bought Long Crichel House soon after the war.

9 December 2000   Mani

Darling Debo,

Here's a picture of the small tower here and flags flying on the 25th March, when the Greek War of Independence broke out against the Turks in 1821, which ended in victory, largely owing to the unofficial influence of Ld Byron, and the scarcely less unofficial naval guns of Admiral Codrington, whose blowing of the enemy fleet to bits in Navarino Bay – referred to in Parliament as '*this untoward event*' – set Greece free. So we fly both flags on the anniversary, but I'm told incorrectly – they should be side by side, not one on top of the other – so don't tell.

'The Lay of the S Glove' was originally inspired by four lines of Regency sporting verse, which I now can't find anywhere. It had two Apollos in knee-breeches, squaring up to each other in a ring, surrounded by gents in beaver hats:

> 'With daddles high upraised, and knob held back
> In awful prescience of th'impending whack
> The Hero stands, and with preclusive spar
> And light manoeuvring kindles up the War.'

I couldn't resist putting it into cockney V-W substitution dialect. I wonder who last heard it? Nobody alive now, I bet, but early 19th-century books are full of it.

I do look forward to Yuletide! It'll be my umpteenth at Dingley Dell, as I always think of it, after the snug Christmas retreat in the *Pickwick Papers*, by Charles Dickens.

Love to all,
    Paddy

[January 2001]   Dumbleton

HAPPY NEW YEAR!

Darling Debo,

Christmas was marvellous and *everyone* enjoyed it. I even managed to get some work done in the sacred Stag Parlour. I've been a member for about 40 years, or I think I have.

It *was* decent to get the 'Three Kings' laid on. It's an odd carol, written by a v High-Church Bostonian, wild about smells and lace and Rossetti, whose name I've clean forgotten.[1] If I'm ever asked again, do you think they could manage 'The Holly and the Ivy'? It's such a strange one, and so seldom heard. I'm particularly fond of it because I remember Xan singing it – with all the words, which I don't know, in Crete at Christmas, 1942, in his strong *basso profundo* voice, while we huddled under the stalactites of a snug cave, roasting cheese on the ends of our Cretan daggers, delicious Cretan rarebits, washed down with tremendously strong wine out of a calabash.

It is a swizz everyone vanishing like this. I spend lots of time writing obituaries. The most recent is one of the Cretan captors of that general. Out of the original party of eleven, only two nigger-boys now remain.

Thank you many many times, darling Debo, and tons of love to all, from

    Paddy

1 The Christmas carol was written by the Rev. John Henry Hopkins Jr, in 1857.

16 January 2001   Dumbleton

Darling Debo,

Yesterday – the Ban on hunting – was a day of mourning, unbelievably depressing. The present government obviously plan to quietly strangle English history in all its aspects.

V many thanks for the glorious fake-library paper – I wish there'd

been room for the Bulge-Slim vol.[1] I look on it as the summit of
my literary achievement. Talking of which I've been sent a long
article in an American literary paper of such gloriously unmitigated
praise, I nearly swooned away.[2] I'll force it on you when I can get it
photo'd. Can't resist.

    Tons of love,
        Paddy

What are the police going to do at Meets when the Ban becomes
law. They'll need thousands of mounted police, and miles of
stabling for captured horses, let alone for raging – or icily polite
– people in scarlet or black. And kennelling? It's somehow
unimaginable.

---

  1 One of PLF's suggested book titles for the false library door was 'Battle of the
Bulge' by Lord Slim. See PLF's letter of February 1964.
  2 In 'Philhellene's Progress', Ben Downing deplored the fact that most Americans had not heard of 'the sublime, the peerless Patrick Leigh Fermor', and set
about correcting this oversight. *New Criterion*, January 2001.

2 May 2001   Chatsworth
                                                        Bakewell

Darling Paddy,
    Foot & mouth continues to wreak havoc not just for the farmers
– I'm told there is no livestock between Dumfries & Blackpool –
but the ripples are waves, the pathos of people who have set up
teashops, bed & breakfasts etc etc even MILES from any outbreak
and are going bust all over the place. It is truly ghoul. Blair pretends
it's all over, well it isn't.[1] The contiguous cull (ladylike word for kill)
is outrageous & even the govt vets are beginning to have a re-think.
Too late for the millions of healthy stock which are dead & lying in
rotting heaps, stinking and bursting often next to the farmhouse.
IMAGINE. No figures are available (i.e. allowed to be published by
the govt) of numbers of healthy animals killed.
    Emma & Toby say the dishonesty & cruelty to man & beast
round them is unbelievable.[2]

Andrew is havering over whether to have a new knee. A big decision, but it is v painful.

Our diamond wedding was last month & the party for the ancients in Derbyshire who have managed 60 years has had to be postponed because of f & m. So, of course, they are dying like flies & I keep getting letters saying My Dear Wife Has Passed Away. Even so 248 pairs are still on the list.

I expect the screams will be heard in Bakewell.

Much love to Joan & you

Debo

1 The foot-and-mouth crisis that broke out earlier that year was not halted until October. The Prime Minister, Tony Blair was anxious, however, to show that it was under control before the June general election.
2 DD's daughter and son-in-law farm on the Scottish Borders.

1 November 2001   Mani

Darling Debo,

Many thanks for *Counting My Chickens*! I read it clean through after dinner to midnight the day it arrived and loved it. Joan too. Your seemingly effortless breezy and unhesitating dash and funny asides at their best. Needless to say, a surprising cheer went up when I got to p. 155.[1] You are clever!

Artemis Cooper has been given the task of collecting all the detached oddments of the past years – on the same principle as yours, really – and putting them into a single vol.[2] So I'll jolly well respond to *your* birthday wishes, with mine. I've just had a letter from somebody who is writing the official biography of Somerset Maugham,[3] and very much wants a full description of my brief sojourn, so I'll dig out the two copies of my letters to you (tucked away somewhere) and do my best. It will be a relief to make it clear that I wasn't horrible, which it might sound like, only tight.

It's wonderful autumn weather here, air clear as crystal so one can see for miles and miles, even picking out the belfries on the

Messenian peninsula, 20 miles away across the gulf, and the sea is very slightly cooler than it was, but I still swim in it for about half an hour every day, which apparently is the very thing for pacemakers, rather unexpectedly.

  Lots of love from
    Paddy

<hr>

1 The appreciation that DD wrote for PLF's eighty-fifth birthday (see p. xv) was reproduced in her bestselling collection of articles and reviews, *Counting My Chickens*, with an introduction by Tom Stoppard.

2 *Words of Mercury*.

3 Jeffrey Meyers, *Somerset Maugham: A Life* (2004).

11 November 2001   Mani

Darling Debo,

  Artemis is being a wonder. Joan hobbles with a stick, rather slowly, and I danced so violently on my name day on the 8th – Feast of SS Michael, Gabriel, Rafael and All Angels, who preside in the small chapel along the lane – that I've done something frightful to my right heel, and now hobble along too (temporarily) with Andrew's smart cane. The feast day was a great success: all the crones and grey beards of the village came, and lots of young. After the mass, the feasting and drinking starts at 8 a.m. and ends with a wild mixture of Ring-a-Ring-a-Roses and Oranges and Lemons, out on to the terrace, then round the fountain. At midday they all vanish, so one can dive straight into the sea to counteract all the reckless swigging that has been going on. We've got a nice stand-in for the faithless Ritsa, whose son's departure for Mount Athos has made her a bit off her nut, but Artemis has been our saviour.

  No more now, except fond love,
    P.

6 March 2002 Mani

Darling Debo,

ITUPMPCISAA.[1] Nearly all my letters ought to start like this nowadays.

I did love being at Chatsworth. What a shame that Pss Margaret's death broke it up, temporarily. I do hope it re-cohered all right. She had always been v decent to me, and I admired her spirit, which I saw put to the test in Italy. She had come to Rome for a week, and I was somehow involved in a series of outings and parties. The thing was, how to dodge reporters. Judy Montagu had arranged a marvellous ride through wild Etruscan hills, backed up by Natalie Perrone, high-jump champion and MFH of the Rome hunt. We were cantering along quietly and were just about to splash through a brook, when all of a sudden on the other side of it, 100 press photographers, who must have been crouching, suddenly shot up and flashed all together in a rather terrifying way, like a series of broadsides. Horses started rearing etc. A cry of 'Come on!' went up and Pss M simply charged on galloping and waving her stick and they scattered like chaff, and we all pelted after her for a mile or two among the trees and the Tuscan tombs, and picnicked quietly in a ruin.

We stayed a couple of nights in Athens on the way out, where we were joined by kind Olivia Stewart, Michael, the Athens Ambassador's daughter, who is a brilliant film-producer in Rome, an angel of kindness who was a great help in our domestic plight.

It was windy, rainy and wild at first, but all of a sudden, today, not a cloud in the sky and masses of blackbirds as if someone had rashly opened a pie.

Lots of love,
Paddy

1 I Take Up My Pen Clad In Sackcloth And Ashes.

11 April 2002   Chatsworth
                                                  Bakewell

Darling Paddy,

We've been in London for Cake's funeral.[1] What a poke in the
eye for the MEDIA that all those people queued night & day in the
freezing wind to see the lying in state. They had to admit . . .

The funeral itself was one of those incredible performances which
can only happen in this country – palace, army, church all at their
tiptop best. My poor friend's[2] steely face made us all realise how
much he loved her and relied on her.

We were taken up front, as it were, in the Abbey. I think it must
have been a mistake, anyway we had a wonderful view of everything.
Bang opposite that wretched little Prime Minister & the frightful
Cherie. Prescott[3] looks like a bare-knuckle fighter of Sackville Glove
fame from the East End. Perhaps he is. I don't know. The King of
Spain was the pick of the foreign royal people, followed by a funny
little chap I couldn't place who turned out to be the Sultan of
Brunei.

Four soldiers carried velvet cushions with her orders, sparkling
diamonds galore. Perfectly beautiful and all in slow motion.

So that was that. We were lucky to be there.

Much love to Joan and you from
    Debo

[1] The Queen Mother died on 30 March, aged 101.
[2] Prince Charles.
[3] John Prescott (1938–). The Labour politician became Deputy Prime Minister
in 1997.

8 May 2002   Chatsworth
                                                  Bakewell

Darling Paddy,

I've been looking at old (very old) papers re when I was in
Washington during the Cuban crisis in the days of Pres Kennedy.
You had sent a telegram to me at the Embassy there – 'Blimey

we're in trouble, 'arf a ton of rubble. Love Fermor.' That must have cheered me up.

I had lunch with Lu Freud the other day. What an extraordinary man, he is exactly the same as he was when 25 & now he's 80, bounding upstairs, darting down the street. Painting away like billy-o & a huge exhib going all over the place to mark his 80th birthday. He's got a grand house in Kensington Church St with a garden planted in 0 but bamboo so you think you're in an endless forest.

    Much love
      Debo

Lady Cranbrook[1] (THE most wonderful woman, dau of Ralph & Coney Jarvis) sent me some amazing beans to plant. All colours of the rainbow, sort of piebald, skewbald, spotted etc. She got them off a market stall in Greece. Her son works at something with Mt Athos monks, who grow ditto, so she asked him to get her some for the Prince of Wales. MT ATHOS GET THEIRS FROM SUTTONS.

---

1 Caroline Jarvis (1935–). Suffolk farmer and campaigner on rural issues, awarded an OBE in 2007 for Services to Red Meat in East Anglia. Champion of British farmers and scourge of the supermarkets. Married 5th Earl of Cranbrook in 1968.

30 November 2002   Mani

Darling Debo,

    Senile decay must have fired a sighting shot across my bows, or I wouldn't be writing this! Did you ask me to Dingley Dell this year or next? Or neither? You see what a muddle I'm in! Please send a calming P.C.

    I went for what must be the last swim of the year last week, 20 days after Guy Fawkes! Wonderful calm autumn days till then – half-an-hour's side-stroke towards the island and back, then a lazy hour a-sprawl on the pebbles, finishing *Twelfth Night* and starting *The Two Gentlemen of Verona* (first time) by W Shakespeare: and then suddenly it all came to an end in deluge, thunder and lightning,

and cats and dogs coming down daily from dawn to dusk. And
there are plenty of the former, viz. cats, indoors as well. A honey-
coloured kitten strolled into the house two years ago, grew up, fell
in love with a village tom, gave birth to six kittens then vanished
into thin air. They are black, gold, orange and lemon skewbalds of
the utmost beauty. Joan and I sit by the fire – plenty of logs from
the olive harvest – while I read aloud from *Carry on Jeeves*.
Meanwhile, the kittens – downholsterers and interior desecrators to
a kitten – demolish all.

    Much love,
      Paddy

4 December 2002   Chatsworth

Darling Paddy,
    YES Christmas THIS YEAR galloping towards us at relentless
speed.
    I keenly suggest that you hire a car from Sunny Dumbleton
because the trains have become ghoul – sometimes they just say NO
TRAINS like when MEAT'S ORF in restaurants in the war.
    I wish you'd got a fax. It is a life saver when wondering whether
Christmas this year or next.
    We all die for you – don't not come.
    Much love. HASTE.
      Debo

(Me saying haste now – it's usually you.)

Sunday [June 2003]   Dumbleton

Darling Debo,
    I loved the service,[1] sunbeams streaming in and the sound of
flocks baa-ing and lots of birdsong coming in and filling in all the
gaps in the liturgy and wild flowers everywhere. It's a mercy having
so many letters to write, because there *are* so many. The worst part –

one of them – in sudden separations like this one is the resemblance
to an interrupted game of tennis, when all the balls served get lost in
the long grass, and masses of arguments and jokes getting cut in half
in mid-act, if you see what I mean.

I'm scribbling away in Joan's old room, looking down over the
lawn where we all hobnobbed afterwards with those trees spreading
shadows as clearly outlined underneath them as dark maps spread
over the lawn. Beyond them are a row of v old apple trees spreading
their branches espalier-wise, like family trees. They must have been
supported by a wall once, now gone.

Darling Debo, I'll write later on and make more sense. Till then
tons of love and to Andrew and to you all, from

    Paddy

1 Joan Leigh Fermor died on 4 June, aged ninety-one. A service was held at St
Peter's Church, Dumbleton, on 12 June.

14 August 2003   Dumbleton

Darling Debo

Many many sympathies about the sad Diana news,[1] though I know it
must have been the end of anguish and anxiety as well as sorrow.

The thing that struck me in those obituaries was that the
whole thing was completely beyond the writers' grasp. They had
never had to tackle such a conundrum before – the flagrant
political unorthodoxy, the lack of subterfuge or hypocrisy and the
v high style, guts and calm dismissiveness – all these were things
the obituarists were quite unable to deal with, however much
editors may have egged them on. Also, they were fascinated and, in
a way, spellbound by the figure they were writing about – the
beauty, the wit, the brains and the civilised bent for literature, the
arts, etc. Quite often this made the condemnation ring flat and
perfunctory, and, somehow, feeble. Some of the nice bits, I feel, Jim
[Lees-Milne] must have had a hand in. What is Mrs de Courcy[2]
like? I wish the editors had shown better photographs, the
extremely beautiful and serene ones.

I thought so much of you these days, as all friends did. I wish we had managed to have dinner at Christian [Carritt]'s. I've just been staying two nights again while she took me under her wing at doc after doc and now *see*, *hear* and *munch* like a basilisk, a Red Indian and a grinding machine, or ogre.

Tons of love, darling Debo, from
Paddy

I long for Greece, but it looks as if I'll have to hang about a bit more.

<hr>

1 Diana Mosley died after a stroke on 11 August, aged ninety-three.
2 Anne de Courcy, author and journalist on the *Daily Mail*, wrote a biography of Diana Mosley published in 2003.

17 or 18 August 2003   Chatsworth
                                                           Bakewell

Darling Paddy,

Your letter was extraordinary. The one which hit all nails on head. THEY can't believe in such a person so honest, straightforward & not pushed or pulled by fashion or views or anything else, as original a product of another age with standards which remained with her till she died.

You are the friend to whom all this shone out & you saw how bamboozled the journalists must be when they are surrounded by the very opposite sort of people.

Wit – perhaps not, it always strikes me as the quick & not kind remark. Nancy YES but Diana I think not. She was very very funny but that's slightly different eh.

It is so odd to have lost someone who was always there. The childhood cry of the seventh, straggling to keep up on stubby legs, of WAIT FOR ME, lives with me. She couldn't.

Now for Swinbrook. The much licked pews,[1] the unbearable memories of the olden days, the Post Office reached by donkey cart, the two-penny bars & acid drops, the village idiot, the blacksmith's shop, Nanny's fabric gloves clutched in the back of the Daimler just before I was sick. Oh well.

Thank you for a wonderful letter, exactly bang on.

Much love
    Debo

1 Diana Mosley's ashes were buried in the churchyard at Swinbrook; it was here that, as children, DD and her sisters used to lick the pews during services.

12 September 2003   Dumbleton

Darling Debo,

I'm busy packing, off tomorrow. I *wish* I'd managed to go up to Dingley Dell, but something always cropped up, and now I've got to go back home after the longest absence for years. It *will* seem strange. The place is being looked after by a charming Wykehamist poet called Hamish Robinson[1] who loves camping and writing in empty homes with lots of books, so it's a godsend.

I hate packing more than anything in the world. I bet I'll forget lots of important things.

Please give fond love to one and all.
    Paddy

1 Poet in residence at the Wordsworth Trust and author of *The Gift Returned* (2005).

23 September 2003   Chatsworth
                                              Bakewell

Darling Paddy,

I telephoned like anything, no reply, & I realised you'd GORN.

The swallows have been in a frightful fuss like you & packing & now they've gone, to join Christopher Gibbs[1] in Morocco I suppose. In a bitter cold May, Mrs Ham used to say in her gloomiest mood 'I can't think why they come'. Anyway the summer's over.

I'm glad you've got the sea. What a comfort. I know you've been longing for it.

And the poet. Is he still there with your books & his pen? Talk about pens, I still pick one up to write & tell Diana about her funeral.

I expect you feel the same about Joan. It is *so odd* them suddenly not being there.

Perhaps luckily you & I haven't got long to go – I can't believe we shall never see them again, or Woman, or Muv & Farve. Though Muv used to worry about getting through all the Chinese before she found any kindred spirit.

Here we rattle on as per. Andrew is very infirm, walking is slow, difficult & painful, but the political rows are keeping him going & he watches the telly sideways (to do with his eyes which don't work properly).

Our exhibition (250 THINGS from here) opened in Las Vegas a couple of weeks ago.

The hotel Stoker & co stayed in has 3000 bedrooms & another 1000 are being built. Our lot were on the same corridor but couldn't visit each other as the distance was about like Piccadilly Circus to Hyde Park Corner.

I'm told your book is on its way.[2] What an excitement. Shall I try to read it? Advise, please.

Much love
    Debo

---

1 Christopher Gibbs (1938–). Arbiter of taste and antiques dealer to the stars, had sold his family home in Oxfordshire to live in Morocco.
2 *Words of Mercury.*

New Year's Day 2004   Chatsworth
                                                    Bakewell

Darling Paddy,

Here we are, all of it, a sort of sainthood has descended on you quite rightly.[1]

Your peers are a rum lot but life is full of peculiar people. I couldn't find it in *The Times*, there were others all beautifully listed but no sign of you. Clever Andrew, who has only got ½ of one eye, did find it. You are called Overseas. Well I don't know. Anyway a million congrats and v much longing to see you soon.

All love & more congrats from

Debo

1 PLF received a knighthood in the New Year's honours list for services to literature and Anglo-Greek relations. DD had sent him a newspaper cutting with the full honours list.

Very early April [2004]   Mani

Darling Debo,

5.55 a.m. Here I sit in the studio, warm as toast, tho' it's a nippy morning, because I'm hosed in your wonderful ribbed woollen stockings, absolutely intact in spite of many a winter and many a mile. The best present ever! Why I'm pre-cockcrow like this is: I woke up bleary eyed, peered at the clock, saw it was 9.20, leaped out of bed, bathed and dressed like lightning, then, flinging doors and shutters open, expecting a radiant cold morning, found it still black as a bag. Sleepy eyes had got the lengths of the two clock hands the wrong way round. Confusion of this kind had been brought on by two things: the hours changed a few days ago into summer time, and Elpida, the girl who does everything, starting with brekker, had turned up the same morning with her face covered with red blotches. It was chicken pox, so she's in hospital for 10 days, as it's harmless for children – when, I *think*, I had it – but much more serious for grown-ups. In a way, it's marvellous; all these dark hours in hand, while sodden slumber still enfolds the world, perfect for what I'm doing this very moment. I've been dogged by the guilty feeling I never wrote to say thank you for my lovely sojourn at Dingley Dell. I absolutely loved it.

I know why the Queen was so *particularly* nice. Before the Honours ceremony at B Palace, a v handsome tall military courtier bore down on me, in blue with a purple fringed sash, red stripe and

box spurs and lots of gold on his shoulders, and said, 'I know all
about you! David Airlie's[1] just been talking to me. Don't worry! I'll
look after you,' and did. Obviously, knowing our sovereign likes to
scatter a few kind words to the honoured ones, but can't always
think *what*, he told her that it was my birthday, and she suddenly
said, 'Many happy returns of the day', and hence my nearly swooning
away.

A few days ago was the National Day, anniversary of the raising
the flag of defiance of the Turks at the War of Independence. We
always fly the Greek flag and the Union Jack on the same pole,
and it's rather a business, climbing up embedded rings to plant the
mast into its sockets. Well, we had only just climbed down, when,
gazing up at the fluttering display, I suddenly noted that I'd
hoisted the Union Jack upside down, a thing that landlubbers
are prone to do; only sailors can spot it. But there are none
here, we're well out of sneering range, so I let them flutter on
incorrectly.

I must go and dole out some 'Whiskers' and 'Kit-E-Kat' to the
still slumbering clowder,* all piebald and skewbald in amusing
patterns. They miss Joan bitterly (they are not the only ones). At
first, when I got back and sat in the chair she huddled over chess
problems in, they would settle all over one, then, one by one
realising I was a fake, wander off. They are beginning to twig that
I'm on their side at last. Under the olives round the terrace, masses
of freesias she scattered there last spring are shooting up in the
grass.

I am sorry about my writing. I'm going to try and reform it. I
don't know what to do about it. Words tend to shrink and huddle.

Christian [Carritt] tells me Andrew has been laid up for several
days, but is better now. Please give him my love, as to all.

And heaps of love to you from
    Paddy

P.S. Day is breaking. Here is an imaginary conversation (my new
genre).

* Correct collective word.

WAKING UP FROM A SIESTA

'Did anyone call?'

'No, sir. Oh yes, only that nice Dr Oblivion. He said he didn't want to wake you up, so he went off with his Gladstone bag full of dates and names. He said you wouldn't be needing them. And he left these flowers.'

'What are they?'

'Forget-me-nots, sir.'

'They look pretty well dead.'

'The others are rosemary.'

'They're on the way out, too.'

'Yes, sir. Rosemary for remembrance . . . He said you could get hold of him any time.'

'Oh, where?'

'Thirteen, Amnesia Grove, sir.'

1 David Ogilvy, 8th Earl of Airlie (1926–). A cousin of DD who was Lord Chamberlain 1984–97.

18 April 2004   Chatsworth
                                                                  Bakewell

Darling Paddy,

Your mention of nice Dr Oblivion has jogged what is left of my memory. Did you know that for many years he was locum at Great Snoring in Norfolk? Much loved, & the people preferred him to Dr Dose (of Happy Families) who put z instead of s in his name. I don't know why, a bit vague perhaps. A sort of sleeping partner & nothing like as good as Oblivion.

The dying forget-me-nots & rosemary are all over the garden here.

Both doctors have retired now. Dr O still has all your names & addresses in his Gladstone bag and Dr Doze is a bit of a pest, he keeps ringing up asking the same question again & again.

BUT Dr Christian Carritt is still as sharp as a needle and as kind as a saint. She arranged everything for Andrew at Ed VII, your adored refuge. I'm sorry to say he is far from well, frightfully depressed & sad, won't eat etc etc. But sometimes he cheers up a bit.

Edensor House, where we lived for 12 years, is being cut up into flats. I went all over it – talk about memories. I could SEE Mr Hore-Belisha[1] sitting up in bed, shouting for newspapers as if we were a hotel. And the bed was the one where Evie (Waugh) slept & made a frightful discovery (according to him) of the filled pot in the bedside table.

And the other visitors' room where Cyril Connolly once slept & complained to me there was lipstick on his pillow, another nail in my housekeeping coffin.

Back to the Drs Oblivion & Doze. Various groups come to see round this old dump, among them a charity to do with an illness. Can't be sure of its name but I think it ends in heimer. *Will they remember to come?*

Oh Paddy, what a muddle we're in.

Much love

Debo

Dr Doze now lives in Sleepy Hollow, next street to Amnesia Grove. He & Oblivion do an act in village halls. The song which raises the roof at every performance is 'You Forgot To Remember'.

[1] Leslie Hore Belisha (1893–1957). The Conservative MP stayed at Edensor House on two occasions, in 1946 and 1948, when attending political engagements nearby.

[May 2004]   Mani

Darling Debo,

This is just a loving message of sympathy to you for sudden event. Poor Andrew,[1] and POOR YOU! It's no good telephoning because you are besieged by all of us. So for the moment, nothing but fondest commiseration and constant thought from

Paddy

I heard the tidings yesterday, coming back from the old soldiers' gathering for the Battle of Kalamata, 1841 – messages from Nicko and Christian, so learnt all news from them.

1 Andrew Devonshire died on 3 May.

23 June 2004   Chatsworth
                                                Bakewell

Darling Paddy,

I've had 817 *cards*, haven't counted the letters but I will when they're answered. Andrew had such diverse interests & acquaintances from every conceivable organisation from all countries in the world.

No Eskimos yet but they'll come. You can't imagine how odd it is reading them. Even from the dullest person there is a sentence which is worthwhile or tells of some generosity to people unknown to me.

It is very strange here without him because he was the hub, everything revolved round him.

Most of the people who look after this place weren't born when he found himself in charge 54 years ago. Odd thought. They've known no other.

So tomorrow is the memorial service at Bolton Abbey. The next day come Jayne Wrightsman, the de la Rentas[1] & an adorable Italian,[2] all part of the summer scene here for years, arranged twelve months ago. Little do they know they are to be joined by Gen Sir Michael Rose,[3] Col of the Coldstream Guards (the one who *did* Kosovo, hero of many) because Andrew planned a Coldstream day here & 800 present or ex-Guardsmen are coming PLUS THE BAND. So that's my entertainment for the American friends.

It will kill me because I've had some wonderful letters from said Guardsmen who were with Andrew in Italy and one who was with Billy[4] when he was killed. 'We were so angry we took no prisoners that day.'

OH DEAR what tragedies that war produced.

That's the coming wk-end. Then London & the service in the Guards' Chapel. Then home for the unveiling of Lucian's amazing *Skewbald Mare* which our works of art fund has bought for this house. An astonishing picture, v moving. At the moment it is in my room but will have to move to the public route when it's unveiled next week.

This feller Robert Hughes[5] is apparently famous (the one who is unveiling). Never heard of him.

Dr Oblivion may be nice but he's a bit of a pest & has taken away Magouche's address when I owe her a letter.

THANKS for v pleasing article.[6]

Much love

    Debo

---

1 Oscar de la Renta (1932–). Dominican Republic fashion designer and his wife, Annette.

2 Federico Fourquet; Italian garden designer and interior decorator.

3 Michael Rose (1940–). The highly decorated general was Commander of the United Nations Protection Force in Bosnia 1994–5.

4 Andrew Devonshire's older brother, Billy, was killed by a sniper's bullet while serving with the Coldstream Guards in Belgium in 1944.

5 Robert Hughes (1938–). The art critic concluded his speech at the unveiling of Lucian Freud's painting with, 'I am filled with admiration for the man who did it and I must say I am filled with jealousy for those who possess it.'

6 PLF wrote an account of Andrew Devonshire's funeral for the *Spectator*, 12 June 2004.

23 July 2004   Chatsworth
                                                               Bakewell

Darling Paddy,

I've never known such frenzied activity in this place as we've seen in the last month. Coldstream Day closely followed Heywood Hill's Prize[1] & was soon overtaken by outdoor concerts on three successive nights with the singers Cliff Richard, Donny Osmond & Tom Jones. Ever heard of them? Well lots of people have. Fifteen thousand came for Cliff. Nine women to one man & for Donny nineteen women to one man. The stout Derbyshire behinds in the row in front of us swayed dangerously & totally happy.

One of the odd things was NO litter. Was it because they were old? Probably.

The Col of the Coldstream, General Sir Michael Rose, is a v impressive fellow. One or two ancients who served with Andrew in Italy came. I asked one what he was like: 'Very good officer, very smart.' Pause. 'No, not very smart but a very good officer.' Incredibly nice of course.

There's a service for A at Lismore first, 4th Aug. The Mayor of Lismore will do a reading. He has the unexpected name of Khan.

Much love
    Debo

1 A literary prize instigated and funded by Andrew Devonshire, which was awarded yearly, 1995–2004, for 'a lifetime's contribution to the enjoyment of books'.

11 September 2004   Chatsworth
                                                    Bakewell

Darling Paddy,

I'm sad you've GORN but glad for you now you can get back into the sea which must be a sort of heaven.

I thought the enclosed,[1] out of Charlotte's amazing task of choosing letters from each to each of my sisters & me over 80 years, might amuse. No doubt you stayed in Harold's dump, probably had that incredible bed/bath room? Throw.

I have been reading them, sort of proof-reading, looking for weeny mistakes & so on. They have taken me back to the olden days like nothing else could, laughing out loud & crying ditto.

Nancy's four years of torture all came back with a bang. Dear me. Would it all have been better now, drs more merciful etc? She would have been told she'd got cancer, no more whispering in the passage with the drs, at least I do believe it's better to know. That came from

America like baring all re drink & drugs. Generally accepted now & easier for all.

Have you got Nancy/Heywood letters?[2] His are *so* good. I'll send pronto if you haven't. Send a P.C. to say Yes/No.

Much love

Debo

Just found, in a drawer from London, Andrew's *grandfather's* garter thing, been there ever since I suppose, & a tin box with my grandfather's letter safely headed Windsor Castle to my father in the Boer War. Please picture. Will the lick on the envelope allow the DNA (or whatever it's called) to answer the question once & for all if he was Clementine Churchill's father? I can't bear the idea of Bay Middleton claiming her (see Mary Soames' book).[3]

---

1 DD enclosed a copy of a letter she had written to her sister Diana in 1975 describing a visit to La Pietra, Harold Acton's villa in Florence. She was reading the typescript of *The Mitfords: Letters Between Six Sisters* (2007).

2 *The Bookshop at 10 Curzon Street*, edited by John Saumarez Smith (2004). Letters between Nancy Mitford and Heywood Hill, founder of the bookshop.

3 DD's grandfather, Algernon (Bertie) Mitford, 1st Baron Redesdale (1837–1916), was long rumoured to have been the father of Winston Churchill's wife, Clementine (1885–1977), the daughter of Redesdale's wife's sister, Lady Blanche Hozier. According to Mary Soames's biography of her mother, another likely candidate was William (Bay) Middleton (1846–92), one of the best horsemen in Britain. *Clementine Churchill: The Biography of a Marriage* (2003), pp. 5–9.

17 September 2004 A.D.   Mani

Darling Debo,

A propos of Dr Oblivion, did I ever send you my first hint of untimely forgetfulness? One is at sea, and at the same instant that one forgets something, a German submarine with a skull-and-crossbones flag surfaces, and fires a shot across one's bows. Then the lid of the conning-tower opens and the top of an admiral, with monocle and fencing scars, sticks out smiling, salutes and says, 'Gut morning! That is just a sighting shot. I am Admiral von Alzheimer. Ve vill meet again!', salutes, and sinks . . .

Your letter was jam all through, and especially your 1975 one to Diana from La Pietra. It WAS a fascinating and eerie place. I remember his ancient parents – father in pince-nez and high stiff collar, bolt upright in their amazing furniture. Derek Hill[1] had been there the week before, and the gardeners had been raking up autumn leaves in a bonfire, next to that little circular fane beside the path. Two elderly English ladies were returning from a stroll, and one of them said: 'What a lot of smoke!', and Harold (imitated by Derek) said: 'Ah! When beautiful ladies like you go by, even the Temple of *LOVE* send za foorth *FIUUMES!*' Harold accompanied Joan and me on foot a little way down the road, and Joan said 'What a business-like walking stick you've got!' 'It *has* to be,' he said, 'Florence is full of RRASKALLS!'

Yes, I did get Nancy and H Hill's letters. I'm up to the neck in them now. He's awfully funny too, and Nancy just as she talked. Joan and I went to lunch twice at the Rue d'Artois, both times with the Colonel,[2] and each time he sat down and picked up his knife and fork, he said '*Aux armes!*', rather nice. I remembered it from his feasts in that lovely palace in Rome. The second lunch was the last time we saw her, and I can see her still, leaning with hands joined behind her on a sort of railing in the hall. I love the way she always sat up straight, hands joined in her lap, eyes sparkling.

There's a marvellous slip of H.H.'s on p. 24, about Mrs Ham – 'There seemed to be more and thicker black net than ever hangin' all round. Why does she not carry a triton?' (Note. Triton, a minor sea-god, son of Poseidon and Amphitrite, with a dolphin's tail, sometimes a horse's forelegs, and blowing a conch.) He obviously meant to write *trident*, with vague memories of the kind of gladiator called *retiarius* ('netman') who fought in the arena naked and only armed with *net* and *trident* (like Mrs H) against a fully armed and helmeted *secutor* ('pursuer'). The netman often won.

Talking of Poseidon, I'm going to dash down those rough steps and dive in.

Tons of love,
Paddy

P.S. Now I come to think of it, I came to that lovely Chelsea-to-Richmond boating party, many summers ago, with a trident and intertwined net (an awful nuisance it was). It must have been the first (or second?) time we met, because I remember Andrew on the gangplank saying, 'I know! You're Xan Fielding's Wife!' But hadn't we met at Royal Coll. of Arts with only heads disguised? Your head in a velvet hunting cap.
P.P.S. Old news of Bay Middleton in my next.

1 Derek Hill (1916–2000). Landscape artist and portraitist to the Establishment.
2 Gaston Palewski.

2 October 2004   Chatsworth
                                                   Bakewell

Darling Paddy,

There is such a lot going on here I don't know which pile of paper to attack first. My fault, for starting things.

Dr Oblivion comes to see me a bit too often. I wish he would just pay attention to you, plenty on his plate I should have thought.

He plagues Robert [Kee], drives him mad.

A letter to me from Diana [Mosley] says about Robert doing Mitterrand,[1] what a good idea etc, & it's dated *1996*. So eight years have rolled & still he struggles.

I've been in the Highlands. Have you ever seen that country? It is too big & threatening for me & the endless evergreen trees are melancholy.

I stayed with the P of Wales in Cake's old house, Birkhall.* That is truly fascinating, all passages lined with Spy cartoons stuck cheek by jowl, all my Granddad's work – he started *Vanity Fair* & engaged Spy.[2] Curtains in tatters & the Prince won't touch them. Cake's hat & mac hanging in the hall. He reveres her & so won't change anything, so right.

* Called Birkhell by my old friend her chef.

My bathroom was a punishment cell, freezing cold LINO ON FLOOR & I didn't take bedroom slippers. Elec towel rail bust. Everything else supreme luxury & I loved the bathroom, back to childhood.

That will have to do for now, must get back to the piles of paper. Much love

Debo

1 Robert Kee was researching a biography of the French President.
2 Thomas Gibson Bowles (1841–1922). DD's maternal grandfather, a politician and journalist, started the popular weekly satirical magazine *Vanity Fair* (unrelated to its modern namesake) in 1868. In 1873 he recruited the artist Leslie Ward, 'Spy', who contributed to the magazine for over forty years. He also founded *The Lady*, still famous today for its classified columns advertising for domestic help.

3 October 2004   Mani

Darling Debo,

I long to hear more about Bay Middleton! I'll tell you why. When I was trudging through Hungary, Transylvania and Rumania ages ago, I stayed ages with a charming Hungarian squire called Elemér von Klobusiçky, living in an old house above the River Maros. We became great pals. He was just old enough to have been a cornet in a hussar regiment in the Great War.

He asked me if I knew anything about Bay Middleton, viz. that he had been a great friend of the beautiful Empress Elizabeth, and always accompanied her out hunting, going over all the worst fences first etc. In fact, a *cavaliere servente*, as they say; but always with the rider '*en tout bien et en tout honneur*' viz. nothing out of order.

Well, once he had been invited to stay at a royal hunting lodge called Gödölő, E of Budapest, where both the Emperor Franz Joseph and the Empss Elizabeth were staying too. He went off to a dinner party in Budapest, and after it, in the small hours, wandered

about in his tails and picked up a v pretty but wicked tart, who
was part of a gang of robbers. She took him, instead of to some
snug alcove, to their den, where he was robbed of everything, *every
stitch of clothing* I think down to his dancing pumps, and then left
in the empty street, lost and, worse still, starkers, and was either
arrested, or found a police station. Something in his extreme good
looks, fine bearing and humour succeeded in impressing them.
There was no common language, except his repeated murmur of
'*Gödölő*', so, puzzled, they wrapped him in a police overcoat and
got in touch with a guard there; then, with some equerry taking
care of him, they smuggled him back to the bachelors' wing, and
all was well, though the tale got about a bit, probably from his
telling it. My pal had heard it from an old courtier who had been
on duty there. Do admit that it's a fascinating tale. Triumph in
adversity with knobs on. He doesn't sound too bad an ancestor to
spring from. Do tell anything you know about him, I long to
know.

I finished Nancy's letters to H.H. Both of them are captivating.
No more now. A dash to the post . . .
Fond love,
   Paddy

20 October 2004   Mani

Darling Debo,
   It's very queer. I'd just finished re-reading your letter about the
hotel where you and Sto & co stayed on the same corridor but
completely out of touch because the distance was the same as
from Piccadilly Circus to Hyde Park Corner – when a postcard of
Hyde Park Corner, dating from *c.*1930, suddenly materialized. Do
look at it carefully. The winged wreath-bearing lady in the chariot
on top of the Wellington Arch was done from my old landlady in
Shepherd Market, where I set off from on my travels, aged 18¾, a
five-minute flight, or less. She was an ex-artist's model called
Beatrice Stewart, painted by Sargent, Sickert, Shannon, Stevens,

Tonks and Augustus John. She was in her seventies, but walked with two sticks because of an accident, and metal leg. You could see she had been a great beauty. I loved her as she was always angelically kind to me, and forgave our noisy parties. In spite of the early date, I can spy only one horse and cart. The Artillery Monument in the foreground always makes me damp about the eyes, especially the recumbent gunner wrapped under his greatcoat and tin hat.

I keep on thinking of things I must remember to tell Joan at lunch, knowing they could make her laugh, rather like you with Diana. Letters addressed to her still arrive from distant parts, but they are dying out now, and it's only subscriptions to be renewed or bright catalogues for pullovers and the like.

Tons of love to you, and to all at Dingley Dell,

Paddy

25 October 2004   Chatsworth
                                                            Bakewell

Darling Paddy,

Lots of things. I've got ANOTHER book on the go, photos of buildings etc within two miles of this old dump.[1]

The inevitable introduction is necessary & one para has this line saying how The house is perfectly placed *between the woods & the water* (like Paddy Leigh Fermor's book). Do you allow that? Sorry to be a bore, but it's true, eh. RSVP one day.

And before Christmas, Amanda [Hartington] has got a carol service in Ripon Cathedral where various fatheads like myself read something from the pulpit all in aid of some Good Cause. She's asked me to read a whack of *A Time of Gifts*. So I looked it up (being proud possessor of *T of G*). It's called 'Christmas 1933', and *I SHALL HAVE TO LEARN GERMAN* to spit it out properly. HELP.

And how do you pronounce Bungen[2] whose inhabitants exchanged greetings? Bung em sounds a bit drear. Or it is BUngen like TUlip? The U I mean? Is the G soft or hard? Oh dear what prarblams.

And help, please, with the names of the carols? One looks like Nancy saying Eet eez too moch in her Czech–ish ladies accent of old.[3]

The last thing is the list of field names of a farm where there is a Stump Cross, a medieval object on a mound which turns out to be a Bronze-Age burial place. Having a good look at that I found the other field names & very nice they are – Dungworth Bank, Sitch, Patch, Interim Furlong, Purchased From Wheeldon, & the one you'll like, Kine Furlong.

When did people stop calling cattle kine? Purchased From Wheeldon seems a long name for a field but that's what it is.

V much love

Debo

---

1 *Round About Chatsworth* (2005).
2 DD misread 'Bungen' for the town of 'Bingen'.
3 As a child, Nancy invented a game in which she played a 'Czechish lady doctor' for which she adopted a thick foreign accent.

27 October 2004   Mani

Darling Debo,

I love the idea of *Between the W and the W* sneaking its way into the introduction. Better still, you sending a chunk of *A.T. of G* through triforium to clerestory in Ripon. 'BINGEN' is the word, and uttered just like the game, viz. BINGO, with EN instead of O. STEELER NACHT, with the CH = Ah!, sounding as a Moslem would pronounce Aly Khan's surname.

(1) ES (2) IST (3) EIN ROS' ENTSPRUNGEN is uttered (1) like an American Ezra Pound fan familiarly dropping his hero's name with the second syllable docked; (2) IST like Hûst!, said by one of the Lost Boys in *Peter Pan*, dropping his H at the sight of a Red Indian; (3) EIN is like the last three letters of the song, Clementine; ROS' like *rows* and ROWS of spectators;

ENTSPRUNGEN is the county of Kent minus its K; SPRUNG is pronounced as it would be in the heart of Ilkley Moor, followed by the tail end of a chicken.

I had a sad loss last week. When bathing I use an old stick to go out to the rock I take off from, and leave it on a ledge. This time a squall blew up, and when I got back, the stick had been whirled away. In the hurry to get down the steps, I had picked up the one Andrew gave me a few years ago, the apple of my eye, black with a silver band – 'PADDY from Andrew, Christmas . . . ?' and the date, back in the nineties. It had become a sort of talisman. Magouche was staying and we hunted up and down the neighbouring beaches for days. It was rather like Excalibur, thrown over the mere by Sir Bedivere and caught by a mysterious shrouded arm, as in the Henry Ford illustration in *The Book of Romance*, one of the Andrew Lang Fairy Tale books, worshipped by me when young.

I slog along steadily here till just before Yule chez Janetta and Jaime in Andalusia and then Morocco, and will think wistfully of you all listening to 'The Holly and the Ivy' on those steps.

Off to the post.

Tons of love,

Paddy

Today is OHI ('NO!') Day, when the Greeks refused the ultimatum of Mussolini's army in 1940, and then drove them all back almost into the Adriatic until Hitler came to their rescue.

Lots of flags, swigging, dancing in a ring and singing. Fun but exhausting.

17 November 2004

Chatsworth
Bakewell

Darling Paddy,

Your German lesson is wonderful. If I get up in the pulpit in Ripon Cathedral (which is what I've got to do) & spout out all that, the audience, sorry congregation, will be all of a dither wondering what's coming next.

I've studied & studied it.

And will have to re-study. It's like a difficult drawing-room game but I'll battle it out somehow. THANKS.

Now for a suggestion. Please buy more paper, use two sheets instead of one and LEAVE MORE SPACE

BETWEEN THE LINES to put your corrections etc. Good idea?
More soon.
Much love
    Debo

Do you realise you're nearly 90? ODD.

23 November 2004   Mani

Darling Debo,

I've just been reading an excellent book by Harold Nicolson called *Good Behaviour*, then wondered why I had bought it, so turned back to the fly-leaf and read: September 1975 'Paddy much love from Debo. So very good to get rid of a book. I *loathe* the things.' I'd obviously asked if I could borrow it from your bedside . . .

Lovely talking to you last night. Lots of bustle here, as the olive harvest is on, acres of spread tarpaulin, the whizz of pruning saws and the pitter-pat of tumbling olives, and, indoors, the shifting round of furniture, everything based on the fireplace, huge baskets of logs and laying of mats and carpets. Ready for anything.

Tons of love,
    Paddy

16 January 2005   Chatsworth
                                                    Bakewell

Darling Paddy,

Your instructions for pronouncing the German words went down a treat. I started by saying what you told me to do & after Entsprungen I gave it up & craved their indulgence of my ignorance.

The Prince of Wales came with us & *he* knew just how to say those words (to the manor born as it were) & he laughed so much & then enjoyed the performance from the pulpit.

It was a very jolly evening made of course by you.

Much love

Debo

14 April 2005   Chatsworth
                                                             Bakewell

Darling Paddy,

So glad I sent you that book with a sensible note in it.

I've had such a rackety time. I ended up in hosp with 'a turn', viz. not quite a stroke.

We did overdo things a bit, a long promised trip with Emma. First night at Bowood, *incredibly* beautiful in all ways, bluebells growing like a crop, dead level & no earth or anything untoward between them, not out yet but all promise. Breakfast in bed at 7.30 unheard of luxury in any stately. Ld & Ly Lansdowne[1] both v nice indeed but it is haunted for me by my Wife & her two bros, killed within 10 days of each other in Aug 1944, my two best friends. I didn't know the Wife then.

Next night Wilbury. A bit of Wiltshire perfection apparently in a poor way till bought by Lady Iveagh[2] eight years ago. She has lavished all on it, so super-luxurious, four different smelling things in every drawer in my room so it's difficult to know what's yours and what belongs to the house when packing.

Ld Londonderry[3] came to dinner. I hadn't seen him for years, *so* funny, good looking and charming. 'I'm a gregarious recluse,' he said.

Amazingly my sister Woman was born there nearly 100 years ago. My grandfather Bowles took the house off & on for 20 years & I suppose my mother wanted to be out of their weeny Pimlico semi-slum. She told me she & her Dad used to ride to Stonehenge, 10 miles, without a fence or obstacle of any kind.

So it had a history for me as well as its beauty. But the trouble with newly acquired houses is the electrically locked gates and all of that which take away some of the magic.

Kindness itself from Ly Iveagh. She has got a Guinness bar in the basement *and a cinema*. I wonder if she could get the *Lives of the Bengal Lancers*, my favourite film.

Then to lunch with Edward Adeane[4] in his mill built over the Avon. The sun came out & it was like England is supposed to be, daffs & willows & rushing water.

Lord Pembroke[5] was there. About twenty-five, bachelor, handsome & charming, he got a FIRST in Industrial Design at Sheffield University, do admit how original. I wish he would invent a tap which doesn't direct water straight on to the plug so it jumps out before you've got enough water to wash in.

So then the wedding,[6] a total ripping success. I sat next to Brig Andrew Parker Bowles[7] one side and a sort of Elvis choir man the other.

It must have been so odd for Andrew seeing his old wife go up the aisle like that. I can't quite imagine it, can you? I know they're all very friendly but even so . . .

The Prince invited Henry & Joan [Coleman] & Stella (housemaid) & Keith her hubby.[8] That's what I love about him. Henry shook hands with Mr Blair & said good luck ('but I didn't mean it'), Mr Howard,[9] & of course found heaps of friends.

Then home.

Got up Sun a.m. perfectly OK & slap bang went wobbly & talked like a drunk person (I'm told, can't remember). Next thing the dr, stretcher, ambulance, hospital. Can't remember much about that either. Room to myself, seventh floor, fantastic view of the hideosities of Sheffield out of vast hermetically sealed window.

Five doctors (or learners, some of them I suppose) at bottom of bed. The chief one was Dr Khan, not exactly Aly but sweet. Eddie Tennant, a saint, stayed with me & ruined his Sunday.

Brain scan ordered the next day. People hate them, Andrew specially loathed it. All I can say is never fear if you have to have one. They put you in a long coffin & shove it up under a cover & bang bang wallop wallop it goes, just about like the train to Eastbourne, no worse. Twenty minutes then they show you the snaps of said brain.

One looked like a dog with a big black nose, one could have been a Picasso drawing of me, a bit frightening, & the rest looked like patterns on hotel carpets, some Gothic, some flowers, quite nice.

Anyway, o untoward was discovered so here I am home again & quite alright except the Dr says I'm to stay on this floor[10] for two WEEKS.

But I'm thankful for mercies, like it not being a real stroke, just a warning.

So there we are. The everyday story of country folk.

The *kindness* in the hosp. was beyond. NHS. But the lunch was yak, I think, certainly no known meat. Perhaps the patients are all from Nepal.

Much love

Debo

---

1 Charles Petty-Fitzmaurice, 9th Marquess of Lansdowne (1941–). Married Fiona Merritt, as his second wife, in 1987. His two cousins, sons of the 6th Marquess, were both killed in action in 1944 within a few days of each other.

2 Miranda Smiley (1940–). Married to Benjamin Guinness, 3rd Earl of Iveagh, 1963–84.

3 Alexander Vane-Tempest-Stewart, 9th Marquess of Londonderry (1937–). The unconventional peer was married to Nicolette Harrison in 1968 and to the ballerina Doreen Wells 1972–89.

4 Edward Adeane (1939–). Private Secretary and Treasurer to the Prince of Wales 1979–85.

5 William Herbert, 18th Earl of Pembroke (1978–). After his father's death in 2003, he left his job as a designer to run his family estate at Wilton in Wiltshire.

6 The Prince of Wales's wedding to Camilla Parker-Bowles, Duchess of Cornwall, on 8 April.

7 Andrew Parker-Bowles (1939–). The former husband of the Duchess of Cornwall had known DD since he was a boy.

8 Keith Mellors was houseman at Chatsworth; his wife, Stella, was housekeeper of the private side of the house.

9 Michael Howard (1941–). Conservative MP and Leader of the Opposition 2003–5.

10 DD's bedroom and sitting room were on the first floor at Chatsworth.

10 July 2005   Chatsworth
                                                               Bakewell

Darling Paddy,

I rattle on here while the Old Vic is being got ready.[1] A huge job as
roof & floors were all wonky. That saint David Mlinaric is giving me a
hand with things like where to put baths & electric points – all the
things you take for granted but must be done. He is so extraordinary,
eye on ball all day, explaining to electricians, plumbers etc in their own
lingo. When I think of the places he's done – Covent Garden, National
Gallery, V&A, Spencer House, ETC ETC – you can imagine the Old
Vic is the smallest fry & just done out of kindness. Amazing.

Nicko Henderson has been here & Robert. It was the weekend
of the concert in the park & the one & only remaining Lancaster
bomber, accompanied by a Spitfire, flew down the river & lumbered
along very low, making a terrific racket. There was Robert, stick in
hand, looking & listening to this elephant slowly turning & offering
to hit the roof of this old dump. It was v moving, all in floods of
course. We asked Robert what it was like[2] & he was *pre-Lancaster*,
flew in a Handley Something, was navigator *and* let the bombs go
when lying more or less on his stomach in the nose of the thing.
Navigation hopeless he told us. Sometimes just on ETA, often when
they met ack-ack fire, they just decided to let the bombs go. 'Perhaps
we're over Hamburg.' 'Oh yes I expect so.' 'Let 'em go.' That sort of
thing.

Jon Snow's[3] telephone went in the middle of dinner. Of course,
we all thought Blair had started another war, but no. It was his
daughter saying Dad, any chance of some tickets for Glastonbury?

Now then. Robert Byron.[4] Alas I never knew him but I bet you
did? Such a fascinating thing, letters galore from Nancy, Tom &
Diana AND MY PARENTS to him have sprung out of the packing
cases the niece is bravely sorting through. I hope to buy them, can't
wait to see. I'll tell you the sort of stuff when (if) they land here.[5]

There is much going on here but that's nothing new.

Much love. Keep on keeping on

Debo

1 Following her husband's death, DD was moving from Chatsworth to the neighbouring village of Edensor.

2 Robert Kee served in the RAF in Bomber Command. His plane was shot down over occupied Holland and he spent three years in a German prisoner-of-war camp, an experience he described in *A Crowd Is Not Company* (1947).

3 Jon Snow (1947–). DD met the Channel 4 News broadcaster through her sister Jessica.

4 Robert Byron (1905–41). Writer whose best-known book, *The Road to Oxiana* (1937), was a record of his journeys through Iran and Afghanistan. He was a friend of the Mitford family and of Nancy in particular.

5 DD was successful in buying the Robert Byron letters.

[August 2005]   Dumbleton

Darling Debo,

It's too queer, when I got here 3 or 4 days ago, bang on top of a pile of letters was a card from you, that managed not to get forwarded, though long out of date.

'Did you know', the text of the P.C. runs, 'that the Vikings called Constantinople Micklegarth? Well, they did. Much love, Debo'

I *did* know it, and have written fruity paragraphs about it in that book called *Mani*. It's really Micklegard, but only a near miss. '*Gard*' and '*garth*' are pretty well interchangeable, and akin to '*grad*' as at the end of Petro- and Stalin-, meaning a 'place' or 'town' – the 'big one' here. Micklegarth was regularly visited by Harold Haardraada – his steeds were always in a muck-sweat – as well as Jerusalem, which he called *Mittelgard*, because he thought it was in the middle of the world. H.H. was later King of Norway, and landed at Stamford Bridge, hoping to capture England before William the Conqueror did; he was helped by a horrible man called Tostig, but got killed by our King Harold, who rushed north just in time, and then marched south again at high speed, just in time for William's landing. A crowded week, ending in the Hastings arrow in the eye.

ENTR'ACTE

25 August 2005.

Debo, I must have written the above illegible stuff three weeks ago, in a maelstrom of old envelopes and bills and I've only just discovered it, and, at the same time, that unless I take care, my writing becomes totally illegible.

I go to London from time to time because of seeing specialists, who are intervening in a few of the minor things that infest the aged and turn the first quarter of an hour at any meeting of those over ninety into an Organ Recital. I ought to be getting back to Greece, so it looks as if meetings will be off till later in the year.

I'm off to spend the Bank Holiday Hol at Antony & Artemis Beevor's house in Kent, which I look forward to. He's a great Cretan War expert and she is my literary executor. Do send news here, when I briefly return, or, if much later, to Greece.

What news of your new quarters?

Tons of love,

Paddy

30 August 2005   Chatsworth
                                                  Bakewell

Darling Paddy,

Micklegarth. I'm still surprised. I can see you aren't. I love them all being in such a hurry, up & down England. Tostig is just the name for a horrid person.

New quarters coming along in the slow way they do. Won't it be odd, moving.

Do you remember when Somerville & Ross had to move to a smaller house, in despair at the fact that 'under everything there is something'.

All love

Debo

13 November 2005   Chatsworth
                                                    Bakewell

Darling Paddy,

Here is chaos. I'm on the brink of moving, trying to undo 46
years-worth of GLUT. My rooms have got cardboard boxes, one for
THROW, one for KEEP, & now I see a third is needed for
UNDECIDED.

Although the Old Vic is huge, it is vaguely smaller than here &
there's no hope of getting even KEEP in.

There are marvellous entertainments called car-boot sales & that's
what I need. You can buy a Rembrandt for a few quid in any old
field. So why not sell a few?

The awful thing about it all is that only I can do it.

I MUST go & fill a cardboard box.

Much love
    Debo

Mid-November [2005]   Mani

Darling Debo,

You'll never guess why I'm writing on this kind of paper.[1] The
reason is that my alignment always seems to get tangled, like the
barbed wire on the Western Front in early films. This makes a move
in the direction of legibility.

I had a shock two days ago. Woke up, opened a book to read,
found the print v smudged on the right-hand page, and *nothing* on
the left hand, so got driven in haste to Kalamata. When I got there, I
found I could read all these rows of diminishing capital letters with
utmost ease. It had all come right, in a mysterious way, caused by
something called a 'blood-spasm' in Greek, so all is well. I long to see
Mr ffytche this time next month.

The book I was reading was Duff's diary edited by J Julius.[2] I
thought it a bit indiscreet at first – then changed my mind, and
enjoyed it a lot. I always liked Duff (I know you didn't) and loved
Diana. I wonder what you would make of it. Antony Head[3] has one

entry in the index, but no mention of the funniest thing about him that Diana used to tell. When he came to stay at Chantilly, Diana showed him his quarters, and said, 'I'm afraid you'll have to share a bath with Duff', to which he immediately answered, 'All right, but bags I the non-tap end.'

    Tons of love, darling Debo,
        Paddy

1 Heavily ruled writing paper.
2 John Julius Norwich had edited a volume of his father's diaries, *The Duff Cooper Diaries, 1915–1951* (2005).
3 Antony, 1st Viscount Head (1906–83). Minister of Defence 1955–7, High Commissioner in Malaysia 1963–6.

14 March 2006   Edensor
                                           Bakewell
                                        Derbyshire

Darling Paddy,

    Eyes. A terrific nuisance. Have yours made reading difficult with their tunnel?[1] Or isn't it like that? RSVP.

    Mine are getting worse, inevitable I suppose, & people's faces are dirty sponges & anyone with their back to the light is a dead loss. Colours have rather gone west, blue & green pretty well indistinguishable, never mind.

    Helen[2] & I have been desperately busy putting together an exhib of Andrew's life in SEVEN rooms at Chatsworth. Your *Three Letters from the Andes* is bunged between his boots & socks & filthy old coat & looks fine.

    Last night was the press evening. It was JUST ready in time. They seemed to like it. Good. One room has fourteen works by Lu Freud, nine oil paintings & some drawings, a bit of a showstopper, & at the end a whole long wall of photos of the funeral procession – amazing. It will all remain for two years.

    I'm having three days hard labour with a French telly crew. Because my daft book has sort of taken off in France[3] so the telly are following up the incredibly & totally unexpected things the journalists wrote after lots of interviews. What a big surprise.

The telly woman is hard work, never a smile & doesn't seem to see the point of anything. I forced them to go to the Farmyard in the snow this a.m. & two schools' worth of five year olds were riveted by watching a cow make a mess. Don't think the cameraman got it but that's typical if you see what I mean, missing the point.

Tomorrow we'll 'do' Alan [Shimwell] & my hens, that'll learn them & I showed them Madame Mère & Pauline B & Napoleon in the Sculpture Gallery[4] which vaguely cheered them. They said 'Do you think it is time to get rid of your royal family?' 'Certainly not' I said 'we'd have a dreary old president.' 'That's what we've got.' 'Yes, so you know?' Heaven knows what the prog will turn out like.

Much love from
　　Debo

1 PLF was suffering from tunnel vision. 'It's called Simplonitis.' (PLF)
2 Helen Marchant (1961–). Secretary to the Devonshires since 1987.
3 *Counting My Chickens* had been published in France as *Les Humeurs d'une châtelaine anglaise*, translated by Jean-Noël Liaut.
4 Marble portrait busts of the Emperor and his mother by Antonio Canova, and of his sister by Thomas Campbell.

[April 2006]   Mani

Darling Debo,

Many apologies if I've sent you the enclosed during the last century, but I've just come across it and send it in hopes of a smile. It's a rather dated 'Meow – meow' campaign 'abolishing the cat' etc. I'm busy wading through old letters, papers etc. Writing is still rather disorderly, but I plan to improve.

Lots of love,
　　Paddy

AFTER LUNCHEON THOUGHTS

For an advertising campaign for KIT-E-KAT

KIT-E-KAT for Felines of Distinction . . .

(Is *your* cat a KIT-E-KAT? You can tell by its whiskers . . .)
Top cats eat KIT-E-KAT
'What are the top cats saying?'
'What's in the MEWS?'
'No mews is good mews, as purr usual.'
'Purr ad ventura . . .'
'Wise witches choose KIT-E-KAT (Quickens acceleration, more climbing power)
Cats have nine lives, but only one KIT-E-KAT!
Why abolish the cat? Give him K-E-K and watch out for the sleekness . . .
K-E-K for dreamless and refreshing catnaps . . .
Lots of love
    Paddy

12 May 2006   Edensor

Darling Paddy,

    Thanks so much for Kit E Cat. It is perfect. Best. V v clever and makes me rush out to buy it in spite of being cat-less (and dog-less too, odd).

Are you in touch with one Dr Mitchell,[1] chosen by his peers to write the life of M Bowra? University Coll Oxford is his grand address.

He wrote to 'The Keeper' Chatsworth asking to see MB's letters to Nancy. So me being her keeper I answered & sent them, only three but never mind.

I told him that Emma's generation when at Oxford called him Old Tragic, an interesting fact which he didn't know *but* on the strength of it he's asked me to lunch in his glamorous diner. *Shall I go?* I rather long to.

When people talk like that, refer to Librarians & co as keepers, I naturally think of them as gamekeepers. Oh never mind.

This house is becoming alright, better than it was when we had the Old People's New Year.[2] I really love it. Can't explain why but perhaps it is the atmosphere.

Much love
   Debo

1 Dr Leslie Mitchell; historian and Emeritus Fellow of University College, Oxford.
2 'Paddy and Nicko Henderson had spent New Year 2006 at Edensor – the first non-family guests as I had only moved in on 14 December 2005.' (DD)

9 July 2006   (The Usual)

Darling Debo,

How I *hate* using this beastly paper, but it's the only way to remain on the rails, I'm afraid. (I must have a serious talk with Mr ffytche.) The only alternative is to use v thin paper, and have a sort of grid underneath. Anyway, to hell with it!

I'm *so sorry* being such a sluggard in writing. I think, subconsciously, it's probably shrinking from this stationery. You note how upright my writing has suddenly become? It's part of my plan to become steadily more legible. Also, note the presence and clarity of the date. In the past, one was lucky if letters had the day of the month. One didn't seem to worry about years.

It's been very queer here recently, but a bit better now. Tremendous heat, for which the local remedy is to keep the windows *and* the shutters firmly shut from the moment it gets at all light at dawn, until after sunset, when one flings them all wide so that cool air can waft about the house all through the hours of darkness. The daylight darkness is a bit eerie. I toil away rather slowly at Vol III of my stop-press youthful travel book. A French critic refers to me as *l'escargot des Carpathes*.

Fond love,
    Paddy

(envelope torn asunder)
Real stop-press!
P.S. I had just sealed the envelope with a letter to you in it, when *your* last letter suddenly turned up under a pile of books, so I rent it open, and I was so amused by the contents that I couldn't do otherwise. I've even been driven back on to unruled paper, so must take care.

First. How did your feast with M Bowra go? There's lots to be said about him, most of it v good but spoilt by a streak of v bad. Anyway, a fascinating theme. Lots to be said when we meet. Maurice adored Joan and gave her all his poems, many extremely funny, some appalling – not in prosody but in content, some not to be read out loud. Joan went through them a year before she died and told me that as she knew he had given similar bundles to Pam Berry[1] and a few others, she would burn her set, which she did next day. The reason being, she said, that they could make many people utterly miserable. All v complex and best explained *unwritten*. But he did far more good than harm, in the sense of being a liberator from inhibitions, family gloom etc. A v. complex case. The editor of his poems behaved extremely nicely to me, wrote and said 'would I mind if the two poems that deal with me were published'. One was harmless, the other not, so he cut them both out of the published vol.[2] Another such brand from the burning was Billa [Harrod]. So he's a good egg. John Betj gets it in the neck, although a great friend. My own private conclusion is that Maurice *could* become v faintly cracked for as long as it took to write a poem, then stepped back into being a marvellously funny, cheerful fellow.

Please send news and gossip,

P

1 Lady Pamela Smith (1914–82). Political hostess. Married, in 1936, Michael Berry (created Baron Hartwell 1968), proprietor of the *Daily Telegraph*.
2 *New Bats in Old Belfries*, a collection of Maurice Bowra's scabrous satires, published in 2005, edited by Henry Hardy and Jennifer Holmes.

29 July 2006   Dumbleton

Darling Debo,

What *is* very queer about tunnel vision is that one suddenly notices that one's interlocutor (or interlocutrix) at dinner has two mouths, four eyes, and four nostrils but by a twist of one's face, I can reduce the features to the normal quota. Sometimes I can manage more or less respectably with no ruled lines at all. It's very wayward, and rather maddening. I think I will try and write in a very clear script, as I'm doing at the moment, as one did when very young. Thank God, I can still (touch wood) read all right, and I'm deep into the umpteenth re-reading of *The Road to Oxiana* by Robert Byron. It's wonderfully funny and clever. I wish I'd known him better. I met him about three times in 1938, once with Sachie Sitwell,[1] once with Bridget Parsons, and once with Mark Grant, but never well. I bet you did, unless you were still too young. Yes I did see him once more, at an exhibition of Willy Acton's[2] paintings. He and everyone was tremendously tight.

I so hope this is more or less legible. One way of dealing with seeing double (turning Salisbury Cathedral into Cologne or rather *vice versa*) is to wear a patch, but I always forget.

With tons of love,

Paddy

1 Sir Sacheverell Sitwell (1897–1988). PLF had been a friend of the writer, youngest of the famous literary trio, and his wife Georgia, since 1937. 'When war broke out, I enlisted in the Irish Guards but they couldn't take me for a month or so and I

lived on tick at the Cavendish Hotel. Sachie and Georgia heard of this, and I was asked to stay with them at Weston, Northamptonshire, until the Guards depot had room for me. I spent Christmas there on leave: total bliss. Talk, music, fun, paper games, fascinating neighbours. It was a wonderful retreat.' (PLF)

2 William Acton (1906–45). Painter and younger brother of Harold Acton.

23 September 2006   Edensor

Darling Paddy,

Harvest Festival here. Alan [Shimwell] has made some little wire baskets lined with hay filled with dark brown eggs, wonderful.

Stella came. We had to be together in a photo for *Vogue*'s 90th birthday come Christmas. So one Mario Testino,[1] famous photographer, came in a helicopter with a crew of makeup, hairdresser, 'fashion editor' etc from London.

I've got a really beautiful dress, grand evening, given me by Oscar de la Renta, so that was my kit. They bound Stella's legs, up to where they join her body, in tartan. A Union Jack flag hung from her waist & her top was what my father would have called meaningless.

Hair skewbald/piebald, all colours & stuck up in bits. THEN they produced 'shoes' with 6 inch heels. More stilts — she could hardly put one foot in front of the other, wobbling & toppling, and being 6´-tall she turned into 6´6˝.

We looked just like that Grandville drawing of a giraffe dancing with a little monkey. I was the monkey.

Fashion is as queer as folks. So that was the excitement, now down to earth with the Harvest Festival.

Much love
    Debo

1 Mario Testino (1954–). The Peruvian photographer took some of the first fashion shots of DD's supermodel granddaughter, Stella Tennant, who married his assistant, David Lasnet, in 1999.

10 October 2006   Mani

Darling Debo,

Is there a copy of *Kim*, by Rudyard Kipling, anywhere about –
viz. the library over at Dingley Dell? I expect it's not quite old or
important enough, but if there *IS*, and a copy illustrated by his father
(John Lockwood Kipling) could you *possibly* get your new librarian
to get a certain picture in it called *The Russeldar*,[1] or something
similar, Hindustani for a retired cavalry soldier, I think, to take a
photograph of it, and send it to me, & note the number of the page it
is opposite, on the back?

This is very complicated. To bore you further, I was going
through old papers yesterday, and came on a colour photograph of a
pretty skewbald cat of Joan's, fast asleep with its head on an open
copy of *Kim*, exactly on this page, with the Russeldar plain as a
pikestaff and Joan's specs across it too; all this is on a square of sofa,
with lovely details of pattern and colour, the cat flat out. It's
marvellously composed, an ideal vision of an afternoon nap, with the
heroine of the scene, viz. Joan, momentarily off stage. I want to get
the text opposite the pussycat correct and turn the picture into
hundreds of P.C.s, which I will use for the rest of my life. I can get
the cards made in Athens or Rome. It will be entitled '*Egyptian P.T.*',

which was the soldiers' name for forty winks after lunch, when serving east of Suez. It would be wonderful if you could help with the context – nothing more, and many many thanks in advance if it can be done. The illustration's *modelled* in relief clay – about 1900, perhaps a bit earlier, by Mr J L K, then photographed.

I'm going to Athens tomorrow for four days, for the memorial service of a chap called David Sutherland, who was one of the great stars of the SBS – Special Boat Service – like Geo Jellicoe, and David Stirling (with SAS), and the Embassy are most kindly sending a car and putting me up, and I'm looking forward to the outing. I wish it were only 20 minutes' drive here from the Rectory, instead of three days. Hamish Robinson was staying here when I came, but has had to return. I've just been talking to Rita, who looks after everything, asking her to send me some Marmite and forgotten clothes. She's the champion of Dumbleton skittles team, and has been covering herself and her side with glory. She's an angel and Jeff our gardener is tip-top, so we're in luck.

The olive harvest has begun. Ladders are propped among the branches of each tree and olives come pattering down on to coloured rugs and tarpaulin, with lots of children and dogs skipping about, and pillars of pale blue smoke from the sawn-off branches floating up into the autumn sky.

Tons of love,
Paddy

1 '*The Ressalder*', a native cavalry captain in the Anglo-Indian army.

[May 2007]   Edensor

Darling Paddy

Nature notes. A daft mallard made her nest in a patch of irises in this garden. I wondered how on earth she would get to the river when the eggs hatched. I thought of penning her in with food and drink so I could catch the lot and take them in the car . . . (but didn't). Yesterday there she was on the lawn with 11 ducklings. Please

picture the hazards ahead – the huge & deep ha-ha into the park, a
hundred yards or more to the main road, the traffic rushing, then
more hundreds of yards to the river. Crows, jackdaws, hawks and
now ravens all spotting them on the open ground.

As though ordered or instructed from on high, the duck jumped
down into the weedy ha-ha & all 11 jumped with her, climbed up
the bank & set off for the road. My excellent neighbour Bridget[1]
followed them & ran past to get to the road before they did,
succeeded & stood there with her hand up stopping the traffic till all
reached the other side. They hurried on such a long trek to the
water, straight as 12 dies.

I know it happens every year, but do admit the power of instinct.
How did she know the way? So extraordinary.

Much love
Debo

---

1 Bridget Flemming (1945–). Photographer born on the Chatsworth estate; semi-
detached neighbour, with her husband, Andrew, of DD in Edensor.

*When this volume went to press, the two correspondents, aged eighty-eight and
ninety-three, were still keeping up a lively exchange of letters.*

INDEX

Stanley, Venetia, 8n5
Starás, Cléarchos, 130
Stephens, Ellen ('Diddy'), 57 & n3
Stergios (Vlach), 123
Stewart, Beatrice, 350–1
Stewart, Damaris, Lady (*née* du Boulay), 113 & n1
Stewart, Sir Michael, 113 & n1, 184, 199, 235, 331
Stewart, Olivia, 331
Stewart-Richardson, Gladys, 53 & n4, 63
Stirling, Colonel David, 73n8, 370
Stirling, Peter, 200 & n1
Stirling, Colonel William, 72 & n8, 78, 200
Stoppard, Sir Tom, 330n1
Strachey, Julia, 205
Strachey, Lytton, 144, 205 & n1, 207 & n2
Strachwitz, Moritz, Graf: 'The Heart of Douglas', 215 & n1
Sturford Meade (house), near Longleat, Wiltshire, 12
Suez crisis (1956), 29n1
Sunday, Bloody Sunday (film), 118
Sunday Times, 290
Sutherland, Colonel David, 273 & n3, 370
Swann, Donald, 48n9
Swinbrook House, Oxfordshire, 8n2, 336 & n1; *see also* Mill Cottage
Swindon *see* Sevenhampton Place
Swiss Cottage, Chatsworth, 52 & n1
Syria, 187

Talassius, 314
Tamarón, Santiago de Mora-Figueroa y Williams, Marqués and Isabella, Marquesa de, 322 & n2
Tangiers, 12–14
Tarmac (company), 224–5, 228, 248
Tássos *see* Eythimíou, Tásso
Tennant, Edward (DD's grandson), 141, 143, 356
Tennant, Isabel (DD's granddaughter), 106 & n2, 259
Tennant, Lady Emma (*née* Cavendish; DD's daughter): at Lismore, 9 & n1; PLF gives vasculum to, 30 & n1; proposes giving skeleton to St Elphin's, 48; shooting, 50; teenage rebelliousness, 57; lost in Greece,

70n4; marriage and child, 106 & n2; in Scotland, 117; at Oxford, 196n2; at Buckingham Palace party, 197; appointed head of National Trust gardens, 199; letter to PLF, 215; makes hooked rugs, 251 & n3; and foot and mouth crisis, 328 & n2; mother's trip with, 355; calls Bowra 'Old Tragic', 365
Tennant, Stella (*later* Lasnet; DD's granddaughter), 117 & n2, 218, 259, 368 & n1
Tennant, Toby (Emma's husband), 107n2, 117, 328 & n2
Testino, Mario, 368 & n1
Thatcher, Sir Denis, 225 & n7
Theodore (drover/guide), 125–6, 130
Thompson, Ernest Thompson: *Wild Animals I Have Known*, 100 & n2
Thompson, Hamilton, 152
Thrapsanó, Grigóris Khnarákis de, 137
Thynne, Lord Christopher, 312 & n2, 313
Thynne, Lady Christopher (*née* Antonia Palmer), 312n2
Timson, Rodney, 210 & n1
Topley, Lady Sophia (*née* Cavendish; *then* Morrison; DD's daughter): birth, 27 & n1, 29; Epstein bust of, 56 & n2; visits Greece with mother, 109; schooling, 117; in Florence, 143; DD stays with in Wiltshire, 286 & n1; marriage to Morrison, 286n1; Christmas 1966 at Chatsworth, 311
Topolski, Feliks, 71 & n4
Toronto, 209
Toynbee, Philip, 192 & n2, 195–6, 207 & n1, 309
Treasures from Chatsworth, The Devonshire Inheritance (exhibition), 184 & n4
Tree, Lady Anne (*née* Cavendish; DD's sister-in-law; 'Tig'), 69 & n5, 109, 243
Tree, Iris (*later* Moffat; *then* Ledebur), 59 & n2, 61, 84, 265
Tree, Michael, 70n5
Treuhaft, Jessica (*née* Mitford; *then* Romilly; 'Decca'): correspondence with DD, xi, 278; invents Society of Hons, 8n2; attends Philip Toynbee's funeral, 196; confounds US telephone company, 206; visit to PLF, 207; aborted *New Yorker* article on,